ORIGINS OF THE NATIONAL FORESTS:
A Centennial Symposium

Edited by Harold K. Steen

Forest History Society
Durham, North Carolina
1992

Work on this book and its publication were supported by
grants to the Forest History Society.

Cover illustration: *The Lone Fisherman* by Hans Kleiber,
courtesy of Buffalo Bill Historical Center, Cody, Wyoming.
Gift of Lucille M. Wright.

Library of Congress Cataloging-in-Publication Data

The Origins of the national forests : a centennial symposium / edited
by Harold K. Steen.
    p. cm.
Includes bibliographical references.
ISBN 0-8223-1272-7

    1. Forest reserves--United States--History--Congresses. 2. Forest
policy--United States--History--Congresses. 3. United States.
Forest Service--History--Congresses. 4. National parks and
reserves--United States--History--Congresses. I. Steen, Harold K.
II. Forest History Society.
SD426.075 1992
333.75'0973--dc20   92-1236
                                               CIP

TABLE OF CONTENTS

NONFEDERAL RELATIONS

OTHER FEDERAL AGENCIES

INDIVIDUALS AND THE NATIONAL FORESTS

Foreword

These proceedings are the product of a conference held during 1991 in celebration of the centennial of the National Forest System. The conference was the first in a series of events designed to celebrate the past, present, and future of the National Forest System. To date, historians and foresters have focused their historical interest on the national parks, the accepted beginnings of the USDA Forest Service in 1905, and the then Chief Forester Gifford Pinchot. The centennial of the National Forest System, however, was an opportunity to shift that focus to the beginnings of what historians themselves call the watershed event in North American conservation history—the Creative Act of 1891 and the birth of the National Forest System. They identify 1891 as the point in which American policy on the disposition of public lands changed, and the true beginning, with the Organic Act of 1897, of conservation in America—the "wise use of natural resources." The first forest reserve was the Yellowstone Park Timberland Reserve established on March 30, 1891. The original portion of the reserve is now called the Shoshone National Forest.

Even within the Forest Service, there are few people with any knowledge of the birth of the national forests and their early management. Forest Service culture is such that the history of the Forest Service is equated with the history of the National Forest System. There is a difference. There have been unfortunate results that have resulted from this lack of knowledge. First, few people are aware of the reasons for which the system was started or the popular sentiment that caused the first 40 million acres to be established as reserves—wildlife and watershed protection. Secondly, the significant contributions of others beside Gifford Pinchot to the beginnings of conservation have been hidden. These include Bernhard Fernow, W.J. McGee, and members of the Boone and Crockett Club. It has even obscured, paradoxically, an awareness of the beginnings of the agency itself. Few know of the agency's origins in 1876 and the early leadership of Franklin Hough and Bernhard Fernow.

There is something more important to this centennial, however, than correcting a few historical footnotes. I hope the centennial and these proceedings stir up an interest and awareness of the National Forest System—and its individual forests, grasslands, and research forests—as a significant entity in itself and a major contribution to American culture. The National Forest System is the most significant piece of scenic, ecologically diverse, and geographically dispersed land under single ownership in the United States. National forests were important to the economic development of the West, are important to today's economy, and will continue to be. To focus, however, as we all too frequently do, on the economic side of the ledger would be missing the primary point. The national forests have served as a crucible for American conservation. American conservation leaders such as Robert Marshall and Aldo Leopold and ideas like the wilderness concept and practical techniques for ecological land management have come from the national forests. The national forests help Americans define how they perceive their country. Open space—the opportunity that we have as a people to enjoy wilderness, protect large herds of wildlife, or enjoy "purple mountains majesty"— separates American culture from European and many Asian cultures. We identify with the natural landscapes rather than cultural artifacts of the past. It is important that the public and Forest Service employees appreciate this more fully.

I hope this conference and the centennial serve as the first step to providing the national forests their just place in American history and the public mind. I would like to see historians and foresters encourage additional conferences and publications on this long neglected topic. I also think they should assume the responsibility of exposing the public to the history of the National Forest System and what it has meant to conservation in America.

Robert L. Hendricks
Centennial Coordinator
USDA Forest Service

Introduction

Centennials and other significant anniversaries often trigger reflection. How did it all get started? How did we get to where we are today? The year 1991 marked the centennial for the National Forest System, and this benchmark did indeed trigger reflection within the USDA Forest Service, the federal agency that since 1905 has managed the national forests.

The proceedings that follow were drawn from a Forest Service sponsored conference held in Missoula, Montana, on June 20-22, 1991 that looked at the origins and significance of the national forests. Included are twenty-one papers that reflect the diversity of issues and priorities and conflicts that a land management agency must address. However, the focus here is on the land—the national forests—and not on the agency that is currently managing them. Afterall, it is the land that is significant in the long run.

The United States landmass is a diversely complex ecosystem, and the national forests—comprising roughly 10 percent of the whole—reflect this diversity. Differences in climate, topography, flora, fauna, and soil are obvious north to south, and east to west. The political geography is also diverse; there is an overall federal system, myriad state systems, and of course the majority of all land that is privately owned, which in turn is governed by federal statutes, state laws, and county ordinances. A dramatic example—the vast bulk of federal extractive resources are in the West, as is the bulk of wilderness, and within the federal ownership is a very significant percentage of private property. People live and work and play on the private lands, and people work and play on the federal lands, but most people live at a distance. Who sets the priorities according to what criteria?

Such questions are not new to the national forests. They were being asked even before the National Forest System began in 1891, they were asked with considerable heat during the first decade or two following 1891, and they are being asked today, at times with heat. Conference authors look at most of the important issues extant in the 1890s and beyond. Water especially, and forage, minerals, and wildlife are examined, as are federal priorities and states' rights. Federal land is looked at from the federal view, state view, and local view. It is looked from other agencies and also from Canada. Included are some of the individuals that made it happen. And what about those who had been living on the land before—long before—who were forced off by those who claimed it vacant? Thoughtful, provocative, informative, only three adjectives that describe the papers.

Conferences stem from ideas, and this idea stemmed from Stephen P. Mealey, while he was supervisor of the Shoshone National Forest in Wyoming, the first reserve proclaimed on March 30, 1891. Steve also participated directly in the conference as master of ceremonies. Centennial coordinator Robert Hendricks implemented Mealey's idea by asking the Forest History Society to make it happen. Rob also contributed a stream of ideas and encouragement. Gerald J. Coutant, chief of the Forest Service visitor services branch, came up with the idea and implemented a concurrent interpretive workshop, drawing upon the historical expertize that the conference provided.

Many others really made it happen: Gerry T. Baertsch, director of conferences, and Sheila M. Stearns, vice president for university relations, both for the University of Montana; Ernest B. Corrick and Edward G. Heilman with the National Forest Service Museum, also in Missoula; Beth Horn, Judson N. Moore, Laird A. Robinson, and Kimberly D. Delgado, all from the Forest Service Regional Office in Missoula. And not the least my associates at the Forest History Society, Kathy Cox, keeper of the numbers, Cheryl Oakes, keeper of the books, and Andrea Anderson, keeper of the paper, for keeping me in line and on track. Since the conference Kevin Foy, Georg Patterson, and Michele Justice brought these proceedings into being.

Harold K. Steen
Durham, North Carolina

GENERAL VIEWS OF

THE NATIONAL FORESTS

The Origins and Significance of the National Forest System

Harold K. Steen
Forest History Society

Statistics on hundreds of millions of acres, hundreds of millions of recreational uses, billions of board feet, thousands of grazing permits, and so forth are obviously impressive—the national forests are significant—but do the numbers tell the whole story? Perhaps not; perhaps the real significance of the forests is the fact that they were created at all, and still exist, and are now permanent features. The fact that we as a nation decided a century ago to keep these forested lands under federal dominion—an atypical decision for the time—shows just how important we believed these lands to be. Important enough to create a major exception to the rule.

A closely related significance is the conservation legacy. Those who were the architects of the conservation movement were invariably involved with the national forests. It is fairly impossible to separate the *notion* of conservation with the *fact* of the forests; conservation superstars like Gifford Pinchot and Theodore Roosevelt played out their roles on a national forest stage. Again, the national forests *are* significant, and the more we study the more we learn just how broad and complex the story really is.

Historians are not think-alike clones of some master interpreter of yesteryear. Sometimes we debate about which is the best vantage point from which to view national forest history. Do we look over Congress's shoulder, do we watch what the outdoors types were doing, do we think that those who used the land for their livelihoods tell the best story? And how about cause and effect? What caused Congress to decide what it did when it did? And so on.

What about us interpreters ourselves? As we sifted through mountains of historical evidence, objectively of course, why did we select that particular small fraction of material as support for our paper?

The papers that follow will allow you to look at the origins and significance of the National Forest System from as many vantage points as there are papers, and reflecting as many biases as there are historians reading those papers. My approach is rather conventional; since it was Congress that authorized the president to proclaim forest reserves—a century ago—I try to figure out what caused Congress to decide what it did. I look at forces and influences closest to Congress and make judgments about the timing and significance of those multiple forces. As you can see from the papers that follow, others will suggest, and rightly so, that a much broader explanation than mine is in order, if we are to achieve full understanding.

The Origins of the National Forest System

I look mainly at that sliver of Congress that was concerned about land—the Interior and Agriculture committees in the House and Senate. Land. When I was in college I received money each month under the G.I. Bill. Generations earlier I would have instead received land, a piece of the public domain as reward for serving my country. If I had built railroads I would have received land. If I had homesteaded, as my Norwegian immigrant grandfather had, I would have received land. As new states entered the Union, they too received grants of the public domain. The national forest story is a story about land—large chunks of the public domain that despite a juggernaut of momentum to dispose of it would neither be granted nor sold.

The numbers are awesome. During the nineteenth century, fully one-half of the nation was transferred from federal ownership to state and private ownership—countless transactions of quarter-sections, full sections, or more. Federal land agents dipping quill pens into inkwells and recording by hand the fruits of three thousand statutes that Congress had passed by 1880 to dispose of the public domain.

An eighth of the nation was granted to the railroads, including 22 percent of Montana. To balance the score, an eighth of the nation was granted to homesteaders. John Wayne movies notwithstanding, the vast majority of homesteaders were rational enough to wait for the train; very few headed West in covered wagons.

The stated goals were simple: settle the West, establish sovereignty, expand the economy. If President Kennedy wanted a man on the moon by the end of the 1960s, Lincoln wanted a railroad to California by the end of the 1860s—both presidential goals were achieved, and it's hard to say which cost the most or which achievement was the greatest for its time.

In the midst of all this, scientists and others were registering concern—even alarm. Pointing to Europe, the scientists held up example after example of abused land

and the resulting erosion, floods, and other ills. This, too, could happen in America they insisted; unchecked forest fires in Colorado could cause floods in Kansas and even in far away Louisiana. The scientists urged, and politicians began to hear; government should devise some means to protect the watersheds of the West.

Political response to scientific concern about forested watersheds appeared in Congress in the early 1870s. By the end of the century, Congress would have considered nearly two hundred bills pertinent to forests; two in particular, passed in the 1890s, are the heroes of my story—a law authorizing the president to proclaim forest reserves and another that prescribed the purposes for which these reserves could be established.

The string of congressional interest began in the 1870s. What to do about floods? After gaining momentum across the Plains, by the time a flood reached Arkansas it could cause devastation over a vast area and could also disrupt river-based commerce. Upstream near the source, a flood might be less dramatic, but still to the local farmer it could be that a vital reservoir was washed out or silted up.

The flip side of flood is drought. Where I was raised near Seattle, drought meant that it was raining less than usual. But in the arid West, drought happened when the streams went dry. Irrigation works, such as reservoirs, would help. Upstream forests would also help, and Congress thought about both flood and drought and how to protect forested watersheds.

The story picks up steam and becomes a bit confusing—are we looking at cause and effect or at coincidence? In 1875 the American Forestry Association formed; by 1890 AFA would be a key player on the forestry stage. In 1876 forestry activity began in the Executive Branch—in the Department of Agriculture through a quirk rather than in the preferred and more logical Department of the Interior. By 1890 the U.S. Division of Forestry had grown in stature adequate to also be a key player along with the American Forestry Association. And it is no coincidence that the driving force in both institutions was Bernhard Eduard Fernow, a German forester who had immigrated to the U.S. in 1876.

Over in the Department of the Interior's Geological Survey, forest-related activity took shape with the 1888 establishment of the Irrigation Survey. Under the direction of scientist/politician John Wesley Powell, the agency aimed to do what its name implied—survey the West for its irrigation needs and potential. Key scientists assigned to the Irrigation Survey, such as Arnold Hague and W.J. McGee, along with Powell, figure large, but I will single out only Arnold Hague—he introduces the Boone and Crockett Club, Yellowstone National Park, and he ghosted the proclamation that created the first national forest. Hague not only deserves a paper just about him, but he deserves a biography, well supported by an especially rich collection of his records held by the National Archives.

I don't want to steal thunder from John Reiger's paper, so let me say only that the Boone and Crockett Club offered a forum and vehicle for Hague, Theodore Roosevelt, and others to swap opinions about conservation. Members of the club clearly influenced the course of conservation history. Yellowstone National Park is important to this story, because while Hague was assigned to surveying the Park's wonderful geology, he became an advocate for enlarging the Park; in fact, when he drafted the proclamation that created the first forest, he thought that he *had* expanded the Park.

The year 1888 is especially significant. Congress had been looking at but rejecting many forestry bills for nearly two decades, and by 1888 the bills were stacking up. The House Public Lands Committee crafted one bill as substitute for twenty-nine others already in the hopper. This bill—HR 7901 "to secure to actual settlers the public lands adapted to agriculture, to protect the forests on the public domain, and for other purposes"—contained twenty-nine sections. Section 8 would authorize the president to proclaim forest reserves and offered basic authority to protect and manage.

HR 7901 passed the House but failed in the Senate. But the concept of forest reserves created by presidential proclamation would survive and surfaced three years later in 1891.

This tidbit is not an exercise in trivial pursuit—for two reasons. First, a committee report accompanied HR 7901, so we can see what the intent of the bill was more clearly than by reading the bill itself. Second, historians—myself included—have managed to maintain a fiction that Congress didn't know what it was voting on when it ratified the process to create forest reserves by presidential proclamation. Two of the several authors who ignored the howls of the historical pack and got the story right appear in this volume—Joe Miller and Ron Arnold, and my thanks to them for leading me down a now obvious trail.

Fernow, Hague, and many others kept advocating—Fernow for some kind of forestry law and Hague to expand Yellowstone National Park. In 1890 and 1891 Congress took on the much overdue task of reviewing and codifying public domain statutes, even to the point of repealing the unpopular Timber Culture Act. The House and

Senate each passed versions of such an act, but with differences. Thus, a conference committee was convened to find a middle ground between the bill's twenty-three sections. In committee, a twenty-fourth section was added—a not that unusual a process for the time—that plucked the essence of the defunct 1888 bill to authorize the president to proclaim forest reserves. However, there was to be no language for purpose or administration; to have included these knotty issues would have derailed the effort.

After much bickering and rhetorical flourish, the bill passed both houses, just as Congress was adjourning. President Harrison had been a strong advocate for forest reserves, and when the bill reached his desk, he quickly signed it on March 3, 1891. Our friend Arnold Hague of the Geological Survey, dejected by still another failure to attain approval for an expanded Yellowstone Park, saw this new law as a means to his end. He hastily drafted a proclamation for a forest reserve south and east of the park and sent it to the secretary of the interior, asking that it be directed to the president. It was, and on March 30, 1891, President Harrison proclaimed the Yellowstone Park Timberland Reserve, the nation's first. On July 1, 1908 the reserve would be renamed the Shoshone National Forest.

A bit more than two months after Harrison signed the law, the commissioner of the General Land Office sent a directive to field agents. The agents were to seek out recommendations for forested watersheds suitable for reserve status, and by this means announce the intent to establish a forest. This notion of prior notice was a crucial part of the process, and when the president ignored it in 1897 and again in 1907, Congress would react harshly. The first time (1897), the reserves narrowly escaped cancellation, and when Teddy Roosevelt did it in a much-celebrated (by him) incident, Congress essentially stripped the president of his authority to proclaim reserves in the West.

So the 1891 act effectively lasted a decade and a half, but during its short life the basic national forest system in the West would be established.

The job was only half done in 1891; still needed was authorization to manage the reserves and clarification of the purposes for which they could be established. Promptly in 1892, Congress began a six-year effort to round out a forest reserve agenda.

A key player was Congressman Thomas McRae from Arkansas, who was principle author of the law that would be passed in 1897. A committee report in 1892 accompanying McRae's initial bill was laced with cumbersome wording, but the essence of multiple use/sustained yield is apparent—timber, water, and forage were to be used but not to the detriment of the reserve itself.

During the 1970s much attention would be given to what Congress was thinking about during the 1890s—the so-called Monongahela decision on clear-cutting and the Supreme Court decision in U.S. vs New Mexico on federal rights to federal water, so it is worth taking a couple of minutes to look for ourselves.

With benefit of hindsight, we know that McRae's 1892 bill survived a half-decade of congressional jostling and scrutiny to provide the framework for what lawyers call the Forest Service Organic Act but what historians call the Forest Management Act. The problem that the courts have had figuring out just what congressional intent was, unlike for the rather prescriptive National Forest Management Act of 1976, that earlier statutes delegated broad authority to Executive Branch agencies. And in this specific case, the 1897 Forest Management Act is an amendment to an appropriations measure and thus lacks much of the usual legislative trail that a full-fledged statute would have.

Congress looked at a wide-range of options on its way to 1897, and what it rejected tells us much about the thinking of the time. Should the statute be prescriptive or delegate broad powers? Congress rejected a bill that was prescriptive. Should water be specifically earmarked for irrigation and industry, or should broader, more general options be put forth? Congress rejected language that would have limited water to use by farmers and corporations. State's rights were examined too; should states receive priority access to the resources on the forest reserves? The answer to this question is less concise because of exceptions, but the record is clear—national interests would not be subordinated to those of a state.

Finally, were the resources to be used—in a commercial sense. Absolutely. Some argued that water was so important that other activities should be proscribed, but this view did not prevail. The resources were to be used under the supervision of a federal officer according to rules and regulations established by the secretary of the interior.

Use but don't abuse—this legacy was repackaged in the 1960 Multiple Use/Sustained Yield Act, and again by the 1976 National Forest Management Act, but the idea has been around for a long time, and is still the theme of conservationists.

One final detail. From 1897 to 1905, agencies in the Department of the Interior managed and protected the forest reserves created by authority of the 1891 act. In 1905 the reserves were transferred to the Department of Agriculture, with its Bureau of Forestry, then renamed Forest Service. In 1907 forest reserves were renamed as national forests.

The book that follows adds much—insights, facts, details, interpretations. But as good, as interesting, as informative as these papers are, more could be written, more angles studied. I suppose this fact offers the strongest sort of evidence that the national forests are truly significant. To capture their story to everyone's satisfaction is beyond the ken. There is always more.

For Further Reading

Arnold, R. "Stepchild of America." In *People of the Tongass: Alaska Forestry Under Attack*, K.A. Soderberg and J. DuRette, eds. (Bellevue, WA: Free Enterprise Press, 1988).

Fairfax, S.K., and A.D. Tarlock. "No Water for the Woods: A Critical Analysis of United States v. New Mexico." *Idaho Law Review* (1979): 509-554.

Gates, P. W. *History of Public Land Law Development*. Washington, DC: Government Printing Office, 1968.

Ise, J. *United States Forest Policy*. New Haven, CT: Yale University Press, 1920.

Kirkland, H. D. "The American Forests, 1864-1898: A Trend Toward Conservation." Doctoral Dissertation, Florida State University, 1971.

Manning, T. G. *Government in Science: The U.S. Geological Survey, 1867—1894*. Lexington, KY: University of Kentucky Press, 1967.

Miller, J. A. "Congress and the Origins of Conservation: Natural Resource Policies, 1865-1900." Doctoral Dissertation, University of Minnesota, 1973.

Pinchot, G. *Breaking new Ground*. New York: Harcourt and Brace, 1947.

Reiger, J. F. *American Sportsman and the Origins of Conservation*. New York: Winchester Press, 1975.

Rodgers, A. D. *Bernhard Eduard Fernow: A Story of North American Forestry*. Princeton, NJ: Princeton University Press, 1951. Reprinted by the Forest History Society, 1991.

Steen, Harold K. *The Origins of the National Forest System*. USDA Forest Service, 1991.

The Forest Reserves and the Argument for a Closing Frontier

Patricia Nelson Limerick
University of Colorado, Boulder

In *Roughing It*, Mark Twain told an essential story about the workings of reform movements. Lost in a blizzard in the Nevada desert, Twain and his two prospector-companions felt sure they would die. Unable to light a fire, they prepared for what they thought would be their last night on earth. A fellow named Ollendorf led off with the first declaration of reform, taking out his bottle of whiskey and declaring that "whether he lived or died he would never touch another drop." Having "given up all hope of life," he "was ready to submit humbly to his fate." Ollendorf did wish that "he could be spared a little longer, not for any selfish reason, but to make a thorough reform in his character, and by devoting himself to helping the poor, nursing the sick, and pleading with the people to guard themselves against the evils of intemperance, make his life a beneficent example to the young, and lay it down at last with the precious reflection that it had not been lived in vain." Ollendorf cast aside his bottle; the other prospector gave up card-playing; Twain himself "threw away" his pipe, and in doing so "felt that at last I was wholly free of a hated vice and one that had ridden me like a tyrant all my days." The next morning these newly virtuous men were doubly surprised: they were not dead, and, with the blizzard cleared, they could see that they had camped just a few feet from a stage station. Humiliated, embarrassed, their joy "poisoned," Ollendorf, and Ballou, and Twain each pursued their separate paths to recover their discarded vices, and then to hide behind the barn. "As I turned the one corner, smoking," Twain wrote, "Ollendorf turned the other with his bottle to his lips, and between us sat . . . Ballou deep in a game of 'solitaire' with [his] old greasy cards."[1] Thus Twain offered a model for summing up the pattern of reform movements—for instance, the story of conservation in the last century. You get people sufficiently worked up with free use of the words "scarcity," "depletion," "exhaustion," or "timber famine." You get them to make some resolutions about how, in the face of these grim threats, they will indeed live more wisely, and be a model to posterity. And then, when no fearful situation of scarcity materializes, they go back to the resource-using equivalent of drinking, smoking, and card-playing. They may smoke and drink a *little* less, or play a few less hands of cards, but they still return to the same kind of behavior that, a resolution or two ago, they were going to give up for all time.

I am hardly the first to say that the beginning of the conservation era added up to something short of a revolution in American resource use. But unlike more skeptical sorts, I also think that good resolutions are worth something, and that sometimes it takes a century or so to figure out what those resolutions really mean and why they might be worth taking seriously. The questions raised by the origins of the forest reserves and the context of their creation go to the heart of how we think about regional history, as well as national history.

One thing is clear: ten years ago, this would have been a much easier essay to write. A decade ago, I was myself more believer than apostate when it came to the old faith that the frontier ended in 1890. If one could accept that premise, then sorts of seemingly unrelated events fall into an extremely manageable pattern. The director of the 1890 census said there was no more frontier line, no more zone of western lands with two to six people, or fewer, per square mile. And that was by no means the end of the year 1890s qualifications as a watershed. A very unpleasant event in human relations took place in South Dakota at Wounded Knee and seemed to signify the end of Indian resistance to white invasion. The Mormons, having pressed their experiment in polygamy as far as, or further than, the federal government would let it go, gave up plural marriage in the Woodruff Manifesto. In this era of watersheds, the western cattle business had jumped the gun by a year or two, with the cataclysmic winter of 1886-1887 killing off both livestock and speculative profits. In the 1890s, western farmers and western miners were restive, encountering a new and frustrating set of limits to their ambitions, and the Populist Party and mining labor organizations recorded their irritable responses to historical change. John Muir was laying the groundwork for the founding of the Sierra Club, an organization that would lead the way in finding uses for nature that did not involve axes, saws, drills, plows, or guns. John C. Fremont, the Great Pathfinder who had led the march of Manifest Destiny, died, financially much reduced, in 1890. Just as the Lilliputians succeeded in immobilizing Gulliver with a web of small ropes, a web of railroads seemed to tie the West in place. Most western territories were now states; the buffalo were almost gone; the Indians were on reservations; the West had cities, and corporations, and schools, and churches, and lots of middle-class white women to serve as dampers on any fun that the survivors of frontier days might try to stir up.

The festivity known as westward expansion seemed to be winding down, running out of refreshments, running out of *spirit*. The West had been, for decades, the kid region, the adolescent region, the region that got itself into occasional messes, but then had to be forgiven because it was young and, in the manner of young things, foolish and charming. But in the 1890s, with the end of the frontier, the obligations and burdens and pains of adulthood descended on the West.

If you accepted this picture of western history, then this speech would write itself. This is how you could tell the story of the origin of the forest reserves. In the beginning, you would say, the continent's natural resources seemed endless. People could chop down one forest, with the assurance that the horizon held another forest. Then, in the late nineteenth century, tremors of encroaching scarcity made themselves felt. A group of sensitive and alert men set themselves to the task of anticipating the approaching end of the frontier. Even if the creation of the forest reserves missed the 1890 deadline by a few months, it made a perfect fit with the other signs and symptoms of the end of the frontier. The American conquest of nature had ended in a victory for the Americans. With that triumph on record, the Americans could afford to be generous winners, protecting nature now that nature had made its unconditional surrender. The end of the frontier made responsible public officials realize that the federal government had to step in and protect resources that may have been infinite in the imagination, but were clearly finite in fact. With the frontier over, an entirely different era of western history began, an era of sensible federal supervision of natural resource use, an era where the frontier's disorder, boom/bust instability, and short-term extraction lived on only in the memories of quaint old-timers. The Mormon renunciation of polygamy, the incident at Wounded Knee, the census results for 1890, the creation of the forest reserves: they were all interlocking pieces in the same easily assembled puzzle, and the name of the puzzle was the end of the frontier.

Ten years ago, the speech putting the creation of the forest reserves into its historical context would have been so easy to write that it would not have been worth writing. Of all the models of explanation dependent on the chronological structure of conventional western history, conservation history was the most dependent. If you could see the origin of conservation as a response to the end of the frontier, then that was all you needed in the way of explanation. Your work in historical interpretation was over virtually before it began.

But the state of thinking in the writing of western history in the 1990s is a different matter. The notion that the frontier ended in 1890 has, for me, collapsed entirely. Since I myself cannot have the pleasures of that kind of certain and clear categorization, it has been the source of some satisfaction to have ended up in a position to ensure that those pleasures of certainty are not going to come easily to anyone else. When I am in the room, people who are about to use the word "frontier," or the term "the end of the frontier," flinch. Instead of relying on old patterns of chronology to sort out western events, we now have to think.

What went wrong with the idea of the end of the frontier? Part of the problem stems from the term frontier, a word that makes a great deal of sense if you are willing to plant your point of view firmly on the Atlantic Coast and to identify wholeheartedly with English-speaking white Americans. The frontier, then, is the edge of Anglo-American settlement, the place, as Richard White puts it, where white people got scarce, or alternatively, where white people got scared. But if you are not willing to let your point of view rest on such grounds of exclusivity, then, if you withdraw its ethnocentricity, the term frontier turns to mush. What can the idea of a frontier, a two-sided line moving through space, say about real places in the American West, places where Indians of different tribes had been living for some time, places where Spanish, French Canadian, even Russian colonizers appeared before Anglo-American colonizers showed up, places where people converged from a number of directions and did not align themselves in a clear division, "our side" of the frontier, and the "other" side?

And what about the end of the frontier? It is, if you are thinking in the conventional terms of western history, easy enough to say when the frontier opens—when white people learn of a resource and rush to exploit it. But when does a frontier end? When it exceeds the population range of two to six people per square mile, Frederick Jackson Turner and the director of the Census thought. But in a mining rush the population instantly exceeds two to six people per square mile. By the conventional definition of a frontier, you would have to declare a mining frontier closed the moment it opened.

Or you could define the presence of a frontier by the factor of risk and conflict. When the whites no longer need to fear Indian attacks or threats to white property-owning, when deserts shift from being life-threatening ordeals for overland travelers to pleasant places for tourists with well-educated taste to observe the play of light and color, then one could say the frontier was over. But as soon as risk revives—if the Indians file a suit to recover land now in white ownership, if the car breaks down in the desert and the tourists in it are better supplied with aesthetic sensitivity than with water—then the threat is back at full-strength, and the frontier snaps back open.

Even if someone could persuade me that frontiers, and the ending of frontiers, could be clearly defined, then it would still be unlikely that this persuasive person could sell me on the idea of 1890 as the end of the frontier. In the American West, too many "frontier-like" events happened *after* 1890—homesteading continued, short-term extraction even accelerated as the western oil, timber, and uranium booms took off, and, contrary to myths of a vanished West, neither Indians nor cowboys disappeared. In extractive industries, the familiar boom/bust cycle continued, while Indian, Hispanic, Anglo, and Asian people continued to search for ways to live together. The westward movement did not stop at 1890; millions more people moved into the West in the twentieth century. If one went by numbers, one would have to call the nineteenth century westward movement the frail prelude to the much more significant twentieth century westward movement. It would be easier to sell me a used car, or a vacuum cleaner, or an encyclopedia set, than it would be to sell me on the idea that the creation of the forest reserves was another sign and symbol of the end of the frontier.

It is, in fact, not an easy matter to find meaning, frontier-related or not, in the passage of the law that created the forest reserves. A conference committee met to discuss a bill with twenty-three sections revising the public land laws, a bill that made no mention of forest reserves. When the bill left the conference committee, it had one more section. Section 24 authorized the president to set aside reserves. When the bill returned to the Senate and the House, it got a favorable vote. The president could create forest reserves, and that was that. Nothing in the 1891 law defined management, or protection, or even what the term reserve meant. Perhaps more important, nothing in the bill provided an appropriation for a staff of managers or protectors.

Why 1891? Is there meaning, frontier-related or not, in the *timing* of this act? Contingency, indirectness, tenuous causality, inadvertence, a sense of purpose far from consensus—they are all at their peak in the story of Section 24. It is, however, perfectly plausible to argue that there is nothing so unusual in this. Contingency, indirectness, tenuous causality, and inadvertence characterize most acts of legislation; Congress is simply too large and unwieldy a body to act with clear direction and purpose in the many bills it passes. And, as Joseph A. Miller and Harold K. Steen have shown, even if Section 24 seemed to appear out of nowhere in the 1891 conference committee, it did have a history in earlier bills and recommendations.[2] Nonetheless, the story of the passage of the 1891 act cannot be made to deliver up a clear and unambiguous meaning; and, in recent years, the concept of the "end of the frontier" has lost much of its power to explain events in Western history.

What now?

Now we can rebuild a structure of significance for the whole package: Section 24, the 1890s, the phases of change in the American West.

Whenever and however it finally ended up incorporated into federal law, the idea of creating reserves is part of a solid and significant story. For the preceding two decades, through the 1870s and the 1880s, a range of people had used the phrase "timber famine," and worried about the future prospects of scarcity.[3] Support was indeed eroding for the idea that full-speed-ahead extraction, without attention to reforestation, was the appropriate treatment of the nation's forests. The origins of this change in thinking had surprisingly little to do with the West. Even if plenty of western trees had undergone a strange journey underground to support mines, or aboveground to build and heat houses, the timber business of the Pacific Northwest and the Rockies had barely begun. The depletion of the Great Lakes forest land was pretty clearly the inspiration for all these remarks about waste, exhaustion, and famine.[4] The reserves did not come out of nowhere: they came out of some people's genuine shift in mood, orientation, sense of the future.

Now we come to the hard part: if we cannot fall back into the old habits of fitting this shift into the idea of the end of the frontier, what larger model should we adopt?

This is what I would propose: a model of first drafts, second drafts, and third drafts. In a shift that registered considerably short of a major watershed, toward the end of the nineteenth century, various Americans (by no means a majority) looked over the process of westward expansion and economic development, and the physical and social results of that process. Their response was one very familiar to writers: the feeling that the outcome needed rethinking. The first draft, produced by several decades of intensive Anglo-American colonization, needed tinkering. The depletion of forests in the Midwest, the aimlessness of Indian reservations, the stubborn distinctiveness of the Mormons, the difficulty of agriculture in semi-arid territory: these were not the optimal outcomes for westward expansion. So a variety of reformers undertook to revise the results, using federal laws as editors use blue pencils. At this stage, however, they were still the kind of editors who think that a few fairly minor changes to the manuscript will take care of its problem. "Preserve for use"—that interesting phrase, used explicitly or in some variation by many of the people calling for forest preservation, illustrates the limits of this round of revision. "Preserve for use" might strike our ears as full of contradiction and tension, but it seemed sensible enough in its time. "Preserve for use" and "rational and scientific management" were the key tenets of the revisers' faith.

The powerful fantasy of white Americans taming and mastering a virgin continent yielded ground to another, also very powerful fantasy: the fantasy of experts wisely managing resources for everyone's benefit. A whole new set of romances bloomed: the romance of the federal government, more precisely, the romance of the Executive Branch; the romance of rationality; the romance of expertise; the romance of reforestation and sustained yield. James Fenimore Cooper, Louis L'Amour, and John Wayne might have had a tougher time making these romances into colorful novels and movies, but they are just as important in the shaping of western history as the fantasies that accumulated around Natty Bumppo, Daniel Boone, Kit Carson, and Buffalo Bill Cody. Traditional western historians have written up the mining frontier, the cattle frontier, the farming frontier, the women's frontier, and so on, but neither they nor anyone else has yet done justice to the bureaucrats' frontier. A proper study would begin with the ground-level reality of the effects of bureaucratic power on particular western places. But it would also examine the myth and symbol of the bureaucrat. It would analyze the dream that the bureaus and services and divisions of the executive branch could provide an escape from, even a cure for, special interest politics, for the tyranny of private property and the profit motive, for the unequal distribution of reward from western resources.

Throughout the twentieth century, intoxicated with the various romances of the bureaucrats' frontier, federal land management agencies tried to oversee the writing of a better second draft of the American West. But the second draft was finally not all that different from the first draft. The profit motive, economic ambition, and commodity-consciousness were allowed—one might even say, had to be allowed—to carry over, nearly unchallenged, from the first draft to the second draft.

Midway through the twentieth century, discontent with this second draft began to gather force. From the wilderness campaign to Earth Day, a number of movements showed the growth of a conviction that a much more searching third draft of the West was in order. This third draft would rest on a fundamental revising of values—away from use, commodity, and profit, and toward a greater loyalty to nature and to a distant posterity. This third draft, if it were ever to become reality, would be a much more fundamental shift than anything that happened in the 1890s. It would mean a basic downshifting in the momentum of the economic development of western resources, a redefinition of ambition, an exploration of whether Americans will forever hear the word "stability" as a synonym for stagnation.

In various ways, this campaign for a third draft of the West challenges, even scorns, the myths and symbols of the bureaucrats' frontier. The romance of scientific management, of an executive branch free from special interest politics, has taken a beating. By this critical vision, federal agencies and private corporations seemed more alike than different in their commitment to the use and commodification of natural resources.

In the late twentieth century, the right way to use and regulate the public lands has again become a subject of heated debate. Thus, we cannot address the issues of 1891 without a full reckoning with the issues of 1991. We can no longer see the creation of the forest reserves as an unambiguous shift away from profligate, short-term resource-development, toward wisdom, restraint, and longterm planning. We must also recognize the ways in which the operation of the forest reserves proved to be business as usual, only in the most superficial way rearranging or revising American economic priorities and ambitions.

Our appraisal of the past requires an honest admission of our hopes for the future. Are we on our way to a more searching and rigorous third draft of the legacy of American westward expansion? Or will we continue to live in a world shaped by the terms of use and commodification set by the first draft and only superficially challenged by the second draft? I am myself something of a believer in the myth and symbol of the bureaucrat—especially the hardy bureaucrat in the outdoors—and in the romance of the federal government. I believe that a shift to permanent federal ownership of forest lands was a step toward fundamental change in American resource use, even if that change was considerably short of complete in 1891, or in 1991. But I am also sympathetic to the argument that an old growth forest is a world apart from a replanted forest crop, and that the Forest Service's cooperation with industry in deficit timber sales is testimony that nothing much shifted in the creation of the so-called reserves.

Appraising the history of conservation in the late twentieth century, we have lost the certainty and complacency that used to come so easily to the aid of western American historians. Without a happy ending, or even a clear ending, to structure the narrative, we have to rethink our understanding of the story's beginning as well. In the 1990s, what may well prove to be the most consequential chapter in the history of the forest reserves will be written by the actions of public officials, business leaders, timber workers, environmental activists, and the owners of the public lands, the American people. Historians cannot be quarantined from this process. Like it or not, the writers of forest history are located squarely at the center of the fray.

Notes

1. Mark Twain, *Roughing It* (1872; New York: New American Library, 1962), pp. 180-183.

2. Joseph A. Miller, "Congress and the Origins of Conservation: Natural Resource Policies, 1865-1900," Ph.D. diss., University of Minnesota, 1973; Harold K. Steen, "The Beginning of the National Forest System," (Washington: United States Department of Agriculture, 1991). The uncertainty over the precise actions of the conference committee in 1891 continues. As

Steen puts it, "Historians generally have offered a similar lament that the record is not complete enough to state with certainty what happened in the conference committee when Section 24 was added. Contemporaries give different accounts. South Dakota Senator Richard Pettigrew says he himself did it; publisher Robert Underwood Johnson says that he himself did it; [Chief of the Division of Forestry Bernhard] Fernow says that Secretary [of Interior John] Noble did it because Noble modestly implied that he had; and some say that [the General Land Office's Edward A.] Bowers was the key. Pettigrew and Johnson 'remembered' their role much later, and it was some time after 1891 that Noble told Fernow that it might be proper for the secretary himself to get some credit. Fernow's correspondence during late February and early March 1891 clearly shows that he was not even aware of the law until 2 weeks after [President Benjamin] Harrison signed it. Finally, according to [Arnold] Hague's account, it was he who brought the news to Noble's attention. And so it goes (p. 22)."

3. Michael Williams, *Americans and Their Forests: A Historical Geography* (New York: Cambridge University Press, 1989), Chapter Twelve, "Preservation and Management, 1870-1910," pp. 393-424; Harold K. Steen, *The U.S. Forest Service: A History* (Seattle: University of Washington, 1976), Chapter One, "Forestry in Agriculture: An Accident of History," pp. 3-21.

4. Williams, *Americans and Their Forests*, Chapter Seven, "The Lumberman's Assault on the Forests of the Lake States, 1860-1890," pp. 193-237; William Cronon, *Nature's Metropolis* (New York: W. W. Norton, 1991), Chapter Four, "The Wealth of Nature: Lumber," pp. 148-206.

The Lands Nobody Wanted:
The Legacy of the Eastern National Forests

William E. Shands
Pinchot Institute for Conservation Studies

The Eastern National Forests—Image and Reality

On the eastern national forests, the Forest Service is steward of a legacy. It is a legacy of human use and misuse of the land, but also a legacy of concern and restoration. Throughout the East there are thriving national forests where less than a century ago there was only charred stumps and brushfields—the lands nobody wanted.[1] An understanding of the origins and history of these national forests is essential if we are to have informed debate over timber harvest levels, wilderness, old growth, biodiversity, and other issues of management and use of the eastern national forests today and in the future.

East of the 100th meridian, the line used historically to mark the divide between the arid west and the water-rich eastern two-thirds of the country, lie fifty national forests.[2] They sprawl across the Ozark and Appalachian mountains and the hills north of the Ohio River. In the upper Lake States they comprise large areas of the region's North Woods. In the south, national forests arc across the coastal plain and piedmont from Texas to North Carolina. Encompassing 24.5 million acres (an area about equal to the state of Virginia), they amount to just about 13 percent of the 191 million-acre national forest system.[3]

Although the western national forests were created from land already owned by the United States, most of the land in the eastern forests had to be purchased from private landowners. It was not until passage of the Weeks Law in 1911 that the federal government was given the authority to acquire land to protect the watersheds of navigable streams. Thus, unlike most of the national forest land in the West, the eastern national forests mainly are purchased forests—land bought from willing sellers on an opportunistic basis. Geology, soil, aspect, a landowner's farming skills and his economic ambition or necessity, all helped determine which lands were made available to the federal government.

19

The image many among the public hold of the national forests are those of the national forests of the West—"ancient forests"; remote backcountry and immense open spaces that bear little evidence of human impact; wilderness areas of hundreds of thousands of acres.

In the East, the reality is much different. Most of the national forests of the East are small as national forests go. All but five are less than a million acres, and about half are less than 500,000 acres. But as available public land in relatively large blocks, they loom large indeed. While there are thirty national forests of more than 250,000 acres, in all the East there are only a dozen other public land areas of this size.[4] In all but a handful of states, the national forests are virtually the only significant areas of public land.

Ownership is fragmented. Considering all the eastern national forests, the federal government owns just over half of the land within the purchase boundaries (the area in which the Forest Service is authorized to acquire land). But on many of the smaller forests, federal ownership within the purchase boundaries is well under 50 percent.

Because of intensive cutting before the land passed into federal ownership, trees are clustered in relatively young age classes—generally less than 100 years. Very few acres of the eastern national forests have not felt "the imprint of man's work," a point that once generated controversy over wilderness standards in the East.[5] There are 119 wilderness areas in the eastern national forests, but they tend to be quite small—only 37 are more than 10,000 acres in size.

At the time they were acquired by the federal government, most of the lands that are now the eastern national forests could hardly have been called "forest." For the most part they were cutover forestland or worn-out and abandoned farmland. Thus, forest rehabilitation has been and continues to be a theme of management of the national forests of the East.

Thanks to the natural resiliency of eastern forests and Forest Service stewardship, the land again supports stands of trees and diverse wildlife. Wilderness advocates and the timber industry conflict over land that was stumps and brush when it came under Forest Service management. Residents of eastern metropolises prize them as open space, playgrounds, and for their environmental and ecological values.

Failure to understand the history of the eastern national forests may contribute to differences between Forest Service personnel and the agency's critics. As one national forest planner put it: "We see the forest as the healing of a near environmental disaster, while our critics view current management as the pillage of a pristine wilderness."[6] Two other factors also are central to an understanding of the national forests of the East.

First, crazy-quilt land ownership, largely determined by acquisition opportunities over the years, virtually ensured that there would be numerous small towns and communities in the national forest environs—and many neighbors. The eastern forests always have had a close—even symbiotic relationship—with the communities and people who live in and around them.

Second, from their earliest days, management of the national forests emphasized improving the quality of life not only for those living in and around the forests, but for residents of urban areas, too. During the Great Depression, the eastern national forests were part of the engine of national economic recovery. Federal funds used to purchase and reforest wornout, often abandoned farmland pumped money into distressed local economies.

The aspirations for these forests were captured in this succinct management direction for a portion of the Nantahala National Forest in North Carolina written by forester Ray W. Brandt in 1937: "Improve social and economic conditions and stabilize local industries to the extent that these can be accomplished through harvesting national forest products on a sustained basis."[7]

The history of the eastern national forests is far more than the story of 24 million acres of federal land; it is the story of land use, society, and economics in the rural East and South over at least one hundred years.

The Forests Before Federal Acquisition

The forests of the eastern United States are dynamic and resilient systems, themselves the product of natural disturbance. A National Park Service botanist who studied forest processes and natural disturbance in the southern Appalachians, advises that "Historical [disturbance] events are important in understanding present composition."[8] Combinations and sequences of events—fire, pests, windthrow, ice storms, drought—all determine the course of forest development.

In recent centuries, the eastern forests have been affected by such natural events as fluctuations in climate over the 400-year span of the Little Ice Age (which ended in the mid-1800s)[9] and widespread pest infestations. Though not totally a natural event (it is caused by a fungus that originated in Asia), the chestnut blight eradicated a major component of the eastern hardwood forests in the 1920s and 1930s.

The effects of even localized disturbances can be substantial. In July 1977 an intense thunderstorm generated "downburst" winds up to 150 miles an hour, leveling trees in a swath 166 miles long and up to 17 miles wide—an area of 40,000 acres—in eastern Minnesota and northern Wisconsin. In March 1987, an ice storm struck an area on the Pisgah National Forest in North Carolina affecting 60,000 acres. In some places, entire stands were leveled, restarting the whole successional sequence. In other places, ice toppled the tall canopy trees, thus releasing well-established understory trees. Over large areas, individual trees were severely damaged, leaving them vulnerable to disease, pests, and drought and accelerating their deaths. Thus, across 60,000 acres of forest, the ice storm left a variety of conditions, creating an almost infinite number of changed successional patterns. Even more recently, in September 1989, Hurricane Hugo ravaged forests in Puerto Rico and the Carolinas; in South Carolina alone, 1.3 million acres required reforestation.[10] Natural disturbances perpetually create a mosaic of age classes and species across the forest landscape.

Early Settlement

Direct human impact on the eastern forests has been long and substantial. Native Americans cleared large areas in the forests to grow crops and repeatedly set fire to the underbrush to stimulate young growth favored by game. Fire historian Stephen J. Pyne writes that "So open were the woods, one author advised with a touch of hyperbole, it was possible to drive a stagecoach from the eastern seaboard to St. Louis without benefit of a cleared road . . . for this condition, Indian fire practices were largely responsible. . . ."[11] Of the effect of the native Americans, historian Michael Williams concludes that ". . . the Indians were a potent, if not crucial ecological factor in the distribution and composition of the forest." Williams adds that "their activities through millennia make the concept of `natural vegetation' a difficult one to uphold."[12]

Later, colonists and pioneers enlarged the openings created by the original forest inhabitants to provide fields for crops. Inexorably over the decades, the amount of forest in the East shrank as the area in farm fields expanded. By the time the logging industry began cutting the forests in earnest in the mid-1800s, much of the Northeast and Central Atlantic had been cleared and settled.[13]

Nonetheless, extensive forests remained in the Appalachian Mountains and to the west of the settled areas. The three upper Lake States—Michigan, Wisconsin, and

Minnesota—especially contained a rich lode of timber. Surveyors in the 1830s estimated that standing pine timber in Michigan amounted to 150 billion board feet, said to be sufficient to build ten million six-room houses. And the size of the trees was impressive. A photo apparently taken in the late 1800s shows a horse-drawn sled with white pine logs three to four feet in diameter stacked three times the height of a man. It was said to bear 100,000 pounds of logs.[14]

In the late 1800s, travelers in the southern Appalachians reported stands of mixed hardwoods with trees more than a hundred feet tall and four to seven feet in diameter. In the coves below Mount Mitchell in North Carolina, government surveyors found "A forest of oaks, hickories, maples, [American] chestnuts, and tulip poplars, some of them large enough to be suggestive of the giant trees on the Pacific Coast."[15]

The Advent of Logging on a Grand Scale

In the middle of the century, the logging industry developed the technology to cut, transport, and mill immense quantities of timber required to satisfy the needs of a growing, westward-spreading population. Between 1850 and 1910, the nation's annual timber lumber production increased eight-fold, from 5.4 billion board-feet to 44.5 billion board feet.[16]

Commercial logging on a grand scale came to Michigan in the 1860s, and shortly thereafter to Wisconsin and Minnesota. The magnificent white pine were cut first, with the timber sent to build Chicago and other Midwest cities. In 1892 some 9 billion board feet of white pine lumber was produced in the three states. That was the apogee of the white pine era in the Lake States; thereafter, the supply of white pine fell precipitously, and loggers turned to other species—maple, oak, hemlock, cedar, poplar, and jackpine, seeking opportunistic markets.[17]

As the supply of trees in the Lake States diminished, the industry turned southward. The lands that are now the Hoosier National Forest were cleared of timber between 1870 and 1910.[18] In 1899 Indiana was first among states in timber production. In the South, intensive harvesting began in the early 1880s and continued well into the current century.

In the southern Appalachians, the industry cut timber with an approach that might be termed extensive high-grading; whatever trees were of value at any given time were cut, without consideration of future species or quality. By the turn of the century, a government forester surveyed the southern Appalachians and found that lands near railroads had been "robbed of everything of commercial value . . ." and "the clearing and culling of a century have made considerable inroads into these forests."[19]

Further south, the Kaul Lumber Company began cutting the longleaf pine on land that is now part of the Talladega National Forest in Alabama in 1908. The timber was not exhausted until 1929.[20] Some areas were intensively grazed following timber harvesting, further retarding regeneration.

The loggers built haul roads and even railroads into rugged mountains in, for example, the Monongahela and the mountain forests in North Carolina. The Shining Rock Wilderness on the Pisgah National Forest still has remnants of the rails that permitted access to timber on the high ridges. On the Monongahela National Forest in West Virginia, hiking trails follow railroad grades used to remove logs in the early 1900s.

In areas where there were deposits of iron, timber was clearcut to make charcoal for the iron furnaces. In the area of western Virginia and eastern West Virginia, now in the George Washington National Forest, there were 54 charcoal iron furnaces in operation at different times throughout the nineteenth century.[21] Depending on stocking, it took between 50 to 150 acres of trees each year to provide charcoal for a furnace. Woodsmen cut virtually every living tree within hauling distance of a furnace, with some stands recut on 30-year rotations. Other lands, such as the Athens District of the Wayne and the Redbird unit on the Daniel Boone were strip-mined for coal.

Soil was degraded by years of abuse. Of the southern Appalachians, a federal forester wrote in 1917, "It is very probable that the productive capacity of forest soils throughout most of this region have been greatly decreased by repeated fires, so that the present forest growth is poorer in composition and quality than it once was."[22] And as will be seen, farming further impoverished thousands of acres of land later acquired for national forests.

The Barren Lands

Photos of the lands when acquired by the federal government are of a piece. Whether the Sumter National Forest in South Carolina, the Sabine in Texas, the Jefferson in Virginia, the Shawnee in Illinois, or the Nicolet in Wisconsin, the scene is largely treeless. In some cases charred stumps and snags mark the landscape. In other cases the scene is impoverished farmland. Of the land that was to become the Ozark National Forest: "Vast areas of some of the finest virgin timber in the country were practically clear cut. Entire watersheds were practically denuded. Fire followed the logging operations, destroying young timber and delayed for generations the renewal of the timber crop."[23]

Of land later incorporated into the Tuskegee National Forest in Alabama, a 1930s report to the Resettlement Administration noted: "The absence of trees on the hillsides is a constant reminder of the exploitation of the forest resources of the purchase area. Creeks where fish abounded twenty years ago are virtually sand beds or mud holes." And the Mark Twain, in Missouri: "After the logging operations were completed, areas were severely burned and many of the remaining trees were killed. Settlers told of days when the air was darkened with smoke and full of cinders for weeks at a time. Fires traveled at tremendous speeds, leaving charred messes [sic] in their wakes."[24]

The situation was much the same in northern Wisconsin, where the Chequamegon and Nicolet National Forests are now located: "The whole world of northern Wisconsin was on fire in those years [the 1920s]. You could choose a high point in any one of today's ranger districts and see miles of cut-over, burned-over land. Tree stubble and smoldering slash littered the landscape."[25] Thus, intensive cutting decades ago left a legacy of degraded soils (in some cases expanses of rock exposed by fire and rain) and timber of low commercial quality clustered in a few age classes that date from the period when regeneration of the forest began.

Not surprisingly, there is very little timber that can be called truly "old" on the eastern national forests. A few substantial stands did escape ax and fire; notable examples can be found in the Joyce Kilmer-Slickrock Wilderness on the Nantahala, and Heart's Content and Tionesta Scenic Areas on the Allegheny in Pennsylvania. But the situation on the Nicolet is more typical. There, the forest staff estimates that only about 1000 acres of the 654,000-acre forest were not cut—and these remnants are widely scattered in blocks of less than 40 acres.[26] The Pisgah and Nantahala National Forests, covering more than a million acres in the mountains of western North Carolina, were not as intensively cutover as most eastern national forests, yet 72 percent of their trees are between 40 and 80 years old.[27]

The people who worked for establishment of the national forests early in this century would be amazed to hear today's arguments over designation of wilderness, biological diversity, and even whether timber sales recover costs. When these lands were acquired by the Forest Service, one had to be very farsighted to recognize their potential.

Origins of the Eastern National Forests

The forests of the East were the crucible of a conservation movement that by the turn of the century had achieved the protection of millions of acres of public forest land—the original forest reserves—in the West. Vermont's Green Mountains were the early laboratory of George Perkins Marsh, whose remarkable 1864 book *Man and Nature: Or Physical Geography as Modified by Human Action* provided the intellectual foundation for the ensuing campaign to protect the nation's forests. Inspired by Marsh, opinion leaders sought to awaken citizens of the need for forest protection. The embryo conservation movement attracted the attention of historian Francis Parkman, who wrote pamphlets on the need for forest conservation.[28]

Passage of the Forest Reserve Act of 1891 was a major achievement of the conservationists. Over the next fifteen years four presidents placed more than 94 million acres of federal lands in the West in forest reserves—the forerunners of the national forests. But national forests came slowly to the East.

Although most of the public domain—land owned by the federal government—lay in the states of the Far West, some remained in a few states east of the 100th meridian—Florida, by virtue of the 1819 treaty with Spain, in the Lake States, because of cessions of territory by the original colonies, and in those states west of the Mississippi acquired in the Louisiana purchase.[29]

However, early forest reservation bypassed these public lands. Then, on July 4, 1901, President McKinley proclaimed the Wichita Forest Reserve in Oklahoma— the first eastern national forest (it was transferred to the Fish and Wildlife Service in 1936 and is now the Wichita Mountains Wildlife Refuge).[30] Six years later in 1907, President Theodore Roosevelt established the Arkansas National Forest (later renamed the Ouachita National Forest) in Arkansas. In 1907 and 1908, a half-dozen forests were established from public land, among them the Ozark in Arkansas, the Ocala in Florida, and the Superior in Minnesota.

But, in those states of the original thirteen colonies there was no federal public domain.[31] Establishment of national forests in the East on a truly significant scale would require that the federal government buy private land. However, there was no clear legislative authority for the government to buy land for national forests. That would come with enactment of the Weeks Law in 1911.

The Campaign for the Appalachian Forests

The campaign had begun more than two decades earlier. In 1893 Charles Sprague Sargent, an early leader of the forest conservation movement, urged that land in the southern Appalachians be protected for outdoor recreation. In 1899 the Appalachian National Park Association was organized to spearhead the campaign for creation of a federal park in the region.[32]

Agitation for a national forest in the White Mountains of New Hampshire dated back to the late 1880s. Flooding attributed to the removal of forests at the headwaters of the Merrimack and Pemegewasset Rivers damaged cotton mills in Manchester and left 6,000 workers jobless. At the turn of the century, a pamphleteering Episcopal minister named John E. Johnson fired salvo after salvo at the timber companies, specifically the New Hampshire Land Company. Johnson's campaign resulted in the creation of the Society for the Protection of New Hampshire Forests, which became the principle advocate of action to establish a national forest in the White Mountains. Meanwhile, states were establishing precedents for the protection of forest land in the East. As early as 1878, Wisconsin had created a forest reservation of 50,000 acres of state land at the headwaters of major state rivers. In 1885, after years of work by forest protection advocates, the New York State legislature established the Adirondack Park from land the state had retained from Crown lands after independence. In the 1890s Pennsylvania set about acquiring land at the headwaters of its major rivers for state forest reservations. And a number of eastern states also rallied behind the campaign to expand forest preserves on public domain in the West, further evidence of broad support for the creation of reserves in the east.[33]

In 1900 the Appalachian Mountain Club and the Appalachian National Park Association of the South Atlantic States sent a memorial to Congress asking for a study of the forests in the southern Appalachians, apparently with an eye to the establishment of a national park. Also in 1900, Congress appropriated $5000 with which Secretary of Agriculture James Wilson was to "investigate the forest condition in the Southern Appalachian Mountain Region of western North Carolina and adjacent states."[34] That the southern Appalachians, like the White Mountains, had superb scenic qualities was apparent even after large quantities of timber had been removed. The forested mountains had significant local value—for jobs, for hunting and fishing, and as a scenic backdrop. Enough forest remained as evidence of what had been lost and what might again be attained. There was also the belief that with some care the mountains could become a major tourist attraction. The petition from the Appalachian National Park Association pointed out that the region was "but twenty-four hours from New York, Chicago, St. Louis, Toledo, and the Gulf states. It is, therefore, within easy reach of millions of people. . . ."[35] Though economics was a motive, local residents apparently believed the area worthy of a national park at a time when the only models were a few great western parks like Yellowstone.

The Wilson Report: "The Conservation of the Forests"

Wilson's 1902 report documented both the best and the worst of the southern Appalachians. First, it described the magnificent forests that remained on the steep mountainsides and hollows. Then it documented the effects of the careless cutting of timber: "The soil, once denuded of its forests and swept by torrential rains, rapidly loses first its humus, then its rich upper strata, and finally is washed in enormous volume into the streams. . . . More good soil is now washed from these cleared mountain-side fields during a single heavy rain than during centuries under forest cover."[36]

Photos accompanying the report showed severe erosion where forested hillsides had been cleared for farm fields. In valleys, soils had been washed away, leaving acres of boulder fields. On steep hillsides, rainfall flushed away the humus, exposing expansive granite outcroppings.

Wilson concluded that the rivers of the southern Appalachians, because of their value for agriculture, water power, and navigation, were "absolutely essential to the well being of the nation."[37] Further, he wrote, "The regulation of the flow of these rivers can be accomplished only by the conservation of the forests." This was important for establishing the constitutional foundation for the federal purchase of land. Instead of a national park, Wilson recommended the establishment of a forest reserve, pointing out that while the federal government had set aside more than 70,000 square miles in the western forest reserves "There is not a single forest reserve in the East."

In recommending the "purchase and creation of a national forest preserve," Wilson asserted that "The states of the Southern Appalachian region own little or no land, and their revenues are inadequate to carry out this plan. Federal action is obviously necessary, is fully justified by reasons of public necessity, and may be expected to have most fortunate results." By action, Wilson meant outright purchase. While there was no direct legislative authority for the purchase of forest lands, Wilson pointed to precedents for federal land acquisition; the federal government had bought battlefield sites for military parks and had purchased land from the Blackfeet Indians that was added to the Flathead forest reserve in Montana.[38]

But for nearly a decade, opponents of federal acquisition were able to deflect bills implementing Wilson's recommendations. Their leader was House Speaker Joseph Cannon, who vowed "Not one cent for scenery."[39]

Success: The Weeks Law

As if to validate Wilson's report of the effects of forest loss and subsequent flooding, violent and tragic floods—like that of the Monongahela River in 1907—struck the East. And the results were devastating. In his *50 Year History of the Monongahela*, C.F. McKim writes that in the forests of northern West Virginia "Exploitation was the order of the day." Then in March 1907, "heavy rains brought flood waters down the Monongahela River . . . the trees and healthy vegetation were no longer there to regulate the rainwater's flow. It devastated all the rich agricultural land in the basin of the Monongahela River, causing some $100 million in damages—a gigantic sum for those times—then descended in all its fury upon the helpless city of Pittsburgh, causing there additional damages of $8 million, drowning people and ruining their homes."[40] To prod Congress to action, the West Virginia legislature enacted legislation permitting the United States to buy land for what became the Monongahela National Forest.

From the southern Appalachians and New England, support for the concept of forest reserves in the East spread to the Ozarks, the Hudson Highlands, the headwaters of the Mississippi, and to Texas. Gifford Pinchot wrote later: "It was this combined pressure that finally overcame the resistance of the House Rules Committee and that of that famous idealist, Joe Cannon."[41]

The Weeks Law was the progeny of the forest-purchase legislation introduced following the publication of Secretary Wilson's report nearly ten years earlier. The Weeks Law permitted the purchase of "forested, cut-over, or denuded lands within the watersheds of navigable streams . . ." deemed "necessary for the regulation" of their flow. At the time, the protection of watersheds was an overriding public concern and a major objective of forest protection in the West and East. However, the emphasis on protecting the flow of navigable streams also was intended to link the acquisition of forest land to the federal government's authority, under the Constitution's commerce clause, to regulate navigation.[42]

The immediate objective of the Weeks Law was the purchase of five million acres of forest land in the southern Appalachians and another million acres in the White Mountains in New Hampshire. It carried an appropriation of $9 million to be spent over six years for forest acquisition in those mountain regions. However, eastern national forest aspirations expanded quickly. Just two years later, a Forest Service study recommended that a national forest be established in Missouri. In 1923 the National Forest Reservation Commission—the committee of federal officials that determined where national forests could be established—recommended that national forests be established throughout the East. The next year, the Clarke McNary Act added "the production of timber" as a purpose for forest acquisition, thus permitting the purchase of land beyond the headwaters of navigable streams.[43]

Acquisition of the eastern national forests occurred in three pulses—the first the period from passage of the Weeks law into the early 1920s, the second a transition period in the late 1920s and early 1930s, and the third during the New Deal administration of President Franklin D. Roosevelt (See Table 1).

Protecting Mountain Watersheds

The first Weeks Law forest—the Pisgah in North Carolina—was established in 1916. Through 1923, ten more forests were established. Seven were in the central and southern Appalachians plus the Alabama (now the William B. Bankhead), the White Mountain in New Hampshire and the Allegheny in Pennsylvania, all justified on their value as protectors of water flows. The establishment of the Allegheny in 1923 brought an end to the first phase of Weeks Law forest establishment. The next ten years were a period of transition from the original Weeks Law forests to the forests of the New Deal.

With the exception of the Huron National Forest in Michigan, created by combining a portion of the Michigan National Forest with some acquired lands, no forests were established for the rest of the 1920s. Acquisition continued at a vigorous pace, however, and land was added to the existing forests. When enactment of the Clarke-McNary Act in 1924 removed the headwaters of navigable streams limitation on acquisitions, purchase units were established in Wisconsin, Michigan, Florida, and Louisiana.

Elected in 1929, Herbert Hoover was, in the words of one historian, "The first conservationist president since President Theodore Roosevelt." An avid fisherman, President Hoover brought to office a deep interest in fisheries and water quality. From existing purchase units, Hoover in 1930 and 1931 proclaimed four entirely new national forests—the Hiawatha and Ottawa in Michigan, the Osceola in Florida, and the Green Mountain in Vermont. During that time, the Kisatchie in Louisiana was established by departmental order.[44]

Table 1. The Eastern National Forests: A Chronology of Establishment.

1901	Wichita, OK	1936 - Transferred to Fish and Wildlife Service; now the Wichita Mountains Wildlife Range
1907	Arkansas, AR	Now the Ouachita NF
1908	Ozark, AR	
	Minnesota, MN	Now the Chippewa NF
	Ocala, FL	
	Choctawatachee, FL	1940 - Transferred to War Dept.
	Marquette, MI	Transferred to the Hiawatha NF
	Michigan, MI	Transferred to the Hiawatha NF and Huron NF
	Superior, MN	
1911	Florida, FL	Combined Ocala and Choctawatachee
	Enactment of Weeks Law	
1916	Pisgah, NC	
1918	Alabama, AL	Name changed to Black Warrior, then William B. Bankhead NF
	Shenandoah, VA	Name changed to George Washington
	White Mountain, NH, ME	
	Natural Bridge, VA	Transferred to George Washington
1920	Boone, NC	Transferred to Pisgah
	Nantahala, NC	
	Monogahela, WV	
	Cherokee, TN	
	Unaka, NC	Transferred to Pisgah
1923	Allegheny, PA	
1926	Ouachita, AR, OK	Name changed from Arkansas
1927	Ocala, FL	Created from portion of Florida NF
1928	Chippewa, MN	Name changed from Minnesota
	Huron, MI	Created from Michigan NF and other lands
1930	Kisatchie, LA	Established by Dept. order
1931	Hiawatha, MI	
	Ottawa, MI	
1932	Osceola, FL	
	Green Mountain, VT	
1933	Geo. Washington, VA, WV	Name changed from Shenandoah
	Nicolet, WI	
	Chequamegon, WI	Created from part of Nicolet and other lands
1936	Jefferson, VA, WV, KY	Created from Unaka and G. Washington NF lands
	Appalachicola, FL	
	Kisatchie, LA	[Proclaimed]

1936	Bienville, MS	
	Holly Springs, MS	
	De Soto, MS	
	Black Warrior, AL	Name changed from Alabama
	Chattahoochie, GA	Created from portions of Cherokee, Nantahala, and other lands
	Francis Marion, SC	
	Sumter, SC	
	Conecuh, AL	
	Talladega, AL	
	Homochitto, MS	
	Croatan, NC	
	Angelina, TX	
	Davy Crockett, TX	
	Sabine, TX	
	Sam Houston, TX	
1937	Cumberland, KY	Name changed to Daniel Boone
1938	Manistee, MI	
1939	Shawnee, IL	
	Mark Twain, MO	
	Clark, MO	Added to Mark Twain
1942	Wm. B. Bankhead, AL	Name changed from Black Warrior
1951	Hoosier, IN	
	Wayne, OH	
1959	Oconee, GA	Created from Bankhead-Jones land
	Tombigbee, MS	Created from Bankhead-Jones land
	Tuskegee, AL	Created from Bankhead-Jones land
1960	St. Francis, MO	Created from Bankhead-Jones land
1961	Delta, MS	
	Uwharrie, NC	
1966	Daniel Boone, KY	Name changed from Cumberland
1985	Finger Lakes, NY	Created from Hector Land Use Project (Bankhead-Jones land)

Data compiled from USDA Forest Service, "Establishment and Modification of National Forest Boundaries: A Chronologic Record, 1891-1973," Division of Engineering, Washington, D.C., 1973.

These forests responded to the economic imperatives of the era, particularly the deterioration of farm-based local economies. And they presented an extraordinary opportunity for Franklin D. Roosevelt. President Hoover established the Nicolet National Forest on March 2, 1933, just two days before his successor's inauguration. Three weeks later the new president had proposed and Congress had enacted legislation creating the Civilian Conservation Corps. From the first camp on the George Washington National Forest—Camp Roosevelt—seventy miles west of Washington, CCC camps spread across the nation. Eventually, the Nicolet would have twenty CCC camps.[45]

New Deal, New Forests

The New Deal forests—twenty-two in number—were created out of the suffering of land and people—land that had been abused and people trapped in economic despair. Proclaimed by President Franklin D. Roosevelt, the New Deal forests reflected his social aspirations and his deep and abiding concern for natural resources.[46]

Scattered across the East, from the Mark Twain in Missouri, to the Chequamegon in Wisconsin, to the Osceola and Apalachicola in Florida, to the Angelina, Davy Crockett, Sabine, and Sam Houston in Texas, their establishment reflected complex needs and aspirations. The first was land rehabilitation. Logging and repeated fires, often combined with careless farming practices, had left large areas biologically impoverished. Something had to be done to restore the land.

The second was economic. When Roosevelt took office farm prices and incomes were in a state of collapse.[47] As farm families abandoned the land in ever-greater numbers, local governments saw tax receipts plummet. Businesses that depended on farm spending also were imperiled. It did not take long for state and local officials to see that federal land purchase and investment in management could provide some relief to hard-pressed local economies.[48]

Meanwhile, President Roosevelt was looking for ways to put the growing army of jobless to useful work. Deciding that the land was a good, wholesome workplace and there was much that needed to be done, President Roosevelt allocated $20 million for forest acquisition from a special emergency fund. For the most part, states and localities were eager to attract federal investment—in land acquisition, road-building, and reforestation. In northern Wisconsin, the Park Falls *Herald* anticipated much-needed jobs building roads in the new national forests, editorializing that "The federal government doesn't do things like that in a small way." There also was the idea that these national forests, many created from depleted farmland, would serve to demonstrate how land could be rehabilitated through stewardship and caring management.[49]

Since World War II only three new forests have been established outright—the Wayne in Ohio, the Hoosier in Indiana, and the Uwharrie in North Carolina. Several other forests—including the newest, the 13,232-acre Finger Lakes National Forest in New York (1985)—have been were established from land that was acquired under the Bankhead-Jones Farm Tenant Act,[50] a New Deal farmland acquisition and rehabilitation program.

Early Management

The first challenge facing managers of these new national forests was simply to acquire enough land to make them viable public forests. The second was to control wildfire. The third was to begin the long course of restoration—a task still in progress.

Acquiring the Forests

The first task was to acquire enough land for a viable national forest. This began well before the forest was officially established by presidential proclamation. The National Forest Reservation Commission—comprised of the secretaries of Agriculture, Interior, and War and two congressmen and two senators—determined where new forests could be established and drew the boundaries of forest purchase units. Only when it was felt that enough land had been acquired within a purchase unit to permit efficient management was a new national forest officially established. This could take some time. The Forest Service got a commitment on the first tract in what was to become the Monongahela National Forest in 1911; the forest was not designated until 1920.[51] In some cases, purchase units were abolished when it proved impossible to acquire sufficient land.

The eastern forests were purchased by the federal government with the approval of state legislatures and (except for a few rare instances) from willing sellers. Under provisions of the Weeks Law, a state legislature had to pass legislation permitting the federal government to buy land. Some states were eager to get federal money into depressed communities. Other states were wary. Wisconsin's original 1925 enabling bill limited federal purchases to only 100,000 acres. In 1933 this was raised to two million acres. Maryland passed then rescinded legislation permitting federal acquisition.[52]

With state approval in hand, the Forest Service moved aggressively to acquire land. Especially during the 1930s, there was considerable competition among states for the limited funds available for national forest acquisition. Local advocates feverishly urged landowners to sell, less the opportunity to gain a national forest be lost.[53]

Overall, purchases were opportunistic. The federal government could not buy only the most productive land, or the most scenic, or land that protected valuable wildlife habitat. Basically, federal buyers had to take what was offered and try to collect enough land into a unit that could become a viable national forest. Some landowners sold their land to the federal government, but retained the right to cut the timber—leaving the Forest Service to reforest it later. When it came to farm land, farmers with better land who felt they could hang on refused to sell. But others with lower quality lands, or inadequate skills, or the need or desire for quick cash sold. Thus, factors both biological and social determined which acres came under public ownership.

Moreover, the federal government did not buy the rights to subsurface minerals over large areas of some national forests—the Wayne, the Hoosier, the Allegheny, the Daniel Boone, the Monongahela, the Jefferson, the George Washington, and the Superior. Ownership of minerals is complex. Of those rights to subsurface minerals not owned by the federal government, outstanding rights—those held by a party other than the landowner when the land was bought by the Forest Service—continue to be the most troublesome. Management problems continue, particularly in the case of coal and oil, although the Forest Service has become more aggressive in exercising its rights to protect surface resources from impairment by subsurface mineral exploration and development.[54]

Controlling Fire

Fire was a persistent threat to the forests. In some cases, the problem was lightening strikes in dry slash left behind by the loggers. But in other areas, particularly in the South, the principle cause of wildfire was arson. In some mountain areas, arson was a traditional way of taking revenge or settling a grudge. And when the federal government began hiring mountaineers to fight fires, there would be a rash of "job fires" to generate employment during lean times. Over the years the Forest Service has been effective in enlisting local residents in anti-fire campaigns, although arson continues as a way of expressing discontent with government programs.[55] It was the eventual control of fire that truly permitted restoration of the forests.

Reforestation and Rehabilitation

For the first forests, the 1920s were a period of custodial management and planning. But as forests were created pell-mell during the 1930s, and with the young men of the CCC as a workforce, attention turned to forest rehabilitation, reforestation and construction of administrative buildings, campgrounds, picnic areas, and roads and trails. Corpsmen planted prodigious numbers of trees; on the Manistee National Forest in Michigan, individual corpsmen planted 1,000 to 1,500 tree seedlings a day. On the national forests in Texas, Corpsmen planted 15,000 acres in a year.[56] On the Hiawatha, red pine plantations planted by the CCCs are large enough to be seen now in high-altitude aerial photographs.

Corpsmen built campgrounds, filled gullies and redirected water run-off to control erosion, and restored fish habitat. Throughout the forests, one can see and use structures that have become monuments to the industry of the CCCs: the Woodstock Tower in the George Washington National Forest; the headquarters building of the Chippewa National Forest in Cass Lake; campgrounds at Ratcliff Lake, Boykins Springs and other recreation areas on the national forests in Texas; Blanchard Springs Dam on the Ozark; and picnic shelters, trails, and bridges just about everywhere on the eastern national forests.

It would be understandable if today's Forest Service personnel, besieged by forest interest groups and consumed with planning, regarded the Forest Service veterans of the CCC era with envy; by all accounts, they got enormous satisfaction from their work. Marvin L. Smith, ranger on the Mineral Lake District of the Chequamegon wrote in 1935: "It is mighty gratifying to all of us to be growing up with the forest. We regret very much the condition of the land that [was] bought [by the federal government] but find additional pleasure in reclaiming many thousands of acres which, were it not for the federal government and its resources, might remain unproductive for a good many years."[57]

Management Today and in the Future

Following World War II, the eastern national forests continued their transformation from barren lands to true forests. Recreation use soared. The amount of timber harvested increased, but so did the amount of wood on the land, reflecting the regrowth of the forest. That restoration continues is attested to by increases in forest growth and the volume of standing timber on national forests in the East. Between 1952 and 1987, the volume of standing timber on the eastern national forests, both hardwoods and softwoods, more than doubled (Table 2).

Table 2: Changes in Standing Timber Volume on the Eastern National Forests, 1952 to 1986

(Million Cubic Feet)

REGION	1952		1986	
	HARDWOODS	SOFTWOODS	HARDWOODS	SOFTWOODS
Northeast	1,983	459	4,127	746
N. Central	2,482	1,336	5,470	3,270
Southeast	2,481	1,991	5,055	2,855
South Central	1,785	3,123	4,502	6,466
TOTAL	8,731	6,909	19,154	13,337

* Source: USDA Forest Service, *An Analysis of the Timber Situation in the United States: 1989-2040*, Tables 77 and 78

Yet managers continue to work with a legacy of resources that are still below their productive potential for wildlife, recreation, water, and timber, and fragmented ownership that imposes increasing challenges to managers.

Actions which the Forest Service believes to be necessary to continue the process of restoration, especially clearcutting, generate angry protests. The controversial clearcuts on the Monongahela in the early 1970s that ultimately resulted in the National Forest Management Act of 1976 were motivated by a desire to replace low-quality cull trees with vigorous new stands in an area that had been extensively high-graded while in private ownership. Nearly twenty years later, clearcutting remains a persistent point of controversy.

So are timber sales. Over much of the eastern forests it costs more to sell the forests' low quality timber than the government gets for it, and Forest Service contentions that timber sales benefit other resources and increase future asset value have not persuaded Forest Service critics.

Meanwhile, there are continued campaigns for wilderness designation and, more recently, demands for management that promotes biological diversity. There is a growing appreciation of the forests' significance as public open space, playgrounds, and of their ecological and scientific resources.[58]

But perhaps the greatest change is that of the public's role. From being users, many have become active, informed *participants* in the management of the forests themselves. Forest users grapple with issues of management in the course of participation in national forest planning, filing of appeals, and legal action. Thousands also contribute ideas and energy as volunteers on the forests.

It is clear that priorities are shifting. Forests are reassessing their timber programs to reduce clearcutting and to produce less timber but of higher quality and value. If one reads the forest plans closely, one sees greater emphasis being given to wildlife, recreation, and water and other non-timber values.

Without the bold initiatives of the Weeks Law, there would be little public open space and recreation land in most states in the East. Acquisition continues, though at a deliberate pace. Although it has been many years since Congress last appropriated money for general forestland acquisition, the Forest Service continues to use its Weeks Law acquisition authority to buy land with money from the Land and Water Conservation Fund. Jack Alcock, regional forester for the twelve-state Southern Region, says that acquisition and consolidation of ownership is the region's "number one priority."[59] Alcock believes that the 1990s may be the last opportunity to buy critical tracts.

And local officials still believe that the forests can diversify and reinvigorate rural economies. At least one long-neglected unit has benefited from new local appreciation of its potential. The Uwharrie National Forest in North Carolina—which the Reagan administration wanted to sell to reduce the federal deficit—recently got $750,000 for acquisition. Local officials, who once opposed land purchases for the fragmented, 48,000-acre forest, now believe that a bigger and spruced up Uwharrie may become the base of a recreation economy.[60]

Restoration is still a theme, but concepts of restoration are far more sophisticated than planting trees to hold soil in place and soak up rainfall. On the Huron-Manistee National Forest, scientists are designing a system of old growth restoration areas; the ultimate goal is to restore old growth on 173,000 acres, or 18 percent of the forest. Virtually every forest is looking at areas for restoration of old-growth forests, though not enough acres to satisfy some critics.[61]

On the Pisgah National Forest, scientists from North Carolina State University, Mars Hill College, and the Forest Service are inventorying animals and plants on sample plots spread across 20,000 acres of the Toecane Ranger District; the objective is to develop a methodology for measuring biodiversity.[62]

The lands that nobody wanted fifty years ago now are the lands everybody wants. Through the forest planning process, forest staffs and forest users are struggling to identify the appropriate roles—environmental, social, and economic—individual forests should play now and in the next century. Nearly fifteen years ago, a report by The Conservation Foundation urged that management of the eastern national forests emphasize "providing public benefits that cannot be supplied by private land, either because resources are unavailable or because an economic incentive is absent." The plan for the Green Mountain echoes those words, stating that the forest will be managed "to provide public benefits that private land does not."[63]

Some forest staffs are looking closely at just what distinguishes the national forest from other lands in their environs and are charting a course that capitalizes on a forest's distinctive values. For example, Ottawa National Forest Supervisor Dave Morton believes his forest "Will continue to escalate in value as a 'wild' place in a populated Midwest region." The staff of the Mark Twain has determined that Forest's primary values are "ecological, aesthetic, wildlife and recreation, in that order." And from the Hoosier: "We will offer you outdoor recreation experiences that accentuate the Hoosier National Forest's unique characteristics and that are not available elsewhere."[64]

The eastern national forests are quintessential democratic institutions. Established with the express consent of the states, they were intended to address serious—even extreme—conditions ecologic *and* economic. And they reflected a public consensus that the national forests were to be managed to address multiple social and environmental goals—to relieve human suffering and restore degraded lands. As the nation approaches the twenty-first century, debate over their management tests our concepts of broad community interest and public consensus. Yet this intense debate over issues—some old, some just emerging—attests to the value of these forests and the foresight of those who, a century ago, believed there should be national forests in the East.

Notes

The preparation of this paper was partially supported by a grant from the World Wildlife Fund and The Conservation Foundation.

1. William E. Shands and Robert G. Healy, *The Lands Nobody Wanted*, [Washington, DC: The Conservation Foundation, 1977].

2. These forests fall in what are now the Forest Service's Eastern and Southern Regions. The westernmost states of these regions are Texas, Oklahoma, Missouri, Iowa, and Minnesota. Though located east of the 100th meridian and a part of the Southern Region (R-8), I have not counted the Caribbean National Forest in Puerto Rico among the national forests of the East. Its history and ecology are sufficiently different to make it unique among all the national forests.

3. Figures on national forest acreage are from "Land Areas of the National Forest System as of September 30, 1990," USDA Forest Service, 1990.

4. Shands and Healy, *The Lands Nobody Wanted*, p. 1.

5. The Wilderness Act. Act of September 3, 1964 (P.L. 88-577, 78 Stat. 890; 16 U.S.C. 1131-1136); Dennis M. Roth, *The Wilderness Movement and the National Forests*, (College Station, TX: Intaglio Press, 1988), p. 40.

6. J. Terry Moore, Nicolet National Forest, letter to author, March 4, 1991.

7. Ray W. Brandt, "Management Plan—Franklin Working Circle, Nantahala National Forest, North Carolina." December 30, 1938. Unpublished report in files of the National Forests in North Carolina, Asheville, NC.

8. Forest Stearns, "The Changing Forests of the Lake States" in W.E. Shands, ed. *The Lake States Forests: A Resources Renaissance* (Washington: The Conservation Foundation, 1988), p. 25; Peter S. White, "Pattern, Process, and Natural Disturbance in Vegetation," in *The Botanical Review*, Vol. 45 No. 3 July-September 1979, p. 230.

9. Forest Stearns, "The Changing Forests of the Lake States," p.26.

10. Orie L. Loucks, "New Light on the Changing Forest," in Susan Flader ed. *The Great Lakes Forest: An Environmental and Social History* (Minneapolis: University of Minnesota Press, 1983), p. 18; Arthur Rowe, ranger, Pisgah District, Pisgah National Forest, North Carolina. Interview, July 15, 1991; Howard Burnett, "In Hugo's Wake," *American Forests*, January/February 1990, p. 17-20.

11. Stephen J. Pyne, *Fire in America: A Cultural History of Wildland and Rural Fire* (Princeton, New Jersey: Princeton University Press, 1982), p.46.

12. Michael Williams, *Americans and Their Forests: A Historical Geography*. (Cambridge: Cambridge University Press, 1989) p. 49.

13. Douglas W. MacCleery has calculated that in the 60 years ending in 1910, forest was cleared for farmland at the average rate of 13.5 square miles per day. Douglas W. MacCleery, "Condition and Trends of U.S. Forests: A Brief Overview," 1990, p. 2. Unpublished paper available from author, USDA Forest Service, Timber Management Staff, Washington, D.C; Williams, *Americans and Their Forests*, p. 118-128.

14. Rolland H. Maybee, *Michigan's White Pine Era*. [Lansing: Michigan Historical Commission, 1960], p. 11.

15. The Southern Appalachian Center, Mars Hill College, "A Socioeconomic Overview of Western North Carolina for the Nantahala-Pisgah Forests," 1979, p. 73. Unpublished report prepared for USDA Forest Service, National Forests in North Carolina, Asheville, NC; James Wilson, *A Report of the Secretary of Agriculture in Relation to the Forests, Rivers, and Mountains of the Southern Appalachian Region*, (Washington, DC: GPO, 1902), p. 23.

16. MacCleery, "Conditions and Trends of U.S. Forests.

17. Williams, *Americans and Their Forests*, p. 222; Maybee, *Michigan's White Pine Era*, p. 53.

18. USDA Forest Service, "Draft Environmental Impact Statement, Land and Resource Management Plan Amendment for the Wayne-Hoosier Forest National Forest, April 1990" p. 3-4.

19. David L. Loftis, Southeast Forest Experiment Station, interview, January 14, 1991; H.B. Ayres and W.W. Ashe, "Forests and Forest Conditions in the Southern Appalachians," an appendix to Wilson, *Report of the Secretary of Agriculture*, p. 45.

20. Robert G. Pasquill, USDA Forest Service, "A Brief History of the National Forests in Alabama with Particular Attention Being Paid to the Forest Conditions at Time of Acquisition," 1991. Unpublished paper on file with the National Forests in Alabama, Montgomery, AL. (Unpaged).

21. George W. Kelley, USDA Forest Service, George Washington National Forest, Harrisonburg, VA. Personal communication to author, February 26, 1991.

22. E. H. Frothingham "Report on Study of Cut-Over Areas in the Southern Appalachians." Dated 1917. Unpublished report in files of the National Forests in North Carolina, Asheville, NC. p. 65.

23. USDA Forest Service. 1962. "History of the Ozark and St. Francis National Forests" quoted in "Ozark National Forest Timber Management Plan," USDA Forest Service, 1978, p. 8.

24. Robert G. Pasquill, "A Brief History of the National Forests in Alabama with Particular Attention Being Paid to the Forest Conditions at Time of Acquisition," unpaged; USDA Forest Service. 1991. "Missouri's National Forest," pamphlet published by the Mark Twain National Forest, Rolla, MO. (No page numbers).

25. The Daily Press [Ashland, WI]. 1983. "Chequamegon: The Making of a Forest," in special supplement, "The Chequamegon National Forest in its 50th Year—1933-1983. November, 1983. p. 3.

26. J. Terry Moore, USDA Forest Service, Nicolet National Forest, Rhinelander, WI, letter to author, March 4, 1991.

27. USDA Forest Service, National Forests in North Carolina, "Final Environmental Impact Statement, Land and Resource Management Plan 1986-2000: Nantahala and Pisgah National Forests," Asheville, North Carolina, p. III-6.

28. George Perkins Marsh, *Man and Nature: Or, Physical Geography as Modified by Human Action* (Cambridge, MA: Harvard University Press, 1965); Howard Doughty, *Francis Parkman* (New York: Macmillan Co., 1962) p. 316.

29. USDA Bureau of Land Management, *Public Land Statistics, 1988* (Washington: GPO, 1989), p. 3.

30. USDA Forest Service, Division of Engineering, "Establishment and Modification of National Forest Boundaries: A Chronologic Record 1891-1973," dated October, 1973. This volume is the source of all dates on forest establishment used in this paper.

31. With the colonies' independence, New York state retained crown lands for itself. Speculators claimed most of these lands, but were not interested in the steep, seemingly inhospitable acres that, a little more than a century later, became the nucleus of the Adirondack Park. Frank Graham, Jr., *The Adirondack Park*, [New York: Alfred A. Knopf, 1978], p. 6. My thanks to Bob Wolf for reminding me of the fact of New York state public domain.

32. Harold K. Steen, *The U.S. Forest Service: A History*. (Seattle: University of Washington Press, 1991) p. 123; Andrew Denny Rodgers III, *Bernhard Eduard Fernow: A Story of North American Forestry*, (Durham, NC: Forest History Society, 1991) p. 247.

33. David Conrad, "The Return of the Forests," p. 46. Unpublished manuscript in files of the USDA Forest Service History Unit, Washington, DC, 1988, 46-47; Frank Graham, Jr. *The Adirondack Park: A Political History*. (New York: Alfred A. Knopf, 1978) p. 105; Rodgers, *Bernard Eduard Fernow*, p. 214, 222, 246.

34. James Wilson, *A Report of the Secretary of Agriculture*, p. 13.

35. Ibid, p. 162.

36. Ibid, p. 38.

37. Ibid, p. 39.

38. Ibid, p. 40, 36.

39. Samuel T. Dana and Sally Fairfax, *Forest and Range Policy: Its Development in the United States* Second Edition (New York: McGraw-Hill, 1980) p. 111.

40. Gifford Pinchot, *Breaking New Ground* (Washington, DC: Island Press, 1987), p. 240.

41. C. R. McKim, *50 Year History of the Monongahela National Forest* (USDA Forest Service, no place of publication or date), p. 3.

42. John Ise, *United States Forest Policy* (New Haven: Yale University Press, 1920), p. 211; Pinchot, *Breaking New Ground*, 240.

43. Act of March 1, 1911 (16 U.S.C. 515); Harold K. Steen, *The Beginning of the National Forest System* (Washington, DC: USDA Forest Service 1991) p. 29; Steen, *The U.S. Forest Service: A History*, p. 125.

44. U.S. Congress. 1930. *A National Plan for American Forestry* (Washington: Government Print-ing Office) p. 1172; USDA Forest Service. 1973. "Open Space for People." No date, no place of publication. p. 6; Shelley Smith Mastran and Nan Lowerre, *Mountaineers and Rangers: A History of Federal Forest Management in the Southern Appalachians 1900-81* (Washington, DC: USDA Forest Service, 1983), p. 29.

45. Donald C. Swain, "Conservation Accomplishments, 1921-1933," in Roderick Nash, ed., *The American Environment: Readings in the History of Conservation* (Reading, MA: Addison-Wesley Publishing Co., 1968), p. 144; According to the "Establishment and Modification of National Forest Boundaries," the Kisatchie was first established by order of the secretary of agriculture in 1930, and then established again in 1936 by presidential proclamation.

46. Arthur M. Schlesinger, Jr., *The Coming of the New Deal* (Boston: Houghton Mifflin Co., 1959), p. 20; Terry Moore, Nicolet National Forest, interview, June 27, 1991.

47. Arthur M. Schlesinger, Jr., *The Coming of the New Deal*, p. 320.

48. Ibid. p. 27; *See*, for example, USDA Forest Service, "Draft Environmental Impact Statement, Land and Resource Management Plan Amendment for the Hoosier National Forest," April, 1990, p. 3-7.

49. C. R. McKim, *50 Year History of the Monongahela National Forest*, p. 12; Ashland Daily Press, "The Chequamegon National Forest in its 50th Year," p.4; Fred Soady, Jr., "The Making of the Shawnee," in *Forest History*, Vol. 9, No. 2, July, 1965, p. 5.

50. Act of July 22, 1937.

51. The National Forest Management Act of 1976 (Sec. 17) abolished the National Forest Reserva-tion Commission and gave the Secretary of Agriculture the authority to identify lands to be acquired; C. R. McKim, *50 Year History of the Monongahela National Forest*, p. 7.

52. Ashland Daily Press. 1983. "The Chequamegon National Forest in Its 50th Year" p. 4; Dana and Fairfax, *Forest and Range Policy*, p. 114.

53. Fred Soady, Jr., "The Making of the Shawnee," p. 8.

54. Stanley Kurcaba, USDA Forest Service, Minerals and Geology Management Staff, Washington, DC, interview with author, June 13, 1991; Shands and Healy, *The Lands Nobody Wanted*, p. 58. *See also* General Accounting Office, "Private Mineral Rights Complicate the Management of Eastern Wilderness Areas," Report to Congress, July 26, 1984; Jack Bills, USDA Forest Service, Minerals and Geology Management Staff, Washington, DC, telephone interview with author, June 12, 1991.

55. Bass, Sharon M.W. 1981. Op. Cit. p.48; Shelley Smith Mastran and Nan Lowerre, *Mountaineers and Rangers*, pp. vi, 34.

56. Alison T. Otis, et. al., *The Forest Service and the Civilian Conservation Corps: 1933-42*, p.61; *The Daily Sentinel*, Nacogdoches, TX, "Forest system benefited from the projects of the CCC" in supplement "Celebrating a 50th Anniversary: National Forests in Texas," Oct. 10, 1986. p. 4.

57. In May 1991, the author had an opportunity to talk with a group of Forest Service retirees from the Eastern Region (R-9), many of whom began their careers in the 1930s. Though they had gone on to achieve much during their careers, it was clear that in many respects, their work on the forests of the 1930s was a high point; Ashland Daily Press, "The Chequamegon National Forest in its 50th Year," p. 5.

58. For a discussion of "the forest as a human environment rather than as a source of commodities" *see* Samuel P. Hays, "The New Environmental Forest" in *University of Colorado Law Review* 59:3 Summer 1988.

59. Shands, W.E. et. al. 1990. *National Forest Planning: Searching for a Common Vision.* (Washington: USDA Forest Service). *See* especially, Chapter II, "The Public's Role in Decisionmaking"; Jack Alcock, USDA Forest Service, Southern Region, Atlanta, GA, letter to author dated March 22, 1991.

60. The Associated Press. 1990. "N.C.'s Neglected National Forest Spruced Up," in the Asheville (NC) *Citizen*, December 31, 1990.

61. "Landscape Ecology and New Perspectives on North Central Forests," *Forest Perspectives: New Directions in Natural Resources Management*, Vol. 2, Issue 2, p. 14; John R. Luoma, "In Wisconsin, a Debate Over Ways to Manage National forest Growth," *The New York Times-The Environment*, Tuesday, October 18, p. 22.

62. USDA Forest Service, National Forests in North Carolina, Asheville, NC, "Nantahala/Pisgah Plan Re-Analysis Update," June 1991 (unpaged).

63. USDA Forest Service, "Record of Decision: Final Environmental Impact Statement, Land and Resource Management Plan, Green Mountain and Finger Lakes National Forests," 1986, p. 3.

64. On the concept of management for distinctive values, *see* William E. Shands, "Beyond Multiple Use: Managing National Forests for Distinctive Values" *American Forests*, Vol. 94, No.3&4, March/April 1988, p. 14; Dave Morton, USDA Forest Service, Ottawa National Forest, letter to author, March 13, 1991; B. Eric Norse and Kathy McAllister, USDA Forest Service, Mark Twain National Forest, "The Mark Twain Perspective," undated and unpaged; Frank Voytas, USDA Forest Service, Wayne-Hoosier National Forest, Bedford, IN, personal communication, April 8, 1991.

Canadian Federal Forest Reserves, 1883-1933:
A Parallel Experiment

Peter Gillis
Treasury Board of Canada

In the years between 1929 and 1933, a series of agreements turned over control of natural resources to the three Canadian Prairie provinces of Manitoba, Saskatchewan, and Alberta. In addition, federal lands set aside in the province of British Columbia to support the construction of the Canadian Pacific Railway and never taken up by the company were turned back to the province. Part of this natural resource patrimony were the federal forest reserves or national forests which had served as the center-piece of Canadian forestry and forest conservation efforts at the national level since the turn of the century.

The reasons for federal abandonment can, on the surface, be easily rationalized on constitutional grounds. The *British North America Act of 1867*, which established governmental structures in Canada, clearly gave control over natural resources to the provincial governments. The Canadian government had emulated its American counterpart in controlling natural resources in the West after the transfer Rupert's land from the Hudson's Bay Company to its control in 1869 in order to use these in fuelling western settlement and national development. By the 1920s, however, many Canadians felt that the role of the Dominion in settling western Canada had been fulfilled. The land had been settled; the railways had been built, if not actually over built; and the western provinces established. The western provinces themselves were adamant in wishing equality of status. They found themselves short of money for local improvements and were sure that management of their natural resources would generate the needed revenues.

These constitutional issues played into the political hand of William Von MacKenzie King, the Liberal Prime Minister through most of the 1920s. National political parties had been shattered in the wake of the conscription crisis of 1917. Regional-ism was rife in the country, and a general political disillusionment had set in. Tax dollars were scarce and the federal government was anxious to cut its commitments. In the West, the Progressives, a farmers' protest movement that had achieved national prominence in the 1921 federal election, saw the resource issue as vital. For King, his primary aim was to rebuild the Liberal Party as the dominant force in the

Canadian federal politics. He assiduously wooed the Progressives, many of whom were former Liberals. In this context, the natural resource issue became an important issue and the federal forestry reserves a political football within it.

The wisdom of the overall transfer cannot be doubted or criticized. The West had been settled, and there was no reason to treat these provinces on a different constitutional basis than any of the others. Unfortunately, in the case of the forest reserves, there was a lack of vision, understanding, and, it must be added, competence. The forest industries were then and continue today as the most important sector of the Canadian economy. The federal government shared jurisdiction with the provinces in other natural resources fields such as agriculture and mining. Federal forestry initiatives were based on American examples where the federal government retained control of large amounts of forest land and shared the costs of forestry programs with the states. As will be discussed later in this paper, this seemed to hold the promise for some truly creative federalism in the forestry sector. Both the Dominion forestry service and a few public critics warned that some federal forest land would be needed in the future and that the federal government was not being responsible in giving it all away. This prophecy had been proved true by the mid-1930s. King, however, walked way for any strong central role for the federal government in national forestry policy. In failing to retain at least some of the federal forest reserves, the Liberal administration immeasurably damaged public forestry and forest conservation in Canada. This paper analyzes the origins of federal forest reserves, their role in early public forestry administration in Canada, and the reasons for their demise.

Origins

The idea of having areas of land dedicated to the production of trees, where forest would be protected and reserved for timber harvesting, had fairly early origins in Canada. The meeting of the American Forestry Congress in Montreal in 1882 had served to focus the attention of Canadian lumbermen on the need to protect existing stands of merchantable timber. Though their interests lay mostly in fire protection and land classification to protect their existing investment in standing forests these lumbermen forged alliances with scientists, horticulturists, and a growing number of middle class professionals concerned about the decline and over-exploitation of eastern Canadian forests to bring about considerable pressure on all governments to take some action on forest conservation.[1]

The provinces of Ontario and Quebec moved to establish the first public forest reserves in the years immediately after the Congress, though the first actions in

Quebec were to be short lived. The federal government, under the leadership of Sir John A. Macdonald, did not react very actively to the Congress recommendations. Preoccupied with the need to attract settlement to the Prairies and concerned about the lack of forest cover in that region, it was not inclined to push forest land classification and other regulatory measures which might discourage settlement and local timbering. Already in the belt of railway lands in British Columbia there was conflict between local lumbermen and the government over the cost of logs, and Macdonald was not willing to place further constraints on the small sawmills in Manitoba, Alberta, and British Columbia.

Instead, the Prime Minister decided that it would be better to study the matter. In late February 1883, a faithful Tory, Joseph H. Morgan, with no previous experi ence in forest issues, was appointed to prepare a study of forestry measures for the West.[2] In 1884 Morgan presented preliminary report which recommended a tree planting program for the region. This report was lost in the excitement over the Riel or Northwest Rebellion of 1885. But concern over the need for increased western settlement after 1885 secure Morgan's reappointment in July 1887 as forestry commissioner, with a mandate similar to 1883, except that he was now to consider ways of "preserving and protecting the forests of the Dominion."[3] Morgan presented another positive report on the planting and went on to recommend protection of the headwaters of rivers flowing from the Rocky Mountains through fire protection and forest reservations. This built on an early amendment to the *Dominion Lands Act* in 1884 which provided for "the preservation of forest trees on the crests and slopes of the Rocky Mountains, and the proper maintenance throughout the year, of the volume of water in the rivers and streams." This was a recognition that forest conservation would play a vital role in the settlement of the semi-arid lands of southern Alberta and Saskatchewan.[4]

Morgan was dismissed from the federal service in 1890 as a result of a disagreement with his boss, A. M. Burgess, deputy minister of the interior, but his work had laid the basis for an approach to federal forestry—tree planting, watershed conservation, and forest reservation. The boundaries for Rocky Mountain Reserve were laid out and some rudimentary forest protection undertaken in the reserve, but these activities were under the control of the Timber, Mineral and Grazing Lands office of the Department of the Interior, which was such more interested in leasing timber berths. This combined with poor economic conditions to slow any further dynamic forestry activities. Only after 1893 did the Conservative government revitalize the forest reserve surveys and move in 1894 to create the first reserve outside the Rockies—Moose Mountain Reserve in present-day southeastern Saskatchewan. But the Tories had lost John A. Macdonald to death in 1891 and could not renew the leadership of the party. They were toppled from power in the federal election of 1896 by the Liberals, led by a French Canadian, Wilfrid Laurier.

Laurier Liberalism and American Influence on Forest Conservation

The Liberal Party under Laurier was an amalgam of interest groups and ideologies stretching from the prime minister's rather traditional laissez-faire liberalism, tempered by political expediency, to Minister of the Interior Clifford Sifton's clear-headed, calculated dedication to material progress. Sifton thought that government should act as the dynamic leader for private enterprise, using regulation as necessary to guide businessmen to serve the public interest.[5] Regardless of ideological orientation, the Liberals had as a priority the speeding up of the economic development of Canada, particularly the West, where they thought they thought efficient and enlightened resource policies would aid the settlement process.

To find these latter policies the Liberal government simply turned to ideas long in gestation within the Department of the Interior. William Pearce, superintendent of mines in Calgary, and E. F. Stephenson, inspector of Crown timber agents, based in Winnipeg, both made recommendations. Pearce favored forest reserves because they would help conserve water needed for irrigation. Stephenson suggested that more and larger forest reserves were needed beyond the areas of water conservation and that all western forests could be protected while not interfering with settlement or commercial exploitation of the woodlands.[6] These suggestions were then given life by Sifton. He strongly believed in centralizing policy for the public lands in the prairies and western forests. An interested observer of American trends, the minister well appreciated the mounting popularity of scientific forestry in that country and the economic arguments provided by men such as Gifford Pinchot to support more efficient resource use.

The Laurier government moved by order-in-council on 24 July 1899 to create a new post of chief inspector of timber and forestry within the existing Timber and Grazing Branch of the Department of the Interior.[7] The chief inspector was to report on the stage of western forest reserves, to survey new areas, and investigate wildfire conditions on Dominion lands. The order also set out new timber lease conditions and set up a system for fire protection on licensed berths. The first chief inspector was Elihu Stewart, a land surveyor with extensive experience, some ambition, and excellent political connections. He was a sound administrator, with an amateur's avid enthusiasm for his newfound vocation. He quickly reinterpreted his vague commission to be the creation of a judicious system of forestry in Canada based on tree planting in western Canada and the formation of more forest reserves. Stewart also made it his mission to escape the limiting confines of the Timber and Grazing Branch.[8]

Stewart turned first to tree planting, meeting western demands for trees to alleviate the bleakness of the plain and to establish windbreaks which would reduce crop damage and water evaporation. To establish a program, he turned for inspiration to the U.S. Bureau of Forestry and projects started by the midwestern states. In March 1901, Norman M. Ross, the first professional forester hired by the Canadian government, joined Stewart to run the tree planting program and establish a station to grow seedlings.[9] This work convinced the government to grant Stewart's wish to separate himself from Timber and Grazing as the new superintendent of forestry for Canada.

Stewart, however, did not have full support for a full-blown forestry program in the West. Some prairie settlers did agree with federal officials that existing forested areas did need to be preserved. Living in a fragile, largely treeless environment, these settlers readily recognized the connection between forest conservation and soil protection. They also knew firsthand the hardships of timber scarcity. The local lumber industry met some of their needs but they still relied on mills operating on the Pacific coast for most supplies. But the majority of settlers and the prairie lumber interests showed little support for forest conservation, which they regarded as the ideas dreamed up by federal bureaucrats and eastern lumber interests and definitely against their immediate economic self-interest.

Stewart saw the first reserves as the key to his forestry program, but he had to create a policy climate in which he could win control over western forestlands. He was supported in this view by no other than Gifford Pinchot. Shortly after taking office, the superintendent had written and then visited Pinchot at the Forestry Bureau in Washington.[10] Pinchot was flattered by the approach and free with his advice. He opined that it was absolutely essential to efficient forest administration that federal forest lands be controlled by one authority dedicated to scientific forestry and that it was absolutely essential that all remaining government-held forestland in the North-West Territories and British Columbia be reserved.[11] Thus at the very beginning Canadian forest policy makers turned to American experiences and advice, apparently believing that the two countries had more in common than was actually the case. This lack of appreciation for the political, constitutional, and cultural differences between the two nations was to eventually lead to some serious policy miscalculations.

In 1899 there is no doubt that the main intention of the Liberal government, as opposed to Stewart, was to meet the western demand for a more aggressive tree planting program. Just before Christmas that year the new deputy minister of the interior, James Smart, an old friend and political confidant of Sifton, requested that Stewart bring together a group of influential Canadians to discuss forming a Canadian Forestry Association which could galvanize efforts for prairie tree planting.[12] Stewart consulted about the meeting with Sir Henri Joly de Lotbiniere, who had acted as president of the Montreal conference in 1882, and was then serving as minister of inland revenue in the Laurier government. Lotbiniere was essential in ensuring that representatives of the eastern lumber interests which were supporting forestry measures were represented at the meetings along with federal ministers, bureaucrats, scientists and, perhaps most important, Thomas Southworth, clerk of forestry, in the liberal administration in the province of Ontario and the stoutest public advocate of scientific forestry then on the Canadian scene.

The first meeting was held on 15 January 1900 and resulted in a call for a public association modelled on the American Forestry Association. A public meeting was to be held to "kick off" the new organization, and Southworth and Stewart worked to ensure that the association would concern itself with "national forestry methods" and "forest preservation" as well as western tree planting.[13] The Railway Committee Room in the Parliament Buildings was filled on 8 March 1900 for the first official meeting of the Canadian Forestry Association. The direction of the new organization was unanimously adopted as support for forest conservation and preservation, including large-scale forests reservation in western Canada.[14] Stewart now had a powerful lobby group to support his activities and with a bit of political gamesmanship in early 1905 he was able to have himself placed in charge of both the forestry and timber-leasing operations within Interior. Political events were to make this a fleeting victory, and Stewart's high-handed approach was to earn him enemies within the government that were to frustrate his larger goals.

Basically, Stewart needed a piece of legislation to firmly establish and expand the western forest reserves. He was working on such a bill when Clifford Sifton suddenly resigned from the Laurier administration over French language education in the West and a growing frustration with the prime minister over his approach to government.[15] Stewart, his staunchest ally for forest conservation, was gone; followed by his deputy Smart shortly afterward. The situation was further complicated by the new minister, Frank Oliver. He was Sifton's political and ideological opposite. His political tenets turned around the federal government not intervening in western development. Founder and editor of the *Edmonton Bulletin* in Alberta, Oliver had built a career in championing western development and values and on paying attention to local issues and grievances.[16]

Stewart, however, still had powerful forces on his side. The government's support for the Canadian Forestry Association was only part of Laurier's strategy to identify with the popular issue conservation. A "Canadian Forestry Convention" had been arranged by Stewart for 10-12 January 1906 to galvanize support for his legislation. The prime minister and other ministers applauded the event as they attempted to leave no doubt that they would be emulating the dynamic measures of Theodore Roosevelt and Gifford Pinchot in the United States, particularly after Pinchot himself agreed to be the conference's keynote speaker.[17] Pinchot was not slow to once again attempt to place his imprint on Canadian forestry policy. He called on the Canadian government to adopt an organized forestry policy; to evaluate land before settlement and to reserve all non-agricultural forest areas; to promote the management of reserves by trained government employees; to improve federal fire fighting, including along railway rights of way; and to encourage tree planting on the Prairies.[18] All other speakers supported or amplified these points, and in the post-convention euphoria Stewart convinced Oliver to introduce the *Dominion Forest Reserves Act.*[19]

The bill had been conceived in November 1904, just a few months before Sifton's resignation. The bill retained the Dominion practice of creating reserves by government order-in-council but established strict legal conditions for their management. In this way reserves could be quickly created in non-agricultural areas of the West regardless of whether or not they were under a current timber license or other lease. Gifford Pinchot would have heartily approved of this power-ful, single-purpose legislation. Sifton too was supportive, returning the bill only to have included in it clauses to provide for wildlife protection in the reserve areas.[20] With Sifton's resignation, needless to say, Frank Oliver was such less enthusiastic. He quibbled that the wildlife protection measures infringed on provincial jurisdic-tion but his real, unstated problem lay with the use of orders-in-council to override established rights. The new minister supported the rights of the individual over government and considered the alteration of a lease to be a breach of contract.

Thus it was with some misgiving that Oliver proceeded to first reading of the bill. Now, with the balance of power shifting in the Department of the Interior, under a new minister and a new deputy minister W. W. Cory, Stewart's rogue attitude of by-passing his superiors and dealing with the political level came back to haunt him. Oliver sought other advice, often cutting Stewart out of the consultation.[21] The political pressure for the forest reserve measure was substantial, however, and all might have been well had not the San Francisco earthquake in April 1906 sent western lumber prices sky-rocketing. Western farmers now became convinced that suppliers were gouging them and their outrage forced the government to appoint a parliamentary Select Committee to investigate price fixing.[22]

Obviously, the forest reserve bill did not directly affect the price of lumber on the Prairies but rumors abounded that it would restrict access to lumber by western lumbermen and thus serve to keep prices high. Oliver not only saw a chance to make changes but was also driven by new political considerations. It was an emasculated bill which proceeded to second reading in May 1906. Timber leases were excluded from the area of forest reserves, as the government declared, to protect leaseholder rights and creation of reserves by order-in-council and the establishment of management rules on the same basis were also eliminated. Clearly, the Liberal administration had backed away from its public commitment to create a new, all-powerful forestry organization. It had placed reserves, which by this time amounted to 2.9 million acres, under a superintendent of forestry and, under intense opposition pressure, had agreed to expedite the conversion of abandoned timber leases into reserve lands.[23]

The Laurier Liberals did not return to forestry legislation until 1911 with the *Forest Reserves and National Parks Act*. The bill was in part an effort to refurbish the conservation ethic of a government soon to face a general election, which in fact it was to lose. A separate National Parks Branch was created but with Frank Oliver still minister, the actual boundaries of the Rocky Mountain Parks were reduced to ensure that they did not stand in the way of economic development. Indeed, the debate and political maneuvering around the bill reveals both the fragility of the concept of forest conservation prior to World War I and the Laurier administration's ambivalence toward it. In the debates over the bill, a number of familiar themes reappeared. Politicians representing western constituencies split from easterners. A prairie populism emphasizing local control was once more pitted against eastern desire for scientific planning and controlled use of natural resources. But western opinion itself remained diverse and complicated the political landscape for Oliver.

Farmers and wealthy ranchers in southern Alberta wanted the forest reserves on the eastern slopes of the Rockies enlarged. Western lumbermen, in contrast, worried that larger reserves would jeopardize their precarious position and that increased forestry regulation would drive them out of business. Finally, prairie settlers remained concerned about what they considered the high price of lumber and resented the eviction of squatters from forest reserves after passage of the 1906 legislation. Robert H. Campbell, Stewart's assistant who replaced him on his retirement in 1907, wished to use the new legislation to obtain control over western timber berths.[24] It rapidly became obvious, however, that Oliver aimed at very specific measures which did not interfere with the existing rights and regulations of leaseholders. He aimed to give national parks a legal definition, similar to forest reserves except that they would be small in size and public access would be guaranteed. He would also enlarge the size of the Rocky Mountain Reserve. The Forestry Branch was given 36 as opposed to the existing 21 reserves with an area that was increased from 3.3 million acres to 16.6 million acres. It also had increased control over fire regulations, including those lands outside reserves and greater control over public access to reserve lands.[25] Too, the Branch was given increased appropriations to cover its new responsibilities.

The government boasted of this expansion as proof that it was dedicated to wise resource planning. The extent of the new reserves was impressive but the accomplishment might have been more meaningful if the minister had chosen to talk about forestry and forest conservation instead of private rights and the utilitarian need to use timber in his speeches in support of the legislation. This gap been the ideals of forest management and the final provisions of the 1911 legislation clearly revealed the vulnerability of the conservation movement to political necessity. Oliver understood this vulnerability, which defined the Laurier government's support of the conservation cause. Now the Liberals would provide ample funding for the Forestry Branch but would not face down the political difficulties or additional expenses of intensive forest management on productive timberlands. From 1911 on the federal government turned to creating and enlarging federal forests reserves as a compromise. The policy would continue to protect "vested interests" in resource exploitation while appearing to adopt modern resource management and land classification ideas.

The *Forest Reserves and National Parks Act* was the last major forest conservation initiative undertaken at the federal level in Canada before World War I. Theodore Roosevelt and Gifford Pinchot again influenced the conservation movement in Canada with their plans for a series of conservation commissions. A Commission of Conservation was established by the federal government in April 1909. The commission had investigatory powers but no executive authority.[26] Under the leadership of Clifford Sifton and its dynamic secretary, James White, it carried on much excellent research, including pioneering work in forest inventory and forest disease and insect control. It did add, however, to the very fragmentation of federal forests management activities against which Pinchot had originally warned Elihu Stewart he must guard. By 1914 four separate agencies divided federal forest administration--the Forestry Branch, the Parks Branch, the Timber and Grazing Branch, all within the Department of the Interior, and the independent Commission of Conservation. The challenge for federal foresters in the early postwar years would be to achieve a single forest authority and to use this to expand the reserves to operating timber berths.

The Limits of National Leadership

The First World War created a sense of dedication to reform and a new order in the field of federal forestry as it did in other domains.[27] The first British Empire Forestry Conference, held in London, England, in 1920 and attended by the rising star of the Forestry Branch, Ernest Herbert Finlayson, gave the impetus to again push for a single forestry authority which controlled all federal forest lands. Finlayson's report roundly criticized the disparate efforts of the Conservation Commission and the failure of Timber and Grazing Branch to adopt forestry measures.[28] The demise of the Conservation Commission in 1921, in the wake of its determined secretarial controversy with the unionist prime minister, Arthur Meighen brought the Forestry Service immediate new responsibilities for working with provincial governments in forest surveys and inventorying, as well as silvicultural and forest insect research projects.[29]

With these changes, the Branch moved quickly to re-establish itself as the single national spokesman on forestry and forest conservation. R. H. Campbell set four initiatives that the Branch would pursue in developing a national forest policy: improvement, protection and expansion of western forests reserves (totalling 23 million acres in 1921); development of a nationwide research program emphasizing cooperation with industry and provincial governments; a national forest inventory; and public education on forestry.[30] A political embarrassment for the Liberal government of William Lyon MacKenzie King, which had defeated Meighen's Unionists in 1921, provided the impetus to keep reform of federal forestry measures on center stage.

The issue was the contentious matter of shipping unprocessed timber to the United States. Most provinces already controlled the export of unmanufactured wood cut on Crown lands and successive federal administrations had been careful to stay clear of the thorny issue. At stake in this case, however, was pulpwood cut on private lands. Basically, pulpwood cut on settler's lands in marginal farming areas of eastern Canada was a prime source of supply to newsprint manufacturers both in Canada and the United States. Canadian manufacturers were convinced that the American trade forced up the price of settlers' pulpwood and aided foreign competitors. They elicited the services of a timber broker turned publicist and self-proclaimed conservationist from Atlantic Canada, Frank J. D. Barnjum, who, through connections in the Montreal business community, finally persuaded the King government to prohibit the export of pulpwood in June 1923.[31]

Immediately the government began to realize the size of the hornet's nest it had kicked. The prime minister backtracked in the face of criticism over interference with property rights and public rumbling from the powerful Liberal premier of Quebec, L-A Taschereau, on the effect of the ruling on the colonization movement in that province. King quickly opted for the time honored approach of a royal commission to fully investigate the pulpwood issues and make recommendations on forest conservation. The work of the commission is interesting in itself, but what concerns us here is that E. H. Finlayson was appointed its secretary. He conducted the research and wrote the final report. It provided an escape hatch from the embargo fiasco and made an articulate plea for better forest management practices across the country. A grateful government responded by allowing the embargo provision to die and then seized the political advantage by announcing its intention to embark on a new national forestry policy aimed at the preservation of Canadian forests.[32]

Finlayson, who was confirmed as director of forestry in 1925 as a result of his work on the Royal Commission, started to push forward these new forestry initiatives even before the final report was completed. He convinced the minister of the interior, Charles Stewart, to sponsor a federal-provincial meeting in Ottawa in January 1924 to discuss improvements to fire protection. Stewart was regional representative in the Cabinet for the western Prairies and a low tariff man with a strong belief in the development of Canadian resources. He became interested in and committed to forestry measures but, unfortunately, he did not enjoy King's confidence (indeed King would have preferred someone else in the Cabinet) and this would make him a pawn rather than a power broker in the future power struggle over the western forest reserves.[33]

The conference was viewed as the first of several to secure federal-provincial agreement on how to deal with problems such as fire protection, forest inventory, and dedication of lands to forest production. Fire protection was chosen as the first topic because of its relatively non-controversial nature. The provinces, for their parts, were facing expenditure and taxation problems which made them willing to discuss measures which might relieve the cost of maintaining their forests. Stewart's opening address to the conference gave the reason for some hope in this regard. The minister commenced with a call for cooperation in fire protection matters which would "bring about some degree of uniformity throughout the country in regard to the preservation of forests". He went on to suggest that the federal government was tentatively considering to aid this process through financial assistance. Further, Stewart said that, though federal officials considered forest disease and insect control as provincial matters, the government might also consider assistance in these areas as well. In return, the federal government wanted a national commitment to the classification of more forest land and the establishment of more forest reserves. A new fiscal arrangement for forestry in Canada was being proposed and this issue overshadowed all other discussions at the conference.[34]

The proposal was rudimentary in nature but it envisioned for Canada a forestry aid system similar to that existing in the United States, where the federal government contributed to state programs. The *Weeks Act*, on which this American scheme was based, had been studied by the Forestry Branch. Outside of the wealthy province of Ontario, the others were interested in obtaining federal aid in forest protection but also too canny to surrender such independence over land classification and forest management standards. The best that could be agreed to was a commitment to further conferences to discuss the basis for agreements. Stewart, himself, betrayed the federal government's lack of clear direction in his closing remarks, where he indicated that he was willing to listen to provincial proposal but held out little hope for direct Dominion assistance in areas of purely provincial jurisdiction. Rather, he claimed that his original remarks had been aimed at "points of contact" between the two levels of government, though he did not stipulate what these might be.[35]

The gains were modest but they did bespeak of the possibilities for a more creative federalism in the forestry field. At the political level, however, the constitutional position during the 1920s and 30s was that forestry was almost exclusively a provincial responsibility and should not benefit from direct federal aid. This constrained the possibilities for innovative federal-provincial solutions until after World War II. Without the power of divination, however, the Forestry Branch was buoyed by the prospect of further federal-provincial cooperation and the promise of a renewed forestry program promise in the wake of the Pulpwood Commission, where the newly named Dominion Forestry Service would be given control of operating timber berths.[36]

By 1926 the Forestry Service was to find how fleeting this promise of progress was to be and how chimerical was the King government's commitment to forestry. It is not overly cynical to suggest that the Liberals had moved rapidly with the recommendations of the Pulpwood Commission because it was facing a general election in 1925. Forestry remained a pre-election commitment and a likely field for popular measures. Stewart, however, did not have enough pull in Cabinet to obtain approval for any type of strong forestry policy. When it was announced in June 1926, the policy dealt only with western lands and was not very adventurous. Rejecting artificial planting and regeneration technique, it responded only to the Service's desire that western forest reserves be extended until they comprised all nonagricultural lands in the West suitable for timber growth. The government also declared its intention to regulate cutting on such land so as to ensure natural regeneration. This was a good deal less than a truly National Forestry Program and even this smacked of a sham since no timetable was announced and actual forest reserve land had shrunk from 23 to 21 million acres during the King years in government.[37]

It rapidly became obvious that progress even on these very limited objectives would be non-existent. That indeed, the highwater mark of the King government's infatuation with the political possibilities of forest conservation had been passed in 1926 to be replaced by disinterest and a desire to abdicate any federal role in forestry. The policy itself disappeared in the political crisis known as the King-Byng Affair where King was forced from power for a short period of time.[38] After the fall of the Meighen Conservatives, King returned to power with a majority government; Stewart once more as minister of the interior and with a new set of political priorities. A major goal was to reach a settlement with the Prairie provinces for the handing over control of the western natural resources, including the timber reserves, in order to strengthen the Liberal party politically and also to economize on administrative costs.

The Abandonment of the Forest Reserves

These priorities conflicted directly with the Forestry Service's own goals and objectives to expand and redefine its mandate. It was in the period leading up to the resources Transfer Agreements that Stewart's lack of stature with King jeopardized the Service's ability to make its case effectively to the Prime Minister. But all can not be blamed on the minister. The Service itself had blind spot on the resource transfer issue. It had been a growing political problem since the end of World War I. Among Canadians there was a feeling that the Dominion's purposes in eastern Canada had been fulfilled and it was time to treat the western provinces like all the others. Those provinces themselves were adamant in wishing equality. They found themselves pressed for money for local improvements and were certain that management of their own natural resources could generate these revenues. At the same time, pressure festered at the federal political level. National parties lay shattered in the wake of the conscription crisis; regionalism was rife and a general disillusionment had set in. In the West, the Progressives, the fragmented farm protest movement which had grown to prominence during the war years, saw the resource issue as important. King set as one of his primary tasks the rebuilding of the Liberal party through the reintegration into it of the progressives, many of whom were disenchanted Grits. Therefore, at various times after 1921, King offered the transfer of western resources as part of a political package which would gain this end, though the prime minister's terms were not particularly generous.[39]

These difficulties perhaps lulled the Forestry Service into a false sense of security. Attached to the "purchase theory" for Rupert's Land, which likened the acquisition of the public domain in the Canadian West to that in the United States, it argued that even if some lands were turned over to the western provinces, extensive timberlands must be retained under federal ownership to accomplish national goals in conserving wood supplies and promoting proper forest management techniques.[40] King, however, subscribed to the more legally sound position that the western provinces had a constitutional right to the control of their resources based on the *British North America Act*. In the desultory federal-provincial negotiations of 1922 this rejection of the American model did not have such impact, because the federal position had included control over western timber. After the political crisis of 1926, the prime minister desperately wanted western political support and the situation was to be different.

King was particularly interested in a coalition with Premier John Bracen's Progressives in Manitoba. Bracken was willing to deal but he wanted the resource question settled first. In July 1928, with both a political coalition and a resource transfer agreement on the table when Bracken travelled to Ottawa, King was more disposed to be reasonable. Manitoba was given control over much of its natural resources, including the Dominion Forest Reserves. All that remained was for a proposed Royal Commission to determine a suitable financial settlement between the two governments.[41] Suddenly and dramatically the ground on which the Service had built a substantial part of its mandate was radically altered. At the political level, the agreement was greeted favorably and there was little that the Forestry Service could do but fight a futile rear guard action to stop the Manitoba formula from being adopted elsewhere.

King, for his part, had not come to the end of his political maneuvering. Happy with his success with Manitoba, and not able to extend this automatically to Saskatchewan and Alberta, the prime minister turned to British Columbia. There the Railway Belt ran through the heart of the province. Most of this territory was largely inaccessible forest land which had not been taken up either by the railways or for settlement. Several forest reserves had been established in the belt and more were planned. The British Columbia government was interested in taking over administration of the area again but a federal Royal Commission on the reconveyance of land to British Columbia had declared in 1928 that the province had no right of ownership.[42] The prime minister now offered up the Railway Belt in order to steal a march on the Conservatives, who were becoming popular there.

Finlayson realized that if the Forestry Service was to make a stand it would be in the Railway Belt where there was no doubt about federal ownership of the land. An effort was made to intervene in the political gamesmanship with proposals for a clause in the transfer agreement which would preserve federal control over substantial forest areas in the belt. The Service contended:

> The primary value and function of the national forest areas is to meet . . . a future emergency, under present conditions, even in the eastern provinces where forest revenues are higher and where market values are greater, the local authorities have found themselves unable to take the necessary precautions in this condition (sustained yield), although Ontario and Quebec are now taking initial steps in that direction. . . . It appears, therefore, a foregone conclusion that the prairie provinces, at any rate, would find themselves unable to carry on the protection and administration of these national forest areas to the extent to which their importance in the national interest demands.[43]

As for the west coast reserves, British Columbia had argued in the recent past that at least part of its forest should be regarded as a national resource and administered at federal expense. The argument had some impact and plans were made for the reservation of four substantial national forests in that province. Finlayson was confident that a truly national role for the Forest Service had finally been recognized, particularly since it would also assume responsibility for two research stations in British Columbia; one on the coast and another in the interior.[44]

Once again, however, all had been done without due regard to the necessities of politics. By late 1929, it was obvious that everything was becoming unstuck. On the broad front, the final negotiations for a resource transfer agreement with Manitoba were completed. The only mention of forestry was a federal admonition that the province provide for professional care of its forests. With another federal election looming in 1930, King signed away the Railway Belt with none of the conditions requested by the Forest Service. The prime minister's only regret was that he could not persuade Alberta to cash in on a federal offer to turn over control of its natural resources. The actual agreements with Alberta and Saskatchewan were to drag into the 1930s and were eventually ratified by the new Tory government of R. B. Bennet. King, however, claimed credit for all the deals, and his major biographer states that they were probably the major achievement of the prime minister's third administration.[45]

Thus in four years the work of over three decades was abandoned and dismantled. The propriety of the natural resource transfers cannot be doubted or criticized. The West had been settled and there was no reason to treat these provinces on a different constitutional basis than any of the others. There was, however, in the case of forestry, a lack of vision, understanding, and it must be added, competence. Examples of cooperative forestry measures were put before the politicians by E.H. Finlayson and his officials time and again and the promise of creative federalism in this area examined extensively. It would appear that provinces such as Saskatchewan, Alberta, and British Columbia may have been easily persuaded to leave substantial reserves under federal control to aid both forest research and experimental work, and timber conservation and watershed protection objectives. This is not to say that federal administration was inherently superior to provincial control but rather that federal forests would have continued to give a such stronger federal-provincial cast to forestry which could have helped to break the constitutional log-jam for a national forestry program. The King government was incapable of recognizing or grasping that challenge.

Ultimately political expediency frustrated the Forestry Service's idealist vision that the state could use the tools of scientific resource management to promote efficient and enlightened utilization of those resources in support of national growth and development. The Service was imbued with the conservation ideas of American progressives such as Gifford Pinchot and later federal-state programs which involved both federal control of large forest reserves and financial support for local efforts. After 1920 it attempted to bring these ideas to fruition in Canada. Though the Service appreciated the extent to which basic management and silvicultural techniques must underpin forestry operations, it also realized that Canada needed the essential structure of a National Forest Policy before the other goals could be met. The Service was convinced that such policy should involve federal control of substantial western timberlands which could be managed for future generations; federal funding and active participation in and leadership of forestry research; and federal-provincial cooperation in fields such as forest inventories, fire protection, land classification, and reforestation. The abandonment of the western reserves cast such a pall over federal forestry that it was not to recover for almost two decades, when some of the visionary ideas of the early 1920s would eventually find their way into the *Canada Forestry Act of 1949*.

Notes

1. For a full discussion of the origins of the forest conservation movement in Canada *see* R. Peter Gillis and Thomas R. Roach, *Lost Initiatives: Canada's Forest Industries. Forest Policy and Forest Conservation* (Westport, Connecticut: Greenwood Press, 1986), Chap.2, The Beginnings of a Movement, pp. 31-50.

2. National Archives of Canada, Records of the Department of the Interior, Record Group 15, vol. 298, file 62441.

3. Ibid., vol. 311, file 69113.

4. Peter Murphy, *History of Forest and Prairie Fire Control Policy in Alberta* (Edmonton, Alberta: Energy & Natural Resources Information Centre, 1985), p. 132; NAC, RG 15 vol. 311, file 69113 and vol. 630, file 235667, pt.2; Canada, *Statutes* 47 Vict., cp 25 and Senate, *Debates* (28 March, 1884), pp. 358-364.

5. For more details on Sifton's career *see* David J. Hall, *Clifford Sifton*, vol.1, *The Young Napoleon. 1861-1900*, and vol. 2, *The Lonely Eminence 1901-1929* (Vancouver, British Columbia: University of British Columbia Press, 1981 and 1985).

6. Canada, Department of the Interior, *Annual Report* (1898).

7. NAC, RG 15, vol. 772, file 523278.

8. Ibid.

9. Canada, Department of the Interior, *Annual Report* (1900) and Murphy, pp. 102-105.

10. NAC, Records of the Canadian Forest Service, RG 39, vol. 267, file 39766 Policy, National Forests.

11. Ibid., vol. 19, file 383, Policy, U.S. Forest Service, E. Stewart to G. Pinchot, 23 Aug. 1899; Pinchot to Stewart, 2 Aug. 1899; Stewart to Pinchot, 29 Nov. 1899; and Pinchot to Stewart, 16 Dec. 1899.

12. For a detailed discussion of the formation of the Canadian Forestry Association *see* R. Peter Gillis and Thomas R. Roach, "The American Influence on Conservation in Canada: 1899-1911," *Journal of Forest History* 30:4 (October 1986): 160-174.

13. NAC, RG39, vol. 232, file 349, T. Southworth to E. Stewart, 24 January, 1900.

14. Canadian Forestry Association, *Report of the First Annual Meeting, (Ottawa, 1900) and Formation of the Canadian Forestry Association's Rod and Gun in Canada* 10 (March, 1900), pp. 192, 202-204.

15. The complicated events surrounding the Sifton resignation are dealt with in Hall, *Clifford Sifton* vol. 2, pp. 162-182.

16. Frank Oliver's career is dealt with in Hall, *Clifford Sifton*, vol. 2, pp. 1-62, 191-192, 199, and 229; and Pierre Berton, *The Promised Land: Settling the West 1896-1194* (Toronto, Ontario: McClelland and Stewart, 1984) pp. 58-59, 94-98, 206-208, 255.

17. Canadian Forestry Association, *Report of the Canadian Forestry Convention* (Ottawa, 1906) and G. Pinchot, *Breaking New Ground* (Seattle: University of Washington Press, 1972), pp. 254-262.

18. G. Pinchot, p. 254.

19. Canada, House of Commons, *Debates* (1906), vol. 1, p. 559.

20. NAC, RG39, vol. 259, file 3805-1-2 "Forest Reserve Act."

21. Ibid., *see* particularly correspondence between Cory and departmental legal counsel, T.G. Rothwell, 5,9 and 1 March, 1906.

22. Canada, House of Commons, "Proceedings of the Select Committee appointed for the Purpose of Inquiring into the Prices Charged in the Provinces of Manitoba, Alberta, and Saskatchewan", *Journals of the House of Commons of Canada* 42:2 (1907) and Hall, *Clifford Sifton* vol. 2, p. 96.

23. Canada, House of Commons, *debates*, 1906, vol. 2, pp. 2832, 3318, 3412; vol. 3, pp. 5416, 5537, 5556.

24. NAC, RG39, vol. 259, file 3805-1-2.

25. Canada, House of Commons, *Debates*, 1911, vol. 5, pp. 8085, 8600-8623, 8650-8659.

26. The Commission of Conservation is discussed in detail in Gillis and Roach, *Lost Initiatives*, pp. 75-76, 192-196.

27. *See* Gillis and Roach, *Lost Initiatives*, Chapter IV.

28. NAC, RG39, file 40129, Finlayson Report.

29. NAC, Records of the Department of Northern Affairs and National Development, RG22, vol. 6, Report of Council on Conservation Commission.

30. Ibid. RG39, Campbell correspondence, file 40129.

31. Canadian Annual Review. 1923.

32. NAC, RG39, Proceedings of the Royal Commission on Pulpwood; and *Canadian Annual Review*. 1924-25.

33. For an analysis of Stewart and the politics of the Cabinet *see* H. B. Neatby, *William Lyon Mackenzie King, vol. 2, The Lonely Heights* (Toronto, University of Toronto Press, 1963).

34. NAC, RG398, Proceedings of the Dominion-Provincial Conference on Forest Fire Protection.

35. Ibid.

36. Ibid., vol. 248, file 28829.

37. Ibid., vol. 271, file 40139-II.

38. For details on this constitutional crisis refer to R. Graham ed., *The King-Byng Affair. 1926: A Question of Responsible Government* (Toronto, 1967).

39. *See* C. Martin, *Dominion Lands Policy* (2nd edition, Toronto: MacMillan, 1973).

40. Ibid.

41. For Brackens' career *see* J. Kendle, *John Bracken: A Political Biography* (Toronto: University of Toronto Press, 1980).

42. Neatby, *Lonely Heights.*

43. NAC, RG39, vol. 95, file 48183.

44. Ibid.

45. Neatby, *The Lonely Heights.*

How Do We Write and Interpret the History of National Forests?

Joseph A. Miller
Yale University

My qualifications, aside from the national forest experience this week, are these: research on how Congress disposed of public lands and created forest reserves and parks in the late 1800s, an editing of letters from the Apache National Forest in 1914-1915, and a paper on the history of sustained yield and community stability.[1] Presently, I am editing letters to and from Gifford Pinchot in the 1890s. Finally, I must note the general interest of a forestry librarian and long-term advocate and practitioner of conservation and environmental history.

This is to let you know at the beginning that I have not tried to write a history of any national forest, or component thereof, nor am I really an interpreter, except in the broad sense of the word. But I have some ideas and opinions, based on the aforesaid experiences, to share with you this afternoon.

My title reads "write and interpret." For historians, interpretation is part of the writing process. But this conference recognizes the differing interests and emphases of historians and interpreters, and I have tried to keep some balance between them in my remarks. It is no small achievement of this conference, by the way, bringing these groups together, and one hopes there will be further meetings during the centennial decade.

How do we write and interpret the history of national forests? My response to this question will, with apologies to Robert Browning, count the ways.

First Way: Bibliographically

It is appropriate to begin with the literature. Certainly there has been more writing than on-the-ground interpretation. What has been done that we can use and build upon? Or modify and correct? Or tear apart with enthusiasm?

Over the past twenty years national forest historical activity has developed rapidly through the efforts of historians (academic, agency, or amateur); Forest Service archaeologists and recreation staff; History Office; historical societies, those in the West as well as the Forest History Society. The quantity and character of historical writing can be seen from the bibliography compiled by Gerry Williams of the Forest Service. Listings in each issue of *Forest & Conservation History* confirm this literature explosion.[2]

Even for a librarian, Williams's bibliography is daunting. There are literally hundreds of contributions, which vary considerably in subject matter, emphasis, locale, and quality. The questions are: how good are these studies as history, what is lacking, how would an interpreter use them?

Improved access to this corpus of writings should be a priority concern for interpreters. I am thinking of an expanded index or guide, building upon the Williams bibliography. In addition, and as a service for interpreters, most of these writings should be held in one place, so that items can be borrowed or photocopied quickly.

Historians would benefit greatly from an essay review or evaluation of national forest histories, particularly with respect to future research directions. I would not be surprised to find that many topics await more detailed treatment—topics in public administration, resources management, community development, or regional ecosystems. The Records Centers of the National Archives overflow with source material on the role of federal agencies in the West, more than enough for hundreds of books and doctoral dissertations on national forest topics, and almost enough to move western history away from its preoccupation with territorial politics and military events.[3]

Second Way: Archivally and Archaeologically

Before literature, or secondary sources, come primary sources, those records of transactions in the past that have survived and that form the basis of historical inquiry. You will hear about these elsewhere during the conference. Here I wish to note the differing roles of historians and interpreters in saving primary sources and the relation of primary sources to practices of records management within the Forest Service.

Historians are not as likely to be involved in deciding what should be saved out of the currently generated flow. A noteworthy exception is the chair of this session, John Reiger, who was instrumental in securing the George Bird Grinnell papers for the Yale University historical manuscripts collection.

Historians usually become involved with primary sources once they reach archives and libraries. Historians identify significant documents during their research and disseminate knowledge of them through their publications. In this research process, historians create or instigate the creation of archival guides. Many new guides to archival sources are needed for national forest history. Those for materials in the National Archives were drafted in the 1940s and 1950s. I doubt there are many guides at all to materials in Federal Record Centers. What are the resources in forest and regional offices? What guides exist to sources of interest in universities and historical societies? Even the most important primary source materials can lack accessibility. Recently, I have had some experience with the Gifford Pinchot papers in the Library of Congress. Hurriedly prepared in the 1940s, the printed guide to that collection only approximates the contents of its more than three thousand boxes of materials.

Having numerous, accurate guides to primary sources is critical to fostering historical research on national forest topics. Those who save records of national forests, then, are usually not historians. They are cultural resources, recreation, and administrative staff in the Forest Service; Federal Records Center managers and archivists; and possibly some librarians.

Some of the saving takes place in the normal course of records management. Retention schedules and other regulations govern disposition of Forest Service. These have been most helpfully summarized in Terry West's "Guide to the Curation of Forest Service Administrative History, Artifacts, and Records" (1988). Then there are non-official records: reminiscences, memories, photos, clipping files, reports and assessments. Some of these are donated to the Forest Service. Artifacts, buildings, archaeological sites are a category unto themselves. Much more should be said about the latter, but I would only betray my ignorance if I tried to do so.

Both categories of records and artifacts are discussed in West's guide. The problem is, of course, that despite administrative regulations many records never reach the Centers, many artifacts are never saved. Paper records can be lost even when retention schedules are followed, because the schedules are not necessarily good predictors of historical value. The resource of experience and activity represented by records and artifacts is usually taken for granted or ignored or perceived as a burden; rarely, I think, is it managed as a whole. In most bureaucracies, the proper disposition of old things is a very low-priority function. The order to throw away is easily given and indicates decisiveness. Many brooms are always ready to sweep clean. The horror stories I have heard at this conference and before make this almost a truism, such as the burning of TR's hunting cabin by a forest supervisor in Region 9. Archival, artifactual, archaeological and historic site resources must receive more systematic consideration and protection if we are serious about the "vital role of history in natural resource management." [4]

Two kinds of administrative awareness or policy changes are called for: The first is to know in detail the process of saving, curating, and discarding historical materials. The time has come, surely, to go beyond horror stories, or anecdotes about the way things are done here, and to describe carefully the actual situation and what should be done in the way of saving and storing.

The second level of administrative awareness would consist of deciding, gradually, what should be saved. "Decisions" now are by default: the material is lost unless someone or some few make an effort to save. What I am suggesting is gradual change to a process of explicit decision-making, which is the way national forests are managed. The same should apply to the experience of national forest management.

Should all maps of national forests be saved? Management plans? Other plans, assessments, and programs. Correspondence received during the planning process? Older material remaining in the regional offices and on the forests that never got into the Archives or any local depository. What about these old work tools from the 1920s in the storeroom we accidentally found, or data sheets from the 1960s. Examples by the score will occur to you. From many questions of this kind could emerge sets of categories and written guidelines.

Decisions to store and save have associated costs, and those overhead costs of caring for historical items must be planned for. I need only mention buildings, and the whole matter of restoration.

Third Way: Administratively

The emphasis on saving historical sources that I propose would require a more structured kind of historical activity within the Forest Service, a place for history in the administrative scheme that would serve all functions—cultural resources, archaeologists, senior administrators, public affairs. The historical effort as it is now organized lacks definition and purpose.

Whatever the structure, I think a strong case can be made for a historical program that pays administrative dividends. Saving and caring for historical sources is another way of saying "records management." The largest dividend from historical records management would fall to the legal branch. Lawyers use the Federal Records Centers more than historians, and lawyers in the Forest Service would benefit immediately and continuously from improved access to records. The second dividend comes from writings. Histories should be helpful in understanding the development of national forest policies and procedures. Those written during the past fifteen years—Rowley on grazing, Clary on timber management, Roth on wilderness policy, to mention only three—center themselves on administration and policy in some detail.[5] The recent study of management practices in the Inter-mountain Region comes closest to my idea of dividends accruing from administrative history. Even if one disagreed with every sentence in it, having such a convenient, documented study of the region's past will clarify issues and provide the basis for intelligent discussion and planning.[6]

Briefer histories or broad analyses from a historical perspective are equally valuable. I was quite impressed with the recent write up of national forests in the South.[7] This publication resulted from collaboration between a retired forester and a staff person in Pubic Affairs. It gets right down to business, sticks to the point, and presents a solid historical background in relatively few pages. Whether long and scholarly, or brief and informative, these historical efforts should contribute to long-term public relations, a third administrative dividend. I would think this activity deserved encouragement, considering the relatively few writings on national forests compared with national parks.

A fourth administrative dividend: The subject of leadership is arousing consider-able interest these days in the natural resources community, and in the national forest system, there are more than eighty years of individual case studies to draw upon. Curt Meine's recent biography of Aldo Leopold makes effective use of old personnel and operations files to discuss Leopold's career in the Forest Service.[8]

I have saved policy analysis—possible the most important—for last. What can historical research tell us about policy? Most policy analysts would say "nothing," since their mode of thinking is closer to simulation modeling and operations research than to the discipline of history. History has, I would argue, much to offer the policy analyst. What has been lacking until now is a conceptual approach that values historical skills. I share with you here my discovery of *Evidence, Argument and Persuasion in the Policy Process*, by Giandomenico Majone (Yale University Press, 1989). In Majone's book, policy analysis is not a logical presentation of options and consequences but a way of ensuring that a given policy is chosen and implemented. "Public policy," he writes, "is made of language." Historically minded persons who aspire to forest policy analysis must read this book.

Fourth Way: Contextually

I mean by context the questions we ask of sources, the topics or subjects of historical effort, and the frames of reference guiding our inquiries. The context of national forest history has been the Romance of the Bureaucrat, to use Patricia Limerick's phrase.[9] It is natural to trace back organizational accomplishments; they are conditions of bureaucratic life. But often this official view gets in the way. We cannot meaningfully impose twentieth century distinctions between Park Service and Forest Service backward in time.

Consider these nineteenth century congressional actions: Yellowstone Park, 1872; Yellowstone Timberland Reserve, 1891. Each is celebrated as a founding event in the histories of Park Service and Forest Service. We trace the lineage of both national park and national forest systems from their enaction.

Yet these events were clearly secondary byproducts of the larger public land disposal system. Congress, not the Executive Branch nor the few voices favoring something like conservation, disposed of public lands. National parks and forest reserves had to fit in with dominant congressional conceptions: of public lands as real estate, of "actual settlers", of discharging legal responsibilities, of using public lands for education, of national security (wood for ships, lead for munitions, gold mining for the Civil War debt.) Parks and forest reserves in the nineteenth century raised legitimate questions of in-holdings, of jurisdiction (federal, state, and local), of the very meaning of the word "reservation" to westerners. I have argued that this interpretive context completely misrepresents the role of Congress, and we lose thereby key elements in the legislative-executive dialogue.[10]

Histories of twentieth century national forest management have dwelled upon legislation and controversies. They move along well worn grooves, considering over and over the same questions. Fortunately, new interpretive contexts are emerging, and not all of them from the centers of historical scholarship. As an example, I would point to the Region 5 interpretive plan, drafted by Linda Lux.[11].

Another emerging context is the multidisciplinary concern for landscape ecology, and the position of national forests within the larger concept of public lands. The public lands are taking on new significance as population grows and development proceeds. The protection of biodiversity—protection or preservation rather than commodity utilization of resources—is rapidly becoming for many the primary function of public lands.[12] This emphasis will continue and become stronger.

To give a personal context, I see national forests as one of many public spaces—with wildlife refuges, national parks, and public domain lands; with state parks and reserves; with urban forest parks and open spaces. My emphasis is on public, open to all, because that is the only constant. Our fine distinctions between parks, forests, refuges, and reserves are lost on all but a minority of the general public. The public's muddled perceptions of land use continue to exasperate resource managers and conservationists. The concept of public, though, is understood, and should be emphasized.

These land saving actions for public benefit, whether of national forest or park or reserve, encourage one to believe the human race is maturing. Consider the changing rationales for public lands—assets to be given away, "pleasuring grounds" of spectacular curiosities, efficient resource utilization, species preservation, ecosystem preservation and biological diversity. These notions of ownership and stewardship have evolved from satisfying our own needs to meeting broader issues of welfare. We must begin to appreciate these changes historically.

Perhaps with the longer view we can begin to realize how scarce and precious open, public space has become. It is the luxury of luxuries, because the model has been discontinued. Yet public and even professional perceptions remain land-rich. That is, with all our concern for parks and forests, we seem unmoved by the loss on private lands of billions of tons of topsoil, or trillions of gallons of ground-water. Or we work to place visitors in two-million acre wilderness areas so they never have to see one another.

In sum, the traditional context of national forest history no longer serves, and newer ones are only beginning to emerge. The context of historical questions and interpretations matters a great deal and deserves far more thought than has been given to it so far.

Fifth Way: Spatially

Histories of national forests or any reserves inevitably become histories of places and spaces. At the practical level, this means maps, photos, and other visualizations, discussed further on; at the conceptual level, it means researching, writing, and thinking like historical geographers, whose province is space and place.

Historical geography or spatial history looks at changes in the land over time, The subject has interested me since 1965, when I wrote two review articles for *Forest History*.[13]

Already studies of national forests from the "environmental" point of view have been completed. The results are somewhat disjointed, which is not surprising, given that spatial-historical studies are exceedingly difficult to research and write. To repeat, this kind of investigation can be improved by studying the works of historical geographers.[14]

It is no surprise to recreation or cultural resources staff that visitors hunger for a sense of place or meaning in their visit. Spatially-related histories can provide interpreters with needed resources. Historical research into the spatial dimension—changes in the land—could also benefit national forest management activities such as habitat evaluation, timber management, ecosystem dynamics, and landscape ecology.

Sixth Way: Graphically

In order to present the national forest story spatially, one must use graphics. This means maps and schematics of all kinds. There are never enough, there are never enough.

Graphics must serve to integrate the text. The task is challenging, I admit, and anyone wishing to further her or his graphics education is encouraged to read Edwin Tufte's *Envisioning Information* (Graphic Arts Press, 1990). Fortunately, for creating graphics, computer software programs have reached new levels of capability, and computer hardware is becoming cheaper. Historians can create graphically new ways of comprehending changes in the land over time. Computer mapping and modelling software can be used with existing historical-geographical data to show relationships undreamed of only a few years ago. Again, the focus on graphics would tend to integrate historical work with the planning activities taking place on all forests and in all regions.

The relationships referred to above include, of course, the built environment, the towns and industrial sites that are part of every locale. Historians and interpreters want to document and present how the townscapes change, how people interact with the surrounding country, what the national forests have meant to the human population.

Photographs: I need hardly tell this audience about the extraordinarily rich Forest Service photo collection at the National Agricultural Library, now accessible on compact disk. Of course, these photos are used all the time, but I would guess mostly for decoration and flavor. One exception is the role of repeat photographs in vegetational change studies. Many national forest photos document pre-settlement vegetation.[14]

I have often wondered, given the millions of quality photos in the collection, why a project has not been undertaken to use thousands of these photos at once in a well conceived film or video. At any rate, the photo resource is unique and should be exploited in every imaginable way by historians and interpreters.

Seventh Way: Communally

Along with communities in space are communities of individuals sharing a common interest in the national forests. These communities and their relationships are varied and complex—within the Forest Service itself, between the Forest Service and users, visitors, interest groups, minorities, professional associations, Congress, other federal agencies, state and local officials, foreign government personnel and nationals.

Mostly we learn of these relationships when they become adversarial, in controversies. We are much less interested in trying to understand their regular functions. But knowledge of the social dimensions of natural resources management gives quite different perspectives on national forest history: as seen through the eyes of Basque sheepherders, contract loggers, small businessmen, Sierra Club and Wilderness Society members, or wildlife professionals.

The previously noted Region 5 interpretive plan recognizes "appreciation of cultural diversity" as one of its four purposes. Interpretive themes encompass the native American, hispanic, black, and Asian experiences in California. One interpretive project involves fire lookout towers that were used as aircraft warning lookouts during World War II. These surviving structures and their wartime uses are linked to the treatment of Japanese-Americans. Imaginative interpretation of this kind must engage visitors, stimulate thinking. It can only be applauded.

Eighth Way: Carefully

Given the previous seven ways of writing and interpreting, the notion of carefulness will not surprise you.

Writing the history of national forests is a test of integrating place, space, communities, ecosystem, human purposes. To do it right requires great sensitivity, abundant sources, a comprehensive contextual viewpoint, and a willingness to experiment with narrative and analysis.

Interpreting the history of national forests is no less difficult. Those who do this work will need to become more critical of the histories they use and take the lead in demanding writings and research relevant to their educational mission.

Having said this, I must confess that writing history seems more difficult to me with each passing year. This summer I have been reading *On History*, by Michael Oakeshott, the British philosopher who died recently.[15] Oakeshott's criteria for writing history are so exacting as to discourage most of us here. Perhaps that is why I have not been able to find a single historical journal review of *On History* since it was published in 1983. Why do I bring this book up here? First, because it is the best thing I have ever read on the philosophy of history, and this paper gives me an opportunity to say so. Second, it sets high standards, and it reminds us that absolute integrity is the foundation of all our historical work.

Ninth Way: Briefly, In Support Of

Sometimes we don't need careful historical studies. Basic data from the past can be used to catch and hold the short attention spans of today's public. Some themes and events naturally stand out. They can be taken from existing writings and presented in illustrated booklets (comics?) for the young or more standard treatment for adult readers. They can be issued as individual publications or supplements to audio-visual presentations.

If this sounds like a brief for using history in public relations, it is. The public has practically zero understanding of what forest management entails. Some of what is done on national forests can surely be illustrated better using a historical perspective. Basic tasks—fire fighting, tree planting, trees planted, habitat creation—have a cumulative significance that is not brought out in standard public information releases. For example, I have seen a brochure on fires that does not tell the reader once that the Forest Service has been fighting fires on millions of acres for decades. Our national forest organization has the largest, finest fire fighting organization on Planet Earth. Why is this basic "story" not told.

Tenth Way: Enthusiastically, with Imagination

This one is easy. Enthusiasm and imagination radiate through this conference. Topics, projects, studies, plans are in the making. This enthusiasm has only to be harnessed and directed. I would be surprised if future meetings did not show remarkable progress in historical activity.

I have counted in this talk Ten Ways to write and interpret national forest history. Librarians prefer enumerations of Ten, perhaps to honor the memory of John Dewey and his decimal classification. Other ways will no doubt occur to you. But enough has been said to spark discussion.

Notes

1. Joseph A. Miller, "Congress and the Origins of Conservation: Natural Resources Policies, 1865-1900, Ph.D. dissertation, University of Minnesota, 1973; "Sincerely yours, Harris: Being the Selected Letters of George Harris Collingwood to Miss Jean Cummings, written by the Young Ranger in 1915 and 1915 while stationed on the Apache National Forest in Arizona," Joseph A. Miller and Judith Rudnicki, eds., *Forest History* 12 (January 1969): 10-29; Joseph A. Miller, Johannes Drielsma, and William R. Burch, Jr., "Sustained Yield and Community Stability in American Forestry" in *Community and Forestry: Continuities in the Sociology of Natural Resources*, Robert G. Lee, Donald R. Field, and W. R. Burch, Jr., eds. (Boulder, CO: Westview Press, 1990).

2. Gerald W. Williams. *Selected References Concerning the USDA Forest Service: Social, Political, and Historical Sources of Information* (Umpqua and Willamette National Forests, 1990).

3. John P. Heard, "Records of the Bureau of Land Management in California and Nevada: Resource for Historians," *Forest History* 12:2 (July 1968): 20-26, 1968.

4. George Leonard, "The Vital Role History Plays in Natural Resource Management," unpublished paper, National Forest History and Interpretation Conference and Workshop, Missoula, MT, June 20-22, 1991.

5. William D. Rowley, *U. S. Forest Service Grazing and Rangelands: A History* (College Station, TX: Texas A&M University Press, 1985); David A. Clary, *Timber and the Forest Service* (Lawrence, KS: University Press of Kansas, 1986); Dennis Roth, *The Wilderness Movement and the National Forests* (College Station, TX: Intaglio Press, 1988).

6. Thomas G. Alexander, *The Rise of Multiple-Use Management in the Intermountain West: A History of Region 4 of the Forest Service* (USDA Forest Service ; Government Printing Office, 1988). Administrative history is well developed in the Park Service. *See* Barry Mackintosh, *Park Administrative Histories: An Annotated Bibliography*, N.p., 1983.

7. Sharon S. Young and A. P. Mustian, Jr. *Impacts of National Forests on the Forest Resources of the South* (Miscellaneous publication no. 25, Washington, DC: USDA Forest Service, 1989).

8. Curt Meine, *Aldo Leopold: His life and Work* (Madison: University of Wisconsin Press, 1988).

9. Patricia Limerick, "Forest Reserves and the Argument for a Closing Frontier," National Forest History and Interpretation Conference and Workshop, Missoula, MT, June 20-22, 1991.

10. Miller, "Congress and the Origins of Conservation," 222-358.

11. Linda M. Lux, Change, *Diversity and Leadership: Windows on California's Past and Its Future Through the Interpretation of Cultural Resources*. Review Draft, August 1990.

12. D. Wilcove, "Protecting Biodiversity in Multiple-Use Lands: Lessons from the U. S. Forest Service" *Trends in Ecology and Evolution* 4:12 (1989): 385-388.

13. Joseph A. Miller, "The Changing Forest: Recent Research in the Historical Geography of American Forests," *Forest History* 9:1 (1965): 18-25; "Forests and the Regional Landscape," *Forest History* 9:2 (July 1965): 24-29. *Americans and Their Forests: A Historical Geography* by Michael Williams (New York: Cambridge University Press, 1989) is the preeminent current example.

14. Jeffrey M. LaLande, *Prehistory and History of the Rogue River National Forest: A Cultural Resource Overview* (Medford, OR: USDA Forest Service, Rogue River National Forest, 1980); Elizabeth M. Smith, *History of the Boise National Forest, 1905-1976* (Boise: Idaho State Historical Society, 1983).

15. Garry F. Rogers, and others, *Bibliography of Repeat Photography for Evaluating Landscape Change* (Salt Lake City: University of Utah Press, 1984).

16. Michael Oakeshott, *On History* (Savage, MD: Barnes and Noble Books, 1983).

NATIONAL FOREST

RESOURCES

Graziers and Reclamationists: The First Foresters?

William Rowley
University of Nevada, Reno

Early government forestry boosters went to great lengths to demonstrate why the various western resource users and developers should embrace forestry. The molding of a consensus of opinion in support of the movement was deemed necessary for the ultimate success of national forests and the reservation of lands for that purpose. Although in many respects the designation of forested lands and their protection was rightly viewed with some fear by western stock interests, forestry propaganda reached out to them. This was never a completely successful campaign prior to the implementation of government forests, but afterwards Forest Service grazing chief Will C. Barnes said of the agency efforts: "The grazing men of the Forest Service were the shock troops that won the West for forestry."[1] But grazier support for forestry was largely an after-the-fact occurrence.

In contrast to Barnes' declaration about graziers' support for the administration of federal forest lands, grazing interests were not as obvious in the ranks of early forest reserve supporters as were irrigationists. Irrigationists in their support of forests and the protection they afforded water supplies often chided grazing interests for the threat they posed to the functions of the forests as "spongy reservoirs."[2]

Problems on the western range began as soon as the open-range system of stock grazing commenced in the West in the nineteenth century. Range use and range rights without ownership of the land promoted overstocking and the destruction of native perennial grasses. Big stock operators wanted range-leasing laws, but many interests opposed this including small operators who felt they would be outbid by larger operators. The result in many areas was confusion, competition for the range, and even range wars. The use of limited forage resource was not monitored by community, by private ownership, and certainly not by federal land law. Stock organizations in several states did impose rules and tradition which state legislatures reinforced with law. But in the more marginal range areas, especially in the high mountain pastures where forest resources also prevailed, the ranges stood open for further use by new arrivals, particularly sheep interests just at a time when forest reserves came on the scene. This meant that cattle and now sheep were being ranged on forested watersheds. The demand for their removal occurred with the creation of forest reserves in 1891, and consequently many grazing interests became hostile to the government forestry movement. In return forestry interests denounced grazing in certain areas of the forest. One government observer from the Bureau of Forestry wrote, "the animals not only check vegetation, but bring such slopes to a condition of barrenness from which recovery is very slow."[3]

Irrigation engineer Frederick Newell and future director of the Reclamation Service noted in 1897 that it was generally accepted that water supplies for irrigation were dependent to a certain extent in quantity and continuity upon the preservation of the forests upon the headwaters of the streams, but he also asserted that stock raising was also impracticable unless water could be drawn from the forests. Although these demonstrative statements are replete in the literature, stock interests remained suspicious of federal forest reserves. Certainly sheep interests feared their wholesale expulsion from the forests. When this did occur, they believed that government officials had fallen totally under the influence of John Muir and his rhetoric that branded sheep as the hoofed locusts of the forest.

Only the protests and reasoned arguments of Oregon sheepman John Minto helped prompt a reconsideration of the policy. In response Frederick V. Coville, a USDA botanist, travelled west in the summer of 1897 to survey the situation in the Oregon and Washington mountains. His subsequent report entitled *Forest Growth and Sheep Grazing in the Cascade Mountains of Oregon in 1898* maintained that sheep grazing could be done safely in the Cascades. The report was a general endorsement of regulated grazing in the reserves. He outlined a program that would grant grazing permits, regulate the number of stock, and the season of grazing. The permits also obligated the graziers to protect against and fight fire in the forests. In other articles Coville noted that he was aware that the adoption of these policies was not in accord with the ideas of those whose conception of a forest reserve is identical with their conception of a national park. He wrote:

> While it is feasible and proper that certain portions of the forest reserves should be maintained for such purposes, it is no less clear that the executive branch of the Government in setting aside such large and much used areas of the forest lands as reserves, and the legislative branch of the Government in specifying the principles under which these reserves should be managed, had chiefly in mind the preservation of these reserves for use, not from use. Rational regulation of all the resources in the reservations is their object.[4]

But these concessions to graziers do not suggest how the grazing men of the Forest Service won the West for forestry as Barnes maintained and confronted what

Gifford Pinchot termed, "far and away the bitterest issue of the time." What is perhaps important to understand about the grazing regulations to be applied by the forest administration is that it did in very limited areas what stock operators or at least established stock operators had been wanting for many years with respect to the range: acknowledgement of grazing privileges (or rights) to the tacit exclusion of new competitors for the resource. The 1905 *Forest Reserve Use Book* put it this way in noting objectives of grazing regulations: the protection of the settler and home builder against unfair competition in the use of the range. All of this could be done under the policies of limiting the numbers on the range for the protection of the forage, soil, and timber resources. Graziers secure in their privileges and protected from the unlimited competition of landless drovers, itinerant drovers, be they new cattle graziers or especially sheep herders, could finally if belatedly become enthusiastic supporters of government forestry and its accompanying range rules and even grudgingly grazing fees.[5]

Graziers, of course, had no way of foreseeing a grazing regulation system in the forests in the long years prior to the establishment of the reserves and their more measured administration after 1905. Many saw only the prospects of complete exclusion from the reserves. But events proved otherwise, and ultimately Will Barnes could make his enthusiastic evaluation of the accomplishment of the grazing programs for the cause of forestry in the West.

In contrast many reclamationists were early converts to forestry. In the formative years of the scientific conservation movement, ardent reclamationists and foresters saw a complimentary relationship between the two. The noted irrigation advocate Francis G. Newlands of Nevada proclaimed the importance of forests for assisting in the storage of water for the irrigation of the West. Although at the outset he believed that each state should have control of its own forests which were valuable for timber and lumber, he also saw forests as the sources of great mountain streams. He asserted in 1891 to the first Irrigation Congress in Salt Lake City ". . . unless the mountains and the hillsides are kept covered with timber, the snows which now practically impound the water and hold it until needed, will melt the quicker in summer and thus make artificial storage more expensive." [6]

Not withstanding these statements, the impression that irrigation prognosticators presented a united front in favor of forest protection should not be completely accepted. Some argued "with a flavor of authority" that the cutting of the forest and even the compacting of the soils by grazing increased run off into the streams and expanded the water supply. From the view of the reclamationist and even the grazier this was a further invitation for the determined and thorough use of both timber and grazing resources. G.K. Gilbert, a scientist geologist who contributed the chapter "Water Supply" to John Wesley Powell's famous 1878 *Report on the Lands of the Arid Region of the United States,* declared that "The cutting of trees for lumber and fence material and fuel has further increased the streams. By the removal of foliage, that share of the rain and snow which was formerly caught by it and thence evaporated, is now permitted to reach the ground, and some part of it is contributed to the streams." He believed that the activities of "the white man" (Euro-Americans) promoted a greater percentage of snow to be melted and a less percentage to be evaporated directly. All of this, he said, ". . . follows from the destruction of trees and grass." His conclusion was that, "By reducing the amount of vegetation he gives a freer flow to the water from rain and melting snow and carries a greater percentage of it to streams, while a smaller percentage reaches the air by evaporation from the soil. By the treading of his cattle he diminishes the leakage of the smaller water channels, and conserves the streams that gather there. In all of these ways he increases the outflow of the land. . . ."[7]

Admittedly these observations backed with scientific authority were made as early as the mid-1870s and might be categorized with other popular doctrines of the day that encouraged the advance of Euro-American civilization into the plains and the mountains such as rain follows the plow. But these views cannot be simply dismissed as premature speculations on the relation of timber cutting and grazing to the outflow of water from the land and into the streams and reservoirs. John Wesley Powell, continuing to elaborate on the earlier observations of Gilbert, in 1890 took essentially the same position. The destruction of forests either by man or by fire increased run-off and therefore this increased volume of water in streams and in reservoirs should be welcomed by reclamationists. In discussing what he called "The Non-irrigable Lands of the Arid Region" in *The Century Magazine,* Powell noted in reference to the forests that in recent years there has occurred "vast destruction of values, together with the enormous ravishment of beauty." These events he said have enlisted for years "the sympathy of intelligent men. Forestry organizations have been formed; conventions have been held; publicists have discussed the subject; and there is a universal sentiment in the West, and a growing opinion in the East, that measures should be taken by the General Government for the protection of the forests." Though he found this subject of profound interest, he also noted that "sometimes factitious reasons are given which detract from the argument for the preservation of the woods."[8]

Powell found the preservation of the forests in the arid regions a many-sided question that could not be reduced to the simple formula later proclaimed by *Forestry and Irrigation* magazine of "Save the Forests Store the Floods." Forests like all vegetation live on water. Plant life drinks up the water and the leaves return all that is unused to the air "where it may float away to form clouds in other regions." Powell estimated that perhaps 40 percent of the rainfall of a region is dissipated in this manner. The consequences for the streams is not important in a humid region, but when streams have a value that increases by their volume as in an arid region the results are noteworthy. Powell asserted that: "Researches on this subject made in the Wasatch Mountains and elsewhere by scientific men show that a great increase in the volume of the streams may accrue from the denudation of the mountains of their evergreen garments." Those looking to increase the water flow from the land and into the streams and to fill the reservoirs should not be so quick to advocate the blanket protection of the forests. Furthermore when mountain declivities are grassy slopes, "the snows of winter drift behind ledges and cliffs and into great banks among the rocks, and they fill ravines and cañons, and are thus stored in compact bodies until they are melted by the summer suns and rains. But when forests stand on the slopes the snows are spread in comparatively thin sheets, and great surfaces of evaporation are presented to the sun and the wind." Powell concluded that "For all these reasons the forests of the upper regions are not advantageous to the people of the valleys, who depend on the streams for the fertilization of the farms."

Perhaps these conclusions to some extent reflect Powell's admiration for the success of Mormon occupation and community control of resource development that had occurred in Utah. Powell did acknowledge in his critique of the general forestry advocates that the "immediate slopes" adjacent to reservoirs "should be forest clad, and that all declivities above, the waters of which cannot be discharged in large part of the sediments before reaching the reservoirs, should also have their woods preserved." Forests on these selected slopes best prevented the sedimentation of natural and artificial storage reservoirs. Therefore it was necessary that in the utilization of timber, "judgment and circumspection will be necessary properly to select the areas to be denuded. It is thus that the people of the valley are interested in the forests of the mountains."[9]

Powell's general declarations in favor of the denudation of the mountain forests for the purposes of increasing irrigation waters did not go unnoticed or unchallenged. Abbot Kinney, a southern California forester and future author of *Forest and Water* (1900), replied in the pages of *The Century* that Powell's views were "revolutionary" and represented "a bald and vague statement against the experience and writings of every prominent forestry man of whom we have knowledge. . . ." Kinney said that riparian trees are "gross water users" the trees upon the mountains "are of a different class, and their effect is, without known exception, beneficial to irrigators and water users in the valleys below."

Kinney incredulously restated Powell's transpiration argument that in arid countries the trees take up and evaporate about 40 percent of the rainfall into the air: that the snows melt faster in forests, and that the volume of water in a stream will be larger if its watershed be bare than if it were wooded. Kinney goes on to cite such authorities as J.E. Brown, Becquerel, Marchand, Siemoni, Hummel, Piper, W.C. Bryant, Marsh, Van Reenan, Surell, Ladoucette, Cantegril, Wex, Berghaus, Maass, Gebenan, Ebermayer, and a host of others "without exception known to me, opposed to this view of Major Powell's."

He wrote that "Time, place and instance have been cited over and over again to show that the denudation of mountain districts is followed by increased torrent or flood action and diminished regular flow in springs and streams, often by the entire desiccation of these, In my reading, as in my observation as a forest officer, I have never read or known of an instance to warrant Major Powell's theory. It is a variance with all the known facts." He goes on to say that the most ordinary power of observation shows that soil remains humid longer in a forest than on bare open lands. So also snow remains longer under trees than in the open. Furthermore, "Powell confutes himself" when he says in reference to storage reservoirs, "Storm waters wash the sands from naked hills and mountains, and bear them on to the creeks and rivers, by which they are carried to the storage basins." This is a description of "torrent action," but it stops at reservoirs, according to Powell, and he does not consider the movement of detritus-laden streams to farmlands below. "As soon as such a stream leaves the steep grades of the mountains its drops it load, fills its bed, and changes its course. No one is safe in the bottom lands," when the mountains are denuded Kinney concluded.[10]

In his consideration of the non-agricultural lands of the arid region, Powell appeared to be more determined to protect the pasturage lands than the forests. He said that the pasturage lands in the arid West were fragile and easily destroyed by improvident use and afterwards replaced by noxious weeds. "To be utilized they must be carefully protected, and grazed only in proper seasons and within prescribed limits." Their protection appeared to assume a much greater urgency than the forests in this article by Powell as he wrote, "Yet they must have protection or be ruined, and they should be preserved as one great resource of food for the people." All of this, in his view, would arise out of a new phase of civilization that was coming to the arid West.[11]

The new phase of civilization would require new institutions for the arid lands. The new institutions would protect the great forest for the use of man, and so also the sources of water and the grasses with which to feed the flocks and herds. In the formation of these new institutions for the arid West Powell said to the general government: "Hands off!" If the people have institutions of justice, they will do the work for themselves. There is no need for appropriations or offices created by the government. He called for new commonwealths in the West to be created within the hydrographic basins:

> In such a basin of the arid region the irrigable lands lie below; not chiefly by the river's side, but on the mesas and low plains that stretch back on each side. Above these lands the pasturage hills and mountains stand, and there the forests and sources of water supply are found. The people who live, therein are interdependent in all their industries. The men who control the farming below must also control the upper regions where the waters are gathered from the heavens and stored in the reservoirs.

It was Powell's conviction that the manner in which these waters were to be caught and the way they were to be utilized was a problem for the men of the district to solve and for them alone. It should be noted that Powell was read out of the national irrigation movement by 1893, which increasingly looked to the national government. [12]

With reference again to the forests, Powell said, the people who live within a district are the same people interested in the forests that crown the heights of the hydrographic basin. The wanton destruction of the forests harms their source of water supply and injures timber values.

> If the forests are to be guarded, the people directly interested should perform the task. An army of aliens set to watch the forests would need another army of aliens to watch them, and a forestry organization under the hands of the General Government would become a hotbed of corruption; for it would be impossible to fix responsibility and difficult to secure integrity of administration, because ill-defined values in great quantities are involved.

Powell then connected the protection of pasturage with the protection of the water supply for agriculture. The same local interests that seek protection of the forests and their water

> can best protect the grasses for the summer pasturage of cattle and horses and sheep. . . . Thus it is that there is a body of interdependent and unified interests and values, all collected in one hydrographic basin, and all segregated by well-defined boundary lines from the rest of the world.

The people in these districts should organize under national and state laws irrigation districts that include entire hydrographic basins and be permitted to make their
own laws for the division of the waters, for the protection and use of the forests,
for the protection of the pasturage and for the use of hydro power. "This, then,"
wrote Powell, "is the proposition I make: that the entire arid region be organized
into natural hydrographic districts, each one to be a commonwealth within itself for
the purpose of controlling and using the great values which been pointed out." [13]

More to the point whether great stands of forests should be preserved or clear cut
was a decision that should be made by local self-government and not by a remote
government bureaucracy that was given the mandate to protect the forests. Laymen
also took up Powell's views that forests hindered the immediate supply of waters
for irrigation purposes. Such voices persisted into the late 1890s when it appeared
that forestry and irrigation interests were amalgamating into a great common cause.
In 1896 Robert Fulton, the head of the Southern Pacific Land Company in Nevada
a subsidiary of the Southern Pacific Railroad, declared in a lengthy communication
published in *Science* magazine that the destruction of forests contrary to what
earlier generations believed did not result in the depletion of adjacent streams "and
to all consequent evils." He echoed Powell's statements on the question six years
earlier when he said, "I endeavor to point out some of the reasons why many close
observers, after long years of study have been led to believe that if there is any
difference in the flow of streams and the size of springs before and after the trees
are cut from above them, the balance is in favor of the open country." [14]

Fulton went on to offer the testimony of many living in the vicinity of the Sierra to
the fact that the removal of timber has facilitated the run-off of water into the
streams. He believed that "the strongest force at work to save our rivers is the
drifting winds which heap up the snow in great banks, and in this the trees are a
constant obstacle." As a result of the development of the Comstock mines, the
eastern slope of the Sierra has been cut over for a distance of thirty miles, covering
the heads of such streams as Hunter's Creek, White's Canyon, Thomas Creek,
Galena, Steamboat and other small rivers, which have furnished water for irrigation since 1860 to the owners of probably twenty thousand acres of land in valleys
below. "The consensus of opinion among this class of citizens, intelligent
American farmers all of them," wrote Fulton, "is that there is virtually no diminu-
tion in the supply of water that reaches them from the hills." Truckee Meadows
rancher G.R. Holcomb said that the supply of water was equally certain if not
more so and attributes it entirely to the drifting of the snows that occurs more
easily without the timber. [15]

Fulton quoted the Honorable Ross Lewers of Washoe County who read a paper
before the American Horticultural Society in which he said that in Nevada "the

water supply from the mountains is greater and more permanent now than it was before the timber was cut off." Continuing to quote Lewers the article stated:

> The reason for this is that the wind has a more unimpeded course, and as all the snow storms come from nearly the same point in the south, the snow is blown over and lodges on the north sides of the ridges where it is piled deep in drifts, and not being exposed directly to the sun's rays it melts very slowly and thus affords a more permanent supply. Spring floods are less frequent and for the same reason. I do not pretend to decide how much, if any, the presence of trees induce precipitation. They may moisten the air, but the humidity is all taken out of the ground by the roots, and I observe that the undergrowth and grass is more luxuriant since the timber was cut off.[16]

Fulton observed that the wind was crucial in piling snow in great heaps and packing it away in deep crevices and in this work "the economy of nature is manifested." He explained:

> The center of the body will not melt at any time and it requires a very warm day to get at the under side of a snow drift. The grass will be growing all around it before the ground underneath it gets warmed up sufficiently to start a stream from it, but let a tree stick its head up through the crust and it will go quickly. I have yet to see the first body of perpetual snow lying among trees. It will hardly do to say that the timber lies below the line of perpetual snow, for there are many banks which only disappear entirely once in ten years or so, when there comes a long dry summer, which have trees growing higher up on the same mountain side.

Despite these comments Fulton hastened to conclude that he did not wish to be seen as favoring the destruction of the forests. He could only say that "Whatever is proven there will always be abundant reasons for preserving extensive tracts of woodland everywhere that trees will grow, and it is time the matter became one of public concern."[17]

Within the month the pages of *Science* magazine contained a rejoinder to the views expressed by Fulton from a prestigious source. B.E. Fernow, chief of the Division of Forestry, U.S. Department of Agriculture, lost little time in sending off a sharp reply under the title, "Pseudo-Science in Meteorology." Fernow saw the Fulton article as an unfortunate attack on "the favorable influence of forest cover on meteorological phenomena and especially on water flow in the western Mountains." Since far-reaching economic policies depended on the answer given to the questions raised in the Fulton article, Fernow justified giving the subject further attention "in order to warn against the many erroneous observations and fallacious conclusions contained in the article referred to." Fernow charged that Fulton had done harm "by neglecting to sift more carefully the untutored and too-often-prejudiced opinions and notions of so-called 'practical' men. . . ." In doing so the article discredited observations of laymen as well as scientists.

Fernow said the main argument is false: that trees are mechanical obstructions preventing snow from reaching the ground, transpiration and greater evaporation under trees reduce the available water supplies and hence that forests as far as waterflow is concerned are an evil. He conceded that the argument had been advanced before by others "with a flavor of authority." He dismissed these arguments and said that the winds at high altitudes promote evaporations and said those who take the Fulton position ignore the influence of forest cover on water-flow, namely "as to the manner in which the rivers receive their water." Surface flow into the rivers is the least important and "means rapid flow, high water stages, alternating with low water, uneven distribution through the year." Subdrainage which the forests and the forest floor promotes means:

> less excessive water stages, more even, steady and persistent flow, for the ground water reaches the river sometimes only several years after it first sank into the soil, and hence equalizes the effects of dry and wet seasons while the surface waters are carried off at once and are responsible for floods, followed by low water. Anything, therefore, that tends to change surface drainage into subdrainage is to be encouraged.

According to Fernow the forests provided this influence. With forest removal, the exposure of soils and with fires and sheep herding all soils became gradually more compact and less penetrable. Then more water flows over the surface and less remains for subdrainage and then ultimately the change is felt in the riverflow. All of this change will be deleterious. Clearly Fernow was perturbed that the Fulton opinions received notice in *Science* because he saw them as inaccurate science and also because they might serve to argue against what he saw as "far-reaching economic policies depending in part on the answer which science or well sustained observation and argument can give to the question. . . ."[18]

Fernow saw the far-reaching economic policies as shifting in natural resources from a *laissez-faire* school to *faire-marcher* school which, of course, embraced government forestry.[19] Fernow used this contradistinction in an address to the

American Association for the Advancement of Science in August of 1895. By this time the forestry movement was moving toward the embracement of other resource users that might become advocates of forestry, especially the irrigationists or reclamationists. By this year speakers at the annual Irrigation Congresses were saying, "I cannot leave this platform and say no word for that twin sister of irrigation whose name is reforestation. Arid America will never be reclaimed without being reforested."[20] Still, the Fulton-Powell views indicated doubters in the ranks, who were ridiculed by Fernow and other high priests of the forestry movement. But irrigationists were soon to be solidly in forestry's camp and vice versa. By 1903 the publication *Forestry and Irrigation* was the official organ of the American Forestry Association and the National Irrigation Association.

The irrigationists were, of course, more interested in water. Hydrologist and reclamationist Frederick Newell, wrote in 1897, "Everything, therefore that affects the supply of water in a land of drought must be looked upon with the keenest solicitude. . . . It would seem, therefore, as though every effort should be made to ascertain the extent, value, and influence of the forest and to guard the perpetuity of the supplies of water and of wood." Simple timber production was almost a secondary value of the forest in his view. "There is a belief prevailing throughout the country that water supply for irrigation is dependent to a certain extent in quantity, and perhaps still more in continuity, upon the preservation of the forests upon the headwaters of the streams." Without this water the arid West is worthless. All of the arid West's industries stand in peril without it: mining, stock raising, agriculture, and urban centers. In short, the miner, the grazier, the irrigator, and the city dweller should be avid supporters of government forestry.[21]

George H. Maxwell, executive chairman of the National Irrigation Association, in a speech on "Irrigation and the Forest" before the 1901 American Forestry Association meeting in Denver declared, "The forests are the source of all irrigation. We cannot irrigate without water. We cannot have water without forests. If we do not preserve them, we will have no irrigation." Other irrigationists referred to the forests as "Nature's Storage Reservoirs," and urged the preservation of the reservoirs which nature has provided for holding back the water in the natural sponges of the forest and the forest floor.

The pages of the American Forestry Association journal, *The Forester*, contained numerous articles illustrating the support offered by irrigationists to forestry. Colorado conservationist Henry Michelson wrote in these pages: "We of the West, should teach the irrigationist farmer unceasingly thus: 'If you wish for an abundance of water, see to the preservation of the woods at the sources of the rivers.'" Editorially *The Forester* by 1899 went beyond touting the forests as nature's great reservoirs by suggesting that man-made reservoirs could supplement the function of protective forests, "but they cannot be substituted for them."

Finally in President Theodore Roosevelt's important address to Congress in December 1901 on the broad questions of forestry and water, he too declared that "The forests are natural reservoirs. Forest conservation is therefore an essential condition of water conservation." But he could not be content with this passive kind of water conservation. He went a step further to lay the foundation of the national reclamation act:

> The forests alone cannot, however, fully regulate and conserve the waters of the arid region. Great storage works are necessary to equalize the flow of streams and to save the flood waters. Their construction has been conclusively shown to be an undertaking too vast for private effort. Nor can it be best accomplished by the individual states acting alone. It is properly a national function, at least in some of its features.[22]

At this point national forests and national irrigation appear as inseparable allies despite some early doubters ranging from laymen or "practical men" to distinguished scientists on the function of forests in relation to water supply.

Yet shortly after the consignment of the two tasks to government agencies, tensions occurred. By 1909 long time reclamationist and forestry supporter Francis G. Newlands found himself in the midst of a controversy between the Forest Service and the Reclamation Service. The Reclamation Service in order to store water in Lake Tahoe was eager to enter into a contract with the Truckee Electric Company to build a dam at the outlet of the lake on the Truckee River. The dam would not only provide storage water in the lake, but also revenues from hydroelectric sales. The Forest Service under Gifford Pinchot was reluctant to grant this long term monopoly to a private company and additional rights of way for power lines. Newlands believed it was clear that "under the broad language of the reclamation act, the power to construct irrigation works also involves the power to construct power works, provided the work done in the construction of the power works is in aid of irrigation."

In a letter to President William Howard Taft, he called for a coordination of the various services on questions that related to water. The coordination should be pursued according to the conservation policies developed over the last decade and the irrigation works on the Truckee-Carson rivers should be so planned as to fit into the ultimate development of rivers for every civilized use. Broad, comprehensive plans should be framed which will involve "the conservation of the forests as the sources of the water supply, and the storage of the waters for both power and irrigation and for the development of the highest power and the greatest area of irrigation that is practicable."

Coordination was the underpinning concept of the Inland Waterways Commission that President Roosevelt created in 1907 and on which Newlands served by presidential appointment. Newlands believed that the coordination of the Forest Service and the Reclamation Service crucial for the development of inland waterways. In the future, he believed, this could be achieved through the creation of another commission that should be known as the National Conservation Commission. The commission, of course, was never created within the government. Although it took various forms, bureaucratic competition in the twentieth century replaced the earlier cooperation between these early allies in the movement for government forest protection on a host of issues relating to forestry, water, dams, and floods.[23]

Notes

1. Will C. Barnes, *Apaches and Longhorns: The Reminiscences of Will C. Barnes*, ed. Frank C. Lockwood (Los Angeles: The Ward Ritchie Press, 1941), p. 202.

2. "Forests and Irrigation," *The Irrigation Age* 3 (August 15, 1892): 138.

3. R. H. Forbes, "The Open range and the Irrigation Farmer," *The Forester* 7 (October, 1901): 257; C.S. Crandall, "Reproduction of Trees and Range Cattle," *The Forester* 7 (July, 1901): 174.

4. Frederick Newell, "The National Forest Reserves," *The National Geographic Magazine* 7 (June, 1897): 179; Thomas R. Cox, "The Conservationist as Reactionary: John Minto and American Forest Policy," *Pacific Northwest Quarterly* 74 (October, 1983): 146-53; Lawrence Rakestraw, "Sheep Grazing in the Cascade Range: John Minto vs. John Muir," *Pacific Historical Review* 27 (November, 1958): 371-82; Frederick V. Coville, *Forest Growth and Sheep Grazing in the Cascade Mountains of Oregon*. USDA, Division of Forestry Bulletin no. 15. Washington, D.C.: Government Printing Office, 1898; Coville, "Grazing and Forest Policy," *The Forester* 4 (February, 1898): 32.

5. Gifford Pinchot, *Breaking New Ground* (New York: Harcourt, Brace & Co., 1947. Reprint. Seattle: University of Washington Press, 1972), 256; *Use Book—Use of the National Forest Reserves*, 1905 (Washington, DC: Government Printing Office, 1905), 20-21; William D. Rowley, *U.S. Forest Service Grazing and Rangelands: A History* (College Station, TX: Texas A&M University Press, 1985), p. 59.

6. Francis G. Newlands, "Irrigation Congress," *The Irrigation Age* 1 (October, 1891): 195-96.

7. Stephen J. Pyne, *Grove Karl Gilbert, A Great Engine of Research* (Austin: University of Texas Press, 1980); G. K. Gilbert, "Water Supply," in John Wesley Powell, *Report on the Lands of the Arid Region of the United States*, ed. Wallace Stegner (Cambridge, MA: The Belknap Press of Harvard University Press, 1962), p. 89.

8. John Wesley Powell, "The Non-Irrigable Lands of the Arid Region," *The Century Magazine* 39 (April, 1890): 919-20.

9. Powell, "Non-Irrigable Lands," p. 920.

10. Abbot Kinney, "Forests and Streams," *The Century Magazine* 40 (August, 1890): 637-38.

11. Powell, "Non-Irrigable Lands," pp. 920, 922.

12. Powell, "Institutions for the Arid Lands," *The Century Magazine* 40 (May, 1890): 113-14; Thomas G. Alexander, "The Powell Irrigation Survey and the People of the Mountain West," *Journal of the West* 7 (January, 1968): 52.

13. Powell, "Institutions for the Arid Lands," p. 114.

14. Robert L. Fulton, "How Nature Regulates the Rains," *Science* 3 (April 10, 1896): 546-47.

15. Fulton, "How Nature Regulates," p. 550.

16. Ibid., p. 551.

17. Ibid., p. 552.

18. B. E. Fernow, "Pseudo-Science in Meteorology," *Science* 3 (May 8, 1896): 706-08.

19. Fernow, "The Providential Functions of Government with Special Reference to Natural Resources," *Science* 2 (August 30, 1895): 257.

20. J. S. Emery, "Forestry," *Irrigation Age* 8 (December, 1895): 247-48.

21. Newell, "The National Forest Reserves," p. 179.

22. George H. Maxwell, "Irrigation and the Forest," *The Forester* 7 (September 1901): 232-33; Maxwell, "Nature's Storage Reservoirs," 5 (August 1899): 183; Abbot Kinney, "The Forest Problem in the West," 5 (September 1899): 200; "The Protection of Irrigation Works," 5 (February 1899): 46; Henry Michelson, "Forests in Their Relation to Irrigation," 5 (January 1899): 10; "Why Persons Interested in Irrigation should be Members of the American Forestry Association," 5 (February 1899): 25; "President Roosevelt's Message: Strong Recommendations Regarding Forestry and Irrigation," 7 (December 1901): 302.

23. Newlands to William Howard Taft, August 14, 1909 and Newlands to Taft, September 5, 1909, Newlands Papers, Sterling Library, Yale University, New Haven, Connecticut.

Cautious Support: Relations Between The Mining Industry and The Forest Service, 1891-1991

Stanley Dempsey
Royal Gold, Inc.

The histories of mining and forestry in the United States are intertwined to a surprising extent. Mining was a latecomer among the nation's industries, but its time of greatest growth and technical advance was contemporaneous with that of the development of modern forest management and conservation. Mining and forestry professionals jointly supported the movement to preserve and manage the nation's forests, and major mining firms were cautious supporters of the national forest system from its beginning.

Local iron mining and manufacturing was underway in all thirteen states of the U.S. when George Washington became president, but large scale copper, gold, and coal mining began only in the middle of the nineteenth century. Modern mining traces its beginning to the California gold rush. Mining historian T.A. Rickard states that:

> The discovery of gold in California by Marshall in 1848 was the most portentous event in the history of modern mining because it gave an immediate stimulus to worldwide migration, it induced an enormous expansion of international trade, and it caused scientific industry to invade the waste places of the earth.[1]

The wealth of California was enormous, and the works undertaken to win the gold were out of proportion to any mining ever undertaken before in the United States. A gigantic system of dams and flumes was built to supply water to dozens of large hydraulic mines. The lode mines were also major undertakings even by today's standards. The Empire Mine at Grass Valley was discovered in 1850 and produced for 105 years, ultimately becoming one of the deepest mines in the world, developed to an inclined depth of 11,007 feet.[2]

Mining in California created a great demand for technically trained people. Much of this demand was filled by immigrants from Europe, and later by American graduates who had received additional training at the great mining academies of Europe.[3] Geologists, mining engineers, and metallurgists soon moved on from California, ready to repeat their mineral successes in other parts of the United States.[4] Much of the history of mining in the public lands states can be traced to people who employed "California methods."

Prospectors and small miners operated all over the West with varied success. Individuals made important discoveries and were sometimes rewarded handsomely for their efforts when they sold to larger firms.[5] Corporations, employing modern methods and trained technical people, grew into mining giants as they exploited major gold, silver, lead, and copper deposits at places like Butte, Lead, Virginia City, Leadville, and Globe.[6] Further east, great copper mines were developed in Michigan, and a major new industry was developed to mine the colossal iron deposits found in Minnesota.

Western miners operated under their own land laws for many years,[7] and the basic mining statutes of the United States, enacted in 1866 and modified in 1872, adopted many of the principles of mining district laws. Under the federal system, miners are free to search for minerals on public lands, and their reward for discovery is ownership. Mining rights are held by the performance of annual labor, and title thus secured and maintained is good against the world. This arrangement has encouraged mine development, and miners have fought tenaciously over the years to keep these laws unchanged.

From earliest times, the mining industry has been a major consumer of forest products. Timber is used for mine support, buildings, railroad ties, and fuel. The waterworks created for California placer mines consumed incredible amounts of lumber. Charcoal was the major fuel source for iron making well into the late nineteenth century. Miners have always been concerned about timber supplies. Likewise, they are interested in the management of rivers and watersheds, particularly to protect water supplies for ore processing and hydropower. As with the mining law, miners have become active politically whenever timber supplies have been threatened.

During the second half of the nineteenth century, mining, like other interests, developed organizations for the sharing of technical information and engaging in political action. The American Institute of Mining Engineers (AIME; now the American Institute of Mining, Metallurgical and Petroleum Engineers) was founded in 1871 to secure a wider dissemination of professional knowledge. The

American Mining Congress (AMC) was founded in 1897. Its purpose was largely political. The Mining and Metallurgical Society of America was formed to provide for support of professional and cultural interests of mining people. In addition, a vigorous, independent mining press was established.[8]

Leading mining professionals became members of technical and trade organizations, and such organizations held conferences and published technical papers much as they do today. Meeting reports and the mining press reflect the many interests of the mining industry and mining professionals over the years. Among these has been a continuing interest and support for modern forest management practices and conservation of timberland and watersheds.

Rossiter W. Raymond was among the earliest of mining professionals to comment on forest issues. A graduate of Brooklyn Polytechnic Institute and of the Mining Academy at Freiberg, Germany, Raymond was, for several years, United States commissioner of mineral statistics. He travelled throughout the mining regions of the West in the late 1860s and early 1870s, preparing extensive reports of his observations on all aspects of mining. In 1870 he used his report to call attention to the "wanton destruction of timber in the mining regions . . . of the West," and asked "what shall be the remedy."[9] He suggested sale of timber to settlers and a free market solution to the problem. In later years, Raymond was active as an editor of both the *Transactions* of AIME and of the *Engineering and Mining Journal* (E&MJ), a leading mining industry publication. As we will see below, his interest in conservation is reflected time and again in the pages of these publications.

Other mining professionals also expressed concern about timber supply, management of forest resources, the need for technical research on forest products, watershed protection, and even the effect of timber clearing on climate.

AIME met in Utah and Montana in 1887. The meeting opened in Salt Lake City on July 6, 1887. After three sessions in Salt Lake the meeting moved to Butte City, Montana, where 4th and 5th sessions were held. They then moved to Mammoth Hot Springs, Wyoming, where a special meeting of the institute was held on July 17. There Arnold Hague of the U.S.G.S., geologist in charge of Yellowstone National Park and a member of AIME, presented a paper describing Yellowstone Park. Thereafter, institute members undertook a five day tour of the park. Hague made a special point of discussing watershed management issues with the visiting miners, saying that:

> Of the present Park area about 84 percent is forest clad, almost wholly made up of coniferous trees. The timber is by no means of

the finest quality, but for purposes of water protection it meets every possible requirement. Much has been said of late years by scientific and experienced persons of the great necessity of preserving the forests near the sources of our great rivers. It is mainly for the forest protection that the proposed enlargement is demanded by the public welfare. In my opinion no region in the Rocky Mountains is so admirably adapted for a forest reservation as the Yellowstone National Park.[10]

Hague would later become a member of the Forest Reserve Commission, the group appointed by the National Academy of Sciences in 1896. He would work with Gifford Pinchot, William Brewer, Alexander Agassiz, and Wolcott Gibbs to produce the report that was the basis for President Cleveland's Washington's birthday withdrawal in 1897. Miners were particularly incensed by the loss of timber supplies to speculators who grabbed timber holdings by fraudulent use of the mining and other public land laws.

The close contact between miners and foresters is reflected in the mining press and the *Transactions* of AIME, and is fully described in *Bernhard Eduard Fernow: A Study of North American Forestry*, the biography of Bernhard Fernow, the German-trained forest engineer who would become the third chief forester of the Department of Agriculture, and some might say the father of the National Forest System.[11] Fernow devoted part of his career to mining and was actively associated with the American Institute of Mining Engineers for most of his working life. He became a life associate of the institute in 1878. Several of the prominent members of the institute were interested in forestry. Rossiter Raymond was the institute's president from 1872 to 1875. Abram Hewitt, an iron manufacturer and partner of Peter Cooper, founder of the Cooper Union, was president from 1876 to 1890, and John Birkinbine, editor of the *Journal of the United States Association of Charcoal Iron Workers*, was president from 1891-1893. Fernow quickly came to the notice of these men and gained their support. Fernow's biographer said that "in the course of Fernow's entire career he had no closer friend than Raymond," that "Fernow undoubtedly won the complete confidence and admiration of Raymond and Hewitt," and that "both aided Fernow's later appointment as Chief Forester of the Forestry Division in the United States Department of Agriculture and as a director of America's first professional forestry school, the New York State College of Forestry at Cornell University." Birkinbine, an engineer, was for many years president of the Pennsylvania Forestry Association and editor of its official publication, *Forest Leaves*.[12] He too was closely associated with Fernow, particularly as a student of charcoal making practices.

Raymond helped Fernow develop a practice as a consulting forest engineer. Rodgers comments that "it is interesting to realize that in part, out of the mining industry originated in America the practice of the consulting forest engineer." He also observed that:

> Perhaps the first professional utterances made formally to urge conserving the nation's natural resources were expressed in the appointment at the first session of the [American] Institute [of Mining Engineers], held at Wilkes Barre, Pennsylvania, in 1871, of a committee of eminent mining engineers "to consider and report on waste in coal mining. . . ."[13]

Fernow delivered a paper at the Philadelphia meeting of AIME in 1878. He raised the issue of forest preservation in general, but focussed specifically on wasteful consumption of wood in the United States, particularly in the charcoal industry. Charcoal, used in smelting iron, consumed fifty thousand acres of woodland annually. Fernow's good friend Rossiter Raymond arose during the discussion period to compliment the author for taking a new and wise direction in proposing an economy (in charcoal making) which tends to preserve forests, and then went on to say that:

> Mr. Fernow deserves special credit, because he did not propose legislative interference and the introduction of restrictive laws, a subject of which he is particularly qualified to speak, and recommendation which might have been expected from him as a late member of the Prussian Forest Department.[14]

Despite their friendship, Fernow felt obliged to reply, saying that he:

> [W]ould like to explain briefly his views in regard to government superintendence in the matter of forestry, which had been alluded to by Dr. Raymond. Although not an advocate of the enactment of laws for which no basis has been laid, he was by no means opposed to the idea of government interference in regard to the preservation of forests. On the contrary he was convinced that it was the highest duty of the government to establish the basis for such legislation. He was convinced also that the time for action had arrived, and that it is dangerous to wait until the financial aspect of the matter had made itself conspicuous; he held that the climatological influence of the woodlands, the existence of which is now undoubtedly established, was a much stronger reason for governmental interference than any commercial question whatever.[15]

Raymond, who advocated free market approaches rather than government supervision to secure forest preservation, may not have wholly concurred in Fernow's prescriptions. However, he backed both Fernow and his successor Gifford Pinchot consistently over the next thirty years, sparing no effort to foster the preservation of forests and creation of an effective agency of government to administer forest lands. He kept up a constant commentary on forestry matters in the pages of the *Engineering and Mining Journal* calling for the creation of "an efficient department of forestry" at the federal level. His support of both Fernow and the cause of forestry continued after Fernow became chief of the Forestry Division in the Department of Agriculture. Raymond also helped Fernow keep the support of miners by explaining that forest reservations and forest legislation had no negative impact on mining rights. A grateful Fernow dedicated his book, *A Brief History of Forestry*,[16] to Raymond.

Fernow, as chief of the Forestry Division, spoke again before a meeting of AIME in 1888. This time, addressing directly the issue of the mining industry in its relation to forestry, he invited western miners to support increased appropriations for forest management and more scientific management of private forests.[17]

Gifford Pinchot succeeded Bernhard Fernow in 1898, becoming the fourth chief of the Division of Forestry. Like Fernow, Pinchot maintained close relations with leaders of the mining industry, and he enjoyed the continued support of Rossiter Raymond in the pages of the *Engineering and Mining Journal*. Raymond wrote in 1901 that:

> We have heretofore referred to the importance of a proper consideration of the forest resources of the United States; and to the fact that this is of even more importance to the mining industry than to many others. The work for this purpose is hardly yet begun and its necessity is appreciated by comparatively few people. The Forestry Division of the Department of Agriculture, under both its late and present heads, is doing much to educate the public up to a proper understanding of the work, and has really done so much for a very modest appropriation, that it has set a bright example to other Government bureaus which might be mentioned. We hope for the success of this work and trust that it will receive the encouragement which it deserves.

Pinchot spoke at a meeting of AIME in February 1898, and one of his assistants appeared before a meeting of the AMC in 1905.[18]

Pinchot, in his autobiography, *Breaking New Ground*, describes some large mining enterprises such as Homestake and Anaconda as "principalities", and gives examples of their use of political power to gain access to timber. But he also sympathizes with the problems Homestake encountered when it tried to work out timber purchases with General Land Office bureaucrats and gives that company credit for supporting the Black Hills Forest Reserve and for agreeing to buy from the government the timber they needed for their mines in Sale No. 1.[19] Pinchot worked directly to gain the support of mine operators like Thomas J. Grier, super-intendent of the Homestake Mine. While Pinchot makes it clear that Homestake looked after its own interests, he acknowledges that they supported both the Pettigrew Amendment to the Sundry Civil Bill in 1897 and the Transfer Act in 1905.[20]

Although the record of mining industry support for modern forestry and for forest conservation leaders Fernow and Pinchot is clear, the politics of public land availability intruded on the relationship, threatening it in the extreme. Pinchot believed that Congress and the president created chaos in the West when they first withdrew forest reserves in 1891. Miners joined other westerners in opposing what they saw as a lock up of public lands in the forest reserves. As Pinchot states in *Breaking New Ground*, the 1891 Act authorizing Forest Reserves "slipped through Congress without question and without debate." It was "the beginning and basis of our whole National Forest System," but it "did not provide for the practices of Forestry on the Forest Reserves . . . did not set up a form of administration . . . [and] merely set the land aside and withdrew [land] . . . from every form of use by people of the West or by the Government."[21]

Although legislation was passed to restore some lands to mineral entry, the problem was still extant when President Cleveland announced the creation of additional reserves on Washington's birthday in 1897. Pinchot was highly critical of the way in which these new reserves were handled, and confessed to understand-ing why the people of the West were so upset when they were created. Pinchot was politically embarrassed by the situation and had to work mightily to bring groups like the miners back into support of forestry.

Following a political firestorm of western protest, and a presidential pocket veto of a bill nullifying the reserves, the Pettigrew amendment to the Sundry Civil Bill was passed and the battle over the reserves was ended. In Pinchot's view, that amend-ment "is the most important Federal Forest legislation ever enacted. It did two essential things: it opened the Forest reserves to use, and it cleared the road to sound administration, including the practice of Forestry."[22]

Pinchot was quick to get the message out to the miners and much of his talk at the AIME meeting in 1898 was directed toward assuring miners that the forest reserves were not withdrawn from mining. Subsequently Pinchot received the support of Homestake and the American Mining Congress for the Transfer Act in 1905.[23]

Leaders of the mining industry were also embarrassed by the unnecessary withdrawal of the forest reserves from the operation of the mining law. Their support for the reserves became cautious until the Pettigrew amendment removed their concern about access to public lands. There is much evidence that the mining giants acted aggressively in securing their timber supply, and it is not unfair to say they acted largely out of self-interest, but they did support Pinchot when he needed help with the Transfer Act.

With the forest reserves finally safe from attack, Pinchot turned his attention to their management. Although Pinchot states in *Breaking New Ground* that his administration "preferred the small man to the big man" and stepped "on the toes of the biggest interests in the West," he and his people soon won the respect of the mining community. His strong support for wise use of all of the resources of the forest reserves, including minerals, and his practical approach to regulation, including transfer of executive power to the field, went over well with miners. Miners took comfort in the language of the Forest Service *Use Book* of 1907 that "it is the policy of the Government to favor the development of mines . . . and every facility is afforded for that purpose. . . ."[24]

Pinchot was particularly skillful in maintaining good relations with the mining industry. When miners began to complain in 1908 about "an excessive price to miners for timber" and "officious" conduct and "red tape" in forest reserves (called national forests sine 1907), Pinchot invited the members of the Committee on Investigation of the National Forest Service of the American Mining Congress to confer with him and other Forest Service officials in Washington. That invitation was taken up and productive meetings were held in Washington and Denver over the next two years.[25] Ravenel Macbeth, secretary of the Idaho Mining Association, had this to say with regard to forestry relations in 1917:

> We have found, in our relations with the Forest Reserve officials, that the personal equation enters, to a large extent, into the matter. We have found in some sections prospectors have been encouraged in their work, whereas, in other sections these officials have failed to give such encouragement—in fact, have so strictly interpreted the provisions of the regulations, that prospecting has been hampered. We would state, however, that since the organization of this Association

in 1913 a much better condition has existed and that constant improvement is being noted by the mining men.

Formerly, in the matter of an examination to secure patent, officials who had no knowledge of the geological conditions existing in the section in which the property was located were appointed to make examinations and frequently, as a result of ignorance, reported adversely, but owing to vigorous representations made to the Department by this Association, such examinations are now made by competent mineral inspectors.

At present we have taken up with the Department the matter of withdrawing certain sections in small areas, over which sheep are now permitted to graze, for the use of prospectors who have found it impossible to prospect in certain sections of the State owing to the sheep having caned up the country and not leaving any feed for their stock.[26]

Following a renewed build-up of complaints by miners in the mid-1920s, E. A. Sherman, associate forester of the Forest Service, spoke before a combined meeting of AMC, AIME, and the American Silver Producers Association at Denver in 1926, addressing the issues involved directly, saying that:

Our officers are instructed to aid and cooperate with the industry in every practical way and to establish cordial relations with the prospectors and miners in their districts. That this policy has been followed in the overwhelming majority of cases is a known fact. That there may have been exceptions to the rule in a few cases is not to be wondered at when we consider the vast territory served and the fact that perfect men are not available for hire by the government say more than by the mine owner. However, a man who fails to cultivate a friendly, helpful, cooperative spirit in his relations with those who are endeavoring to develop the mineral wealth of our mountains has no place in the Forest Service. In seeing that this policy of cooperation is carried out we have welcomed, and will continue to welcome helpful, constructive criticism from the miners and prospectors and from your associations.

The American Mining Congress several years ago through a committee undertook to investigate complaints against the actions of Forest officers made by mining claimants, but not in one single

instance—I am happy to say—did the committee find any just ground
for criticizing the action our officers had taken. The Forest Service
regretted to see the committee discontinued and would welcome its re-
establishment, although we shall constantly strive to so handle our
work that it will not be needed.[27]

Although it is clear that leading mining engineers and the professional managers of
large mining firms were supporters of Fernow and Pinchot and their cause, it
would be an overstatement to say that miners universally supported federal control
of forests. Many small prospectors and miners who enjoyed access to the public
lands, and who had an equal opportunity to strike it rich under the 1872 Mining
Law, did not always accept the leadership of the large mining corporations. As
John Ise states in *The United States Forest Policy*, "there was much opposition to
the reserves from the very first, and in almost every session of Congress (between
1891 and 1897) war was waged on the reservation policy." He goes on to explain
that:

Two classes in the West were particularly hostile—the stockmen, who
found their privileges restricted by the reservation of these lands, and
the miners, who were at first entirely shut out of all forest reserves.

The prohibition of mining was an unnecessary hardship, for mining,
properly conducted, would not have interfered seriously with the
purposes for which the reserves were created, and in 1896, certain
reservations in Colorado were opened to miners . . . and the day after
Cleveland created the thirteen reserves, Secretary of the Interior
David R. Francis requested the chairman of the Senate Committee on
Appropriations to insert into the Sundry Civil Bill a provision opening
all forest reserves to mining. Such a provision was inserted in a later
Sundry Civil Bill [the 1897 Act]. . . .[28]

Gifford Pinchot was clearly a gifted organizer and promoter. He built upon
Fernow's relationship with the mining industry and used every possible public
relations tactic to keep the support of miners and other user groups. Though many
of Pinchot's accomplishments were highly visible and meant to be that way to
bring support to the Forest Service, he also gained the respect of miners when he
showed himself to be objective and capable of working out problems behind the
scenes. J. Parke Channing, a highly respected mining engineer who is credited
with development of the large Miami copper mine in Arizona, relates that Pinchot
helped make land available for tailing storage at Miami by signing an order delet-
ing a sagebrush covered parcel from a forest reserve, and did so at the time when
the Cabinet was discussing his dismissal.[29]

Subsequent to the Fernow and Pinchot years, the tradition of communication between the major mining organizations and the Forest Service continued. Often motivated by a desire to keep pressure from building in the public or in Congress for revision of the mining law, miners have worked cooperatively with Forest Service officials to deal with a number of surface management issues, supporting legislation and regulation that were required to deal with problems that arose out of changing public demands on National Forest System lands. Mining support for the Common Varieties Act of 1955 is well-documented, as is the cooperative effort between the Forest Service and the AMC in the development and implementation of the Surface Management Regulations which are now used to protect surface resources from damage by mining activities.[30]

Today, both users of forest resources and the Forest Service itself are under enormous pressure from preservationists to use planning authorities to essentially lock up National Forest System lands. The nation will sort these issues out politically as it always has, and it is fair to predict that miners will continue to be active participants in the process. The very proper collaboration between leaders of the mining industry and the Forest Service during the past century has been productive of changes in laws and regulations that were required to meet changing public requirements and attitudes toward use of forest lands. Hopefully, the spirit of mutual respect and openness that has characterized this relationship will continue as we all struggle with mining and forestry issues of the future.

Notes

1. T.A. Rickard, "The Discovery of Gold In California, University of California," *Chronicle*, April 1928, as quoted in Rickard, *A History of American Mining* (New York and London, 1932).

2. John R. Wagner, *Gold Mines of California* (Berkeley, CA: Howell-North Books, 1970).

3. Clark C. Spence, *Mining Engineers and The American West, The Lace Boot Brigade, 1849-1933* (New Haven, CT: Yale University Press, 1970).

4. Rickard, *A History of American Mining.*

5. The success of prospectors at Leadville is well documented. The Gallagher brothers sold two mines for $250,000 in 1878, and Horace Tabor sold his interest in the Little Pittsburg mine

for $1 million in 1879. Don L. and Jean Harvey Griswold, *The Carbonate Camp Called Leadville* (Denver: The University of Denver Press, 1951).

6. William S. Greever, *The Bonanza West: The Story of the Western Mining Rushes, 1848-1900* (Norman: University of Oklahoma Press, 1963); Rodman W. Paul, *Mining Frontiers of the Far West, 1848-1880* (New York: Holt, Rinehart and Winston, 1963).

7. Charles Howard Shinn, *Mining Camps: A Study in American Frontier Government*, ed. Rodman W. Paul (New York, Harper & Row, 1965).

8. A. J. Wilson, *The Pick and the Pen* (London, Mining Journal Books Limited, 1979); Wilson, *The Pick and the Pen*, 263.

9. Wilson, *The Pick and the Pen*, 94; Rossiter W. Raymond, *Statistics of Mines and Mining* (Washington DC: Government Printing Office, 1870), 342.

10. Transactions AIME XVI 783, 803 (1887). Despite the unbroken record of cooperation between the principal mining organizations and the Forest Service, both parties are often embarrassed by the actions and words of opportunists and crooks who hold themselves out as miners, but who are really people who honor the mining law in its breach. The Forest Service has had to contend with all manner of illegal occupancy and trespass problems, ranging from attempts to use mining claims for summer home sites, to claims staked for marijuana cultivation. These situations are of great concern to the legitimate mining industry, as miners are worried that these fraud situations will bring pressure on a mining law that is generally quite favorable for real miners. The American Mining Congress has recently advocated toughening up enforcement of the surface management rules and has, in the past, assisted the Forest Service directly with efforts to end the abuse of illegal occupancy.

11. Andrew Denny Rodgers III, *Bernhard Eduard Fernow: A Study of North American Forestry* (Princeton, NJ: Princeton University Press, 1951). Reprinted by the Forest History Society, 1991.

12. Ibid., 23, 26.

13. Ibid., 18.

14. B. Fernow, "The Economy Effected By the Use of Red Charcoal," *Transactions of the American Institute of Mining Engineers* 6 (1878): 199.

15. Ibid., 206.

16. "The Government Timber Suits and the Preservation of Forests," *Engineering and Mining Journal* (April 20, 1889): 364; "Common Sense in Forestry," *Engineering and Mining Journal* (August 15, 1891): 184; "Mining Claims Within Forest Reservations," *Engineering and Mining Journal* (March 19, 1898); Fernow, *A Brief History of Forestry in Europe, The United States and Other Countries* (Toronto: University of Toronto Press, 1907, 1911).

17. B. E. Fernow, "The Mining Industry in its Relation to Forestry," *Transactions of the American Institute of Mining Engineers* 27 (1888): 264.

18. Editorial, *Engineering and Mining Journal* (February 16, 1901): 201; Gifford Pinchot, "Mining and the Forest Reserves," *Transactions of the American Institute of Mining Engineers* 28 (1898): 339; R.E. Benedict, "Forest Reserves in Their Relation to the Mining Industry," *Proceedings of the American Mining Congress* (1905): 67.

19. Gifford Pinchot, *Breaking New Ground* (New York: Harcourt Brace, 1947. Reprinted 1972 by University of Washington Press, Seattle), 131, 115, 174. *See also* "Homestake Forest Products Company," in *Homestake Centennial 1976*, unpublished pamphlet available at the Denver Public Library, which relates the history of the Black Hills Forest Reserve and Homestake's forest products operations in the Reserve.

20. Pinchot, *Breaking New Ground*, 198, 114.

21. Ibid., 85.

22. Ibid., 116.

23. Judge Curtis Lindley, the foremost commentator on the mining law of his time, described the confusion surrounding the forest reserves and their impact on mineral entry in his treatise on the *American Law Relating to Mines and Mineral Lands* 3rd edition (San Francisco: Bancroft-Whitney Company, 1914). He refers to Pinchot's paper delivered to AIME in 1898, saying that Pinchot "points out that it was not the intention of the government in creating the national forests to antagonize the mining industry; Pinchot, *Breaking New Ground*, 198; *Report of Proceedings of the American Mining Congress* 7 (1904): 35.

24. Pinchot, *Breaking New Ground*, 263, 259; USDA, Forest Service, *The Use of the National Forest Reserves: Regulations and Instructions for Use of the National Forests* (July 1, 1907), 36.

25. *Official Proceedings*, American Mining Congress (1908): 36; *See* Pinchot to the Special Committee on Mining in National Forests, American Mining Congress, April 24, 1909.

26. *Mining Congress Journal* 7 (1917).

27. E. A. Sherman, "Mining in National Forests," paper read at a meeting of the Western Division of the American Mining Congress, the American Institute of Mining and Metallurgical Engineers, the American Petroleum Geologists, and the American Silver Producers Associations, September 1926.

28. John Ise, *The United States Forest Policy* (New Haven, CT: Yale University Press, 1920), 130.

29. *Transactions of the Mining and Metallurgical Society* (December 31, 1915): 312.

30. Harold K. Steen, *The U.S. Forest Service: A History* (Seattle: University of Washington Press, 1976. Reprinted 1991), 296, 297; *See* Stanley Dempsey, "Forest Service Regulations Concerning the Effect of Mining Operations on Surface Resources," *Natural Resources Lawyer* 8 (1975).

Wildlife, Conservation, and the First Forest Reserve

John F. Reiger
Ohio University, Chillicothe

In 1975 the writer published *American Sportsmen and the Origins of Conservation*, which argued that "sportsmen"—those who hunted and fished for pleasure rather than commerce or necessity—were the spearhead of a conservation *movement* originating in the 1870s. With the University of Oklahoma Press's publication of a revised, paperback edition in 1986, the book has become available to a new audience interested in the roots of environmental concern. This paper, "Wildlife, Conservation, and the First Forest Reserve," is an amended version of one small part of the thesis contained in that monograph.

Although their first concern was always wildlife, sportsmen-conservationists of the late nineteenth century quickly perceived that their many efforts in behalf of game mammals, birds, and fishes was a solution to only half the problem. It would do little good to conserve wildlife if its habitat continued to shrink, for eventually both would be gone. That part of the environment most immediately threatened was the forest.

Possessing an Old World code,[1] sportsmen saw forests not as a challenge to the American mission of progress, but as one of the essential settings for that important activity called sport. Free from the prejudices of the frontiersman, farmer, and logger, sportsmen viewed trees as something more than a hiding place for Indians, an obstacle to ploughing, or a source of financial gain. Woodlands were both the home of their quarry and the aesthetic backdrop for that avocation which many considered more rewarding—in a noneconomic sense—than their vocation.

As in the case of wildlife depletion, the appearance in the early 1870s of the first national sporting periodicals, *American Sportsman*, *Forest and Stream*, and *Field and Stream*, helped focus sportsmen's anger over woodland eradication and unite them against it.[2] When *American Angler* appeared early in the next decade, another voice for forest conservation was added to the sporting press. Like the other journals, *American Angler* endeavored to keep its readers informed of the most up-to-date information on "natural history," and that included the disastrous effects of unregulated logging and pulpmill discharge on rivers and their inhabitants. In addition to attacks on water pollution, the paper also explained in detail how uncontrolled lumbering ruined fishing waters by causing such habitat changes as bank erosion and higher water temperatures.[3] Like the other periodicals, *American Angler* illustrated a remarkable understanding of ecological principles.

Of the four major papers, *American Sportsman* and *Forest and Stream* proved to be the most concerned with forest conservation. Founded in 1871, the former journal repeatedly lamented the extent and ramifications of woodland destruction, as a solution to the problem, it suggested that European forestry techniques be adapted to American timberlands.[4]

When *Forest and Stream* was founded in 1873, it quickly proved that it was even more dedicated to forest conservation than its predecessor. Editor Charles Hallock stated every week in *Forest and Stream*'s subtitle that his paper was "Devoted to . . . Preservation of Forests," and he lived up to that claim by frequently calling attention to the depletion of timberlands and the need for their protection.[5] Hallock's interest in this issue may have been spawned, in part at least, by George Bird Grinnell. Although Grinnell did not join the paper's staff until 1876, he was associated closely with it from the beginning as a writer, financial supporter, and natural history adviser. Since his graduation from Yale in 1870, he had also kept in touch with scientific developments through his close association with Othniel C. Marsh, a sportsman and paleontologist who was then one of the university's most prominent faculty members. Grinnell assisted Marsh on his 1870 fossil-collecting expedition to the Far West, entered Yale's Sheffield Scientific School in early 1874, and received a Ph.D. under Marsh in 1880.[6]

Grinnell first concentrated on defining "sportsmanship" and conserving wildlife after becoming *Forest and Stream*'s editor and owner in 1880. It did not take long, however, for him to understand that more was also needed on the subject of forest conservation. In April 1882, therefore, he began his editorial drive to transform the nation's orientation toward its woodlands. Years earlier, Hallock had pointed the way by drawing attention to how rapidly the timberlands were being depleted and by suggesting Europe's system of managed forests as an alternative to the wasteful methods of American lumbering. But Grinnell went far beyond his predecessor in publicizing the European science of forestry.

In "Spare the Trees," the opening editorial of his campaign in behalf of the forests, he manifested awareness of the interrelationship of all natural resources. "If we have the most perfect code of game and fish laws which it is possible to devise," he wrote, "and have them ever so thoroughly enforced, what will they avail if there is no cover for game nor water for fish?" Employing the ideology of the

business-farm community, he called for Americans to use their "proverbial thrifti-
ness and forecast" to achieve "the proper and sensible management of woodlands."
The forests must be seen as a "crop . . . which is slow in coming to the harvest,
but it is a sure one, and is every year becoming a more paying one." In addition,
"it breaks the fierceness of the winds, and keeps the springs from drying up, and is
a comfort to the eye. . . . Under its protecting arms live and breed the grouse, the
quail and the hare, and in its shadowed riles swim the trout. . . ." Although the
lesson was a simple one, it had not yet been learned by the American people: "No
woods, no game; no woods, no water; and no water, no fish."[7]

Ever since the early days of *Forest and Stream*, the weekly's editors had been
interested in the possible applicability to American conditions of European developments in sport, natural history, and science. Particularly significant in this
regard was the Europeans' attitude toward their woodlands. In an 1883 editorial,
"Forestry," Grinnell reported: "In parts of Europe forestry is a science, and
officers are appointed by the governments to supervise the forests; and only
judicious thinning of young trees and cutting of those which [have] attained their
growth is allowed. . . ." He pointed out that the system was used not only on
government lands but on private holdings as well, "the theory being that the
individual will pass away, but the forest must remain forever." He contrasted the
continental emphasis on continuous resource management with the situation existing in America, where the sovereignty of private ownership allowed an individual
to "buy a tract of land in the great water producing region of the state and for his
own pecuniary benefit render it forever sterile." Grinnell suggested that laws
regulating forest use, like those already existing in Europe, should be immediately
passed in the United States. As in the case of game legislation, he believed that
statutes protecting the forests would have democratic results and "work well for the
people at large."[8]

In 1884 *Forest and Stream* stepped up its campaign to educate the American people
in the principles and methods of forestry. In March Grinnell used the recent floods
of the Ohio and Mississippi Rivers as illustrations of "the terrible effects of our
criminal waste of woodlands." He asked for massive reforestation along the rivers'
banks and the creation of state and federal forestry commissions. Later that spring,
he went further and demanded that the national government immediately appoint
"A Competent Forestry Officer," a "trained professional" to lead in "the inauguration of a system of forest conservancy." In the five-part series, "Forests and
Forestry" (1884-85), Grinnell consistently used almost the entire front page of his
weekly to explain the fundamentals of the European science. He argued that
forestry's concepts were applicable to every country. Although American trees and
soils were not exactly like those in Germany and France, the continent's expert

foresters were "capable of adapting general principles to changed conditions." And "pending the theoretical and practical training of young Americans," these foreign professionals should staff the forestry bureau.[9] Under their direction, it could become an animated, functioning department.

At the same time that Grinnell, through *Forest and Stream*, was beating the drum for general forest conservation, he was also leading a campaign that aimed, first, to define the meaning of Yellowstone Park for the American people and, second, to establish for it an effective administration. The 1872 act creating the reservation had for its object the protection of a natural "museum" of "wonders"—geysers, hot springs, and canyons. The park was *not* intentionally preserved either as a wilderness or a game refuge. The only concern of those few interested in the area was that the "curiosities" be made available to the public as soon as possible.[10] Instead of believing that the park should remain in a pristine state, most of these individuals assumed that it would soon be "improved" by a multitude of hotels, roads, and other conveniences.

During the rest of the 1870s and the very early '80s, most of Congress, as well as the general public, virtually forgot about the park. Because of its inaccessibility, there was at first little danger to it outside of the depredations of commercial hunters, who were killing all the reserve's big game for the money their hides would bring in markets to the east.

But by 1881, the tracks of the Northern Pacific Railroad had approached the vicinity of the reservation. "Soon after," Grinnell recalled in his autobiography, "its [the railroad's] President, . . . [Henry] Villard, took out a special train carrying a number of guests—railroad men, capitalists, and scientific men—to show the public the country traversed by his road." And "among those who then visited the Park were some . . . who saw its possibilities as a pleasure resort, and realized that the privileges offered to lessees through the Act establishing the Park would have a money value to those who might secure them."[11] Soon these men would begin their efforts to exploit the reserve, inspiring Grinnell to launch a campaign aimed at protecting the park by clarifying its status.

In large measure, Grinnell's crusade was the outgrowth of his experience in the West. Because the boundaries of Yellowstone Park were drawn with little real knowledge of the terrain, a number of expeditions were sent into the region to see exactly what Congress had, in fact, preserved. One of these was an 1875 reconnaissance led by engineer William Ludlow. As the expedition's official naturalist, Grinnell became thoroughly familiar with the park and its problems, the most obvious of which was hide hunting.[12]

Although all species of big game were being systematically slaughtered, he was most alarmed by the destruction of the buffalo, in this, their last stronghold. For seventy years, the dream of western expansion had fed on buffalo meat, and the animal had become the symbol of the new land, the game Old World aristocrats and New World patricians—Grinnell and Theodore Roosevelt among them—had to shoot, as a kind of initiation rite into frontier Americanism. Now, with the establishment of Yellowstone National Park, there appeared to be a possibility that the bison might be preserved, though the founders of the park had not conceived of it as a game refuge.

Although Grinnell's conception of the national park as a wildlife preserve was articulated as early as 1877,[14] it took several years for him to realize that if his idea were to become a reality, something more was required than sporadic protests. On December 14, 1882, he provided that "something more" by launching a crusade in *Forest and Stream* to define the status of Yellowstone National Park and protect it from commercialization. Only after a continuous campaign of a dozen years would his goal be achieved.

The first editorial, "Their Last Refuge," covered the whole front page and was both a plea for the buffalo and a detailed analysis of the deficiencies in the act creating the reserve. He pointed out that the statute put the destiny of the reservation completely in the hands of the secretary of the interior. This official had the power to grant leases to private persons and corporations for the purpose of building roads, hotels, and other facilities, and to decide what regulations should be devised for the park. With regard to wildlife, only their "wanton destruction" with "the purpose of merchandise or profit" was specified as one of the offenses the secretary was to "provide against."[15]

Grinnell's editorial made it clear that the vagueness of the act subjected it to a number of interpretations and left huge loopholes for those who sought to use the reserve for their own profit. An example was the section on wildlife, which seemed to suggest that individuals or corporations could kill all the game they wished, just so long as they were not too "wanton." The greatest deficiency, of course, was that the act provided no machinery for carrying out any regulations the secretary of the interior might promulgate. As Grinnell later recalled, the secretary's rules "soon came to be regarded as a dead letter. Anyone was at liberty to cut down the forest, kill the game or carry away natural curiosities, and all these things were constantly done. . . ."[16]

He cogently summed up the problem in the 1882 editorial: "This 'great and glorious government' has again stultified itself by enacting laws without supplying the means to enforce them. The Park is overrun by skin-hunters, who slaughter the game for the hides, and laugh defiance at the government. . . ." In fact, "the curse of politics has entered into the management of the reservation," with "the little money appropriated for its maintenance" being "wasted by incompetent and ignorant officials. It is leased to private parties, who desire to make a peep show of its wonders."[17]

Grinnell would soon have aid in his efforts in behalf of American forests in general and Yellowstone Park in particular. The establishment of the Boone and Crockett Club, named after two of America's most famous hunters, would be that help. After Grinnell became friends with Theodore Roosevelt in the mid-1880s, he emphasized to him the need for an effective sportsmen's society, to do for the larger mammals what the Audubon Society—founded by Grinnell in 1886—was doing for birds. Roosevelt agreed. Accordingly, in December 1887, the latter invited a number of his big-game hunting friends and relatives to a dinner party in Manhattan at which the Boone and Crockett Club was born.[18]

It was probably Grinnell who first pointed out that some provision should be made for club membership for those who were not big-game hunters but who had worked for wildlife preservation. Examples were his two friends, geologist Arnold Hague and Supreme Court lawyer William Hallett Phillips; the latter was also an enthusiastic angler. They had labored for Yellowstone Park, which entitled them to membership, even though neither man had killed any big game.[19]

After some consideration, it was decided that nonhunters could be elected to associate or honorary membership.[20] In time its members would include many of the most famous and respected men in America, individuals like Henry L. Stimson, Henry Cabot Lodge, Elihu Root, Owen Wister, Wade Hampton, Gifford Pinchot, and many others. As a result, the organization's influence would prove far in excess of any ordinary association of similar size. In fact, the Boone and Crockett Club—and *not* the Sierra Club—was the first private organization to deal effectively with conservation issues of national scope.

As is usually the case, the work of the organization was accomplished by only a small number of members, the rest being content merely to attend the annual dinner. Of these active members, Grinnell was the most influential. He formulated almost every idea the club came to stand for; he brought up most of the issues it became involved in; he did a great part of the work on the Boone and Crockett book series on hunting and conservation; and he effectively used *Forest and Stream* as the "natural mouthpiece of the club."[21] In 1896 George S. Anderson, then superintendent of Yellowstone National Park and a regular member of the Boone and Crockett Club, expressed the belief that without Grinnell, the club could not continue to exist. And in a letter to Grinnell a year later, Roosevelt acknowledged him as one of the two or three "leaders of our organization."[22]

A subsequent director of the society, the noted explorer and naturalist of Alaska, Charles Sheldon, went so far as to declare: "The Boone and Crockett Club . . . has been *George Bird Grinnell* from its founding. All its books, its work, its soundness, have been due to his unflagging work and interest and knowledge." Because the statement was substantially correct, its significance lies in the fact that some of the most important figures in the first conservation movement—including its two future leaders, Roosevelt and Pinchot—were members of the club. "When Theodore Roosevelt became president," former secretary of the interior Stewart Udall has pointed out, "the Boone and Crockett wildlife creed . . . became national policy." Forests and water could be included in that "creed," for in time the club took as its basic approach Grinnell's idea that all renewable resources benefited from continuous, efficient administration.[23]

The club's interest in the conservation of big game naturally turned it toward Yellowstone National Park. Describing his early relationship with Roosevelt, Grinnell later recalled that "the original attempt by a certain group of men to secure for their own profit control of all the important attractions of the park had been defeated before I knew him well, but as soon as he understood about the conditions in Yellowstone Park, he gave time and thought to considering its protection."[24] It would not be long before he joined Grinnell, Phillips, and Hague in actively working to establish a "government" for the park that would adequately protect its wildlife, especially the big game. With the arrival of 1891, the leaders of Boone and Crockett galvanized themselves for a new effort in behalf of the Yellowstone. The club's annual dinner was going to be held on January 14 at the Metropolitan Club in Washington, D.C., and Roosevelt wanted to use the occasion to emphasize to government officials the need for action. At the time, Grinnell was so busy with *Forest and Stream* matters that he thought he would be unable to attend. He changed his mind only after receiving an urgent plea from Roosevelt. The dinner was kept informal,[25] even though Roosevelt had invited a gallery of notables. As president of the Boone and Crockett, he presided over the table. On his left sat Secretary of War Redfield Proctor, and on his right, Speaker of the House Thomas B. Reed. Grinnell sat opposite Roosevelt, with Secretary of the Interior John W. Noble on one side and Samuel Pierpont Langley, physicist and secretary of the Smithsonian Institution, on the other. A few members of Congress, including Henry Cabot Lodge, as well as Arnold Hague, and William Hallett Phillips, also attended.[26]

At a business meeting beforehand, Grinnell and Roosevelt drew up a series of resolutions that were read at the dinner: "*Resolved*, That the Boone and Crockett Club, speaking for itself and hundreds of [sportsmen's] clubs and associations throughout the country, urges the immediate passage by the House of Representatives of the Senate bill for protection and maintenance of the Yellowstone National Park. *Resolved*, That this club declares itself emphatically opposed to the granting of a right of way to the Montana Mineral Railroad or to any other railroad through the Yellowstone National Park."[27]

After Roosevelt and Phillips made short speeches on the requirements of the reservation, one of the congressmen asked a number of questions that were answered by Hague and Roosevelt. "We then got to the subject of . . . large game," Grinnell reported to his friend Archibald Rogers, "and Langley, in response to a request from Roosevelt, said that he believed from what he had heard, that the large game of the Continent would be practically exterminated except in such preserves as the Yellowstone National Park, within the life of the present generation of men." The secretary had probably obtained this viewpoint from Grinnell. The two had been in communication on wildlife matters for some time, and Langley had already incorporated at least one of Grinnell's suggestions. This was his idea for having the National Zoological Park, which the Smithsonian controlled, acquire the Yellowstone reserve's surplus bears and other unwanted predators, rather than destroying them as formerly.[28]

After the secretary had made his comment, "Roosevelt . . . asked me to say something of the way in which game had disappeared in my time," Grinnell continued in his letter to Rogers, "and I told them a few 'lies' about buffalo, elk, and other large game in the old days." Clearly, Grinnell's long and varied experience in the primitive West had entitled him to Roosevelt's esteem.[29] When he finished his description of "the old days," a general conversation followed until about eleven o'clock, when the group broke up.[30]

Grinnell felt that the dinner had been a success, because "we excited a real interest," and he was now "more hopeful than . . . for two or three years." Despite his optimism, the railroad lobby proved successful in keeping the House from considering the Senate bill before the end of the session.[31]

In *A Brief History of the Boone and Crockett Club* (1910), Grinnell explains that "the attempt to exploit the Yellowstone National Park for private gain in a way led up to the United States forest reserve system as it stands to-day," because "as a natural sequence to the work that they [the club's leaders] had been doing" in regard to Yellowstone Park "came the impulse to attempt to preserve western forests generally." Since their original concern had been the park, it might seem odd that concrete results on the forestry question were obtained three years before the passage of the 1894 Yellowstone Park Protection Act. The reason for this was simply that the battle over the park took place in a public arena against determined western opposition, while the results in forestry were achieved by circumventing the popular forum. Nevertheless, the interrelationship between the two issues is shown by the fact that the first forest reserve President Harrison chose to set aside in 1891 was the Yellowstone National Park Timberland Reserve adjacent to the national preserve. "In essence," says one observer, "the Yellowstone became the birthplace for both the national parks and national forests."[32] He might have added that the systems for managing both were created largely by members of the Boone and Crockett Club.

As in the case of Yellowstone National Park, Grinnell led the club on the forestry issue. The editorial effort he began in 1882 to transform the nation's orientation toward its woodlands continued unabated through the decade.[33] The central thrust of these sophisticated but simply stated expositions was that "the Federal government must husband its resources and place them under systematic management," the purpose of which was exploitation without waste. Grinnell emphasized, in fact, that not to use resources was in itself wasteful: "The proposal to lock up the forests and prevent all further utilization of their products is one that cannot be entertained."[34] The latter statement was made in 1888 and matches exactly the policy that would be established in future years by two other Boone and Crockett members, Gifford Pinchot and Theodore Roosevelt.

While Grinnell was acting in his usual capacity as the instigator of public opinion, the Supreme Court lawyer, William Hallett Phillips, was busy in his customary role as a behind-the-scenes negotiator. Like others in the Boone and Crockett Club, he had arrived at his interest in forestry via his involvement in the crusade over the Yellowstone. "In 1887 Phillips . . . had succeeded in interesting Mr. [Lucius Q. C.] Lamar, Secretary of the Interior, and a number of Congressmen, in the forests, and gradually all these persons began to work together. At the close of the first Cleveland Administration, while no legislation had been secured looking toward forest protection, a number of men in Washington had come to feel an interest in the subject."[35]

In 1889 President Benjamin Harrison appointed John W. Noble of Missouri secretary of the interior. As in the case of his predecessors, Noble received the "treatment" from the directors of the Boone and Crockett as soon as he entered office. This consisted of personal visits from Phillips, Hague, and Roosevelt, and invitations to the club's dinners. But the one all-important difference was that Noble, unlike his forerunners, was highly receptive to the organization's expression of concern for the forests.

Why this should be true is not entirely clear. Although Noble was later an associate member of the Boone and Crockett Club, it is not known whether he ever hunted for recreation or accepted the environmental obligation inherent in the code of the sportsman. But it is known that he believed field sports helped individuals who pursued them to make a success of their lives,[36] and this, of course, is one of the basic themes of the sporting tradition.

Regardless of whether Noble was a sportsman himself, he seemed to enjoy the attentions of the prestigious Boone and Crockett Club, and he was in close touch with at least two of its members, Phillips and Grinnell, by 1889. In fact, the latter believed that it was Phillips, who was already a good friend of the secretary of the interior, who was most responsible for involving Noble in the effort to preserve western forests.[37] It would seem that *Forest and Stream*'s editor knew what he was talking about, as he worked with both men in behalf of the same end.

Grinnell's relationship with Noble began in the spring of 1889. In addition to his conservation work, Grinnell was also a dedicated champion of the Native American. After trying for months to oust an Indian agent who was exploiting the Blackfeet of northwestern Montana, he suddenly achieved success when the new secretary of the interior interceded personally in the affair after being alerted by Phillips.[38] From that time to the end of Noble's term in office, the secretary and *Forest and Stream*'s editor were in frequent communication on conservation matters and Indian affairs.

Following the position advocated earlier by *Forest and Stream*, Noble came to agree that in order to save the timberlands, they would have to be withdrawn from the public domain. The means for accomplishing this end were provided on March 3, 1891, when "An Act to Repeal Timber Culture Laws and for other Purposes . . . " was signed by President Harrison. Pushed through at the close of the Fifty-First Congress, the legislation was an effort to revise the land laws of the United States. Those who worked hardest among the members of Congress to have the bill approved were Bernhard Fernow, chief of the Division of Forestry, and to a lesser degree, Hague and Phillips.[39]

The granting of power to the president to set aside timberlands was not an obvious part of the act, but the last of twenty-four sections, being "inserted in [the] Conference Committee in the last hour of Congress by the insistence of Mr. Noble, that he would not allow the bill to be signed by the President unless the clause was added." Grinnell later recalled that it "had little or nothing to do with the title, or indeed the purpose of the bill. . . ."[40]

Soon after the passage of the bill, Hague "saw Secretary Noble and [suggested] . . . the setting aside of the Yellowstone Park Forest Reserve adjoining the Park. . . ." His aim, as Grinnell explained at the time, was "protection for the territory south and east of the Park, which it has so long been hoped might be added to the reservation." Noble liked Hague's idea, but before acting, he wanted to be sure there were no hidden pitfalls of a legal nature. To resolve this question, Hague returned the next day with William Hallett Phillips, Noble's friend and adviser, and all three discussed the legal question. After dismissing all doubts, Noble carried the project to the president, who promised to give the order. The dimensions of the proposed tract were discussed in several conferences between Noble and Hague and, finally, on March 30, 1891, President Harrison issued the proclamation setting aside the first forest reserve. Calling the tract the Yellowstone National Park Timberland Reserve, Harrison defined its boundaries in *exactly* the same language Hague had used in his proposal to Noble.[41]

Though this land would be administered differently than the national park, it eventually obtained real protection when the Forest Service eliminated wasteful logging and uncontrolled fires, the two factors which had previously threatened its existence. In one sense, therefore, Harrison's proclamation was the culmination of the effort Grinnell had begun in 1882 to have Yellowstone Park extended on the east and south, an effort which Phillips and Hague had later taken up.

The Yellowstone reserve contained 1,239,040 acres, all in Wyoming, and was the inauguration of the national forest system, totaling today about 191 million acres. Shortly after its announcement, Roosevelt, representing the Boone and Crockett Club, endorsed the action and commended Harrison and Noble. Grinnell did the same in *Forest and Stream* and urged the public to accept the reserve and the policy it represented. Some years later, Noble would gratefully acknowledge the aid Grinnell and "his very popular and influential paper" had given him, before and after the forest reserve system was initiated.[42]

Though historians have only recently begun to pay attention to the role of sportsmen and their allies in the making of the original conservation movement, the members of the Boone and Crockett Club were central to the establishment of the first forest reserve. And the goal of conserving wildlife, especially big game, proved to be at least as important an objective as watershed protection.

Notes

1. John F. Reiger, *American Sportsmen and the Origins of Conservation* (Norman: University of Oklahoma Press, 1986), chapter 1.

2. The interest shown in this subject by *American Sportsman*, *Forest and Stream*, and *American Angler* will be documented shortly. For *Field and Stream*, see, for example, "Game—Its Extinction: The Cause, and the Remedy," *Chicago Field* (later name of *Field and Stream*), August 3, 1878, IX, 392; "Why the Prairies are Treeless," Ibid., January 29, 1881, XIV, 394; "Tree Planting," *American Field* (later name of *Field and Stream*), July 21, 1883, XX, 49; "A Public Park," Ibid., December 22, 1883, XX, 577; "State School of Forestry," Ibid., July 16, 1884, XXII, 49; and "Nurseries for Game," Ibid., October 24, 1885, XXIV, 385.

3. *American Angler*, May 17, 1884, V, 310; Ibid., May 24, 1884, V, 328; Ibid., December 20, 1884, VI, 386; "Destruction of the Trout and Trout Streams of Central New York," Ibid., January 1, 1887, XI, 8-9; "How Shall We Preserve Our Water Supply?" Ibid., March 5, 1887, XI, 145-46.

4. "Forest Legislation," *American Sportsman*, October 25, 1873, III, 56; "Foreign Sporting Notes," Ibid., March 7, 1874, III, 361; "Wood and Forest," Ibid., November 21, 1874, V, 120; Ibid., March 13, 1875, V, 377; "Our Trees," Ibid., March 20, 1875, V, 392; "Forest Preservation in Europe," *The Rod and the Gun* (later name of *American Sportsman*), July 10, 1875, VI, 231; A. S. Collins, "Decrease of Brook Trout in the United States," Ibid., August 7, 1875, VI, 280; "Waste Land and Forest Culture," Ibid., March 18, 1876, VII, 390; "Are We Drying Up?" Ibid., January 20, 1877, IX, 246.

5. The very first issue of the paper (August 14, 1873) stated: "For the preservation of our rapidly diminishing forests we shall continually do battle. Our great interests are in jeopardy . . . from the depletion of our timber lands by fire and axe." For some other examples of Hallock's interest in the subject, *see* "Woodman Spare that Tree," *Forest and Stream*, August 21, 1873, I, 26; "The Preservation of Our Forests," Ibid., September 4, 1873, I, 56; "The Adirondack Park," Ibid., September 11, 1873, I, 73; "What the Germans Say About Wood Cutting," Ibid., September 18, 1873, I, 89; Ibid., September 25, 1873, I, 101; "The Waste of Timber," October 2, 1873, I, 121; "The State Park," Ibid., October 9, 1873, I, 136-37; Ibid., October 16, 1873, I, 149; Ibid., November 27, 1873, I, 244; "The Forests and their Effects on Man," Ibid., December 25, 1873, I, 321; "Adirondack Park and the Preservation of Our Forests," Ibid., March 19, 1874, II, 88.

6. Grinnell became natural history editor in 1876. For a detailed discussion of his early career, *see* John F. Reiger, ed., *The Passing of the Great West: Selected Papers of George Bird Grinnell* (Norman, OK: 1985); first published in 1972. Based on Grinnell's previously unpublished "Memoirs," which trace his life from 1849 to 1883, this work blends his words with the editor's commentary to paint a picture of the virgin West's last years.

7. *Forest and Stream*, April 13, 1882, XVIII, 204.

8. Ibid., July 19, 1883, XX, 481.

9. "Unheeded Lessons," Ibid., March 27, 1884, XXII, 161; May 15, 1884, XXII, 301; "Forests and Forestry V," Ibid., January 22, 1885, XXIII, 502.

10. Roderick Nash, *Wilderness and the American Mind* (New Haven: Yale University Press, 1982), 108-13; "The Yellowstone National Park," *Scribner's Monthly*, IV (May, 1872), 121, cited in Nash, 113.

11. Grinnell, "Memoirs," 94, George Bird Grinnell Papers, Yale University.

12. John Ise, *Our National Park Policy: A Critical History* (Baltimore: Johns Hopkins University Press, 1961), 21-22; Reiger, ed., *The Passing of the Great West*, 117-19.

13. For Grinnell's buffalo hunting, *see* Ibid., 58-72; also, *see* Grinnell's "Last of the Buffalo," *Scribner's Magazine*, XII (September, 1892), 267-86, for his poetic tribute to the vanished multitudes. The weathered skulls of the bull and cow bison he describes picking up on the prairie, "to keep as mementoes of the past," are on exhibit in the Birdcraft Museum of the Connecticut Audubon Society, Fairfield; Roosevelt first went west to shoot a trophy buffalo; James B. Trefethen, *Crusade for Wildlife: Highlights in Conservation Progress* (Harrisburg, PA: 1961), 2.

14. Reiger, *American Sportsmen*, 99-100.

15. *Forest and Stream*, XIX, 382.

16. Ibid., 382-83; Grinnell, "Memoirs," 95.

17. *Forest and Stream*, XIX, 382-83.

18. Grinnell to T. E. Hofer, January 15, 1919, Letter Book, 269, Grinnell Papers, Yale University; Reiger, *American Sportsmen*, 118-20.

19. Grinnell to W. H. Phillips, June 5, 1889, Letter Book, 354; Grinnell to Arnold Hague, February 22, 1888, Ibid., 297; Hague, however, applauded the "healthy, manly sport" of hunting and relished eating the game others killed! *see* Hague, "The Yellowstone Park as a Game Reservation," in Theodore Roosevelt and George Bird Grinnell, eds., *American Big-Game Hunting* (New York, 1901), 257; and Joseph P. Iddings, "Memorial of Arnold Hague," *Bulletin of the Geological Society of America*, XXIX (1918), 45. The former work first appeared in 1893.

Phillips was "a resident of Washington [D.C.], a Supreme Court lawyer, with a large acquaintance there." Because of this position, and the fact that he was a member of "one of the oldest and best-known Washington families," he was "tuned in" to all the latest legislative and political developments; *Forest and Stream*, May 15, 1897, XLVIII, 381; and Grinnell to N. P. Langford, July 25, 1905, Letter Book, 742-43. Besides being Grinnell's close friend, he was also his lawyer; Grinnell to W. H. Phillips, September 3, 1888, Ibid., 476-77.

20. Because of Grinnell's influence, Hague and Phillips in fact became *regular* members, but they seem to have been the only nonhunters to receive that honor. And despite the rule that

21. Grinnell, ed., *A Brief History of the Boone and Crockett Club With Officers, Constitution and List of Members for the Year 1910* (New York, 1910), 20. After talking with Grinnell's co-workers in the Boone and Crockett, a later member claimed: "His [Grinnell's] sane judgement guided the [Boone and Crockett] Executive Committee" and "in facing every problem that confronted the Club throughout its entire life, the court of last resort always seemed to rest within the mind of this one man. No course of action was determined until his judgment had been sought and no conclusions reached until his opinion had been given"; John P. Holman, "A Tribute to George Bird Grinnell," in "Boone and Crockett Club Officers, By-Laws, Treasurer's Report and List of Members for the Years 1938-1939" (July 1939), 29-30, Boone and Crockett Club Papers, Club Headquarters, Dumfries, Virginia.

22. Anderson to Grinnell, January 29, 1896, Boone and Crockett Club Papers; Roosevelt to Grinnell, November 30, 1897, Theodore Roosevelt Papers, Library of Congress, Series 2. Also, *see* Roosevelt to William Austin Wadsworth, February 4, 1898, in Elting E. Morison and John M. Blum, eds., *The Letters of Theodore Roosevelt* (Cambridge, MA: Oxford University Press, 1951-1954), I, 768.

23. Sheldon to W. Redmond Cross, May 3, 1926, Boone and Crockett Club Papers; emphasis in the original; Udall, *The Quiet Crisis* (New York publisher, 1967), 161.

24. Grinnell, "Introduction," *The Works of Theodore Roosevelt*, National Edition (New York, 1926), I, xxiii.

25. Grinnell to Arnold Hague, January 13, 1891, Letter Book, 183; Grinnell to Archibald Rogers, January 17, 1891, Ibid., 186-88.

26. Since the summer of 1886, the park had been under the control of the army; Grinnell, ed., *A Brief History of the Boone and Crockett Club*, 16-17; "Boone and Crockett Club Meeting," *Forest and Stream*, January 22, 1891, XXXVI, 3.

27. Ibid.; a third resolution endorsed "the efforts now being made to preserve the groves of big trees [giant sequoias] in California" and thanked "the Secretary of the Interior for his interest in this matter."

28. Grinnell to Archibald Rogers, January 17, 1891, Letter Book, 186-87; "Cages in Place of Bullets," *Forest and Stream*, August 21, 1890, XXXV, 85; Ibid., January 8, 1891, XXXV, 489.

29. An important manifestation of the regard Roosevelt had for *Forest and Stream*'s editor is the fact that he very much wanted Grinnell to be his hunting partner, which for Roosevelt was the ultimate compliment. *See* Grinnell to James Willard Schultz, May 24, 1888, Letter Book, 361; and Grinnell to Archibald Rogers, August 8, 1888, Ibid., 444.

Another example of Roosevelt's admiration for Grinnell is an 1894 letter of his to their mutual friend, Madison Grant. In it, he urges Grant to send Grinnell some photographs of Roosevelt, apparently showing the big-game animals the future president had just bagged in the West; Roosevelt to Grant, October 10, 1894, in Morison and Blum, eds., *The Letters of Theodore Roosevelt*, I, 401.

30. Grinnell to Archibald Rogers, January 17, 1891, Letter Book, 187.

31. Ibid; "The National Park Bill," *Forest and Stream*, March 12, 1891, XXXVI, 145.

32. Grinnell, *Boone and Crockett Club*, 21, 23; Ernest F. Swift, *The Public's Land: Our Heritage and Opportunity* (Washington DC: 1963), 7.

33. "Utilize the Streams," *Forest and Stream*, August 11, 1887, XXIX, 41; "Forests of the Rocky Mountains I," Ibid., October 25, 1888, XXXI, 261-62; "Forests of the Rocky Mountains II," Ibid., November 1, 1888, XXXI, 282-83; "Forests of the Rocky Mountains III," Ibid., November 8, 1888, XXXI, 301-02; "Popular Forestry Instruction," Ibid., December 6, 1888, XXXI, 381; "Practical Forest Restoration I," Ibid., February 28, 1889, XXXII, 105; "Practical Forestry Restoration II," Ibid., March 14, 1889, XXXII, 149; "Practical Forest Restoration III," Ibid., March 21, 1889, XXXII, 169; "Practical Forest Restoration IV," Ibid., March 28, 1889, XXXII, 189.

34. "Forests of the Rocky Mountains I," Ibid., October 25, 1888, XXXI, 261-62.

35. Grinnell, *Boone and Crockett Club*, 23.

36. Reiger, *American Sportsmen*, 45.

37. Grinnell went so far as to claim that it was "through the influence of William Hallett Phillips [that] . . . a few lines inserted in an act passed by Congress March 3, 1891, permitted the establishment of forest reserves . . ."; Grinnell, "Big-Game Refuges," in Grinnell, ed., *American Big Game in Its Haunts* (New York publisher, 1904), 443. Although Noble is generally credited with having actually obtained the insertion of those all-important lines, Grinnell was probably correct in believing that the "influence" of Phillips—a friend of the secretary and an active worker for forest preservation since the mid-'80s—played a key role in the evolution of Noble's commitment to the woodlands.

For an example of Phillips' early dedication to the forests of the Yellowstone, see *Forest and Stream*, February 11, 1886, XXVI, 41. In "Secretary Noble's Monument," *Forest and Stream*, March 9, 1893, XL, 203, Grinnell wrote: "It will be remembered that *beginning* [my emphasis] with the Yellowstone National Park, which was brought to the notice of Mr. Noble early in his administration, he has given much attention to the question of our parks and timber reservation[s]"; this statement undoubtedly refers mainly to Phillips.

For examples of the close working relationship between Phillips and Noble, *see* Grinnell to Phillips, May 25, 1889, Letter Book, 322; Grinnell to Noble, May 25, 1889, Ibid., 321 [letter crossed out and apparently never sent]; Grinnell to Phillips, May 28, 1889, Ibid., 329; Grinnell to Phillips, June 5, 1889, Ibid., 354; Grinnell to Phillips, November 7, 1889, Ibid., 453-55; Grinnell to Phillips, December 4, 1889, Ibid., 16; and Grinnell to Phillips, April 24, 1891, Ibid., 383.

For the fact that Noble is usually credited with obtaining the insertion of the important lines in the 1891 act, *see* John Ise, *The United States Forest Policy* (New Haven: Yale University Press, 1920), 115. Although he admits that the history of this issue is extremely vague, Ise nevertheless accepts Bernhard E. Fernow's later claim that he and Edward A. Bowers, of the American Forestry Association, "had educated Noble up to the point" of demanding the insertion of the forest-reserve clause. While Fernow and Bowers deserve credit for exerting some influence, Phillips was probably easily as important—despite the fact that, unlike Fernow, he left no readily accessible documentation of his role. (For an alternative view, *see* Harold K. Steen, *The Beginning of the National Forest System*, USDA Forest Service, 1991). Like many other patrician pioneers of conservation, "he . . . labored long and earnestly for the public good [but] . . . preferred that his efforts should not be known, and that others should receive the credit for what he did"; "William Hallett Phillips," *Forest and Stream*, May 15, 1897, XLVIII, 381. This citation refers to an unsigned obituary of Phillips written by Grinnell; the former had drowned near Washington, D.C., on May 9, at about the age of forty-five.

38. From the late 1880s on, *Forest and Stream* and Grinnell's Letter Books are replete with examples of his efforts in behalf of Native Americans; Grinnell to Phillips, May 25, 1889, Letter Book, 322; Grinnell to Noble, May 25, 1889, Ibid., 321 [letter crossed out and apparently never sent]; Grinnell to Phillips, May 28, 1889, Ibid., 329; "Secretary Noble and the Indians," *Forest and Stream*, May 30, 1889, XXXII, 373; Grinnell to Phillips, June 5, 1889, Letter Book, 354; and Grinnell to Noble, June 19, 1889, Ibid., 380-81.

For some examples of Grinnell's efforts to get the Indian agent removed, *see* Grinnell to Commissioner of Indian Affairs, November 20, 1888, Ibid., 497-502; Grinnell to Commissioner of Indian Affairs, November 30, 1888, Ibid., 39-66; Grinnell to J. W. Schultz, December 4, 1888, Ibid., 7-9; Grinnell to L. H. North, December 13, 1888, Ibid., 34-35; Grinnell to Joseph Kipp, December 20, 1888, Ibid., 86-87; Grinnell to George Gould, December 26, 1888, Ibid., 96-97; Grinnell to H. H. Garr, January 3, 1889, Ibid., 180; Grinnell to Garr, January 7, 1889, Ibid., 128-29; Grinnell to William Russell, February 13, 1889, Ibid., 212; Grinnell to Gould, April 26, 1889, Ibid., 267-68; Grinnell to Garr, May 11, 1889, Ibid., 282; and Grinnell to J. B. Monroe, April 29, 1913, Ibid., 27-28.

39. Arnold Hague to Grinnell, April 11, 1910, Grinnell Papers, Yale University.

40. Bernhard E. Fernow to Grinnell, April 12, 1910, Ibid; Grinnell to John W. Noble, February 28, 1910, Letter Book, 910.

41. Arnold Hague to Grinnell, April 11, 1910, Grinnell Papers; *Forest and Stream*, April 9, 1891, XXXVI, 225; Arnold Hague to Grinnell, April 11, 1910, Grinnell Papers.

42. A copy of this resolution, dated April 8, 1891, is in the Boone and Crockett Club Papers; *Forest and Stream*, April 9, 1891, XXXVI, 225; Ibid., October 22, 1891, XXXVII, 265; Ibid., December 3, 1891, XXXVII, 385; Noble to Grinnell, March 11, 1910, Boone and Crockett Club Papers; Noble to Grinnell, March 15, 1910, Grinnell Papers.

The Historic Canyon Creek Charcoal Kilns

Michael Ryan
Beaverhead National Forest

What have charcoal kilns and the production of charcoal to do with Forest Service history? An honest answer has to be—not very much. Not very much if you are looking for a direct historical linkage between mining history as it unfolded in Canyon Creek and the early forest reserves or the later national forests. However, the mining history in Canyon Creek, and the role played by charcoal production in that history, provide a background or context for understanding the kinds of use early forest reserve officers and later Forest Service officers were expected to bring under control and management in the late nineteenth and very early twentieth centuries. Canyon Creek represents just one of many possible examples of free access or free use of forest resources taken as a right by industrial, agricultural, and individual interests throughout the West during the nineteenth century.

Other prominent local examples of nineteenth century industrial use of public resources are numerous in both the timber and livestock industries. However, the mining industry in Montana was the first, most important, and arguably the largest user of natural resources in southwestern Montana. Timber and water were critical to the development of any ore body. Mining companies exploited these resources freely without regard to conservation or compensation to anyone but owners or stockholders.

Geographic Setting

Southwestern Montana can be characterized as a region of basin and range topography. A number of important rivers including the Beaverhead, Big Hole, Red Rock, and Ruby occupy broad, alluvial valleys flanked by rugged mountain ranges. These ranges include the Ruby, Beaverhead, Tendoy, Highland, and Pioneer mountains. Elevations in these mountains often reach over 10,000 feet. The valleys are broad areas of open, rolling grassland covered by native fescue, blue bunch wheatgrass, and sagebrush. Above the foothill zone timbered mountain slopes support stands of lodgepole pine, Douglas-fir, and Englemann spruce at higher elevations.

Canyon Creek is a major easterly flowing tributary of the Big Hole River. It enters the Big Hole River near Melrose, Montana, at a point about halfway between Dillon and Butte. Canyon Creek in the area of the charcoal kilns is a narrow, flat-flood canyon with steep walls to the north and south. The kilns lie at about 6,500 feet in elevation and are surrounded by a mosaic of timber and sagebrush-grassland along the canyon floor. On adjacent forested slopes lodgepole pine is the dominant species, with juniper, curley-leaf mahogany, and Douglas-fir also present.

Historical Overview

Mining in southwestern Montana was the earliest impetus for a host of other development. The placer gold discoveries at Bannack, Virginia City, Nevada City, and numerous other locations in Alder Gulch brought Montana Territory its first large influx of immigrants from "the States" and surrounding territories. Mining provided the base from which other development grew. Agriculture in the Gallatin Valley, the Beaverhead Valley, the Deer Lodge Valley, and a few other areas of lesser importance developed to serve the needs of miners. The first early cattle drives from Oregon into Montana Territory were designed to take advantage of a ready market in southwestern Montana. It was no accident that one of Montana's earliest and largest livestock enterprises (Poindexter and Orr) was established in Beaverhead County adjacent to the rich placer mines and their throngs of busy miners. When Nelson Story drove the first herd of Texas cattle into the Gallatin Valley in 1866, he too had his eyes firmly fixed on the growing population centered around Bannack and Virginia City.

Large-scale placer mining began in Montana with the discovery of free gold in the gravels of Grasshopper Creek during the summer of 1862. Bannack, the first territorial capital, grew up at the new diggings virtually overnight. Although immensely wealthy, the placer deposits at Bannack were short lived. By the summer of 1863 Bannack was already being eclipsed by discoveries of rich deposits of placer gold made in Alder Gulch some fifty-five miles east. Virginia City, Montana's second territorial capital, grew to be the most important of several mining camps in the Gulch. Working from Bannack and Virginia City, prospectors spread throughout the surrounding mountains to locate other strikes. Some enjoyed success in new locations, but none ever duplicated the strikes on Grasshopper Creek and Alder Gulch. The era of placer mining in southwestern Montana lasted at a much reduced level for many years (indeed in continues today). But by the late 1860s and early 1870s the best placer deposits were largely depleted and emphasis shifted to lode mining.

Trapper Creek and the adjacent Canyon Creek were prospected in the early 1870s. The discovery of large silver lodes in Trapper Creek is the quintessential story of accidental strikes on the mining frontier.

William Spurr and James A. Bryant located a promising silver lode in 1872. They called their Trapper Creek discovery the Forest Queen. Neither partner worked the claim, and the following year the lode was open for relocation. Bryant, P.J. Grotevant, and a number of partners organized a fur trapping expedition to the headwaters of Trapper Creek. While there Bryant intended to relocate the silver lode found the previous year. That being done the partners went about their business of trapping. Grotevant was out on Trapper Mountain searching for lost horses when he accidentally came upon an outcrop of the Trapper Lode. He reportedly sat down to rest on the outcrop and idly kicked a rock at his feet. As the rock turned down-side up Grotevant saw almost pure silver in the stone. He quickly returned to camp and convinced his partners that their time would be better spent staking claims than trapping pine martin and beaver. After staking their claims the party traveled to Bannack to record their find. Word of the new silver strike leaked out and in a matter of a week dozens of men were in Trapper Creek staking claims.

Among the newcomers was Noah Armstrong. Armstrong located the Cleve, Avon, Alta, and Atlantis lodes. These mines quickly became the leading producers in the Bryant (later the Hecla) Mining District. Working from this base of highly successful producers, Armstrong soon bought other properties until he owned the bulk of the mines in Trapper Creek. One of his acquisitions was the Cleopatra, which together with the Atlantis became the two most profitable mines in the district.

Log cabins and tents sprang up immediately, and Trapper City was born in 1873. In addition to the miners' dwellings, there were several saloons and a "hurdy gurdy." Looking to the future Armstrong chose a spot on Trapper Creek about ten miles below Trapper City to build a smelter. The first cabins around Armstrong's smelter appeared in 1873 and the town of Glendale was established. The smelter had two seventy-ton blast furnaces. Apparently not content to wait for the smelter to become operational, Armstrong and other mine owners shipped ten tons of high-grade silver ore to Swansea, Wales, for refining that first year.[1]

Trapper City flourished only briefly. It soon became apparent that the properties located about a mile up the gulch on Lion Mountain (such as the Atlantis) were potentially more important than those near Trapper City. The Trapper Mine shut down just as the Atlantis was coming into production. A new settlement called Lion City grew at the foot of Lion Mountain. Trapper City's last inhabitant gave up and moved to Lion City in 1878.[2]

Lion City boasted two general stores, three saloons, two hotels, boarding houses, a school, and a post office by 1878. Inhabitants included skilled miners, laborers, merchants, teamsters, gamblers, and prostitutes. Lion City served the needs of people at the mine mouth. Glendale served a very different function, and it too was growing. Early lode miners were faced with a number of serious problems. After securing sufficient capital for development, they had to get heavy mining equipment and milling machinery to the lode. Once equipment was in place and working tons of ore had to be hauled to distant places for processing. Hauling ore any great distance was very expensive. The mining records are replete with examples of ore being hauled from southwestern Montana to Corrine, Utah, and shipped by rail to the west coast. There the ore was placed in ships for the trip to Swansea, Wales, and eventual smelting. This option worked for only very high-grade ore which could pay the cost of transport. A preferable solution was to be establish smelters as close to the ore body as possible. This is exactly what Noah Armstrong did. Strengthening his mining, milling, and smelting interests Armstrong formed the Hecla Consolidated Mining Company in 1877. He continued to build up the Glendale smelter, and with the smelter, the town.

Armstrong's original smelter burned down in 1879 at a reported loss of $100,000. Construction of a new smelter began immediately. Prompt reconstruction was imperative. The Glendale smelter was not only processing ore from the Lion Mountain mines, but also from mines in the adjoining Districts of Highland and Vipond.[3]

A glimpse of the nonindustrial side of Glendale in the late 1870s is possible from a contemporary source. Alma Coffin arrived in Glendale in 1879. Her father was the newly employed school teacher. She described the settlement as having one main street ". . . winding up the gulch," and small frame houses and log cabins scattered on the hillside. Miss Coffin also mentioned the smelter, roaster, company office, assay office, warehouse, blacksmith shop, iron house, powder house, coal sheds, stables, hospital, a Masonic Lodge, an Oddfellows Lodge, racetrack, roller skating rink, opera house, and brewery.[4]

Affairs seemed to be going well for Noah Armstrong, and the Hecla District, as the 1880s dawned. Ore from the mines was smelting at $1000 per ton. Base bullion was being shipped by wagon and train from Glendale to Omaha, Nebraska, where it averaged $100,000 in value over a period of several months in 1880. Despite its apparent vigor, Armstrong's company was $77,785 in debt as of January 1881. Armstrong decided to sell his interests in the Hecla Consolidated Mining Company to E.C. Atkins of Indianapolis, who owned the Atkins Saw Works. Atkins employed Henry Knippenberg as manager of the saw works. Knippenberg accepted the position of general manager of Hecla Consolidated. He arrived in Glendale with his family in April of 1881.[5]

Knippenberg set about an immediate reorganization of Hecla's operations. That Knippenberg was an able general manager, and his reorganization successful, is seen from the company's balance sheet. By December of 1881 Knippenberg had erased the debt owed by Armstrong and showed a year-end profit of $237,730.[6]

The mid-1880s saw Glendale's smelter and community growing. The smelters three fifty-ton blast furnaces were supported by two crushers, and a large roaster. The vigor of the Hecla District's production and community growth were assured by the arrival of the Utah and Northern Railroad. The tracks reached Melrose, Montana, in the spring of 1881. The railroad was finally completed to Butte in December of the same year.[7] It is clear that Knippenberg's successful reorganization of the Hecla Consolidated Mining Company was aided immeasurably by completion of the railroad. The Hecla District was linked with Butte on the north and Salt Lake City on the south—two major centers of east-west transcontinental rail traffic.

The 1890s began well for the Hecla Mining District. Glendale was important enough to appear on a map of Montana's leading towns and cities in 1892.[8] The Sherman Silver Purchase Act of 1890 was a boon to the silver interests in Montana. It required the United States government to purchase twice as much silver as it had previously. It also added to the amount of silver money in circulation. However, the act threatened to undermine the nation's gold reserve. President Grover Cleveland was convinced that the act helped precipitate the Panic of 1893. The president called Congress into special session, and in 1893 the Sherman Silver Purchase Act was repealed.

This was a serious blow to the silver producers in the Hecla District. These external forces were only the beginning of Hecla's problems. Production from the mines declined rapidly after 1893. The Cleopatra Mine played out in 1895. The Atlantis followed soon after—although it continued small scale production until 1903. The end was in sight for Hecla Consolidated. Ore reserves were depleted, and national trends greatly reduced the value of silver. Yet the company managed to show a profit for stockholders. It paid annual dividends of 6 percent between 1870 and 1900.[9] The Glendale smelter was closed down and dismantled in 1900. Low grade ore, and slag, were shipped to Omaha for smelting; mining on a large scale was over by 1903.

In the history and development of lode mining in Montana, the Hecla District ranks as one of the most important and productive silver and lead districts in the state. Geach called the Hecla District the ". . . treasure house of Beaverhead County, having produced ore valued at nearly $20,000,000." Commentators of the period pointed to the Hecla Mining District as equal in importance to any in Montana's famous "silver triangle:" Butte to Philipsburg to Helena.[10]

The Use of Charcoal in Smelting

Early blast furnaces represented a significant undertaking for mining companies, but one which some chose to accept for a variety of reasons—mostly economic. These early blast furnaces needed to be small enough to transport, especially prior to rail access. They needed a source of power, usually a steam boiler, to operate the machinery, and in the case of hot blast furnaces, to heat the air forced into the furnace. The furnaces needed fire brick to line the fire box.[11] The only other special need was available water, which in the case of Glendale was brought by ditch and flume from Trapper Creek.

The ores smelted at Glendale were not refractory. They did require blast furnace treatment because ore with a silica content greater than 4 percent needed a blast furnace. The ore was not sulfurous so roasting in a reverberatory furnace was unneeded, or little needed. To "charge" a blast furnace a highly controlled mixture of ore, flux (for example lime, dolomite, or iron ore) and a solid fuel were placed in the furnace. The commonest smelter fuels were coke, charcoal, or a combination of the two.[12] Prior to the arrival of railroads, coke imported from the northeastern United States was too expensive for southwestern Montana smelters. With access to eastern markets provided by the Utah and Northern Railroad there was a change from reliance on charcoal as blast furnace fuel to a mixture of coke and charcoal (the shift in fuel preferences happened at numerous localities in the mining West). This shift occurred at Glendale after 1881. Coke was shipped to Melrose from Pennsylvania. In 1895, for example, the Hecla Company imported 1000 tons of coke. This coke cost $16.65 per ton delivered at Melrose, and an additional $2.35 per ton to haul the 10 miles by wagon from Melrose to Glendale. The smelter consumed 10 tons of coke per day.[13] So the stockpiled 1000 tons would last only about 3 months. At this rate of consumption it is clear why the Hecla Company continued to absorb the additional expense of charcoal production for a portion of the blast furnace fuel.

The actual production of charcoal involves locating a source of cordwood, felling the trees, limbing, bucking into cordwood lengths (4 feet), transporting the wood to the burning site, and burning—or "coaling" the wood. Cordwood was reduced to carbon by two methods. It could be burned in earth-covered mounds, called "pits" by the charcoal burners. It could also be burned in brick or stone kilns designed for the purpose.

The amount of labor in kiln burning was less than that required for pit burning. The kiln burning process was easier to control and the condition of the charcoal could be better determined throughout the process. Kiln productivity was greater than pits. Pits produced from 30 to 35 bushels of charcoal per cord. Kilns would yield 45 to 50 bushels per cord. The yield was 15 to 20 percent greater, and the cost of operation 30 percent less. Finally, kiln burned charcoal was cleaner as it was not mixed with dirt and sand from an earth cover—therefore it burned cleaner and hotter.[14] The only obvious drawback to kiln burning was a lack of mobility. When nearby stands of timber were cut pit burners simply moved operations to another area. As nearby stands of timber were used fallers had to move increasingly greater distances from stationary kilns, thereby greatly increasing the cost of transporting wood to the kilns.

Doubtless, the Hecla Company's need for charcoal was filled by the pit method in the early years. That was the pattern throughout most of the mining West. Pits required less capital, less skill to construct, and probably somewhat less skill to operate than kilns. As a mining district developed the pit method was sometimes supplanted; sometimes it existed side-by-side with charcoal kilns. This second situation applied to the Hecla District. In 1895 the Hecla Company produced charcoal in thirty-eight company owned kilns (not all were in Canyon Creek) and also purchased pit-burned charcoal from independent burners.[15]

Kiln Construction

Charcoal kilns came is several shapes and many sizes. The form and construction depended upon the builder's preferences, skill and knowledge, and the dictates of terrain. They could be rectangular, circular, or conical. Fuel quality did not differ from one to another. The principal drawback to round and rectangular kilns, which were declining in popularity by the mid-1850s, was their structural instability. They were more prone to crack in the joints, and therefore, required more repair. All kilns expanded and contracted with the fluctuations in temperature. Metal bands or wire ropes were placed around them for support. These bands did not prevent cracking in the round and rectangular kilns, and the cracks could not be permanently sealed. The constant cracking and recracking introduced unwanted air into the kilns and made the burning process difficult to manage.[16]

The 23 charcoal kilns on Canyon Creek are 20 feet high and 25 feet in diameter. They represent the conical type, made usually of brick, and most common in the charcoal industry after 1850. These kilns hold between 35 and 45 cords of wood.

The cost of kiln construction was greatly influenced by local factors. Most important of these were the availability and cost of material and labor. It cost $500 to build a conical kiln of 35 to 50 cord capacity in New York. A similar kiln in Michigan cost $600. Murbarger quotes the cost of a brick or stone kiln in Nevada, similar in size to those on Canyon Creek, at between $500 and $1000 each. It was more cost-effective to build smaller kilns (between 160 and 180 cubic meters in capacity). The cost of more structures was offset by a higher quality charcoal.[17]

Kiln Operation

The operation of a charcoal kiln can be divided into three parts: charging the kiln, burning the wood to charcoal, and discharging (or "drawing") the kiln.

The act of "charging" a kiln referred to filling it with cordwood. The wood was not simply pitched in, but stacked very precisely to allow complete, even burning. The cordwood was four feet long. The diameter was not important, although a uniform diameter was helpful for even burning. The kiln was filled from the main charging door on the front of the structure until it was no longer possible to reach the top of the wood stack. The upper portion of the stack was laid in from a smaller charging door: usually at the upper rear of the kiln. Charging a conical kiln thirty feet in diameter required the labor of four men and two horses for one twelve-hour day.[18]

The "burning" process reduced wood fiber to charcoal by driving off the volatile gases and moisture in an oxygen poor environment to produce an almost pure form of carbon. The entire art and science of producing a good grade of charcoal centered on the manipulation of the kiln vents, and the ability to understand conditions inside the kiln from external signs. Once the kilns were fired the charcoal burners never left the site until the burning was completed. They watched the smoke coming from the three rows of vent holes around the bottom of the kiln. Thick white smoke came from the topmost row of vents, usually for three to four days. This signaled water being driven out of the wood as steam. In about four days yellowish smoke began to appear. Blue smoke followed next. Blue smoke indicated the kiln was very hot and the burning process was almost complete. After the first twelve hours the top vents were closed and the second row of vents opened. In another twelve hours the second row of vents smoked blue. They were then closed. The bottom row of vents were opened and the fire was taken down to the very bottom of the kiln. When the burners judged the bottom of the kiln to be thoroughly burned the bottom row of vents were closed and sealed.[19]

The burning time for a thirty-five-cord kiln was between six and eight days. When the kiln was completely fired all vents were closed by inserting a brick and mortaring it tight. The kiln was allowed to stand for two-and-one-half to three days. Eight to ten barrels of water were then thrown into the kiln from the top charging door. The charcoal could usually be drawn the next day. Two men working a twelve-hour day could "draw" or "discharge" a conical kiln about the size of those on Canyon Creek.[20]

Wood Fiber and Charcoal Production at Canyon Creek

A locally available source of good wood was critical to the success and growth of a mining district. Timber was consumed to provide domestic fuel and building materials, both in the form of rough lumber and round logs. It was a source of industrial and commercial fuel to fire steam boilers. The miners were voracious users of timber for mine studs, lagging, and all the other supports needed to keep a mine from collapse. The need for a good smelting fuel further encouraged intensive timber harvest. Coke was unavailable, too expensive to import, and often remained too expensive to use exclusively in the blast furnaces. So mining companies turned to local fuel for their smelting works. As White noted ". . . without adequate and readily accessible timber even the simplest and least capacious furnace was fated to economic failure."[21]

Charcoal burners were not fussy about which species of wood they used; whatever was available worked. In the eastern United States both hard and soft woods were burned. In timber-poor areas such as Nevada virtually anything was burned. Pinyon pine, juniper, mountain mahogany, even sagebrush found their way to the kilns.[22] The Hecla District was favored with large stands of lodgepole pine, some fir, and a few lesser species. This timber was cut in Trapper Creek, Canyon Creek and the large plateau north of Canyon Creek known as Vipond Park.

A brief review of the rate of charcoal consumption will focus the discussion on the rate of timber removal in the Canyon Creek area. The smelters in Eureka, Nevada, processed an ore similar to the makeup of that in the Hecla Mining District. Smelting one ton of silver-lead ore in 1880 required 25 to 35 bushels of charcoal. In that year all the smelters at Eureka consumed 1.25 million bushels. At this rate of consumption 42,857 cords of piñon pine were needed to produce the charcoal.

Depending upon site productivity, between 8 and 10 cords of wood could be harvested from 1 acre. That is, it required somewhere between 3,571 acres and 5,357 acres of piñon-juniper woodland to fuel the Eureka smelters for 1 year. The equivalent of 8 square miles fell to the woodcutters axe in a single year.[23]

In the same year, 1880, the 8 smelters at Leadville, Colorado, were using between 76,791 bushels of charcoal for the smallest to 1,094,870 bushels for the largest. These smelters were fueled by Colorado's pine forests which doubtless produced more wood fiber per acre than Nevada's piñon-juniper woodlands. Still, the timber needed to support only Leadville's portion of the Colorado mining industry must have been staggering. Emmons noted that in 1880 these smelters used between 3,600 cords of wood for the largest to 400 cords of wood annually for the smallest smelter operation—just to fire their boilers![24]

In attempting to calculate the impact of charcoal production on the timberlands of the East Pioneer Mountains, a number of questions arise. Some assumptions must also be made. Lee Harry (Beaverhead National Forest silviculturist) is personally familiar with the Canyon Creek and Vipond Park areas. He provided the following information on wood fiber yield. These calculations apply to a pure lodgepole stand, even though a small amount of Douglas-fir is present in the area. Lodgepole in Canyon Creek produces about 7,000 board feet per acre. Two cords of fuelwood can be produced per thousand board feet. Therefore, about fourteen cords per acre can be cut in these lodgepole stands.

This number seemed rather low considering the apparent density of the stands in the area, especially since the most productive sites in central Nevada's piñon-juniper forests produce only two cords less. Harry approached the problem through a different set of calculations. There are approximately 200 lodgepole per acre in Canyon Creek. Assuming an 8-inch diameter breast high (DBH), and an overall usable height of 60 feet for mature lodgepole, each tree yields .07 cords or 14 cords per acre. Both calculations estimate 14 cords of fuelwood per acre. That estimate is therefore used for stands present on the site historically. Harry and I have personally observed cross-cut sawn stumps in lodgepole stands adjacent to the Canyon Creek kilns. It is assumed that they represent a historic harvest of the area for cordwood. These stumps are consistent with an 8-inch DBH, and the distance between the observed stumps is comparable to the distance between current living stems.

Determining the acres harvested for charcoal production was made a great deal easier by the location of "annual reports" from the Hecla Consolidated Mining Company's officers to their stockholders. These annual financial reports, authored by Knippenberg and other major company officials, were a comprehensive listing of earnings and expenses for the year. They also included narratives concerning ore reserves, capital improvements, and similar topics of interest to owners. Annual reports for every year except those between 1894 and 1896 are held in the collections of the Beaverhead County Historical Museum. Among the expenses itemized are the number of bushels of charcoal used by the company in the Glendale smelter annually, and the cost for that charcoal. Estimating the number of acres harvested annually by the Hecla Company for charcoal requires dividing the annual reported consumption of charcoal by 45 bushels per cord to determine the number of cords of wood required to produce the indicated number of bushels. The number of cords can then be divided by 14 to arrive at the number of acres harvested. For example, in 1881 the Hecla Company consumed 461,177 bushels of charcoal in the blast furnaces at Glendale. If one could expect to get 45 bushels of charcoal[25] per cord of wood, then it would have required 10,248 cords to produce 461,177 bushels of charcoal. At a rate of 14 cords per acre, 732 acres of lodgepole pine were harvested to produce the 461,177 bushels of charcoal used in 1881.

This figure (732 acres) and the others displayed in the following chart [*see* p. 133] represent a minimum number of harvested acres each year. They do not account for domestic and industrial fuelwood, building materials, or mine supports. Not all of the wood fiber used came exclusively from Canyon Creek and Vipond Park. Other charcoal kilns were located in Trapper Creek. The "Acres Harvested" represent an approximation of the Hecla Company's wood fiber consumption for a single industrial product which illustrates the magnitude of unrestricted usage on the public domain. Based on the rate of charcoal consumption in the company's "annual reports" in 16 years, the equivalent of 18.2 sections of timber were cut for charcoal alone.

I have attempted to indicate the immensity of natural resource consumption by early mining entrepreneurs through consideration of a single industrial need of the Hecla Consolidated Mining Company. If the almost ten years of mining prior to the Knippenberg era are included, and the myriad other uses for wood fiber are considered, it is likely that the indicated rate of timber harvest would double at the least. Hecla was by no means the largest of hundreds of mining enterprises operating in Montana between 1864 and 1900. Most were equally rapacious in their consumption of natural resources.

YEAR	BUSHELS	CORDS	ACRES CUT
1881	461,177	10,248	732
1882	685,323	15,229	1,088
1883	931,962	20,710	1,479
1884	827,894	18,398	1,314
1885	1,008,827	22,418	1,601
1886	1,035,164	23,004	1,643
1887	670,535	14,901	1,064
1888	477,788	10,618	758
1889	331,589	7,369	526
1890	222,857	4,952	354
1891	214,348	4,763	340
1892	198,714	4,416	315
1893	136,543	3,034	215
1894	?	?	?
1895	?	?	?
1896	?	?	?
1897	61,000	1,356	99
1898	66,328	1,474	105
1899	18,800	418	30

1900   Glendale smelter shut down and dismantled

TOTALS   16,308 cords   11,665 acres

* From published "annual reports" for the Hecla Consolidated Mining Company for each of the years indicated.

Notes

1. Oren Sassman, "Metal Mining in Historic Beaverhead," (Unpublished Master's Thesis, University of Montana, 1941), 238; Thor N. Karlstrom, *Geology and Ore Deposits of the Hecla Mining District, Beaverhead County, Montana* (Montana Bureau of Mines and Geology, Memoir No. 25, 1948), 4.

2. Sassman, "Metal Mining," 241.

3. Ibid., 228; Karlstrom, *Geology and Ore Deposits*, 5.

4. "Not in Precious Metals Alone, A Manuscript History of Montana, 1976", Montana Historical Society, 156; Roberta Carkeek Cheney, *Names on the Face of Montana* (Missoula, MT: Mountain Press Publishing, 1983), 119.

5. Sassman, "Metal Mining," 243.

6. Ibid., 242.

7. Muriel Sibell Wolle, *A Guide to the Mining Camps of the Treasure State* (Newbury Park, CA: Sage Books, 1963), 190; *The Atlantis* (Glendale, MT: 1880-1881).

8. *The Daily Tribune*, 27 March 1892.

9. Karlstrom, *Geology and Ore Deposits*, 6.

10. Ibid., 1; R.D. Geach, *Mines and Mineral Deposits of Beaverhead County, Montana* (Montana Bureau of Mines and Geology Bull. 85, 1972), 111.

11. *Conservation Study: Birch Creek Charcoal Kilns, Targhee National Forest* (Idaho State Historical Society, CSW Architects and Preservation Services, 1984), 2.

12. Ibid., 5.

13. Sassman, "metal Mining," 243.

14. T. Egleston, "The Manufacture of Charcoal in Kilns," *Transactions of the American Institute of Mining Engineers*, No. 8, 1880.

15. Wolle, *Guide to Mining Camps*, 142.

16. Egleston, "Manufacture of Charcoal Kilns," 374.

17. Ibid., 197, 374; Nell Murbarger, "Forgotten Industry of the Frontier," *Frontier Times* (April-May 1965): 27.

18. Egleston, "Manufacture of Charcoal Kilns," 393.

19. Ibid., 388.

20. Ibid., 389, 395.

21. John R. White, "Early Nineteenth Century Blast Furnace Charcoals: Analysis and Economics," (The Conference on Historic Site Archeology Papers, No. 15, University of South Carolina, 1983): 113.

22. Charles D. Zeieer, "Historical Charcoal Production Near Eureka, Nevada: An Archeological Perspective," *Historical Archeology* 21:1 (1987): 84; Otis E. Young, *Western Mining* (Norman: University of Oklahoma Press, 1979), 113.

23. Ibid., 117; Zeier, "Charcoal Production," 86.

24. S.F. Emmons, "Geology and Mining Industry of Leadville," *Monographs of the United States Geological Survey* 12 (1886): 638.

25. Egleston, "Manufacture of Charcoal Kilns," 374.

Vulcan's Footprints on the Forest: The Mining Industry and California's National Forests, 1850-1950

Kevin Palmer
Modoc National Forest

Seventeen national forests blanket 20 million acres of California comprising about 20 percent of the land area. The state comprises a complex series of eleven geomorphic zones; ten of these cover national forest land and embrace provinces ranging from the semi-arid, chapparal covered slopes of the Transverse Range to the North Coast Range's humid hills. Eighteen mineral types rest within national forest land and range from antimony, chromite, and gold to tungsten. However, only seven of these substances are historically significant with gold being Region 5's [California] predominant element.

Mining in California began 12,000 years ago with Indian use of volcanic glass flows. Hematite and other deposits served as the local Indian paint store for rock and body art. Ironically, gold's soft nature made it useless to Indians and it held little attraction for them.

European immigrant extraction of minerals on what would become national forest land[1] began with the Spanish Colonial Era, establishing a tradition of titanic footprints which can be seen today on any national forest in the state. Mountains and deserts, coupled with a lack of navigable rivers and natural harbors, isolated California and forced the Spanish to limit their colonization efforts to the coastal corridor. This insularity also concentrated Spanish mining activity on the southern coastal portion of the state. Spanish immigrants focused their mining efforts on extracting building materials and gold. The lack of easily obtainable wood in southern California forced the Franciscan padres to substitute building stone, asphaltum, and adobe earth in the construction of religious and secular structures.

Contradictory evidence abounds over which national forest the Spanish mined first—local "fakelore" abounds. The Angeles National Forest's San Francisquito placer deposits, Los Padres National Forest's Antimony Peak and La Panza gold district vie for the Spanish Colonial Era honor.[2] Following the end of Spanish rule in 1822, extractive efforts began to increase on national forest lands. Early mining centered on the southern forests, specifically the Los Padres, Angeles, and San Bernardino national forests.

Truckloads of popular and academic histories have been published on the 1849 Gold Rush to California. The influx of prospectors and miners forever altered the character of the state and its forested land. Americans seemed blinded by an urge to tap the rich resources and quickly rushed to the task. The Mother Lode lay west of the Sierra Nevada's spine, consequently funneling early placering away from current Forest Service lands. As the numbers of miners began to swell and the easy placer gold deposits shrank, a torrent of miners began to stream eastward into future national forest lands in search of unclaimed riches. Miners quickly found the task unpleasant and extremely laborious. Cooperative mining companies formed rapidly to divide the labor.

Vernacular engineering, a trait dominant in mining world wide, came into play after California's initial gold rush. Hydraulic mining, a form of extraction originally unique to California, was used to process large-scale, low-grade placer deposits. Edward Matteson, working with Eli Miller and A. Chabot, invented a prototypical hydraulicking system on the Tahoe National Forest's American Hill District during 1852.[3] This water cannon system eroded hillsides and carried the gold bearing silt into sluice boxes.

Hydraulic mining is based on the premise of mass production. Despite the initial high expenditure of capital, once established, the cost of staffing is very low in comparison to other forms of alluvial mining except dredging.[4] A crew of six-to-seven miners could process 2,000-5,000 yards of gravel in a ten-hour day. This does not compare to the 1.5 yards of gravel processed by a placer miner panning in the same time period. As with any mining system, hydraulicking left its signature on the land. Water companies and miners scratched out thousands of miles of water ditches on varied terrain. Flumes, dams, and pits pockmarked California's timbered lands.

By 1857 gold production slumped, inspiring miners to look elsewhere. Prospectors turned their gaze eastward and opened up new excavation districts on eastern California Forests such as the Inyo and Toiyabe. By 1860 this "Rush in Reverse" sent miners scurrying into east-central Nevada and Colorado.

The bulk of mining activity during this time shifted northward from the southern woodlands and tended to be confined to the west slope of the Sierra Nevada and northwestern forests. The Plumas and Tahoe national forests dominated gold production in this period. Few early gold rush mining areas became established in the southern Sierra Nevada range. Northwestern gold mines began contemporaneously with the Sierra Nevada gold rush.

Mining on the northern California Klamath, Shasta-Trinity, and Six Rivers national forests had one bonding element: gold-bearing rivers flowed through those lands. Unlike the Sierra Nevada, hydraulic mining never slowed on these forests. The vocal down-stream farmers in the Sacramento Delta's rich farmlands successfully retarded hydraulicking and its gravel debris by-product. However, the north coast's rugged topography discouraged settlement and agricultural development along the drainages.

The 1872 Mining Law: A Pernicious Legacy

The location and development of rich mineral deposits spawned permanent habitation in formerly isolated areas of California. This happened because the support needs of miners and mining operations aided the introduction of railroads and communication lines, in addition to other social and cultural accoutrements. In the spirit of Manifest Destiny and the Myth of Overabundance, westerners viewed miners as a positive settlement force. The Mineral Land Act of 1866 placed few restrictions upon miners and mirrored legislative efforts to incite mineral development which westerners perceived as tied to national expansion. This act established the mineral patent proviso, further augmented by the ensuing 1872 Mining Law. This legacy dotted national forests with countless recreation residences located on patented claims.

As "Magna Carta" of the mining trade, the 1872 Mining Law has essentially hamstrung all public lands agencies, including the Forest Service. In all fairness, the act reflected the mining industry's inherent risks and acknowledged the difficulty and expense of establishing a mine—often in isolated locales. This statute merely put the laws that miners had developed at the mining district level into a forum covering federal lands. The system seemed appropriate in 1872, although multiple-use of forested land never entered the minds of the mining law framers— profit and growth served as their guiding principles.

Preservation Conservation, Nineteenth Century Style

Initial environmental regulation in California focused on hydraulic mining and its debris discharge, which fouled downstream agrarian and navigational needs. The amounts of water used for hydraulic mining operations are staggering. During the early 1880s, the Spring Valley Mine located at Cherokee Flat (just west of the Plumas National Forest), consumed 36 million gallons of water in a twenty-four-hour period, three times the City of San Francisco's daily water requirement at that time.[5]

When hydraulic mining reached its height in the mid-to-late 1870s, massive quantities of silt introduced into watercourse systems flowed downstream ruining farm land in the Sacramento and San Joaquin valleys. Farmers formed the Anti-Debris Association in an effort to shut down the destructive mining activity. The plaintiffs won the battle with the 1884 "Sawyer Decision" in the *Woodruff vs. North Bloomfield Gravel Mining Company* case, which put severe restrictions on hydraulic mining.

The Caminetti Act of 1893 created the California Debris Commission, which allowed hydraulic mines to operate with dams to contain hydraulic effluvia. Hydraulic mining nearly disappeared in the Sierra Nevada region, consequently leading to the dominance of lodegold mining in succeeding decades. Placer gold production dropped until the turn-of-the-century, when placer miners found an answer to their problem, the gold dredge.

The Forest Reserve Act

Mining played a duet with the nineteenth century "cut and run" mentality that despoiled countless acres of California timberland. Western forests fueled hungry locomotive steam engines hauling raw ore to smelters. These forests also provided the timber to construct bridges and rail lines, to help supply mining towns, to line mine tunnels, and to drive steam boilers for crushing mills. Certainly the relationship of the resource-rich West and the immense needs of the post-Civil War eastern industrial Gilded Age (1865-1890) encouraged the disfigurement of California's forests.

Comstock Lode chronicler William Wright wrote,

> The Comstock Lode may truthfully be said to be the tomb of the forests of the Sierras. Millions on millions of feet of lumber are annually buried in the mines, never to be resurrected.[6]

Devastating spring floods followed this pillage. Although it may never be known how much timber Comstock mining operations stripped off the Sierra Nevada, an estimate of 600 hundred million board feet, along with 2 million cords of firewood, has been suggested.

Ironically, this anti-conservation appetite for timber ultimately promoted a call for watershed protection and regulation of timber cutting by urban sophisticates, resulting in the 1891 Forest Reserve Act. The act halted the widespread disposition of public timberland and established reserves to slow erosion. Virginia City's thirst for timber exemplifies why the act came into being. Nineteenth-century miners ignored their tracks on the environment and set the tone for generations to come.

High Grading and the Rise in Low Grade Ore Mass Production Technology

By the time the 1891 Forest Reserve Act created a new public lands administrative system, demands from the post-Civil War industrial boom had pared away the bulk of western high-grade ore bodies. The last great nineteenth century American gold rushes took place when the forest reserves were coming into being.

The national monetary standard specie issue snowballed during this time between the "goldbugs" and "silverites," typified by William Jenning Bryan's 1896 "Cross of Gold" presidential campaign platform. Indeed, the deficiency of federal gold stores directly produced the Panic of 1893. The depletion of high grade, precious metal ore bodies promoted the development of low grade processing technology. Mining became increasingly sophisticated during this era to cope with the massive amounts of low grade ore that it was necessary to process to feed the eastern industrial boom.

For decades, California gold miners used the ancient mercury amalgamation gold recovery process, with its low efficiency rate of 75-80 percent. A conservation mentality simply did not exist within the mining industry because,

> The backward state of the arts of mining and metallurgy in the United States was actually attributable to the fact that rich mineral outcrops were readily available.[7]

Mining engineers had to restructure their approach to one stressing the mass production of low-grade ore. Chemistry and new gold strikes worked to alter this lack of gold. The McArthur-Forrest cyanide leaching process, invented in 1889-1890, improved gold recovery significantly.[8] Demand for gold fostered yet another round of prospecting in previously unexplored regions, and this gold flood nearly doubled the world's supply by 1898. Previously worked out hard rock gold mines on national forest lands sprang back into production when miners began utilizing the cyanide technology.

Enter the Dredge

First developed in New Zealand in 1882, and introduced to California in 1898 at the Oroville gold deposits, the dredge greatly revitalized placer mining in the state. Dredging essentially strip mined river beds with a floating gold processing plant. A well designed dredge could profitably mine a gravel bar which carried nine cents of gold per cubic yard.[9]

Dredging in California concentrated in the upper Sacramento Delta and took place on Forest Service lands in northern California on the Scott, Klamath and Salmon rivers in Siskiyou County. The La Porte area on the Plumas National Forest served as the scene of Region 5's most intensive dredging activity, due to its proximity to the Oroville dredging fields. Dredge activity left a landscape behind which resembled the work of an elephantine burrowing mole. Dredging reached a peak during the 1930s and continued in California until 1968.[10]

Despite the hand writing on the wall that ore reserves had depleted, the mining industry did not make any attempt to conserve mineral resources other than improve ore processing and extractive techniques. Mining historian Duane Smith commented,

> The mining industry would never be converted voluntarily to prudent use unless it could be demonstrated that the change would be economical. . . . This refusal meant that mining would pay the price of eventual public condemnation.[11]

The Organic Act and Pinchot's Forest Reserve "Chinese Wall"

While the Forest Reserve Act withdrew vast tracts of timber from former Government Land Office (GLO) holdings, administrative implementation required funding. Passage of the Forest Management Act in 1897, (now referred to as the Forest Service Organic Act) provided for the organization and management of the forest reserves. Lag time between the enactment of the Organic and Forest Reserve acts essentially produced a lock up of these tracts of land, resulting in an adverse reaction from traditional users of forested lands.

Miners became further antagonized by President Grover Cleveland's stealthy creation of the Washington's Birthday reserves—which established 21 million acres of additional forest reserves in 1897. Generally,

> The mining industry, among others, watched with amazement and disgust this change in government philosophy, wishing to continue its business as usual with no interference, light or heavy. It did not like the way the wind was starting to blow off the Potomac.[12]

Corporations and prospectors alike girded to halt the trend and initiated a battle with the federal government which has endured for almost a century.

As a concession to miners' opposition to the creation of the forest reserves, the Organic Act

> permitted mining entry on designated mineral lands of the reserves, it also directed the federal government to make and enforce rules and regulations which would 'preserve the forest thereon from destruction.'[13]

This proviso provided a component which has confounded the Forest Service for generations. The 1872 Mining Law forced the Forest Service into a subordinate relationship with the western mining industry. The Service has been harnessed with the duplicitous role of boosting mineral extraction while simultaneously preventing ecological abuses. Whether it liked it or not, the Forest Service entered into policing the mining business—an industry which held that it had a God-given right to pursue its business unimpeded.

Utilitarianism and Its Influence on Forest Service Minerals Policy

Gifford Pinchot, chief forester from 1898 to 1910 and architect of policies which have guided the Forest Service since 1905, had an approach to conservation with a twentieth century utilitarian bent. According to one author, Pinchot stressed

> opposition to the domination of economic affairs by narrow "special interests" [a turn-of-the-century euphemism for large and often corrupt business firms] and a fundamental belief in rationality and science.[14]

This belief ultimately brought about Pinchot's downfall; his "trust buster" convictions fueled the Ballinger Alaskan coal field controversy. Pinchot had accused the secretary of the interior of improbity over Alaskan coal claims, and President Taft obliged the forester by firing him.

Pinchot strongly supported the position that mining fit into forest management. He held that the forest resources should be actively managed to satisfy the needs of those who would benefit most from their use. He said,

> the object of our forest policy is not to preserve the forests because they are beautiful . . . or because they are refuges for wild creatures of the wilderness . . . but [the object is] the making of prosperous homes. . . . Every other concern comes as secondary.[15]

Following Pinchot's 1898 appointment as chief of the Division of Forestry, he addressed the American Institute of Mining Engineers at Atlantic City. He attempted to appease the mining industry by explaining the federal position. Naturally, Pinchot's primary concerns covered the use of timber and water by miners as well as fire prevention. He summarized the Organic Act's regulations and how they applied to mining.

> Where timber in large quantities has been taken without charge in the past, some share of the cost of caring for and preserving it must hereafter be borne by the men who benefit by such protection. . . . [The regulations] give without charge timber to the value of one hundred dollars on the stump to prospectors and miners whose claims do not furnish sufficient material for their own use, and they provide for the sale of timber in large quantities to meet the demands of larger operations.[16]

Pinchot stressed the need for timber management to supply a reliable source of wood for miners and provided examples where Colorado miners had stripped the slopes making it difficult for other prospectors to obtain timber. He coined the term "fire follows the prospector" in this presentation, and claimed

> Cutting has done but little harm in comparison with the great damage caused by fire. The government is the only agent capable of attacking this giant evil, and even the government is helpless unless it can permanently control the areas with which it must deal. This is the first and most important meaning of forest reservations.[17]

The Unerring Mining Industry and Early Relations With the Forest Service

In a case typical of the confusion following the Forest Reserve Act, the Homestake Mining Company cut timber from the Black Hills Forest Reserve without obtaining permission from the General Land Office. This action resulted in an 1894 lawsuit against Homestake in which the Federal government sued for $700,000 in damages.[18] Perhaps in a conciliatory move a few years later, the federal government auctioned off its first timber sale to the Homestake Mining Company in the Black Hills Reserve.

As the new kid on the block, the Bureau of Forestry (renamed the U.S. Forest Service in 1905) had to barter with two elements of the mining industry in addition to a parasitic third party. Mining consisted of two factions: large corporate entities and the small time "snipers" or itinerant miners. Pinchot's "trust buster" attitude led him to favor the "everyman" mining enterprise rather than large corporate cabals. In the words of one conservation scholar, protection of the small-scale producer at the expense of big business and efficiency was a principal governmental dilemma of the era.[19] Land grabbers played the third part in this trio by milking every legal loophole with their "strawmen" or "dummy entrymen" who functioned as front men for the would-be land barons.

One case in northern California depicted this predicament with precision. At the turn-of-the-century, Henry H. Yard, a *sub rosa* representative of the Western Pacific Railroad, filed 265,000 acres of placer claims along the Plumas National Forest's Feather River drainage. Under the guise of the North California Mining Company, Yard's men claim jumped a large number of established miners in an attempt to slash a right-of-way for a new rail line.

Reform minded California State Mineralogist Lewis Aubury, along with Gifford Pinchot, initiated an investigation of Yard's claims in 1906. A horde of Forest Service, U.S. Geological Survey, and General Land Office mineral examiners uncovered Yard's plan to establish a series of lumber camps on the placer claims. These camps would ferry out the lumber once the Western Pacific Railroad line became functional. Indeed, government mineralogists ascertained no mineral value existed on 24,000 of 25,000 of the Yard claims. GLO officials dethroned Yard in the 1908 decision, *United States v. H. H. Yard, et al.*[20]

Coal Lands and Petroleum—a Stab at Pinchot

Following reports of front men staking spurious mining claims in Alaska, President Theodore Roosevelt ordered 84 million acres of western coal and oil lands withdrawn from mineral entry between 1905-1909. This was Roosevelt's attempt to stymie corporate monopolization of mineral tracts through antiquated land laws. It ultimately translated into the well chronicled Pinchot-Ballinger controversy, when Pinchot accused the secretary of the interior of improbity over Alaskan coal claims.

Another Foreshadow of Environmentalism

Regulation of the California mining industry had its inception in the 1884 Sawyer Decision, and the Forest Service stance on this issue illustrates the Progressive Era's employment of scientific management principles. Californians had grown less tolerant of miners' impacts on their lands as the state's population diversified. Despite his reformist nature, state mineralogist Lewis Aubury typified the industry's haughty environmental stance when he wrote on fumes bearing sulphur dioxide wafting from a Shasta County copper smelter. In a 1905 report on California copper mining, Aubury noted that the vapors had killed vegetation over a large adjacent region, and this has given the company some trouble; but in justice to the industry it may be said that the destruction is less serious than it would be in many other districts, owing to the trifling extent to which agriculture is carried on in that particular neighborhood and to the small size and low value of the trees of the region.[21]

The Forest Service differed with Aubury over this position. Between 1910-1919 the Service prosecuted the Shasta Lake area copper smelters for smoke nuisance which denuded portions of the Shasta National Forest surrounding the mining towns of Kennett and Keswick.[22]

Industrial Needs in a Wartime Setting

The Panic of 1907 and ensuing financial depression became the primary economic issues influencing mining until July 1914. Increasing hostilities in Europe prompted the close of the London Stock Exchange, and financial institutions in the United States followed suit shortly thereafter. A recession precipitated by World War I in Europe combined with a labor shortage, which forced many gold mines to stop or reduce production. Gold mining remained at a relatively low level until the 1930s, when a surge in production occurred when Franklin D. Roosevelt set the price of gold, increasing its rate from $20 to $35 per ounce by 1935.

During World War I, formerly unprofitable American deposits became valuable when German U-boats began to sink merchant ships. This constricted the flow of foreign raw ore sources entering the United States via shipping lanes. As Grecian and Asia Minor sources became strangled, chromite mines across California forests opened to supply the demand for this steel-hardening mineral. The renewed extraction of chromite on the High Plateau, Copper Creek, Low Divide, and other Six Rivers National Forest districts during 1917 embodied this trend. These mines shut down immediately following the 1918 Armistice.[23] Chromite mines on the Los Padres, El Dorado, Shasta-Trinity and Plumas national forests mirrored this event.

The European conflict aided technological developments in radio technology and electronics, producing an additional requisition for copper. Shasta County copper production followed a steady course from 1907 to 1914 with a peak during World War I. The war effort called for tungsten, yet another steel alloy component used in armor plating, rifle barrels, high-speed tools, and radio tubes. The eastern Sierra Nevada area mines on the Sequoia and Inyo national forests opened in response to this need. With the halt in tungsten exports from British colonies in 1915, prices skyrocketed and encouraged domestic production until the war's end. Many of the mines operated intermittently until the onset of World War II in Europe in 1939, which stimulated a revival of the industry. Virtually all tungsten mining operations in California ceased after World War II.[24]

The Mining Claim Problem in the National Forests of California

A veteran Forest Service mineral examiner conducted an investigation of Region 5 during 1937. In a harshly worded report (which made no attempt to disguise its Forest Service bias) the Depression Era study devoted a major portion of its text to the placer claim tenants of the 1872 Mining Law—and the loss of surface rights which penalized the Forest Service and public. The writer had uncovered a high degree of mining law misuse on the southern California forests which contributed less than 1 percent of the gold production (in Region 5) and furnished 81 percent of the mineral locations contested" (by the Forest Service).[25]

Apparently the demand for recreation residences in the highly urbanized area surrounding the Angeles National Forest resulted in a "local mining location boom," making this Forest "one of the leading mining claim forests of California".[26] Scenarios like this demanded intensive agency claim validation work, drained Forest Service coffers, and depleted the traditionally thin work force.

The review concluded that 10 percent of Region 5 mining claims showed performance of their required $100 annual assessment work, and argued that submarginal gold deposits located along mountain streams, often occupy lands of high recreational value and while there is no reason for preventing individuals from obtaining the small returns from these gravels, it likewise is not good management to permit individuals to destroy the higher values that may exist there nor to prevent the public use of these area through the exclusive control of the surface allowed by the mining law.[27]

From Depression to War

The catchword for this wartime era became "new uses for old metals." The World War II effort demanded enormous amounts of copper, tungsten, magnesium, and aluminum for hardened steels, aircraft construction and electrical devices. As with World War I, Axis Power submarine warfare severely curtailed the bulk shipment of raw ore to manufacturing centers. Again, the United States found itself cut off from foreign sources and suddenly low quality ore ignored in peacetime became highly desirable. Supplies of chromite from Rhodesia and New Caledonia were choked off, sending extraction at the Del Norte County mines on the Six Rivers National Forest spiraling upwards. Manganese, critical to steel production, also flowed out of mines located on this forest. Tungsten mines on the Inyo and Sequoia national forests, shut down after the end of World War I, leapt into productivity.

While this was a time for war, it was also a time for increased governmental regulation of mining. The war effort birthed new federal bodies such as the Metals Reserve Corporation (MRC) and the War Production Board. The MRC mission centered on obtaining foreign metals rather than developing domestic sources. A scholar wrote:

> Throughout the war years western miners and mining associations complained about the MRC's import policy, its price levels, the MRC's import policy, its price levels, the ambiguities of federal policies and increasing bureaucracy, the labor shortages in the mines, the lack of access roads, and the seeming dominance of the large corporations in the industry.[28]

If this was not egregious enough, War Production Board Order Limitation Order L-208 shut down non-essential gold mines in 1942 and slapped miners in the face who had enjoyed the Depression Era surge in price. This directive "had a decidedly negative effect on the West while having virtually none at all on its supposed prime goal-increasing the production of other metals." [29] Like it or not, this action served as a portent for ensuing decades, particularly for the small miner.

The account of Charlie Brown, a chromite miner on the Tahoe National Forest in search of an access road to his mine, painted a representative tale. In Brown's words

> We called in the service of our Tri-County Chrome Association, which got busy with Washington and San Francisco authorities. Investigation showed there were so many agencies concerned in the expenditure of this small sum that the project was bogging down in red tape. The Tahoe National Forest office was concerned, also the forestry departments at Washington, their Salt Lake headquarters, and their San Francisco Office. Then the Bureau of Mines in Washington and the Bureau's Salt Lake and San Francisco offices were concerned. But not one of all the officials of these agencies knew what had become of the matter. . . . The red tape and delay . . . caused us to shut down for the winter and quit making deliveries of chromite.[30]

In contrast to Brown's experience, the Forest Service entered into partnerships with several mining corporations in the Access Mine Road Program, initiated in 1942. This project involved collusion with major mining corporations such as Anaconda and U.S. Vanadium due to the wartime labor and equipment shortage.[31] Certainly, this must have further alienated small-time miners such as Charlie Brown, increasing the rift between this special interest group and the Forest Service. Following the war, the GLO which had administrated mining procedure on Forest Service land was merged with the Grazing Service into the Bureau of Land Management.

Epilogue—Multiple Use and Environment Reaffirmed

By the 1950s, mining law that authorized desecration on Forest Service land persisted. Greedy individuals propelled a flow of events which drove the Service into the legislative forum to correct this matter.

Secretary of Agriculture Charles Brannan commissioned the National Forest Advisory Council to undertake a study of this problem in 1950, which the council released two years later. The expose rang with reverberations of the prior 1937 review and contained much of the same finger-pointing relative to the 1872 Mining Law. The Advisory Council's primary concern stemmed over how the surface rights problem made it impossible to achieve a balanced multiple use approach, for "mineral uses take precedence over all others. The authors computed that western mining claims held 2 million acres of national forest land hostage, blanketed by 7 billion board feet of merchantable timber valued at $57 million. The Advisory Council concluded

> Prospecting and mining continue to be important in the national forests as elsewhere but there is an imperative need that they be given their proper place in the pattern of multiple use management which has been established for the national forests, the balance of which has been and continues to be upset by the inability of the Forest Service to administer non-mineral resources on mining locations.[32]

This conservation conflict involved two opposing factions. The National Wildlife Federation, the Izaak Walton League, and the American Forestry Association gathered on the Forest Service side, while the Mining Congress, the U.S. Chamber of Commerce, and the Western Mining Council lined up in opposition. The American Forestry Association (AFA) served as an intermediary force between the Departments of the Interior and Agriculture and the mining interests.

This exchange resulted in the passage of the Multiple Use Mining Act (or Common Varieties Act) on July 23, 1955. Reformist amendments filled some of the 1920 Mineral Leasing Act loopholes. The most critical revisions pertained to the misuse of "common varieties" such as sand and gravel, upon which land grabbers had established claims for the purpose of "mining" timber. The new act enabled mineral managers to sell cinder, pumice, and gravel at their will and prohibited any activity other than mining to take place on unpatented claims. Perhaps most importantly, the act handed back control of nonmineral surface resources (timber and water, etc.) to the Forest Service.

Changes in the American psyche attacked extractive industry during the 1960s. As Duane Smith summarized,

> Miners could usually count on the public eventually to lose interest; that expectation no longer seemed viable. Now the miners were reaping the consequences of their indifference, insensitivity, expediency, and gross exploitation.[33]

Criticism of the Forest Service by environmental and recreation interests promoted enactment of the 1960 Multiple-Use Sustained Yield Act (MUSY). "The bill was an important victory for the Forest Service, which thereby maintained its discretion over the national forest management. . . . Even though the questions raised by the Sierra Club were ignored by others in 1960, their challenge to Forest

Service assumptions about conservation dominated the discussion of forest and range policy in the next fifteen years.[34]

Despite its utilitarian orientation, stirrings of Thoreau transcendentalist-style conservation interjected itself within the agency. Under the stewardship of Aldo Leopold and Bob Marshall, the 1929 "L-20" and 1939 "U" regulations created an evolving wilderness emphasis within the Forest Service.

"Injury to wilderness," Roderick Nash wrote in his classic work *Wilderness and the American Mind*, "is best understood as injury to people who value wilderness".[35] Miners' appreciation of wilderness centered over the mineral values locked within high mountain peaks, and they hotly debated the creation of wilderness areas as untouchable preserves. As the smoke cleared, neither mining nor wilderness advocates had won a clear cut victory. The Multiple-Use Act allowed mining in wilderness areas; however, legislators inserted important provisions governing miners. Again, the mining lobby's muscle allowed it to bend environmental policy.[36]

Influence of the sixties bridged the 1970s with the National Environmental Policy Act (NEPA) and baptized the mining industry with a plethora of ecological legislation. If Tahoe National Forest miner Charlie Brown felt he had been tripped up in the leviathan bureaucratic labyrinth during the 1940s, the ensuing regulation would have turned him pallid. The tide continued to turn against the industry and threatened it as never before. Generally,

> larger companies took most of the blame for the problems, but they also had most of the resources for making the changes that the times required. The financial impotence of the small miner threatened him with extinction.[37]

The 1973 Arab oil embargo and resulting energy crisis brought home the magnitude of California's thirst for petroleum products. Prior to the Energy Crisis, oil and gas exploration and development on Region 5 land had been primarily limited to the Los Padres National Forest's Sespe oil field. Indeed, the legacy of being the birthplace of the freeway still has a powerful influence on California— current figures reveal the state is the third largest consumer of petroleum in the world. A 400 percent price increase in foreign oil stimulated a new interest in geothermal and domestic oil exploration and development on national forest land.

In 1974 the agency adopted regulations to directly monitor mining operations. Although not a Forest Service inspired piece of legislation, the Surface Mining

Reclamation Act of 1977 ensured that national forest lands would be restored in a fashion that would allow multiple use to rebound. In Region 5, thousands upon thousands of acres with boulder-strewn riparian settings made unproductive by placer mining testify to the need for this sorely needed mandate. In retrospect it seems strange that the agency did not press for such a regulation long ago.

As the "invisible gold" boom blossomed during the eighties with the heap leach cyanide system which captured microscopic gold particles, mining came under further federal and state regulation centering around hazardous waste and environmental issues, trimming profits.

Over the years the Forest Service has been forced to serve a duplicitous deputation—one which requires it to serve as a promotional deputy for the mining industry while safeguarding the land against environmental degradation. The American public continues to regard miners as environmental vandals. However, the bottom line is that the public wants to have its aesthetic cake, and yet eat a nice slice of minerals-exhausting consumer goods.

America's nineteenth century bequest of the myth of superabundance still plays a major role in the nation's collective consciousness. Conflict will continue until the public decides how much it is willing to sacrifice when it comes time to pay the piper—electric toasters, gold jewelry, or Vulcan's footprints on the forests?

Notes

1. Forest Reserves/National Forests did not exist until after 1891. In this paper, lands that would *become* national forests are so-called.

2. Raymond W. Rossiter, *Statistics of Mines and Mining in the States and Territories West of the Rocky Mountains* (Washington: GPO, 1872b), 108; Bennie W. Troxel and Paul K. Morton, *Mines and Minerals Resources of Kern County, California. County Report 1* (San Francisco: California Division of Mines and Geology, 1962), 56; William Irelan, Jr., *Eighth Annual Report of the State Mineralogist for the Year Ending October 1, 1988. Report 8* (Sacramento: California State Printing Office, 1888), 531; Herbert A. Franke, "Mines and Minerals of San Luis Obispo County," *California Journal of Mines and Geology* 31 (Sacramento: California State Printing Office, 1935): 422; William B. Clark, *Gold Districts of California. Bulletin 193* (San Francisco: California Division of Mines and Geology, 1970), 179.

3. Phillip Ross May, *Origins of Hydraulic Mining in California* (Oakland, California: Holmes Book Company, 1970), 40-42; William S. Greever, *Bonanza West: The Story of the Western Mining Rushes, 1848-1900* (Moscow, Idaho: University of Idaho Press, 1963), 50-51.

4. C.S. Haley, *Gold Placers of California. Bulletin 57* (Sacramento: California State Printing Office, 1923), 38.

5. May, *Origins of Hydraulic Mining*, 10.

6. Duane A. Smith, *Mining America: The Industry and the Environment, 1800-1980* (Lawrence: University Press of Kansas, 1986), 12.

7. Harold Barger and Sam H. Schurr, *The Mining Industries, 1899-1939: A Study of Output, Employment, and Productivity* (New York: No. 43 of Publications of the National Bureau of Economic Research, 1944. Reprint, New York: Arno Press Inc., 1972), 99.

8. Greever, *Bonanza West*, 308; Otis E. Young, Jr., *Western Mining* (Norman, Oklahoma: University of Oklahoma Press, 1970), 284.

9. Ibid., 132; Lewis E. Aubury, *The Copper Resources of California. Bulletin No. 23* (Sacramento: California State Printing Office, 1905).

10. Clark, *Gold Districts of California*, 6-8.

11. Smith, *Mining America*, 57.

12. Ibid., 56.

13. Gregory Randall Graves, "Anti-conservation and Federal Forestry in the Progressive Era," Ph.D. diss., University of California, Santa Barbara, 1987: 156.

14. Paul J. Culhane, *Public Lands Politics* (Baltimore: John Hopkins University Press, 1981), 4.

15. Glen O. Robinson, *The Forest Service: A Study in Public Land Management* (Baltimore: John Hopkins University Press, 1975), 55.

16. American Institute of Mining Engineers (1899), 343.

17. Ibid., 345.

18. Graves, "Anti-conservation and Federal Forestry", 308.

19. Ibid., 142.

20. Ibid., 110-128.

21. Aubury, *The Copper Resources of California*, 72.

22. Philip A. Lydon and J. C. O'Brien, *Mines and Mineral Resources of Shasta County California*, County Report 6 (Sacramento: California State Printing Office, 1974), 29, 33, 34.

23. Kathy Heffner, *History of Mining in Del Norte County, California, 1850-1950* (Six Rivers National Forest: USDA Forest Service, 1984), 43.

24. L.A. Norman and Richard M. Stewart, "Mines and Mineral Resources of Inyo County," *California Journal of Mines and Geology* 47 (1951): 85-98.

25. USDA Forest Service, *The Mining Claim Problem in the National Forests of California* (San Francisco: USDA Forest Service Region 5, 1944), 24.

26. Ibid., 34.

27. Ibid., 47.

28. Gerald D. Nash, *World War II and the West: Reshaping the Economy* (Lincoln: University of Nebraska Press, 1990), 19-20.

29. Ibid., 27.

30. Ibid., 23.

31. USDA Forest Service, *The History of Engineering in the Forest Service (A Compilation of History and Memoirs, 1905-1989)* (Washington: USDA Forest Service, 1990), 406-422.

32. National Forest Advisory Council, *Report on the Problem of Mining Claims on the National Forests* (Washington: USDA Forest Service, 1953), 2, 6, 10.

33. Smith, *Mining America*, 140.

34. Samuel Trask Dana and Sally k. Fairfax, *Forest and Range Policy: Its Development in the United States* (New York: McGraw-Hill Book Company, 1980), 204.

35. Roderick Nash, *Wilderness and the American Mind* (New Haven: Yale University Press, 1967), 271.

36. Paul W. Gates, *History of public Land Law Development* (Washington: Public Land Law Review Commission, 1968), 763; Harold K. Steen, *The U.S. Forest Service: A History* (Seattle and London: University of Washington Press, 1976), 313-314.

37. Smith, *Mining America*, 156.

Influence of the Forest Service
on Water Development Patterns in the West

Pamela A. Conners
Stanislaus National Forest

"Controversy" and "water" are words often spoken in the same breath. In fact, the etymology for the word "rival" is rooted in the Latin word "rivalis" to express "one using the same stream as another." Thus, at heart, this paper is about controversy, because it explores the patterns of water and hydroelectric development from 1850 through 1920 and the influence of the United States Forest Service on those patterns in the early twentieth century.

Though the geographic focus of this inquiry is the area which is now the Stanislaus National Forest, the Stanislaus seems to be an analog for water development patterns in the western forests. The Stanislaus Forest Reserve, located in California's Central Sierra, was one of the dozen other western reserves created by President Grover Cleveland in 1897 during the lame duck period of his term. The Stanislaus has four major watersheds, all with their headwaters near the Sierra crest and all of which run in a southwest direction, through the San Joaquin Valley and eventually into the Pacific Ocean. The northern boundary of the Stanislaus is formed by the Mokelumne River, the southern boundary by the Merced, while the Stanislaus River roughly bisects the forest from north to south, and the Tuolumne River—emanating from the Mount Lyell glacier in Yosemite National Park—runs between and generally parallels the Stanislaus and the Merced rivers.

There can be no doubt that the imprint of water development on the western landscape has been swift and deep. In only a hundred years, the vast majority of the West's major rivers have become components in a huge plumbing system. Moreover, in the national forests, it is difficult to find any substantial high or mid-elevation meadow or small natural lake catchment that has not been pressed into service for water and hydroelectric purposes.

Historic-era water development on the Stanislaus can be viewed as four major distinctive periods. The first preceded the forest reserves, from 1850 through 1895. The next, from 1896 through 1910 represents the formative years for both the Forest Service and the hydroelectric industry. The third, from 1911 through 1920, was the jelling of the roles and relationships between the Forest Service and the water and hydroelectric industry. The last era examined here is the creation and ramifications of the Federal Water Power Act of 1920.

Liquid Gold, 1850-1895

The more extensive, pioneer water developments—the ones which stretched from the foothills and into what would later become the Stanislaus Forest Reserve—were born out of the needs of gold mining. Gold occurs most predominately in the foothill region of the Southern Mother Lode, where water is more scarce. And except for small scale mining processes, gold recovery methods demanded copious quantities of water, or liquid gold, as it was often termed. Typical of the water developments and the imprint they left during this era was the Tuolumne County Water Company. Organized in the summer of 1851, after more localized sources of water had been tapped and outstripped, this company was initially comprised of a group of miners who needed to transport water to their claims in the Columbia basin.

After first reaching the modestly sized Fivemile Creek, the Tuolumne County Water Company (TCWC) soon extended its system to the South Fork of the Stanislaus River. The twenty-mile-long ditch and flume system was completed in August of 1852 and was the longest water project in California at the time.[1] Like most of the larger systems, the extension of the project was very expensive. The need for more sophisticated and costly engineering works—trestles, flumes, ditch enlargements, reservoir and dam construction—took its toll in terms of local shareholder control. In short order after incorporation in 1852, most of the founders were bought out and the TCWC was under the control of Sacramento financier, D.O. Mills and other business interests from San Francisco.[2] By 1856 the TCWC had virtual dominion over the South Fork of the Stanislaus and was able to deliver year around water through a series of upcountry reservoirs in addition to its earlier lower elevation reservoirs. The upcountry dams were called Herring Creek, Big Dam, Upper Strawberry (or Middle Dam), and Lower Strawberry, now Pinecrest Lake.

The TCWC's arch rival was the Columbia and Stanislaus River Water Company (C&SRWC). Organized in 1854 as a group of Columbia area miners disgruntled with the water rates charged by the TCWC, they decided to take matters into their own hands and build what came to be called the "Miners' Ditch." The labor force was comprised principally of miners paid in scrip redeemable for water upon completion of the system. Reflective of the miners' sentiments, the diggings they left in order to work on the ditch, flume, and tunnel works were protected by tombstone-shaped notices posted at the corners of their claims which read: SACRED TO THE MEMORY OF $6 A DAY . . . that being the disputed charge for water.[3] Their first foray for water was a twenty-eight mile system which tapped the South Fork of the Stanislaus. But vehemently protested in the courts by the Tuolumne County Water Company, the C&SRWC did not wait for the court ruling before they decided to abandon the "trifling rill" of the South Fork and move to the Middle Fork of the Stanislaus.[4] Finished in late 1858 and over sixty miles long, the system began about one mile above Donnell Flat (now Donnell Reservoir) and included a 3250 foot tunnel cut through the lava cap divide that separates the Middle and the South forks.[5]

The Columbia and Stanislaus River Water Company's strategy contrasted with that of its rival in that virtually no reservoirs were built and the ditch was engineered to handle an unusually large volume of water. The ditch was specified to be 15 feet wide at the top, 9 feet wide at the bottom and to flow with water 3 feet deep. Amid a great deal of bitterness, acrimony, and rhetoric revolving around the "monied monopoly's control over the care-worn working man," foreclosure proceedings were soon brought against the C&SRWC by its anxious creditors having apparent ties with D.O. Mills and the Tuolumne County Water Company. The Miner feets Ditch had cost just over $1,000,000 with, again, the loss of local control occurring hand-in-hand with the greater scale of the system. It was bought by its rival, the Tuolumne County Water Company, just a year and one-half after its completion, for under $150,000.[6]

These are just two of a host of early water systems created before any significant attempts were made by extra-local governmental forces to exercise control over the pattern of water development beyond the basic legal doctrine of appropriation and its theorem that the first in use is the first in right. Water systems of this era had several commonalities: First, they were spawned to serve gold mining districts and were virtually single-purposed—to bring liquid gold to the scene of mining. Second, they depended, initially, on local initiative and capital and later were supported by larger, more distant financial structures. Third, they depended on user labor for the bulk of the initial construction. Last, many of the systems would later figure into those that emerged in the next era of water development.

From Liquid Gold to White Coal, 1896-1910

The next period of water development, from 1896 through about 1910, was characterized by the push-pull between enterprise and regulation. It was a time when both the Forest Service and the hydroelectric companies involved in long distance electricity transmission were in their infancy.

The creation and evolution of the Forest Service had a profound influence on the scale, character, and patterns of water development in the twentieth century West. Concomitantly, the influence of the water and hydroelectric industry in the West made a major and lasting imprint on the development of the Forest Service. As a corollary, the national forests can be viewed as artifacts of policy and the administration of policy. That is, the national forests are not natural things; they were created by and for people. To provide a context for this argument, a sketch of the Forest Service's beginnings and the young agency's developing posture toward hydroelectric proponents is helpful.

The Early Forest Service

The Forest Service grew out of a conservation movement that gained national political recognition in the early twentieth century. Just a century before, forest conservation would have been a bizarre concept to the early non-native settlers in North America. Their Medieval ancestral traditions equated forests with evil, and "wilderness" was synonymous with "forests." Forests were the home of witches and "wilder men," they were places where people were "bewildered" and seduced to the ways of satan. In Anglo-Saxon, "wylder ness" meant "lair of a wild beast" or places that were beyond human control.[7] Allegorically and, perhaps, more concretely, clearing forests meant gaining the upper hand over darkness and evil. But by the latter half of the nineteenth century, a growing circle of thinkers considered North America's forests not as threatening, but as a source of indispensable raw materials and economic benefits that were fast being decimated. The federal government began to take note through such legislation as the 1873 Timber Culture Act and the 1891 Forest Reserve Act.

The Timber Culture Act was intended not only to privatize public land and encourage agriculture—that is, to convert unsettled, unused public lands into private, income-producing lands—but to cultivate trees as well. Trees were thought to improve weather and rainfall associated with ample forests. The act was also intended to promote self-sufficiency by helping to supply building materials for homes, fences, and fuel. The Forest Reserve Act was the result of adamant demands to reform public land laws—laws that, instead of promoting agrarian values, settling the country, and contributing to the national economy on a farmstead scale, were playing into the hands of ever-growing corporate interests that seemed to counteract these goals. This act repealed the Preemption and 1878 Timber and Stone Acts and was distinguished by deviating from the earlier public land laws that had all been fashioned to facilitate rather than restrain the passage of public lands into private hands. The act authorized the president to establish forest reserves on public lands in the West, thus closing them to further would-be land patentees and making it the federal government's business to assume stewardship over these lands in behalf of the nation as a whole. Important for water development, the 1891 act also provided a means for private parties to secure rights-of-way over these reserves if they were for the purpose of irrigation.[8]

With Theodore Roosevelt's assumption of the presidency after the assassination of William McKinley in 1901, conservation moved to the top of the domestic political agenda. Likewise, TR's friend and fellow crusader for conservation, Gifford Pinchot, gained in national influence. Water, a key issue in the conservation movement, was clearly on TR and Pinchot's minds when they collaborated on TR's first message to Congress:

> The forest and water problems are perhaps the most vital internal questions of the United States . . . [The forests are essential in providing the life blood to the nation, but] the forests alone cannot fully regulate and conserve waters of the arid region. Great storage works are necessary to equalize the flow of streams and to save the flood waters. . . . These irrigation works should be built by the National Government. The lands reclaimed by them should be reserved by the Government for actual settlers, and the cost of construction should so far as possible be repaid by the land reclaimed. . . . Our people as a whole will profit, for successful homemaking is but another name for the upbuilding of the Nation.[9]

Pinchot, steeped in Progressivism, opened wide his window of opportunity and wasted no time expanding his small Division of Forestry, of which he was the newly appointed head, and surrounding himself with extremely capable men and women who shared his zealous vision of regulating the forests' resources for the economic and moral uplifting of the nation. Forests were seen as a vital crop. And like TR, Pinchot's brand of Progressivism was strongly moralistic, business-like, and idealistic in the belief that technocrats could harness nature for rational, efficient use in the service of the public good. When the new Forest Service was created in 1905, with Pinchot appointed chief forester, the agency's mission statement, largely written by Pinchot, read like a Psalm:

> . . . all land is to be devoted to its most productive use for the permanent good of the whole people, and not for the temporary benefit of individuals or

companies. All of the resources of the forest reserves are for USE, and this use, must be brought about in a thoroughly businesslike manner, under such restrictions only as will insure the permanence of these resources. . . . Where conflicting interests must be reconciled the question will always be decided from the standpoint of the greatest good of the greatest number in the long run.[10]

The early twentieth century was a time of exponential business expansion, and with it brewed a national preoccupation with the "tyranny of concentrated wealth." Businesses which sought to control water and hydroelectric power sites were one of the interests with which the young Forest Service had to develop a relationship by virtue of the nature and location of the resources over which the agency had stewardship. That is, western National Forests encompassed lands at the headwaters of major river systems and included their most dramatic elevation differences and, thus, their greatest hydroelectric potential. To use the Stanislaus national forest as a typical illustration, elevations range from 1,000 feet to 11,575 feet. Elevation differences in the major river canyons can range from 1,000 feet to 2,000 feet in a half-mile or less.[11]

The Tuolumne Electric Company

The Tuolumne Electric Company (TEC) is an example of a small company in this second era of water development whose owners later became enmeshed in large scale hydroelectric development schemes. The TEC also provides an illustration of an early hydroelectric developer and the struggle of local Forest Service agents to cope with this new "use" of the forest.

Formed on March 18, 1903, the TEC had by June 1905, applied to the Forest Service for rights-of-way for a hydroelectric development. Unlike many applicants for water developments, TEC filed under the Act of February 1, 1905, exclusively for the purpose of generating and transmitting electricity. This electricity was to be generated at the Tuolumne River and used at local mines owned by TEC officials. The surplus was to be offered to other mines and for sundry uses in the vicinity.[12]

The grandmother of today's special use permits—applications to the Forest Service for use of resources under its stewardship—were called "Special Privilege Agreements." Though the states controlled actual water rights, the Forest Service controlled any land within a forest reservation that was to be occupied or used to develop the water. The Forest Service levied modest charges for the privilege of taking lands out of general public use or for extracting resources from the land.

For example, a fee had to be paid for the acreage occupied for impoundments, power sites, sawmills, housing, and other necessary facilities, while charges were made in terms of miles of right-of-way for water conveyances, electric transmission lines, and roads. A formula was also applied to hydroelectric systems for using the benefit of the natural flow of the streams and their fall—measured in kilowatt hours of energy metered at the powerhouse. Forest officers were required to complete Report[s] on Special Privilege Applications, and among the questions were asked to determine: "Will the desired privilege involve monopoly?" and "[i]s the desired project consistent with the reasons for which the reserves were established?" Competition for valuable water development sites was extraordinarily intense at the turn of the century, and before Special Privilege permits could be issued, forest rangers had to report on the use fees the enterprise should pay as well as to determine necessary stipulations for protection of any roads, trails, or other existing improvements in the path of the project.

Unknown to the TEC, however, the Department of the Interior (DOI) had, in early 1905, withdrawn a number of reservoir sites on the Tuolumne River "because of their great value in connection with the operations of the Reclamation Service." On the strength of the DOI's objection, TEC's application was rejected by the Forest Service and, in turn, was promptly appealed by TEC. TEC's lawyers righteously argued that applications for viable projects should not be rejected "because of projects . . . [contemplated] in the dim future. . . . Certainly [improvements] ought not to be interfered with because it is dreamed or imagined, that in some future age the waters of the Tuolumne River may be utilized at some point for irrigation purposes. What we require now is confirmation of our right of way, in order to carry out a great public utility project for the immediate locality which requires it now. . . ." The appeal went on to offer that TEC's project would take water from the Clavey River—a major tributary flowing into the Tuolumne—for power generation at a point above that necessary for irrigation and return the water to the Tuolumne "undiminished in quantity."[13]

TEC's application was ultimately approved, based on the company's affidavit that it would use the waters of the Clavey for power generation and not diminish those of the Tuolumne. To underscore the rapidity and comprehensiveness of water rights claims in the Central Sierra, by the close of 1905, the director of the U.S. Geological Survey, Charles Walcott, reported that "the numerous streams which flow from the Sierras to the San Joaquin Valley, the only one that remains available for the Reclamation Service is the Tuolumne River . . . it is, therefore, highly important that this stream be held for the further use of the United States in irrigation development."[14]

Either for speculative purposes or anticipating shortfalls by using the lesser Clavey River, TEC secured rights from the Forest Service for several water storage basins toward the head of the watershed. These rights were gained to the detriment of established uses at these meadow basins by cattlemen who brought their herds there for the summer under Forest Service permit.[15]

As the powerhouse was being completed in early 1908, TEC's officials formed a sister company, the Tuolumne Transmission Company, to distribute the electricity and extend the system beyond their personal mining interests.[16] During this same period, the Forest Service began hiring a number of professionals with hydroelectric engineering expertise in order to judge the validity of proposed projects and to be able to choose between competing proposals and suggest options that promised greater public benefit.[17] Concurrent with these events, Roosevelt's presidency was coming to a close. He and his supporters in government feared an incoming administration not so bold and bully on conservation. Pinchot, Overton Price, and George Woodruff of the Forest Service (Woodruff transferred to DOI in 1907) joined forces with Frederick H. Newell of the Reclamation Service and outgoing Secretary of the Interior James Rudolph Garfield to, in Pinchot's brash words . . . "sew up every opening, tie down every loose end, make every possible resource safe against everything less than an open attack on T.R.'s Conservation Policy."[18]

Through various means, Roosevelt withdrew from entry, along sixteen western rivers, power sites amounting to 1.5 million acres. In the Forest Service, many of these withdrawals took the form of securing lands for ranger stations. As Pinchot stated: "Some of these Ranger stations we located deliberately on water-power sites, in order to ensure some form of Government control until regular power-site withdrawals could take their place, which they did in practically all cases. . . . T.R. did not have, and could not get from Congress, specific authority of law for these withdrawals, but neither was there specific authority for the Louisiana Purchase by Jefferson, or for freeing the slaves by Lincoln, or for the acquisition of the Panama Canal by T.R. himself."[19] Withdrawal for the Las Vegas ranger station at the locale of the TEC's upper Clavey reservoir site appears to have been executed in this spirit.

Within the Forest Service, there was deep and broadly based dissent on the issue of the morality of the highest use principle, particularly with regard to water power sites. Coert DuBois, a district inspector who would later be district forester in California, wrote a heart-felt memorandum on the dispossession of the permitted dairy cattle grazers in one of the meadows speculated as a reservoir site by the TEC:

> It seems to me that the only vital question is who in justice has the most
> equitable claim to the use of Belle Meadow, a hard-working rancher . . . or
> a power company who will use it when they get around to it for additional
> development of electric power for sale. The relative importance of the two
> uses . . . are all minor considerations to the fact that the Forest Service is
> working an injustice to a user of a Forest. . . . The fact that the Faheys [the
> permittees] are allowed to occupy the meadow until the power company
> chooses to flood it does not help matters a bit.[20]

Though Inspector DuBois' opinion did not prevail, local officials on the Stanislaus
outspokenly agreed with him, and because of the company's lack of action to
develop the upper watershed sites, they firmly believed that the TEC was holding
onto the reservoir sites purely for speculation. In the end, TEC was given a
deadline for commencing construction on the upper reservoir sites and failed to
meet it. Within three years, in 1911, TEC reapplied for a permit for one of these
reservoir sites, but again failed to meet a deadline for the commencement of work.
The permit was revoked in 1913. After December 1916, TEC ceased generating
electricity along the Tuolumne and its assets were, in 1920, taken over and
subsequently abandoned by the Pacific Gas and Electric Company.[21]

Steering a course in administering the TEC's permit which was consistent with
Forest Service ideological principles, with embryonic agency policy, with evolving
law and with what seemed to be the just demands of competing and divergent
parties vexed Forest Service officials. Other problems surfaced in the TEC case:
How should payments for special privileges on national forests—termed "conservation charges"—be figured, and were they fair at all? Why should the Forest
Service "tax" a water developer for creating a beneficial public use where there
was only unharnessed, "wasted" water before? Further, why should the Forest
Service be so prickly to the activities of corporations? After all, the water
developers argued, vast capital investments were required to build great water
systems—especially hydroelectric ones and especially in the formidable Sierra
Nevada—and corporate financial systems were one of the few entities equipped to
bankroll such nation-strengthening ventures.

The Main River Water Company

Another pattern typical of this era in hydroelectric development is that reflected by
the Main River Water Company (MRWC). Of no direct importance in terms of a
physical imprint on the land, this company illustrates the formative evolvement of
a relationship between the Forest Service and water development proponents and,

importantly, introduces Oscar C. Merrill, who would later play a key role in federal hydroelectric policy.

Appropriation of water rights in the name of the MRWC began in 1905 with the concept to largely use the old Columbia and Stanislaus River Water Company system—including its tunnel separating the Middle from the South Fork of the Stanislaus River. Water was then to flow into the old ditch of the TCWC before being diverted to the Phoenix power plant, which had been built by the successors of the Tuolumne County Water Company. In 1909 the MRWC proponents filed for rights-of-way over the Stanislaus National Forest under the act of March 3, 1891, that is, for the prime purpose of irrigation.[22]

O. C. Merrill was the Forest Service's chief engineer in Washington, D.C., whose responsibility it was to approve or deny the application. Due to the TCWC successor's prior and quite inclusive water rights and interests on both the Middle and South forks of the Stanislaus River, the MRWC devised an alternative plan that would return the waters it used from the Middle Fork high enough on the river to not infringe on those prior rights. The problem was the MRWC's insistence that the rights-of-way were needed mainly for irrigation purposes. Merrill could not be convinced that a hydroelectric plant generating 65,000 horsepower at 80 percent efficiency was merely a by-product of the system. Merrill rebuked the MRWC, commenting:

> In the whole twenty miles of length of the conduit there are probably not ten acres of land that are agricultural or that could ever require water for irrigation. . . . Not only are there no irrigable lands along the line of the conduit, but there are none for the forty miles between the end of the conduit and the above mentioned point of diversion. . . . No more flagrant example of false certificate has ever come before this office.[23]

Thus, though Merrill rejected the MRWC's application under the March 3 Act, it was shown that another viable hydroelectric project could be carved out of the remaining water resource on the Middle Fork of the Stanislaus.

The Sierra and San Francisco Power Company

The Tuolumne Electric Company and the Main River Water Company, as well as a host of other turn-of-the-century hydroelectric prospectors in the West, began as independent corporations and virtually all of them soon became small parts of larger concerns anu consolidations. A third example, very briefly mentioned here, is the Sierra and San Francisco Power Company (S&SFPCo). This company straddled both the second and third eras of water and hydroelectric development and conceptually bridged the hallmarks of those eras.

Succeeding the 1905 Stanislaus Electric Power Company, and that company being the successor to a consortium of interests active on the Middle Fork of the Stanislaus River, the S&SFPCo was organized from the outset primarily to generate hydroelectric power and transmit it to distant users.[24] The S&SFPCo forged an increasingly symbiotic relationship with the Forest Service through its prolific and generally thoughtful correspondence and frequent meetings between the company's representatives in Boston and San Francisco and Forest Service officers in Washington, D.C. and San Francisco. Though the Forest Service and S&SFPCo wrangled over a great number of issues, there seemed to be a genuine regard and respect between the parties and a consciousness that the policies they hammered out had a significance well beyond the case at hand.

A product of this developing rapport between the Forest Service and hydroelectric proponents was an interesting shift whereby the Forest Service began to accept and guardedly welcome "good" proposals while the hydroelectric industry looked to the Forest Service to protect its interests from competitors having relatively lesser proposals.

Water on the Wheel, 1911-1920

There was no clear demarcation in law, politics, or technology, but the continued weight of these factors in relation to hydroelectric and massive water developments in the West gradually evolved into a new era. Electricity for power, lighting, and heating had proven itself, and large sectors of the nation were fast becoming dependent upon hydroelectric developments as a cheap source of energy. The difficulties of long distance transmission had been overcome as were engineering limitations for large dams and electrical generation apparatus. Pumping systems for the water itself, usually powered by their sister electrical developments, were perfected to aid and defy gravity in pushing the water to irrigation, manufacturing, and household customers. The western states were the most devout patrons of electricity. By the beginning of the second decade of the new century, the average per capita consumption in the West was over twice that of the nation as a whole. Further, the hydroelectric potential of the West was estimated at twenty-two times that of the eastern United States. Demonstration homes featuring various household uses and advantages of electricity sprang-up in large metropolitan areas in California, including San Francisco, Oakland, Sacramento, and Los Angeles. By only 1910, in areas served by central electrical distribution stations, 75 percent of California's homes were wired for electric service. The use of electricity to power urban railroads was second only to manufacturing in the West.[25] The smoke stacks that had characterized the skylines of western industrial centers were being replaced by streams of high voltage wires.

By virtue of their characteristic locations that often covered the headwaters of the chief watersheds conducive to hydroelectric and expansive water developments, this circumstance had broad implications for the Forest Service in the West. Ninety-seven percent of the net area of the national forests was in the Pacific and Mountain states. Moreover, as noted by O.C. Merrill:

> Of the potential water powers in the national forests, 99 3/4 percent is in the Mountain and Pacific states. Water powers on the national forests within these two groups of States amount to 42 percent of the total estimated minimum and 43 percent of the total estimated maximum of potential water powers within the groups.[26]

In California, repeated attempts to better regulate the state's water resources culminated in creation of the State Water Commission of December 19, 1914. With passage of this act, water rights were acquired by application to the State Water Commission and project proponents were monitored for due diligence.[27]

The Federal Water Power Act of 1920

On the national level, nearing the second decade of the new century, there became a focused call for more coordinated, more consistent, and more comprehensive national direction and authority for water developments. It came from many quarters, including the primary federal departments concerned with water developments—Agriculture, Interior, and War—from several states, particularly the Pacific and Mountain regions, and from a large contingent of the water power industry that was frustrated with the problems of overlapping governmental authorities, unfavorable regulations, and uneven application of the laws.

Several federal power regulatory proposals had been before Congress but failed. In the spring of 1918, the House Committee on Water Power began hearings on a new proposal. The lone representative from California was John E. Raker, famous for the Raker Act which gave the City and County of San Francisco the green light to develop its Hetch Hetchy project. The primary representative for the federal government was Oscar C. Merrill. Merrill was considered the foremost expert on hydroelectric power with government, and he was one of the chief authors of the proposed federal water power bill.

In his opening testimony presented for the absent Department of the Interior secretary, Merrill's words reflected the Forest Service's rather spectacular shift from being remarkably wary of giant corporations to guardedly standing in the corporate corner. He testified that conservation of water power resources could best be promoted by large public utility corporations that monopolized immense market areas but whose developments and rates were regulated by public agencies. Merrill continued:

> This particular tendency toward concentration need by no means be of ill omen. Monopolization of the supply in any given territory makes possible through diversification of load, economics of operation that would not be possible for isolated independent stations.

Thus, interruptions of service would go down, efficiency would rise and cost to the customer would decrease. California and Montana, where 90 and 89 percent respectively of the total primary power was owned by public service corporations, were touted as examples of the public good that could come from watch-dogged monopolies or near monopolies. Despite the established trend in California and Montana, Merrill testified that hydroelectric power development was still largely in a "primitive state of isolated independent development" much like the "early and chaotic" railroad days where local, independent, competitive lines were inefficient and did not serve the public well.[28]

Under the proposed bill, Merrill explained that all contenders for a water development that submitted complete applications would receive a preliminary permit. Approval to build would be based on the comprehensiveness of public benefits to be derived from the planned development. As a check against tying up power sites for speculation, time periods for preliminary permits were not to exceed three years. Further, preference was to be given to proposed federal or municipal applications that could equal or better private proposals. The Federal Water Power Commission was another feature of the proposed bill. Designed to more consistently apply rules and to provide coordination between responsible government departments, the commission was to operate independently from those departments, yet be comprised of the secretaries of agriculture, interior, and war. This was thought to also promote improved utilization of water resources by crossing departmental and political boundaries such that the commission could consider water developments on a grander scale than previously practicable.[29]

Notes

This paper has been drawn from: Pamela A. Conners, "Patterns and Policy of Water and Hydroelectric Development on the Stanislaus National Forest, 1850 to 1920" (unpublished MA thesis, University of California, Santa Barbara, 1989).

1. James M. Young, "Columbia and The Miners' Struggle for Water" (unpublished MA thesis, California State College, San Jose, 1963), 29-30, 32.

2. Ibid., 36-40.

3. William S. Hutchinson, "An Early-Day Memory," *Overland Monthly* 22 (September 1893): 258.

4. David H. Johnson, "The History of the Columbia and Stanislaus River Water Company" (unpublished MS, Tuolumne County Historical Society, 1988), 25-26. The case was the Tuolumne County Water Company v. Columbia & Stanislaus River Water Company, California Supreme Court, October term, 1858.

5. Young, "Miners' Struggle," 73. *See also* Johnson, "Columbia & Stanislaus River Water Company," 16.

6. Sources vary on the selling price of the system. Johnson, for example, reported the price as $78,650. *See* Johnson, "Columbia & Stanislaus River Water Company," 38.

7. John R. Stilgoe, *Common Landscape of America, 1580 to 1845* (New Haven, CT: Yale University Press, 1982), 7-12.

8. Paul W. Gates, *History of Public Land Law Development* (Washington, DC: Government Printing Office,1968), 399, 550-551, 563-566.

9. Gifford Pinchot, *Breaking New Ground* (New York: Harcourt, Brace and Company, 1947. Reprint 1987, Washington, DC), 188, 190-191.

10. Ibid., 261-262. This document was written by Pinchot, W.J. McGee and, undoubtedly, others in Pinchot's circle.

11. USDA/USFS, "Draft Environmental Impact Statement for the Land and Resource Management Plan, Stanislaus National Forest" (Pacific Southwest Region, 1990), III-1.

12. Mark V. Thornton, "Struggle for Power: A History of the Tuolumne Electric Company and Tuolumne Transmission Company" (unpublished MS, n.d.), unpaginated. *See also* letter, U.S. Geological Survey to the Commissioner of the General Land Office, July 1, 1905 (NARS, accession 095-51B0080, location 1232879, box 35).

13. Tuolumne Electric Company v. The United States General Land Office (n.d.). (NARS, accession 095-51B0080, location 1232879, box 35).

14. Letter, director of the USGS, Charles Walcott, to the Secretary of the Interior, Mar. 9, 1906 (NARS, Ibid.). Pinchot and Walcott were personal friends as well as professional colleagues.

15. W. J. Rushing, "Report on Special Privilege Applications" for Alpine Valley, Las Vegas and Tamarack Flat, September 15, 13 & 16, respectively, 1906 (NARS, accession 095-51B0080, location 1232879, box 35).

16. Special Privilege Agreement, for transmission lines, designated October 12, 1907, and attachments, including TTC incorporation papers (NARS, accession 095-51H-0080, location U006032E, box 36).

17. E.g., W. E. Herring, "District Engineering Report," to Assistant Forester James B. Adams, September 18, 1908, written from an August 19, 1908 field visit (NARS, asccession 095-51B0080, location 1232879, box 35).

18. Pinchot, *New Ground*, 379.

19. Ibid., 389.

20. N.n. [but unmistakably written by Coert DuBois], "Tuolumne Electric Company - Reservoirs-January 5, 1906 - Stanislaus," (NARS, accession 095-51B0080, location 1232879, box 35). In today's terminology, what had been the district organizational level is now called the regional level.

21. Application 5146, Railroad Commission Decision 7032 (NARS, accession 095-51H0080, location U006032E, box 36). The application was presented in January 1920, but the effective date was back-dated to the last day of 1919.

22. W. L. Huber, "District Engineer's Report on Application of Main River Water Company for a Right of Way for a Reservoir at Sand Flat" (unpublished MS, March 18, 1912), 1. [Oscar C. Merrill's "Engineer's Report Upon the Application of the Main River Water Company and Wm. P. Miller for Conduit and for Reservoir Site Rights of Way," dated March 26, 1910, is an unpublished MS appended to the Huber Report.]

23. Merrill, "Wm. P. Miller," 20-21.

24. Frederick H. Fowler, "District Engineer's Report on Application of Sierra and San Francisco Power Co. for Final Water power Permit," (NARS, accession 09562A0447, location A587E, box 1, 1917), 1-4.

25. Robert Sibley, et al., *The Story of California: Supreme in Electrical Development* (pamphlet printed by *Journal of Electricity and Western Industry*, 1922), 4, 12-13.

26. Hearings before the House Water Power Committee, 65th Congress, 2d Sess. (pts. 1-4, Mar. 18 - April 4, 1918) (Supplemental material presented by Oscar C. Merrill), 121-123.

27. George C. Pardee, *Address on the 'Water Commission Law' at the Hanford Session of the California Development Board* (pamphlet, 1913), passim.

28. "Hearings," 5-14, 122.

29. Ibid., 21.

NONFEDERAL RELATIONS

Indian Land Use and the National Forests

Richard White
University of Washington

Gradually, over the last thirty years, what might be called the master narrative of the national forests has changed. In the original story there was once a vast and bountiful nature. Americans exploited this bounty to build a civilization, but abundance bred waste and carelessness. Far-sighted men, recognizing that the resources were not unlimited, wisely saved a remnant of the original abundance by withdrawing it from the public domain. Carefully nurtured, these lands have yielded profusely as skilled managers have made sure that what is taken is replenished.

Recent studies of the national forests have not been kind to this narrative, but my particular concern here is with the people either initially left out altogether or who were subsumed under a "vast and bountiful" nature. I mean, of course, Indian peoples.

Indian peoples connect with the national forests in numerous ways. They once lived in them, shaped them, and used them. The formation of the forests usually shut Indians off from accustomed resources and the use—or misuse—of national forest lands often greatly affecting adjoining Indian reservations. National forests are not socially neutral. They reward some groups and hurt others. In the past, Indians have rarely been among those rewarded.

But how the history of the national forests has affected Indian peoples is too large a subject for a single paper. My goal instead is to look at how Indians shaped the lands that became national forests. I want, in particular, to look at two very different things. First, I want to examine how Indians used fire and the impact of fire on the landscape. Second, I want to look briefly at how Indians sacralized place; how they created holy ground. Both uses tend to subvert our own constructions of what is natural and what is holy.

National forests are arbitrary remnants of much larger sections of land inhabited by Indian peoples. And a large portion of these lands experienced burning, often regular burning, when under Indian occupancy. Europeans, in effect, moved across

173

the country in a pall of smoke as Indian fires burned in front of them. Europeans noted such fires from the first settlement. In early seventeenth century New England Thomas Morton wrote in his *New English Canaan* that: "Savages are accustomed to set fire of the Country in all places where they come; and to burn it twice a year, at Spring and the fall of the leafe. . . ."

Similar quotes covering the next two and a half centuries and the rest of the continent abound.[1] The study of fires, particularly Indian fires, became something of a cottage industry in the 1970s and 1980s. Not only historians like Stephen Pyne, but also anthropologists like Henry Lewis and wildlife biologists, foresters, and ecologists have all done basic research. Stephen Arno and George Gruell did some of the finest and most innovative studies out of the Northern Forest Fire Laboratory in Missoula. They used an interesting amalgam of techniques to create a fire history: fire scars, repeat photography, and interviews, along with more conventional documentary sources. The results are not undisputed, but a general consensus on the influence of Indian set fires has emerged.[2] Taken together, these studies have revealed that to speak of Indian-set fires as if they were a homogeneous phenomenon with a single purpose and a single result is false and misleading. The frequency, seasonality, and location of fires all varied enormously, and with them the consequences of fires. There were usually a range of rationales for burning in a given area. Indians lit signal fires, which were more common in the West earlier in the nineteenth century than later. They set fires to clear land or otherwise alter the habitat. They burned forests to make travel easier. They used fire as a hunting technique and as a weapon in war. And they burned accidentally when fires escaped from campsites.

The skill with which Indians used fire varied from group to group. At their most skilled, as Henry Lewis has suggested for Indians in California and northern Alberta, Indians knew how to use burning to establish and maintain desired plant and animal communities. By controlling the frequency of fires and the season of burning, and the conditions under which it took place, they achieved particular goals. In California, for example, Indians burned the foothills of the Sacramento Valley and "reduced brush cover to favor a park land of grasses and intermittent stands of brush. Higher in the mountains, burning created more open, park-like forests.[3]

Not all burning by Indians reached the levels of sophistication—levels approaching management—that Henry Lewis has posited for California, but even more haphazard burning had environmental consequences that shaped the lands that would become national forests. Determining the consequences of Indian set fires is, however, a tricky proposition because it depends on both the frequency of such fires and the ability to distinguish them from natural fires. It also means correlating them with other environmental factors such as drought.

In some forested areas where lightning fires are extremely rare, early land surveys which record extensive burned areas before white settlement provide relatively clear evidence of Indian burning. In one partial township on the east coast of Camano Island in Puget Sound, for example, nine of ten 640-acre sections had been burned. The unburned section was an Indian village site. Since lightning fires are extremely rare in the Puget Sound region, these fires, which predate white settlement, were almost certainly set by Indians. In western Washington fires set near villages could burn into and alter the forests, at least in dry years.[4]

Where lightning fires were more common, the very success of fire suppression and the records kept by the U.S. Forest Service on lightning fires gives us a baseline for the frequency of natural fires. Studies which use fire scar sampling, charcoal deposits, etc., have given us some idea of fire frequency and intensity well into the historical past, and these records can be compared to modern records establishing the frequency of natural fires. Such data in the West supports strong correlations between Indian occupancy and fire frequency. They show a much smaller interval between fires in the nineteenth and in the twentieth centuries.[5]

Research in western Montana, for example, indicates far greater frequency of fire in Indian inhabited areas than in less frequented areas before 1860. Similarly, studies in Redwood Mountain in the Sierra Nevada show a marked decrease in fires after removal of the Indians.[6] This connection of burning with Indian habitation has certain obvious consequences for national forests. Because Indians made only seasonal use of higher areas—and less frequent use of heavily forested areas—their impact was greatest on lower elevations and greatest along the routes that they travelled most often. Here the effect of burning was the most obvious. But the same actions by Indians yielded different results in different years. In dry years fires spread into higher and more remote areas where they could burn for extended periods. It was such fires that led to John W. Powell's belief in the 1870s that Indian fires threatened the forests of the Rocky Mountains. "Everywhere throughout the Rocky Mountain Region the explorer away from the beaten paths of civilization meets with great areas of dead forests . . . in seasons of great drought the mountaineer sees the heavens filled with clouds of smoke. In the main these fires are set by Indians." The fires, Powell concluded, "can be curtailed by the removal of the Indians," and, "once protected from fires, the forests will in increase in extent and value."[7]

In general Indian fires helped make the national forests far different landscapes than they are today. At lower elevations and in drier intermountain valleys, they encouraged perennial grasses. They discouraged sagebrush, particularly big sage-brush. Burning by Indians represented a device for the deliberate maintenance of grassland over shrubs or other successional species. Lands dominated by shrubs consisted largely of dry, stony sites. Such lands, with less vegetation, burned less hot and less often.[8]

Similarly, Indian fires probably restricted pinyon-juniper communities, as they appear to have done along the Wasatch Front in Utah, and they shaped oak-brush chaparral communities. In California, Arizona, New Mexico, Colorado and Utah, fires set in grasslands spread up into chaparral and prevented the development of the old, homogeneous communities that now dominate so many areas. Fire created more of a mosaic of successional communities.[9]

At higher elevations less frequent Indian fires and lightning fires kept forest stands open and park-like. They kept trees out of mountain grasslands. The restriction of fires allowed Douglas-fir, which is not fire resistant in its early stages, to spread. In the Bitterroot Mountains repeat photography showed an increase in conifers and shrubs after the virtual elimination by fire at the turn of the century. Studies of Redwood Mountain in the Sierra Nevada showed an increase in understory vegetation following the suppression of Indian light burning. Subalpine forests—lodgepole pine, Engelmann spruce—red fir were the least affected by Indian burning. Here, natural fires probably had a greater impact.[10]

In sum, we find that the suppression of fire, suppression of Indians, and the conservation of the forests were all intimately linked in the late nineteenth and early twentieth centuries. This dual suppression allowed the various Indian landscapes to be either recategorized as wilderness or else managed for watershed, timber, and grazing. Indian use which created these landscapes was dismissed as wasteful or else ignored when areas were submerged into the category of "natural"—a category which came to include Indians as well as wilderness.

Ironically, this naturalization of Indians was helped along by a second use that Indian peoples made of what became national forest lands. Indians sacralized certain lands as religious sites, and whites confused this sacralization with nature worship.[11] As a very rough generalization—one with numerous exceptions—Judeao-Christian religions tend to make time sacred while many Indian religions make place sacred. This is true even among calendrical religions like those of the Pueblos. The Tewa, for example, bound their world with the four sacred mountains. They also have four sacred Tsin or flat-topped hills and numerous shrines around villages. Among other Indian peoples the most obvious sacred places are vision quest sites, or sites that commemorate specific sacred events.[12]

Such sites occur all over the country on Indian lands, private lands, and federal lands. And because mountains and high country with their proximity to heavens play a large role in sacred geography, large numbers of these sacred sites are on national forest land. Unlike Indian burning these uses continue and have become the basis for claims that challenge Forest Service uses of sacred land. In one famous case, Blue Lake, the result was the return of land to the control of Taos Pueblo.

The most notable of the conflicts over sacred lands has been the Northwest Indian Cemetery Protective Association et al. vs. the United States, or the G-O Road case as it is commonly known. The case concerned Yurok, Karuk, and Tolowa sites in the Blue Creek roadless area of Six Rivers National Forest. The Indians won in the lower courts, but the Supreme Court, in a 5-3 opinion (1988) written by Sandra Day O'Conner, overturned it. The court rejected the first amendment claims of the Indians and asserted the right of the government to use "its lands."[13] Indians, however, have continued to exert religious claims to the land even in the face of the G-O Road decision. Currently the Havasupai seek to stop mining near Red Butte in Kaibab National Forest because it will violate a Havasupai shrine. The *Albuquerque Journal* quoted Don Watahomigie, the Havasupai Chairman, as writing: "The site . . . is the abdomen of our Mother Earth . . . destruction of that location is the destruction of the Havasupai religion, our Mother Earth, and our culture. It cannot be permitted." The Blackfeet, meanwhile, are seeking to stop exploratory drilling in the Hall Creek area of the Badger -Two Medicine drainage of Lewis and Clark National Forest for similar reasons.[14]

Indians continue to make such claims despite defeats in court and the very feeble protection that the American Indian Religious Freedom Act offers them. The courts have ruled that to fulfill the requirements of the act, agencies only have to consider the religious use Indian's make of the land. They do not necessarily have to protect it. It is a law without any teeth.[15]

Now for many whites this dual legacy of Indian practice on the lands that became the national forests seems both contradictory and frustrating. We want our Indians simple. We want them as symbols, not as complicated subjects in their own right. We choose our Indians, as it were, according to our management categories. In wilderness areas we have sacred Indians; in multiple use areas we have Indian managers. But Indians, as a people of history rather than as symbols, insisted on burning wilderness and making sacred land that we clearcut. These are our categories, not theirs, and these categories allow us to impose a continuity that disguises the sharp break that national forests imposed on the use of the land.

For, whatever else they were, national forests were an exercise in power. The changes in the land marked the changes in power. And those changes in power still become visible whenever a resource dispute forces national forest managers to confront not symbolic Indians but living, breathing Indians who demand a say in how the land is used.

Notes

1. Stephen Pyne, *Fire in America: A Cultural History of Wildland and Rural Fire* (Princeton, NJ: Princeton University Press, 1982): 48.

2. For disputes over data, Emily Russell, "Indian-set Fires in the Forests of the Northeastern United States," *Ecology* 64 (1983): 80-83.

3. Henry T.Lewis, *Patterns of Indian Burning in California: Ecology and Ethnohistory*, Ballena Press Anthropological Papers, no. 1 (Ramona, Calif.: Ballena Press, 1973), 7, 24-35. Henry Lewis, "Why Indians Burned: Specific Versus General Reasons," *Proceedings—Symposium and Workshop on Wilderness Fire; Missoula, Montana, November 15-18, 1983. U.S. Department of Agriculture, Forest Service. Intermountain Forest and Range Experiment Station, Ogden Utah, General Technical Report INT-182*, 75-80.

4. Richard White, *Land Use Environment and Social Change: The Shaping of Island County, Washington* (Seattle: University of Washington Press: 1980), 23-24.

5. George E. Gruell, "Indian Fires in the Interior West: A widespread Influence," *Proceedings—Symposium and Workshop on Wilderness Fire; Missoula, Montana, November 15-18, 1983. U.S. Department of Agriculture, Forest Service. Intermountain Forest and Range Experiment Station, Ogden Utah, General Technical Report INT-182*, 69; Stephen F. Arno and George E.Gruell, "Fire History at the Forest-Grassland Ecotone in Southwestern Montana," *Journal of Range Management* 36 (May 1983), 332-336; George E. Gruell," Fire and Vegetative Trends in the Northern Rockies: Interpretations from 1871-1982 Photographs," USDA, Forest Service, Intermountain Forest and Range Experiment Station, Ogden, Utah, *General Technical Report, INT-158* (December 1983), 5, 105-107.

6. Gruell, "Indian Fires," 69; Stephen W. Barrett and Stephen F. Arno, Indian Fires as an Ecological Influence in the Northern Rockies," *Journal of Forestry* (October 1982), 647-650.

7. Pyne, *Fire in America*, 80; Gruell, "Indian Fires," 71.

8. Stephen F. Arno, "Ecological Effects and Management Implications of Indian Fires," *Proceedings—Symposium and Workshop on Wilderness Fire; Missoula, Montana, November 15-18, 1983. U.S. Department of Agriculture, Forest Service. Intermountain Forest and Range Experiment Station, Ogden Utah, General Technical Report INT-182*, 81-82.

9. Ibid.; Dan L. Flores, "Zion in Eden: Phases of the Environmental History of Utah," *Environmental Review* 7 (Winter 1983), 329.

10. Gruell, "Indian Fires," 69; Barrett and Arno, "Indian Fires as an Ecological Influence," 650; Arno, "Ecological Effects," 82-84.

11. For a survey of Indian attitudes, but one which verges on the sacralization of all nature, *see* Donald Hughes and Jim Swan, "How Much of the Earth is Sacred Space?" *Environmental Review* (Winter 1986), 247-259.

12. Alfonso Ortiz, *The Tewa World: Space, Time, Being, and Becoming in a Pueblo Society* (Chicago: University of Chicago Press, 1969), 18-20. ; Ake Hultkrantz, *Belief and Worship in Native North America*, edited by Christopher Vecsey, (Syracuse: Syracuse University Press, 1981), 123.

13. For the original decision, *see* Northwest Indian Cemetery Protective Association v. Peterson, 565, F. Suppl. 586 (N.D. California 1983).

14. *Albuquerque Journal*, August 19, 1990. *High Country News*, May 20, 1991.

15. Hughes and Swan, "Sacred Space," 254-255.

The First Sagebrush Rebellion: Forest Reserves and States Rights in Colorado and the West, 1891-1907

Michael McCarthy
University of Denver

In Nevada in the summer of 1979 the Sagebrush Rebellion began its long sweep across the American West. Five years later, like a stream that overflows its banks, spends itself, recedes, and dies, it was gone. In its brief life it constituted a virtual war between the federal government and insurgent westerners over the question of federal ownership and regulation of western public lands. In a region where the government owns a landmass larger than western Europe, and where massive regulation goes hand in hand with ownership, the rebels of '79 simply came to believe that federal "landlordism" was destroying their economic lives. By eroding the economic development of western people, they also believed the government crippled the states in which they lived. Attacking "federal colonialism" and "boodle-passers" who had "taken charge of our assets," they insisted, like the Idaho Cattlemen's Association, that they had become "serfs" in their own homes, unable to control their "destiny" while, as one said, "Washington controls the land." As Governor Ed Herschler of Wyoming expressed it, "the system is badly out of kilter. Federal encroachments on state and local governments are at an all-time high."

From the beginning, the heart of the rebellion was the belief that excessive federal control and regulation of the western public domain stripped people and states of their rights—rights to graze cattle on the public domain, rights to mine it, rights to generate tax base from it, rights, echoed Senator Orrin Hatch of Utah, to control their own "destiny." To reverse the trend, to regain lost "rights," the Sagebrush Rebellion attempted two things: in the short run, improved, "fairer" federal management of the public domain, and in the long run, cession of federal lands to the states in which they lay. In the end, it got neither; the question of rights remained as unresolved as before, and the rebellion ultimately flared out and died. In its brief life, however, it stunned all who witnessed it, and it set all its observers to wondering where it had come from.

In fact, it came from the past. It was not the first Sagebrush Rebellion, it was the second—a distant echo of an earlier conflict that crisscrossed the West in the 1890s.

180

In 1979 it was as if an old script had been found, dusted off, and transported into the present for another reading. On one side, once again, was the West, and on the other the federal government. In the middle were the familiar old questions about land, rights, and power. In 1979 westerns spoke of an excess of federal sovereignty in their midst, mostly on and around the land, and a hundred years earlier they said the same thing. In 1979 they warred with the government to correct the problem, and in the 1890s they did the same thing. Ten decades passed between the two rebellions and nothing was learned and nothing changed—proving, if nothing else, the relentless redundancy of history and the inability of people to profit from lessons before them.

In the last decade of the nineteenth century and the first decade of the twentieth, America witnessed one of the greatest domestic upheavals in its history. The so-called "conservation movement" triggered the greatest sectional conflict the nation had seen since the Civil War, and one of the greatest it had experienced in 200 years. Some called it the "silent" revolution, but it was, in fact, not silent at all. It was deep, angry, often violent, and frighteningly divisive. And it left scars—as the second Sagebrush Rebellion later proved—that have not healed today.

The genesis of the conservation conflict, of course, is well-documented. Through-out most of America's life, as the "East" moved steadily west, the nation's attitude toward its timbered environment was simplistic and lethal. Clinging to the belief that the land existed for exploitation and no other reason, the mythology that the rich bounty of the West had been purposely set aside by God for the use of man, pioneers cut and slashed their way across the country with abandon. The evangels of the new age "civilized," to be sure. But in the process they also annihilated some of the most magnificent forests on the continent. Only in the last years of the Gilded Age, with the end of the century in sight, did the process slow. And only when it did, and America caught its breath, did its people begin to see what had happened: the virtual looting of the "Garden of the World." In the early 1890s, prodded by Frederick Jackson Turner's pronouncement that the frontier had "ended," many Americans, especially Easterners, concluded that the time had come to reassess the nation's great developmental ethic. So they did. And out of their fear that what had happened in the past would continue, without counterac-tion, to happen in the future, they launched the conservation movement. Their first target, not surprisingly, was the Great Forest.

Congressional passage of the Creative, or General Revision, or Forest Reserve, Act in 1891 began federal attempts to save the vanishing timberlands of the western public domain. The effect of the new policy on the West was profound. Almost immediately it changed it physically by constricting growth patterns, channeling growth *away* from public lands for the first time in American history and forcing it elsewhere. It changed it economically by impacting mining, farming, and stockraising, by locking up taxable land and stunting the growth of state revenues. It changed it politically by setting Democrats against Republicans with a particular new fury. But, most of all, it deepened an already broad political gulf that existed between the federal government and sovereign western states, between the "West " and the "East," and made the conservation issue, as much as anything else, a question of "rights"—the rights of western people as opposed to those of the East, and the rights of western states as opposed to those of the federal government.

In the 1890s, three events triggered the controversy: the Creative Act of 1891, Grover Cleveland's 1897 "Midnight Reserves," and the so-called Organic Act of the same year. Together they strung a virtual tripwire for protest all across the West, but nowhere was the protest longer, uglier, or more significant than in Colorado.

For several days the passage of the Creative Act caused little movement in Colorado. There, as everywhere in the West, where the new law was little known and less understood, homesteaders, miners, and small cattlemen continued to conduct business as usual on the public domain. But as the distant abstractions of the act slowly translated into reality—as the region's first forest reserves were carved out of the land on which they lived—the pioneers' world quickly changed. So did their attitude, which swung from unconcern to anger overnight. In Colorado the first flashpoint for protest was the two-million-acre White River Timber Land Reserve created by Benjamin Harrison across the White River Plateau on October 16, 1891. But within a year, by Christmas 1892, with Harrison's creation of the Pikes Peak, Plum Creek, South Platte, and Battlement Mesa reserves, controversy had spread across virtually all of central Colorado. Initial protest was predictably inchoate; then, as later, ignorant pioneers were confused about the law itself and inarticulate in expressing themselves against it. Even so, however, a central theme quickly developed among them; the savaging of the region's rights by the federal government. As a White River lawyer asked a crowed of homesteaders one autumn evening in Glenwood Springs, "is it fair to the people who have come out here to upbuild the country and their own lives to have, after years of earnest endeavor, someone take these resources from us?"

For two years, from the hard country along the White to the Grand Valley below, in homesteader and cattlemen's meetings, and in the nearly rabid editorials of the local press, this question was asked again and again. Arguing against the withdrawals, for example, the angry *Meeker Herald* urged its citizens to "arise in your might and protest this damnable outrage," to fight "that government outfit" that had no right to "drive you from the homes that you have acquired by years of toil." Before a packed house in the Denver Chamber of Commerce Building one October evening, Bear Creek cattleman H. H. Eddy denounced federal policy as a tyranny "not equalled since the days of William the Conqueror." And countless others—the emerging theme of "rights" always foremost among them—said the same. But it did no good. The protests failed. Other than creating a straw man with which to do battle—a distant federal monolith with "esthetic Eastern people" behind it, ready to "plaster the West with reserves that would retard and cripple the hardy pioneers"—insurgent Coloradans might as well have shouted to the wind. By 1893 Harrison's five Colorado reserves (and ten more in other western states) stood essentially unchallenged.

In the fall of 1893 the growing fight over reserves spread from the backwoods of the West to the floors of Congress. There, for the next three years, debate over the so-called McRae Bill—the conservationists' master plan to add an administrative component to the Creative Act (which had effectively "locked up" public timber-lands and literally left them to burn)—allowed Westerners a second arena in which to voice their rage.

For the first time the states' right broadsides of 1891 and 1892 broke down into specifics. At least three themes began to emerge: fear that reserve resources would be siphoned off by eastern business, to the detriment of local settlers; fear that land lost to the states for disposal would impair their tax bases; and anger at the fact that Westerners were denied the same access to abundance and equality that had been accorded their fathers on earlier frontiers. Colorado's congressional delega-tion, for example, opposed the bill's stipulation that "merchantable" timber be sold to the highest bidder; its belief was that an "unfriendly" Interior Department would sell primarily to eastern timber combines instead of local settlers with little money and less influence. "Now comes the average Eastern congressman," said the *Rocky Mountain News*, "full of ignorance, and seeing the opportunity to make a dollar or two by the sale of timber proposes to do damage beyond estimate." The "tax base" question was equally controversial. As one Coloradan argued, the state's Rio Blanco County, home of the White River Reserve, was only three years old, and others were not much older than it; while forest protection was inherently good, forest lock-ups cost them all dearly in "revenue, pleasure, and liberty." If withdrawals continued in the future as they had in the past, so the argument ran, states would lose land sales, tax revenue would continue to shrink, and services would disappear. It was an argument with increasing frequency in Colorado in the middle 90s.

The McRae Bill had several incarnations between 1893 and its final death in 1896, and Coloradans opposed them all. But any celebrations they might have held were short-circuited by Cleveland's 1897 withdrawals—21 million acres of timberland from Wyoming to Washington. Although the reserves did not directly affect Colorado, the "principle" of their withdrawal did. In this case what galled insurgents was the method by which the action had been taken: attacking Washington with renewed anger, they and others everywhere charged that the central issue was the "rights" of the affected states in the entire process. They maintained, first (and primarily), that the territories had been withdrawn at the request of eastern "theorists, enthusiasts, and cranks"—Cleveland's six-man "National Forestry Commission"—who had never actually seen the land in question, and authorized by an eastern president angry at the West for opposing his presidential candidacy in 1892. They maintained, second, that, spurning the age-old practice of advise and consent, he had not consulted western congressmen in advance of his action, nor did he advise them of it later. The trouble with Cleveland, said the *Denver Republican*, "is that he is imbued with the idea that the people of the West are ignorant." The result was the complete loss of "individual rights and the rights of the communities."

In April 1897, after four years of effort, congressional insurgents finally forced a showdown on the reserve issue. In a passionate three-month debate over South Dakota Senator Pettigrew's essential antiforestry amendment to the year's Sundry Civil Bill, Coloradans led the pack in its support. In a debate that broke sharply along East-West lines, they argued, with Pettigrew, that the Cleveland withdrawals should be suspended for at least one year, that reserved areas should be resurveyed and nontimbered lands eliminated from them, and that no future reserves should be established except to protect the forests within the reserve, establish favorable conditions of waterflow, or to furnish a continuous supply of timber for the use of citizens of the United States. They also agreed that the free use of timber should be granted all "bona fide" local settlers, and (to their later chagrin) that the secretary of interior be given the power to make future rules and regulations for the reserves.

Throughout the debate Coloradans focused on an increasingly familiar theme; eastern-federal "paternalism," sectional politico-economic leverage, and the assertion of one region's rights over another's. Congressman John Bell of Montrose, near Battlement Mesa, insisted that neither he nor his constituents opposed legitimate "conservation;" what they opposed was the federal *brand* of conservation that, on the Battlement, for example, took in vast amounts of nontimbered agricultural, pastoral, and mining lands along with timber stands, leaving local settlers with nothing. "It is of this injustice," he said, "this indiscriminate setting aside of reservations that the people of my district complain." John Shafroth of Denver, however, painted protest with broader strokes. Focusing on eastern political and economic interests that he believed had created the reserve policy for their own benefit, he said that "it is most brazen for conservationists to tell us that they desire to protect us against ourselves. This proffered guardianship over western interests we most earnestly protest against. You may have the power, but it is not right." On June 4, 1897, William McKinley signed the Sundry Civil Bill and the "Pettigrew Amendment" with it. The so-called Organic Act of 1897, embodying all of Pettigrew's original goals, appeared to be a victory on the insurgent West. Shafroth, Bell, and their colleague apparently had their point.

In a game of highest stakes, though, the government held the ace. And in late June 1897, with the establishment of the reserves' first regulations, it played it.

On paper, at least, the new regulations appeared to be a radical departure from the government's past forestry policy of reserve-and-abandon. On paper, at least, the forest reservations now were officially unlocked for the first time in six years and opened to local settlers. Mineral prospecting, livestock pasturing (except for sheep), and the free use of water and timber for the legitimate purposes of settlers living in or near the reserves were all allowed. But from the start a gulf developed between perception and reality—between what the regulations promised and what they actually delivered. The Organic Act clearly held that the reserves now were open, and from 1897 on it was clearly the federal perception that they were; in Colorado, along the rim of Battlement, in the valley of the Yampa, along Plum Creek, from Gunnison to Rifle to Meeker, the reality, to the settlers, was that they still were not.

Complaints began immediately, and they never stopped. Their primary focus was loss of pasture and timber access. Permits for timber cutting, they said, took months to acquire, and those wanting timber had to submit petitions citing the precise diameter of the trees in question, the number of trees, per acre, whether the timber had been killed by fire or disease, whether or not the trees had attained their full growth, how their cutting would improve the forest in general, and whether or not their removal would impair the overall objectives of the reserve. Then they had to submit to inspection by government men largely unfamiliar with the local forest terrain, and endure months of delay in Washington. Even they could be, and often were, denied. The net result was that homesteaders found it virtually impossible to build cabins and fencing in the small mountain meadows in which they lived. Prospectors suffered for the same reason: lack of timber for sluicing and the shoring of deep mines made it nearly impossible for them to hunt for mineral. For stockmen, permits for cattle grazing were difficult to obtain and more difficult to

keep, and for sheepmen, of course, they were impossible. For years the government insisted that the charges were untrue, the reserves were open. But the widen-
ing gap between what it promised and what local settlers thought they received
quickly ignited a new round in the conservation wars.

Still trying to define their position on the reserves, Colorado pioneers continued to
argue both for their own individual "rights" in a system they now considered
permanently turned against them, and for those of the "state" that supposedly
shielded them. After 1897, refining old themes into new, they essentially argued
three things: that the reserves had been created by eastern men with no knowledge
of the West, that reserve rules formulated from the Organic Act were written by
eastern men with no interest in the West, that the reservations were protected by
eastern men ("timber agents" and federal "rangers") who had no sympathy for the
West—and that the entire process had led to a wholesale breaching of the rights of
western citizens and states.

It enraged them, for example, that forest reserves had been created by largely
eastern Congress with no land of its own to lose to the system. It angered them
more that by 1906 the state's eighteen reserves (12 million acres of land) had been
authorized by two men, one from Indiana, one of new New York, one (Harrison)
who never set foot in Colorado in his life, and the other (Theodore Roosevelt) who
barely did. Worse, to them, was the fact that the withdrawals were based on
information furnished largely by eastern "conservationists" who never saw the
West either. To upcountry pioneers it was a little wonder that the reserves included
so many millions of acres of nonforested lands with them (and, once included,
rarely eliminated); from Cleveland's Forestry Commission, which viewed
fragments of the West from the luxury of a fast-travelling Pullman car before
recommending the withdrawal of 21 million acres of land, to the operatives of
Theodore Roosevelt, who performed exactly the same way, the government's
approach to western withdrawals was cavalier in every way. This was why the
West saw no justice in the application of conservation in its midst. Expressing,
again, the theme of lost rights, one White River rancher speculated that "if that
great (western) domain passes to the general government, we people of the West
will not be considered. The capital of the East will set the laws and we will follow
them." By 1897, in fact, many would have argued that the process had already
started.

If the creation of the reserves was an issue in the high country, the daily regulations that governed them was an even bigger one. Attacking the General Land
Office and Forest Service bureaucrats" who wrote the laws, insurgents again
insisted that their rights had been lost in the process. Their charge—by now a

familiar one—was that the new regulators were uniformly eastern men who knew nothing of the West and its conditions, who did not care, and who promulgated ignorant regulations that crippled local western economies. Congressman Herschel Hogg blasted them as "goggle-eyed, bandy-legged dudes from the East" and "sad-eyed, absent-minded professors and bugologists." Senator Henry Teller, who said that Roosevelt knew "no more about conditions in the West than a woodchuck," dismissed the bureaucrats as "distant dictators with only a theoretical knowledge of the West"—men "who had absolutely no acquaintance with the subject, who were too indolent to go over the country and examine its geography, who simply sat in their offices and made the laws, doing the utmost injustice to the people." Even Gifford Pinchot agreed that "the abysmal ignorance of the Washington office about conditions was outrageous." In other words, in this whole process, asked the West, when every word on every page of every regulation affected the very existence of people on the ground, where were citizen rights? And where, again, were the rights of the protector states?

To Westerners, the points at which "rights" seemed to be most directly abrogated was the point at which federal agents actually applied the regulations to specific reserves. It was here, on a summer afternoon, perhaps in a wilderness clearing, in a timber stand, on a fast-moving stream, where government actually met settler face to face, and where reality and the appearance of reality most clearly diverged.

Organic Act or not, insurgent pioneers insisted that federal agents deliberately impeded their access to reserves and reserve resources. They routinely denied grazing permits. They delayed and denied timber cutting permits. They hamstrung prospecting. And they did it all with a sense of hostility, even malice. The problem, again, said Westerners, was the fact that early "timber agents" were virtually all Easterners and either spoilsmen or appointees of spoilsmen— watchmakers, bookkeepers, veterinarians, saloon operators, protegees of eastern party bosses—whose primary goal was personal gain and not forest protection. As an angry Colorado Senator Edward Wolcott stated it, "they tumble all over each other in the western states, broken-down politicians from the Eastern states. They are not fit to stay at home so they are unloaded on the West. These people are worse than any timber thieves the East can imagine."

In time, of course, the GLO's timber agents gave way to the rangers of the United States Forest Service. But in the insurgent mind the evils of ignorance and corruption were only replaced by the worse evil of zealotry. To Gifford Pinchot, his men were passionate, almost evangelical, but only in pursuit of the public good. To Westerners, however, who commonly depicted them as whip-cracking "cossacks," the new rangers were simply fanatics carrying out a fanatical policy. As the

Leadville Press bitterly editorialized, ranger law had locked up the reserves even more tightly than before, and left westerners "buncoed, robbed, and treated like serfs of English landlords." The *Eagle County Blade* wrote that "the fellows who spilled tea in Boston Harbor were not the only ones who had a righteous cause for revolution." Speaking specifically of ranger rule, a central Colorado cattleman added that "if your ancestors had come to America with mine, if as many of them had fought battles for freedom from King George, if you had breathed the spirit of liberty for thirty years on Colorado mountain tops, you would hate it as I do."

In the decade after the passage of the Organic Act, insurgents increasingly converted rhetoric to action. And at the heart of the action was still the question of rights.

Of all the insurgent groups, the most active was small cattlemen who fought for years against what they insistently called an "absentee landlord system" that made Coloradans "tenants of the federal government." In hundreds of local and regional meetings, especially in the early 1900s, they put pressure on the government to excise rangelands from the reserves and facilitate the granting of grazing permits. They fought the transfer of the reserves from the Department of the Interior to the Department of Agriculture, arguing that it would only increase the influence of men from "some codfish district of Massachusetts" who know "no more about western conditions than a Filipino does about Latin." At Public Lands Commission hearings in Denver in 1904, they fought federal leasing proposals and the question of grazing taxes, arguing that "Uncle Sam has been paid a thousandfold already for the land by the blood and bones" of cattlemen and others. In the meantime they also created a condition of anarchy on the states back ranges, contesting federal laws whenever they could and forcing rangers to arm themselves and maintain the law at gunpoint.

Behind the cattlemen and other high country settlers stood the state's political establishment, which expanded an almost manic energy in its efforts to roll back conservation on all levels. In the ten years after 1897 Colorado's governors, legislators, and congressmen, almost without exception fought what Teller acidly called "the fostering and kindly hand of the national government" and emphatically agreed with Teller that "we want it taken off."

In Congress, no state in the West produced a more rabidly anticonservation contingent in the conservation era than Colorado. Whether fighting the McRae Bill, the hostile application of reserve regulations, or supporting passage of the "Fulton Amendment" to the 1907 Agricultural Appropriations Act (mandating congressional approval for all future national forests), its relentless negativism rested on a single, inflexible premise: that in conservation matters the federal government had usurped the rights of the western states and the citizens who lived in them. When Hogg said that "I do not think in any area of government there has been such a reckless exercise of power" as conservation and when he raked the "forest crank" and "dreamer" responsible, he reflected the attitudes of a generation of colleagues, Democrat and Republican alike.

At the state level Colorado produced a stable of intensely anticonservation states rights governors who stirred up antigovernment sentiment at regional and national governors' conferences for fifteen years. Charles Thomas spoke routinely about federal "abuses of power." John Shafroth, who moved from Congress to the Colorado statehouse, maintained that "serious wrongs" had been inflicted by the government to the extent that back country pioneers had become virtual "criminals" on their own land. Pueblo Democrat Alva Adams launched a campaign to force federal cession of public domain lands to the states in which they lay. "Such a change of control," he said, would "give the state home rule over its entire territory and exempt every citizens of Colorado from the liability of being a trespasser" in his own region. "Such a transfer," he concluded, would also "promote the dignity of the state and advance the welfare of the people." Cession, of course, never happened, but the idea gained enough advocacy Westwide to create serious federal concern. Not insignificantly, too, it provided a precedent for the second "Sagebrush Rebellion" nearly a century later.

A few steps from the governor's office the Colorado state legislature besieged Washington with a decade's worth of petitions and memorials, all of them arguing that the state's sovereignty had been destroyed by federal conservation initiatives. In 1907, in fact, fearful that Colorado was sinking into a quasi-civil war with the government over the issue, it was the legislature's passage of such a memorial that ultimately brought the first conservation era—the first Sagebrush Rebellion—to an end. "Assuming all the rights of a private landowner," read the memorial, the government had "undertaken the active administration of the lands composing national forests, utilizing them for the benefit of the government" at the expense of the state. By withdrawing fully one quarter of Colorado from entry, disregarding its "implied obligations to the state in the process," by "developing its resources for the benefit of the general government" and "engaging in business in competition with our citizens," the government was guilty of nothing less than "usurping the rights of the state and its citizens." To remedy the wrong, the legislature called for a "public lands convention" to be held in Denver later that year. It was the legislators' hope that at the meeting the government would be pressured either to defend and make sense of its policy, modify it to meet western needs, or abandon it forever.

The convention's basic objectives were clearly reflected in questions posed by its program committee. Did the federal government possess "the constitutional right to hold the public lands within the borders of new states in perpetual ownership and under municipal sovereignty without the consent of the state?" When the general government derived revenue from the reservations—through fees and resource sales—was such action in the interests of the states," or did it turn government into a profit-taking landlord? Did the whole program, in fact, "retard the settlement and development" of the American West and place it in an inferior political and economic position with regard to other regions and older states? Insurgents, of course, believed they knew the answers. With regard to what they saw as sixteen years of "landlordism, exploitation, special privilege, and carpetbag government"—what Teller called the government's "Russia policy for the West"—all that remained was vindication.

But, of course, it never came. For three days in June, federal officers sent to Denver by Roosevelt faced down insurgents from all over the West. When it was over the West knew the worst: federal policies were legal, they were immutable, and they would be enforced. In three days the president suffocated the insurgent movement, essentially forever, and ended a decade of disorder in its tracks.

From the moment the gavel fell in Denver, the central issue of the convention was the central issue of the conservation wars: state and individual rights. From the stage of the Broadway Theater, before a crowd of hundreds, western speaker after speaker spoke of the "outrages" of sixteen years. The litany by now was familiar. The government "usurped" land that belonged to the West. In the process it violated the rights of pioneers who relied on the land for survival. And it made it impossible for the states to grow. To the bitter end Teller insisted that "the government does not have the right to seize the land," and fellow senator Thomas Patterson said that "we do not want more than a fifth of our state taken from the people and turned into a federal preserve." Speakers from every state in the West repeatedly agreed. But it meant nothing, not to Roosevelt and not to the other architects of conservation. It was an old song, often sung, and by 1908 it had simply grown too old.

In the final hours of the convention, Gifford Pinchot confronted his enemies for the last time. He told them clearly, emphatically, that the government was right, that it would not back down, then he walked away, leaving them mute. The insurgents never recovered. In the next few days they drifted slowly back to the mining camps and summer range from which they had come, and for all intents and purposes they were not heard from again. Over the next few years the cry of "states' rights" occasionally rang down from the high country, but it quickly died. The first Sagebrush Rebellion was over. And few believed it would ever come again.

Given all this, then, what exactly *was* "states rights" in Colorado? What did the doctrine *mean* to those who invoked it? When pioneers attacked the federal government and eastern policy makers on conservation issues, what, precisely, were they trying to *say*?

In general, of course, "states rights" was several things in one, not one thing alone, and for all its political overtones, its roots were decidedly economic. Put another way, multiple issues, political in spirit but economic in origin, made up the doctrine, and it was under that banner that Colorado arranged and acted on its many angers.

Four central themes, all interconnected, finally underpinned the states rights argument: first, what was commonly referred to in the western press as "laissez faire"—the pioneers' belief in the fundamental right of American citizens to earn a living off the land; second the western idea of "mission"; the insurgent notion of "equal footing" (an idea that resonated through the Sagebrush Rebellion as well as the first); and fourth, the ancient charge of "colonialism."

The first theme was clear and self-explanatory, and it was present in every statement the insurgents made. Westward-moving pioneers believed passionately that they had the right to convert western lands, especially timberlands, to their own personal use for the purpose of economic survival. Immersed in the spirit of late nineteenth century laissez faire capitalism and mindful of the fact that their fathers and their father's fathers had made living off the land with no governments restricting them, they simply asserted the same "rights" as those before them had. Forest reserves, to them, abridged basic rights by denying them access to historically "public" resources. Cordoned-off watersheds, for example, meant less (if any) timber for homes or fencing. Rules and regulations meant fewer grazing pastures and patented mines. Decreased enterprise, then, meant decreased income, and decreased income negated all the individual dreams that fueled the westward movement in the first place.

A second part of the states rights argument—that meshed perfectly with the first— was the old American idea of "mission." With regard to it, Coloradans worked a very simple equation: as God's children in a new world, they had a mission (what earlier generations would have called "Manifest Destiny"); the mission was to "civilize;" "civilization," by definition was the creation of viable new governments (states), strong economic institutions (farms, mines, ranches, ancillary businesses), and stable societies in areas (like Colorado) where they did not exist before; and the western landscape (including the forest) was the stage on which it all was to be carried out. The problem was, however, the government demolished the stage. When it created the forest reserve system, withdrew land from entry, and established rules and regulations for its future use—no matter how well-intentioned it may have been—it created a massive net effect for the West. Settlement was stunted in and around the reserves, the use of the land itself was restricted, and because of the cavalier approach to withdrawals by eastern policy makers who had no familiarity with the land, huge amounts of nonforested territory were withdrawn to begin with. In the end, then, one thing was clear to an angry West: on and near the reserves, at least, viable governments, strong economic institutions, and stable societies simply did not develop. "Civilization" was stillborn. The great mythic "mission" had failed.

What was not clear to the West in this matter was why the federal government had suddenly changed the rules of the land disposal game to begin with. It was the unshakable impression of the West, insurgent or otherwise, that the whole intent of the Founding Fathers in creating the public domain in the first place had been to hold it in trust only so long as it took to dispose of it to individual ownership. Moreover, it had been on the assumption that the lands would always be open to settlement that western states had relinquished claims to public lands within their borders as conditions of statehood. In other words, the federal role in the West, said its people, was temporary custodian, not permanent landlord—and it had been so for over a century. The advent of reservations and regulations, then constituted, at very least, a breach of faith. If the reserve situation was what it seemed to be—a calculated departure from a century of rapid disposal and settlement and the beginning of a generation of revenue-generating landlordism—it was, said Henry Teller, "the most extraordinary proposition ever presented to an Anglo-Saxon, self-governing people." And it threatened to reduce them to the level of "servile peons."

It must also be remembered, at least in passing, that the whole withdraw-conserve process hit the West at a particularly bad time, a fact that exacerbated the entire conservation conflict. In 1891, when the Creative Act was passed, the cattle kingdom was in decline all across the West. Within two years the great silver frontier disintegrated. Back-country agriculture, like its downstream cousin (for which the forest reserves were created in the first place), stumbled throughout the entire period. At any other time the region may have been better able to confront the "failure" of laissez faire and mission and to absorb the shock of the new disposal system. But at the turn of the century, with the frontier "closing" and depression hemming them in from all sides, pioneer settlers equated shrinking land access with shrinking opportunity, and shrinking opportunity with economic destruction. Adopting, out of desperation, a "last stand" mentality that permitted them no flexibility, they mourned more keenly than ever their lost rights.

Above all, however, what galled Westerners was the belief that the kinds of restrictions placed on them had never been placed on the East. On earlier, more easterly frontiers, they argued, free men working free land had carved great personal fortunes out of them, as was their right. And in the process they had built powerful sovereign states around them. In Illinois and Pennsylvania and points between pioneers had transformed the Great Forest into the ever-elusive "civilization," and they had done so at great personal and regional profit. Then they refused the West the same opportunity. "After their states have been settled," said Thomas Patterson, "after their resources have been developed, after all this they start a (conservation) movement intended to cripple the mountain states and shut them out of the race for prosperity on equal terms with the other states."

The result was a sense of betrayal that existed everywhere. As one embittered insurgent said, "I think it is with considerable effrontery that a man comes to a western state after having gotten the benefit of the liberal policy of the government as to the public lands in the state of Ohio, and says that now since we have eaten our cake we want you people of Colorado to divide your cake with us." To some extent, of course, the charge was shallow and overdrawn. To some extent, it made the East the West's great straw man, its suppressiveness more imaginary than real. But the West's "equal footing" argument—that its states supposedly entered the Union with the same rights as the rest—still had validity. Westerners' belief that without the same access to the land that established states had they could never gain equality still had a truth that rang through the years.

Technically, the western argument was simple. When western states entered the Union—most of them in the second half of the nineteenth century—their admission bills contained the understanding that they entered on "equal footing" with other states. But, so the argument ran, this did not happen in fact; instead, as a condition of admission, the states were forced, one by one, to relinquish title to the single most important thing that may have guaranteed that equality: the public lands lying within the states. (Colorado's Enabling Act, for example, clearly said that the state would "forever disclaim all right and title to the unappropriated public lands" lying within it, and that the lands would "remain at the sole and entire disposition of the United States.") For the relinquishment each state received two sections in every township for schools, but nothing more, and early on insurgents were convinced that they lost more than they gained. Then, when the conservation era began and they lost *access* to the lands they had already *given up*, they were more convinced than ever.

If the government, then, used conservation as a mechanism to perpetuate *un*equal footing, all Westerners had to do was determine why. Actually, applying a kind of "devil theory" to their own history, they already knew, and they articulated what they thought in a kind of long, even elegant, syllogism. The Creative and Organic Acts, they said, made it impossible for small settler-entrepreneurs to make good livings on or near the forest reserves; the inability of individuals to prosper, in turn, impeded the growth of strong communities and states around them; the net result was that the absence of strong western states allowed the East to keep the region in its historic condition of economic and political servitude. The net result of the federal forest reserve policy, then, whether intended or not, was really colonialism. In other words, said insurgent pioneers, as long as easterners wielding federal powers could keep western lands out of the hands of western settlers, and keep their state governments weak and impotent around them, the East could exploit the region to its own benefit, as it always had. Colonialism, they said—in states rights terms—was the way of the West. "Conservation" was just another way to maintain it.

The colonial theme was not insignificant; in the West it had a long and bitter history, and among anticonservation pioneers it was the final ingredient in "states rights." Like others, Coloradans were blunt in expressing their premise about the conservation-colonialism connection.

The East, they said, had dominated the West economically since the first days of the Republic; wherever there had been an "East," there had been a "West," and wherever it had been, it had been subjugated. In the 1890s, having exhausted its own land and resources, and finding control of the West both profitable and necessary, the East sought to continue it. The way to neutralize an emerging West (attempting to control its own destiny through the manipulation of its own resources) was essentially to take them away from it. This the East effectively did through "conservation." As for the federal government, filled with Easterners, not Westerners, it sanctioned it all. Specifically, it pushed the conservation movement not necessarily to save watersheds and downstream agriculture, as it claimed, but more as the means to an end: the shattering of the West's infant economic independence, the continuation of eastern economic supremacy, and the continuing dependence, in every colonial way, of West on East. Conservation, insisted westerners, was not about trees, but power.

In the final analysis, then, "states rights" was primarily an expression of rage by western people and states who felt economically damaged by conservation in general and forest reservations in particular—all of it, they believed, engineered by a hostile eastern political establishment anxious to tighten the colonial yoke. But the expression still begged a critical question: colonialism and lack of economic opportunity aside, did western states and people really lose their *rights*? The answer, of course, was in the eye of the beholder. In the federal eye the answer was no, but in the insurgent eye it was yes—and the difference in perceiving the question of what constituted the violation of rights and what was not was exactly what gave life to the conservation conflict in the first place.

Technically, constitutionally, of course, individual rights were not abridged. "Laissez faire" and "mission" obviously carried no constitutional guarantees and never had. Federal disposal policy, as unfortunate as its timing was, was completely legal. Pioneers had no sacred right to the land, whether they worked it or not, whether they tamed it or not, and whether their economic livelihood depended on it or not. Whether or not they ultimately failed may have been a moral question, but it was hardly unconstitutional.

The same was true with reference to the "rights" of the states; western arguments about "equal footing" were compelling but legally baseless. First, the doctrine had no constitutional foundation. Neither the phrase nor the concept of equal footing appeared in the constitution, and without constitutional roots it had no force at all. Second, the assertion that western lands were signed away to the federal government was not totally accurate. While federal pressure did exist, much of the West gave up its land willingly in return for the two townships. Some states hoped to cash in on the rising value of township land. Others hoped to avoid the staggering expense of public land maintenance and let its government shoulder the burden. In essence, the states sold their birthright only to renege on the agreement later by calling for cession and other concessions. Third, under any circumstances, decades of American history and tradition affirmed the power of Congress to hold and manage (and dispose of) the public domain any way it saw fit.

Still, in the mind of the West, a final point needed to be made: the fact that in the insurgent West (except for its quasi-legal approach to "equal footing"), "rights" were not simply a question of constitutionality in the first place. Whether the result of convenience or naivete, anticonservation Westerners consistently framed their concept of rights less in statute and law than in what they might have called "morality." Preaching an almost Lockean doctrine—that human or civil rights transcended the policies of states when those policies "abused" those governed—they still insisted, constitution or not, that they were wronged. If their constitutional rights had not been violated, in other words, they stubbornly held that their civil (or "moral") rights were.

Were they wrong? Except for a single, important caveat, the answer is no.

First, the caveat. While most of the insurgents, by far, were honest men and women—part of what A.B. Guthrie has called "thousands of people just trying to get along"—there was a small element among them that emphatically were not. And while the honest majority invoked "states rights" in the true belief that it had been harmed, the back country spoilsmen who simply raped the land, then invoked their rights" when the government crushed them, used the doctrine as a shield. The states rights movement was never primarily deep cover for looters, but they did exist in it and their rhetoric was always cynical and self-serving.

As for the rest, though, there was truth in all they said.

Colonialism, for example, *did* exist, and it always had. And it *did* negatively effect Westerners in their confrontation with conservation. As far back as they could remember, they had been plagued by railroad abuses, high tariffs, gold standards, the monopolization of western economic fields by eastern corporations, and a host of other mechanisms assuring eastern economic supremacy in western regions. For generations the West had lived with control. Like railroad abuses, high tariffs, and gold standards, "conservation" was just another form of it.

The most salient truth, perhaps, was the fact that the East *did* force the Creative Act and everything that followed it. The West's first reserves *were* surveyed by eastern scientific "experts" and withdrawn by eastern presidents. The reserves' initial regulations *were* written by eastern men—GLO law clerks and others ill-trained for the job—and enforced by cadres of eastern political spoilsmen on the ground. The post-1900 conservation program *was* run by eastern progressives more interested in the application of science and "efficiency" to western conservation problems than in mitigating their effects on western people. And, despite repeated federal contentions to the contrary, the regulations of 1891 were *not* fairly adminis-tered across the West, and the national forests *were* largely inaccessible. In other words, eastern policy *did* have a negative effect on the West. Operated from a distance, even with the best of intentions, the early reserves simply did not work for Westerners. In its headlong pursuit of the general good, the government simply ignored too many individual goods for this to happen.

In the end, because of these facts, the insurgent West believed it had every right to say—in moral terms if not legal—that its rights, personal and state alike, were compromised away in the collision with conservation. Perhaps it was right. Perhaps it was not. No one will ever know, and now it does not matter. What matters now, simply, is the fact that the expression was made. A hundred years ago it gave a generation of Americans, East and West alike, the opportunity to look into the soul of the West to try to understand the complex relation existing there between men, land, and rights. Unfortunately, it largely failed to do it. But in so doing, it sent a message to the future.

The message is this: that a maddening dynamic—federal government versus the West over the question of landed rights—exists in the western psyche, that it always had, that it always will, and that sooner or later it must be confronted once and for all if it is to stop causing the deep sectional and national agonies that it has in the past. When it appeared the first time, a hundred years ago, no one learned anything from the bitter controversy it caused. When it happened again in 1979, the result was the same. Now, a century and two Sagebrush Rebellions later, perhaps it is time to approach the dynamic again, East and West alike, states and federal government alike, not to defend or condemn it, for this no longer matters, but simply to acknowledge it, dissect it, and attempt to understand it. To do less will guarantee two things: a West perpetually at war with its demons, and, because of that, new convulsions out of old.

Private Lands Within National Forests:
Origins, Problems, and Opportunities

Dennis L. Lynch and Stephen Larrabee
Colorado State University

Origins of Private Lands and Important Paradigms

Imagine that you are living on a small homestead or mining claim. You are all alone in a vast land with no neighbors for miles. Suddenly, word comes through a passerby that you have a new neighbor. A very large and powerful neighbor, who isn't sure what to do with his land, but who may restrict what you have been doing or are likely to do in the development of your land. Who now controls the adjacent land you had been hoping to claim and develop. Who may restrict the use of land that has come to be regarded as common property of the people in this area. That new neighbor is known as the "Forest Reserve." It is a new type of governmental creature. Created, not by the public will, but by an assertive, perhaps even deceitful, conference committee of Congress. A creature that engulfs vast acreages of land by simple proclamation, nothing more, of the president of the United States.

To some settlers this may have sounded like good news, but to many others it must have sounded like the beginning of hard times. In the vernacular of our day, these people had just been caught in a paradigm shift. It was a sudden and distinct change from the prevailing "land development" paradigm to something new called "conservation."

Land Development

Land had been the key commodity Congress used in its effort to build a diverse and powerful nation. Land had become the trading stock for the development of transcontinental railroads. It was the enticement for immigrants to brave the ocean passage and trek to the edge of the wilderness. To land hungry Europeans, it was their hope for a new life. They were accustomed to population densities that numbered people per hectare. In America the equation was reversed. Here it was square miles per person. Thomas Jefferson expressed the land development paradigm in his statement, "It is too soon yet in our country to say that every man

198

who cannot find employment but who can find uncultivated land shall be at liberty to cultivate it, paying a moderate rent. But it is not too soon to provide by every possible means that as few as possible shall be without a little portion of land. The small land holders are the most precious part of a state."[1]

In 1785 Congress had provided a rectangular land survey system to aid in public land disposal. After surveying, lands could be sold at auction for cash to the highest bidder, but at not less than $1 per acre. The first patent to public land was issued by the government in 1788. Alexander Hamilton, then secretary of the treasury, submitted a plan in 1790 to Congress for the disposal of the public domain. He contemplated the raising of revenue to retire the public debt through the sale of land and the provision of homes for settlers on small tracts of land.[2] Following this, the government made a series of land acquisitions from France, Spain, and Mexico. These acquisitions were followed by land disposal activities primarily designed to raise funds for the federal treasury. Grants of land also began to be made to the states.

To maintain some semblance of order on the public lands, Congress passed legislation (2 Stat. 445) which forbade anyone to settle on or occupy public lands until authorized by law. The president could direct the marshal to remove trespassers and to use military force as necessary.

The Act of September 4, 1841 (5 Stat.453) introduced three unique ideas. Certain states were allowed to share in the revenues from public land sales, states were also to receive 500,000 acres of land as they were admitted to the Union, and a privilege to individuals, known as a "preemption privilege" provided an opportunity for citizens to settle upon and purchase not more than 160 acres of public land at a minimum price of $1.25 per acre. Preemptors had to live on the land, improve the land, confirm that the land was solely for their use, and supply proof of their settlement within one year.

In 1848 James Marshall and John Sutter discovered gold in the Sacramento valley of California. By the spring of 1849, approximately 50,000 people invaded California in search of gold and by the end of the year the number had swelled to 100,000. During the period from 1850 to 1860, similar gold and silver booms occurred in several western states.[3] No formal policy existed to authorize this use of the public lands. Legally, these hordes of people were trespassers under the Act of 1807, but enforcement of governmental interests was virtually impossible.

By 1850 grants of public land were being made to railroads to encourage them to construct new lines. The trespass situation on public lands had reached proportions that merited the appointment of special agents to suppress timber trespass.

In 1862 the Homestead Act (12 Stat. 392) authorized citizens to enter 160 acres of unappropriated public land and secure a free patent if they would reside on or cultivate the land for five years. Or, they could purchase the land at its regular price of $1.25 per acre after a period of only six months following filing (a practice known as "commutation").

It is hard to describe what the homesteading opportunity meant to the people of that day. Arthur Ruhl, writing in *Harper's Magazine*, describes a scene in northern Idaho where Mr. Isadore Selig, a tailor by trade, becomes an instant national celebrity by winning the drawing to have first choice of a homestead. He could look over what to most European immigrants would seem a principality—hundreds of thousands of acres of beautiful timber and lake country—and pick out what pleased him most. He would have to work for it, to be sure; live there for five years, pay the government's fee, and make the slight improvements necessary to "prove up." Otherwise, it was his for the taking.[4]

Also in 1862, Congress made massive grants of land to the Union Pacific and Central Pacific railroads. First granting them the odd numbered sections of non-mineral land for ten miles either side of the railroad line and then extending it to twenty miles either side of the line in 1864. The Northern Pacific Railroad received grants of odd numbered sections in the territories for forty miles each side of the line and twenty miles within states. After completion of the construction of the railroad, any lands remaining were to be sold by preemption to settlers at not more than $1.25 per acre (later raised to $2.50 per acre). The railroads were also required to transport government mail, troops, and supplies at fair and reasonable rates under regulations set by Congress.[5]

The Morrill Act of 1862 provided that each state which had public lands within its boundaries would receive 30,000 acres for each senator and representative from that state. This was for the purpose of establishing a fund for the use of colleges of agriculture and mechanical arts.[6]

By 1866 interest in the development of minerals in the West and the severe trespass problem, led to legislation (14 Stat. 251) which provided that mineral lands of the public domain were open to exploration and occupation by citizens. If the mining claims proved to be valid according to local rules, lode claims could be purchased at $5 per acre. In 1870 placer claims up to 160 acres in size could be purchased for $2.50 per acre.[7]

The General Mining Act of 1872 (17 Stat. 91) recognized mineral lands as a distinct class of public lands and modified the 1866 Act. It codified much of the local mining law and provided for survey and sale of lode and placer claims.[8]

The Timber Culture Act of 1873 (17 Stat. 605) offered 160 acres of land to any citizen who planted 40 acres to trees and kept them growing for a period of ten years. However, a homesteader who could show that 10 acres of trees had been cultivated for a two year period was entitled to receive a patent in lieu of the Homestead Act residence requirement.[9]

The Desert Land Act of 1877 (19 Stat. 377), permitted the sale of 640 acres of nontimber, nonmineral land unfit for cultivation and without irrigation to any settler who would irrigate it within three years after filing. The cost was $.25 per acre at filing and $1.00 per acre at time of final proof.[10]

The Timber and Stone Act (20 Stat. 89) of 1878 provided for the sale of 160 acres of surveyed, nonmineral land that was valuable for timber or stone and unfit for cultivation for not less than $2.50 per acre in the states of California, Oregon, Nevada, and Washington. The act prohibited unlawful cutting or wanton destruction of timber on any public lands. It granted permission to miners and farmers to clear land and use timber for necessary improvements. In 1892 the law was extended to all public land states (27 Stat. 348).[11] Janel M. Curry-Roper (1989) in studying the effects of the act in Minnesota, found a relationship between the volume of Timber and Stone Act entries and the price of timber. In times of low timber prices, entries were occasional, of small size, and were not contiguous with other entries. In times of high timber prices, there was a higher volume of sales, larger sized entries, and the parcels were usually contiguous. The concentration of entries and their relatively large size shows that timberland sales were often speculative at that time. On the day before a township opened, people lined up outside the land office hours before the opening, at times braving sixty mile an hour winds and temperatures of thirty below zero. The purchasers came from all walks of life and in this Minnesota case, most were from towns in the area or nearby population centers.[12]

To say that all of this activity to dispose of the public lands was as noble as Jefferson had envisioned it would be most naive. Railroads didn't build some of the rail lines anticipated, but kept the land. Entrymen would file on a piece of land and immediately relinquish their rights to another for cash, move on and do the same again and again. Or they would live six months on the entry, apply for commutation, get it, and resettle on another entry. At the end of a year, they would own

320 acres. They then might seek a mortgage on the property, receive the cash and abandon the property and move on. People actually turned a six month summer experience on the frontier into lucrative land fraud, got back on the train and went home. Lumbermen practiced wholesale fraud by getting locals to file on property and then quickly sell the land back to the company.[13]

Emory Best, then assistant commissioner of the General Land Office, made a defense for the disposal of the public lands on the basis:

> that a wise and beneficent system has peopled the country with thrifty and energetic settlers, and this is pointed to as one of our greatest achievements.

He estimated that by 1897, about 247,000,000 acres of land had been sold for cash, including commuted homestead entries, for which the government had received about $280,000,000.[14]

By 1891 sufficient evidence of land fraud and destruction of public forest lands existed to cause numerous groups and individuals who were concerned about "conservation" to call for legislation (26 Stat. 1095) which repealed the Preemption Act of 1841 and the Timber Culture Act of 1873. Also included in this legislation were requirements to stop auctions of public lands, to remove commutation from the Homestead Act, to improve the Desert Land Act, and to confine withdrawals for irrigation sites to the lands actually needed. The last provision, Section 24, of this act expressed the new "conservation" paradigm, by empowering the president to set aside, by simple proclamation, public lands covered with timber or under-growth, whether of commercial value or not, as "forest reserves."

A Sudden Introduction to Conservation

It is really a misnomer, but Section 24 is often referred to as the Forest Reserve Act of March 3, 1891.[15] Section 24 was, in fact, added in conference committee without further review by the originating committees. The power of the conservation paradigm, though strongly held by many, had been insufficient to bring about change on its own merits.

Frederick Newell, chief hydrographer, United States Geological Survey, commented on the inclusion of this clause in the legislation.

> If we admit that something should be done to secure the perpetuity of the great public forests, the query at once arises as to what it should be and how

we should go about it. The most direct way would undoubtedly be to at once reserve all forest lands, have them surveyed and examined, appoint suitable men to take charge of them, to protect them from fire, to designate trees that may be cut, and to attend to the details of the utilization and preservation of the tree growth. A system of this kind once fairly under way would unquestionably be more than self-sustaining and would bring to the government a considerable and constantly increasing income, besides furnishing a perpetual supply of timber, protecting the sources of water, and adding to the natural attractions which draw tourists to remote parts of the country. *But such a step involves many radical changes. The people as a whole are not educated up to it.* (emphasis added) Those in the West are afraid of interference in local concerns, and those of the East are fearful lest large expenditures should be incurred. As a compromise, therefore, the friends of forestry have proposed that, instead of taking all the forests, certain specified spots should be designated, and that these should be reserved for forestry purposes in the hope that later some provision might be made for carrying out a system outlined above, and that the system, if it proved efficient, might be extended gradually further and further. *Accordingly, many bills have been introduced into Congress, but have all failed from one cause or another.* At length, after many failures, *a clause was inserted in the Act* (emphasis added).[16]

Ise, Dana, as well as Clawson and Held, all take the position that this hastily added provision was really not understood by Congress or the public. Further, they think that if it had been understood, it would not have had the slightest chance of passage. Steen, however, points out that considerable effort by very knowledgeable and concerned people to establish such authority proceeded the addition of this provision. Notably, the January 11, 1890 "Memorial of the American Association for the Advancement of Science in Behalf of a Proper Forest Policy," which called for immediate action to insure the perpetuity of forest cover on the western mountain ranges to preserve favorable hydrologic conditions. All authors agree that it is unlikely that anyone imagined the impact of this clause on the future of land management in the United States.[17]

On March 30, 1891, President Harrison began the process of implementing the new paradigm by issuing a proclamation establishing the Yellowstone National Park Timber Land Reserve of Wyoming. This was followed by the proclamation establishing the White River Plateau Timber Land Reserve of Colorado on October 16, 1891.[18]

Initially, there was little interest in the forest reserve proclamations. Publication of the proclamations in western newspapers appear as stark copies without journalistic comment or editorials. For example, the reservation of the White River Plateau in Colorado appears in the Washington news column of the Sunday *Denver Republican* just as it was issued, with no introductory remarks or commentary. This curiosity has been explained by Fairfax and Yale who note that, at the time, land reservations were an unfamiliar concept. Neither Congress nor the public was clear about the purpose of the reserves.[19]

It is important to realize that Congress had been busy with the deliberate, methodical process of public land disposal, the attracting of development, and the settlement of the country. The West was now teeming with people who had come to regard the public lands as virtually theirs for the taking. Suddenly, without much grassroots discussion, forest reservations were superimposed over all this activity. Significantly, no one really understood what the probable result would be. Those who generated the idea of the forest reserves must have been confident that the results would be better than the fraud and exploitation which had become so widespread. Even they, however, could not have anticipated all the impacts to settlers and developers of the West who had been encouraged and authorized by Congress to take up and use public land. Thus, when one views the historical opposition to the forest reserves, it should be done with the realization that the sudden establishment of the forest reserves created real problems for basically honest, unsuspecting people.

Harold Langille, an early forest inspector, commented on the situation as he found it in 1902 in the Mt Hood area of Oregon:

> Let us pass up the criminality and moral turpitude of the times: the land fraud cases; the wholesale theft of timber through connivance with supervisors; grand and petty larceny in the allocation of range, flagrant violation of rules and regulations. Not that these conditions, or any of them were to be found in every reserve. They were not. *There were earnest, honest endeavorers doing the best they knew in the absence of coordinative understanding, and these constituted a majority.* (emphasis added)[20]

Problems and Opportunities for Private Landholders

One of the most immediate problems was the interpretation by the secretary of the interior that the reservation of the land meant that no use whatsoever was to be made of it. This very quickly threatened the survival of the forest reserves. Many reserve supporters rushed to correct this misconception. Robert Underwood Johnson in 1894 wrote of a conversation he had with Senator Hearst of California regarding a plan he and John Muir had discussed for reserving the upper Tuolumne:

> When I mentioned the subject to Senator Hearst, he broke out: "Reserve the Tuolumne? Why, I'd favor reserving the whole of the Sierra top from Shasta down. It includes very little agricultural land, the region has been pretty thoroughly prospected and, of course, mining and other private rights would not be interfered with."[21]

B. E. Fernow, writing in *Science* during 1897 as chairman of the American Forestry Association Executive Committee, reviewed the history of the forest reserves and stated:

> In absence of specific legislation the Secretaries of the Interior construed the reservation of these lands as a withdrawal not only from sale and entry, but from all use whatsoever, the Department being powerless to protect or utilize the same. *This was never the intention of the projectors of the forest reservations.* (emphasis added) This sudden withdrawal from use of such a vast area, some of which was occupied by mining and lumbering industries dependent upon wood supplies, created strenuous opposition in the Senate and led to the adoption of a clause in the Sundry Civil Appropriations Bill at once restoring these reservations to the public domain. . . . The bill did not become a law, not being signed by the President.[22]

Extracts from the report of the committee appointed by the National Academy of Sciences, published in *Science*, concurred with Fernow:

> According to a strict interpretation of the rulings of the Department of the Interior, no one has a right to enter a forest reserve, cut a single tree from its forests, or to examine its rocks in search of valuable minerals. Forty million acres of land are thus theoretically shut out from all human occupation or enjoyment. Such a condition of things should not continue, for unless the reserved lands of the public domain are made to contribute to the welfare and prosperity of the country they should be thrown open to settlement and the whole system of reserved forest abandoned. Land more valuable for its mineral deposits, or for the production of agricultural crops, than for its timber should be taken from the reservations and sold to miners and farmers; settlers within or adjacent to the boundaries, unable to procure it in other ways, should be authorized to take such material from reserved forests as is necessary for their needs, and prospectors should be allowed to search them for minerals.[23]

One can see that if this no use interpretation was so frightening to the forest reserve supporters, it certainly would have a sudden, devastating impact on the settlers within the forest reserves. Despite the expressed concern for the preservation of private rights, problems continued to exist for the settlers and this, in turn, brought pressure to gut the reserves.

Problems

Problems for Local Government

The local governmental units of the western states, the counties, were immediately affected by the creation of the forest reserves. When the deeding of government lands was stopped or greatly curtailed by the creation of the reserves, a protest was at once heard from the counties. They were in need of funds for schools, roads, and governmental functions. The people were counting on the settlement of the land to increase the taxable land base. They were pleased to see government timber lands converted into taxable property by whatever means. To meet the objections of the counties, a provision was made to pay them 10 percent of the government receipts from the sale of timber within the county. By 1906 the amount paid to road and school funds of the counties amounted to $75,000.[24]

Problems for Miners

The first serious discussion of the private land problems created by the forest reserves is in a report from the Committee on the Public Lands to the Committee of the Whole House, entitled "Forest Reserves in Colorado." The Committee on Public Lands had reviewed a proposed bill "To open the forest reservations of the State of Colorado for the location of mining claims" and offered a substitute for it. The report included the following discussion:

> The particular reservations . . . are in the mountains of Colorado. . . . They were created by proclamation, upon the petition of the citizens of the State of Colorado, for the purpose of preventing the destruction of shade trees and underbrush in the high mountains, so as to preserve the snows from melting until midsummer, when the water would be most needed for irrigation in the valleys and plains below. Your committee is informed that the people of the State of Colorado would never have petitioned for these reservations if it had been understood that the miner thereby would be excluded from making

mining locations thereon. In one part of these reservations a large number of mining claims have been located and by reason of the impossibility of obtaining title under the present laws a chaotic condition of affairs exists there. Mining claims there are held by the uncertain right of possession only, which causes an unsettled condition of society and greatly retards the development of the mines in the district.[25]

Thus, one of the first concerns was how to perfect title to land within a forest reserve. In this case, the problem was how to carry a foothold interest in a mining claim to patent. A second concern was the whole question of exploration and development of minerals as it had previously been practiced. It is clear that neither of these problems had been envisioned when the proclamations were made. Further, the no use interpretation was regarded seriously enough to produce "An Act to Open Forest Reservations in the State of Colorado for the Location of Mining Claims" (29 Stat. 1) 1896.

Problems for Homesteaders

In 1899 concerns began to surface in the Black Hills Forest Reserve. There, questions about homestead locations made prior to the reservation became an issue. A proposed amendment to the Sundry Appropriations Bill to remedy this problem was referred from the Committee on Appropriations to the General Land Office for review. The apparent purpose of the amendment was to offer relief to persons who settled and improved land prior to the proclamation and prior to the survey of the area.

These people had settled on long narrow stretches of agricultural lands situated along streams with rough mountainous land to either side. The subsequent survey compelled them to take lands by legal subdivisions (aliquot parts) and release some of the land which they had used and improved. This also caused them to embrace large areas within their entries of rough, stony, and worthless character. The effect of the reservation was to prohibit them from refiling on the better agricultural lands which they had believed they were holding. The amendment proposed to permit metes and bounds surveys to incorporate the irregular shape of these lands and to allow new homestead entries upon them. The General Land Office, while noting that this problem existed in the other forest reserves, was concerned that opening the forest reserves to metes and bounds homesteading would only open the reserves to entry by squatters and speculators. It could also open the door to possession of long strips of land along streams which would monopolize water supplies as well as restrict access to other properties. The General Land Office suggested that any legislation should address all forest reserves and the problem might be solved by permitting entry, under these specific circumstances, to contiguous tracts of twenty acres embracing only the lands actually used.[26]

In the June 30, 1901 annual report of the General Land Office (reported in Senate Report No. 212), additional problems for settlers on the forest reserves were identified. The G.L.O. noted that a class of claimants existed who from ignorance, carelessness, and one reason or another, failed to observe the homestead law which required filing of their entries within three months after the survey had been completed and the township plat had been placed in the local land office.

Their entries were, therefore, cut off as a result of the proclamation. It actually served as an adverse claim to their entry. In cases on appeal for adjudication, it had been held that the claimant who failed to assert his claim within the statutory period could get no relief through executive action. In many cases, this was a very serious hardship for settlers who had made bona fide entries and spent years of labor, improvement, and cultivation. The General Land Office stated:

> there are honest settlers who have devoted years of toil and hardship to the establishment of homes, whose claims have been embraced in forest reserves unknown to them, and who, through ignorance or a misunderstanding of the requirements of the law, or of inability to obtain information promptly in remote localities, have failed to get their claims of record within the required period. These people ought not to be allowed to suffer because of the necessarily strict construction of proclamations creating the reserves, and some relief should be afforded them.[27]

The situation cited above and the plight of the settlers in the Black Hills were joined together in a Committee on Public Lands report:

> As a rule these were old time settlers many of them having made their homes upon their claims for from fifteen to twenty years and having made valuable improvements upon them. And these improvements are, practically, all that they possess representing the labor and accumulation of years. This bill is designed to relieve a most worthy class of settlers, whose cases come entirely within the spirit of our settlement laws. By reason of conditions for which they are not justly responsible, they have been deprived of an opportunity to enter their lands. In many instances these are the pioneer settlers who have braved the dangers and hardships of life upon our frontiers to establish a home for themselves and their families. It would be in the nature of a public as well as a private calamity to deprive them of their homes.[28]

The committee then offered a bill for the relief of bona fide settlers in forest reserves.

Problems like these had become so significant that in 1904 the House Committee on Public Lands considered a bill for the entry of agricultural lands in forest reserves. This bill and others like it were implicit threats to the forest reserves in that widespread entries could undermine the intent of the reserves and leave them with only symbolic status. A House report stated: "The purpose of the forest reserves is that they should be for the benefit of the people. As far as possible they should be so managed as not to unnecessarily interfere with the settlement of any region where they are located. This bill was drawn with a view to permitting the occupation under the homestead law of such tracts as are chiefly available for agriculture and yet necessarily surrounded by the forest reserves." This bill, again, included the idea of a metes and bounds survey to cover irregularly shaped areas of agricultural lands.[29]

In 1906 Mr. Clark of Wyoming, from the Senate Committee on Public Lands, submitted a report on a bill to extend the provisions of homestead laws to certain lands in the Yellowstone Forest Reserve. Apparently settlers in the valley of the Shoshone River had experienced problems similar to settlers elsewhere in the forest reserves.[30]

After further work by the Committee on Public Lands, the Forest Homestead Act of June 11, 1906 (34 Stat. 233) authorized the secretary of agriculture to open for entry, through the secretary of the interior, forest reserve lands chiefly valuable for agriculture which were not needed for public purposes and which in his judgement might be occupied without injury to the forest.[31]

To comply with this act, a large program of land classification became necessary. Hundreds of small forest homesteads, referred to as "June 11ths," were surveyed and opened to entry. The surveys were by metes and bounds and no stands of merchantable timber were included, as had been the case in thousands of previous homesteads. The worth of most of the lands opened to entry for growing crops was negligible, and a large number of the claims, as soon as patented were sold and used for pastures.[32]

Thus, the forest reserves barely escaped being gutted. It is quite easy to imagine how the wording of the act and its interpretation could have reduced the reserves to one large agricultural "pasture" and opened these areas to widespread entry.

Grazing Problems

For nearly 100 years, people in the West had allowed their stock to graze freely on the public domain. In fact it became a custom for persons to make a business of gathering herds of cattle or sheep, raising them, and fattening them for market upon the unenclosed lands of the government of the United States. In 1890 the Supreme Court of the United States held in Buford v. Houtz (133 U.S. 320) within the territory of Utah that an implied license to graze the public domain had arisen and no one was bound to keep their cattle confined within their own land. The court recognized that keeping stock confined within private lands was ill-adapted to the nature and condition of the country at that time, since there was a scarcity of means for enclosing lands and there was such great value of the use of the public domain for pasturage. If, on the other hand, a person cultivated their lands and did not want stock grazing on it, it was then the duty of that person to fence their lands against the stock.[33]

This practice continued within the forest reserves after their withdrawal by proclamation. In 1908 Shannon v. U.S. (160 F.870) was brought before the Ninth Circuit Court of Appeals for the District of Montana. In this case, the court held that the implied license to pasture on the public domain had been terminated by inclusion of the land in the Little Belt Mountains Forest Reserve. The court viewed this as an appropriation of the implied license by the federal government. Further, the court held that the secretary of agriculture was vested with authority to establish rules and regulations for the administration of these areas and that the states could not restrict that authority by state legislation.[34]

This question appeared again in 1911 before the Supreme Court, in Light v. U.S. (220 U.S. 523), which was a Colorado case occurring within the Holy Cross Forest Reserve. The general rule in operation within this forest reserve was that "all persons must secure permits before grazing any stock in a national forest." In this case, Mr. Light would turn his cattle loose on his property and they would then wander across the public domain and onto the forest reserve which, because it had fewer stock grazing had superior grass and water. When notified to remove his cattle, he declined to do so and threatened to resist if they were driven off by a forest officer. He justified his position on the ground that Colorado statutes provided that a landowner could not recover damages for trespass by animals unless the property was enclosed with a fence of designated size and material. He claimed that unless the government put a fence around the reserve, it had no remedy.

He further contended that Congress could not constitutionally withdraw large bodies of land from settlement without the consent of the state where the land is located. Thus, he argued that the Act of 1891 was invalid and the area of the reserve should be treated in the same way as the public domain, specifically that an implied license to graze stock existed. This part of the case, the constitutional status of the forest reserves, had been developed by the Colorado state attorney. The state joined with Mr. Light to test the authority of the federal government over state rights and law in cases involving public lands and the forest reserves.

The court stated, "the Nation is an owner, and has made Congress the principal agent to dispose of its property." It cited several previous cases which established the power of Congress to determine the conditions for the disposal and use of the public lands. It pointed out that Section 3, Article IV of the constitution stated, "Congress shall have the power to dispose of and make all needful rules and regulations respecting the territory or the property belonging to the United States," which was at least, a grant of power to control the property of the United States.

The court noted that fence laws of a state do not authorize wanton or willful trespass or afford immunity to those who loose their cattle with the intention that they graze on the lands of another. It believed that Mr. Light's actions were such that it was the equivalent of driving his cattle onto the forest reserve with malicious intent. It held that he was properly enjoined from doing so by the lower court. This made it unnecessary to consider if the United States is required to fence its property, or the other constitutional questions involved.[35]

From these cases then, several key points were established. First, that with the proclamation of a forest reserve the implied license to graze these areas ceased. Second, the government had the power to regulate the use of these lands. Third, the forest reserve lands did not have to be fenced against trespassing stock from private lands or the public domain. And finally, that permitted stock within the forest reserve would have to be fenced out of private lands if the land owner did wish to have the stock grazing his lands (based on the State fence law).[36]

Even though the forest reserves had prevailed in these cases, that did not mean that the public readily accepted these ideas. The *Denver Republican* of May 2, 1911 carried a headline, "FOREST RESERVE BATTLE IS LOST," LIGHT CASE WON BY THE GOVERNMENT, COLORADO BEATEN WHEN FEDERAL SUPREME COURT DECIDES UNITED STATES ALONE HAS POWER OVER PUBLIC LANDS.[37] The next day the *Denver Republican* commented on the decision in the Light case: "Monday afternoon the champions of arbitrary federal control in respect to the national forests and the federal lands in general were filled with glee over a report that the supreme court of the United States had decided in the Light case that the fencing law of Colorado was null and void and as worthless as so much waste paper so far as the forest reserves where concerned." The paper went on to castigate those conducting the case and to defend Colorado's rights in the public lands particularly in respect to water.[38]

If an immigrant's background brought him from an area where sheep grazing had been his way of life, he hardly had any support among those promoting the reserves. Division of Forestry chief Fernow had stated more than a decade earlier:

> There is one industry, and one only, that finds no consideration in this policy. It is that of the sheep herder. Not that his business is considered illegitimate as such, but, carried on as it has been, it is incompatible with all the other interests which the forest may subserve. . . . Just as the proverbial incompatibility of goat and garden, so the growing of wool and wood on the same ground is incompatible.[39]

Nuisance Problems

There was also the possibility that general nuisance problems could arise when private property was adjacent to public forest lands. For example, if some one discovered valuable minerals adjacent to your property, you were apt to suffer the nuisances of blasting, noise, dust, water pollution, or increased traffic. As esthetic values became more important this might also include unsightly scars on the landscape. Holes in the earth, created by mining activity, might trap livestock legally grazing on the forest. Until the Multiple Use Mining Act of July 23, 1955 (P.L. 167) was passed, individuals who really did not intend to mine might use the mining laws to establish a summer home or fence off portions of the forest for their use, thus denying those areas to more legitimate users.

Problems Created by Intruding Pieces of National Forest Land

Lastly, there was the problem of how to obtain title to forest land which intruded into private property. For example, if two mining patents lay side by side, but had a small strip of forest between them, that area of forest reserve was subject to all the rules, regulations, and public privileges as was any other area of the reserve. No administrative mechanism existed to provide for the disposal of such small tracts to the private landowner, and a special private act of Congress was required until the passage of the Small Tracts Act of 1983. In the meantime, a special use permit was required from the Forest Service to legitimize use of these small areas and this was usually accompanied by a fee.

Problems for Railroads

Prior to 1888, the Arizona Mineral Belt Railroad Company was organized to construct a railroad from Flagstaff to Globe, Arizona. Thirty-five miles of the road was constructed when it was sold out, under a foreclosure. After the foreclosure it was reorganized under the laws of the Arizona Territory and started to complete the road. A change in plans, however, resulted in a decision to entirely change the course of the road to better serve Jerome, Camp Verde, and the Verde valley. In the meantime, however, the San Francisco Forest Reserve was created in 1898. The railroad sought a special act of Congress to give it a right of way over the forest reserve. A Senate report noted, "The only hindrance to the building of the road is the failure of the company to have a right of way over said reserve, which can be had only by a special act of Congress."[40]

Opportunities

While it is important to recognize that the withdrawal of the forest reserves resulted in serious problems for private landholders, it is just as important to identify a number of opportunities and benefits that accrued to them. As the forest reserves were patrolled for fires, settlers received some benefit in the form of aid and protection from wildfires. This became more significant through the years as fire prevention and suppression cooperation between the federal government and the states increased. After regulations for the reserves had been developed, settlers had the opportunity, under permit and without charge, to use timber from the adjacent forest lands for their own use. If they wished to purchase timber for manufacturing of products or to sell to others, they could purchase a permit for commercial cutting.

Settlers could obtain a grazing permit for a fee, which allowed them to graze a specified number of stock for a certain period on a defined area of the forest. Although this probably reduced the number of stock they would have liked to graze, there was possibly a greater value in not having to compete with other grazers for the available forage, as was common on the public domain. For example, ranchers in the public domain adjacent to the Park Range Forest Reserve near Craig, Colorado, passed resolutions to petition Congress to extend the boundaries of the reserve to "give us a protected range and to make it possible for us to maintain our homes by making our ranches profitable again." In this case, a few large non-resident cattle outfits had overcrowded the range and had so dominated it that the small man could not run cattle at a profit.[41]

The protection from fire and the management of forest and range resulted in pure, consistent water supplies of benefit to the settler and his stock. For some, the construction of roads into the forest by the government brought improved access to their property as tourism became more popular, settlers could provide lodging and services to tourists, who tended to use the forest areas for fishing, hunting, and related activities. Since state game laws were often enforced by the forest rangers, some benefit accrued in reduced poaching of valuable game.

In more recent years, private land values within the forests have increased since the owners had the benefit of using adjacent public lands for recreational pursuits. Thus, increasing the "effective" size of their holdings by the presence of nearby open space areas.

If, after the above opportunities had been weighed against the problems and the settler was unsatisfied with his ownership within the forest reserve, there was a final remedy. He could, under the 1897 Forest Lieu Selection Provision (repealed in 1905), relinquish the entry and select an equal acreage of vacant unreserved public domain outside the forest reserve.

Whether opportunities outweighed problems for those who stayed is problematical. What should be noted is that private rights within the reserves were the forces that actually defined the nature of the forest reserves. Perhaps the most amazing aspect of this story is that the national forests *and* the private lands within them *both* continue to coexist. One can easily see that on several occasions either could have led to the demise of the other. It seems likely that this interplay of private rights and public good will continue to define the role of national forests with the inholdings. Can they continue to live together in the future?

Footnotes

1. Thomas Jefferson, "Letter to James Madison, 1785," quoted in *The People's Land*, p. 3, Edited by Peter Barnes (Pennsylvania: Rodale Press, 1975).

2. Emory F. Best, "The Utilization of the Vacant Public Lands," *The National Geographic Magazine* 3:1 (January 1897): pp. 49-57.

3. Joseph M. Petulla, *American Environmental History* (San Francisco: Boyd & Fraser, 1977), pp. 157-159 mining, 176-178 land speculation, 266-276 forest reservations.

4. Arthur Ruhl, "What Happens to Pioneers," *Harper's Magazine* 145:866 (July 1922): p. 137.

5. Samuel Trask Dana, *Forest and Range Policy, Its Development in the United States* (New York: McGraw-Hill, 1956), pp. 372-425.

5. Samuel Trask Dana, *Forest and Range Policy, Its Development in the United States* (New York: McGraw-Hill, 1956), pp. 372-425.

6. Ibid.

7. Ibid.

8. Ibid.

9. Ibid.

10. Ibid.

11. Ibid.

12. Janel M. Curry-Roper, "The Impact of the Timber and Stone Act on Public Land Ownership in Northern Minnesota," *Journal of Forest History* (April 1989): pp. 70-79.

13. Seth K. Humphrey, "What is the Matter With Our Land Laws?" *The Atlantic Monthly* 102:1 (July 1908): pp. 1-9.

14. Best, "The Utilization of Vacant Public Lands," p. 50.

15. Dana, *Forest and Range Policy*, p. 100.

16. Frederick H. Newell, "The National Forest Reserves," *The National Geographic Magazine* 8:6 (June 1897): p. 185.

17. John Ise, *United States Forest Policy* (New Haven: Yale University Press, 1920), p. 117; Dana, *Forest and Range Policy*, p. 101; Marion Clawson and Burnell Held, *The Federal Lands* (Baltimore: John Hopkins, 1957), p. 28; Harold K. Steen, *The U. S. Forest Service: A History* (Univ. of Washington Press, 1976), pp. 26-27; Memorial of the American Association for the Advancement of Science In Behalf of a Proper Forest Policy, Message from the President of the United States, Executive Document 36, Jan. 20, 1890.

18. Len Shoemaker, "Forest and Range Conservation Also the National Forests," unpublished article, November 15, 1966, Western History Department, Denver Public Library, Denver, Colorado, p. 46.

19. "The Denver Republican," October 18, 1891; Sally K. Fairfax and Carolyn E. Yale, *Federal Lands* (Washington, D.C.: Island Press, 1987), p. 17.

20. Harold D. Langille, "Mostly Division `R' Days," *Oregon Historical Quarterly* 57:4 (December 1956): pp. 301-313.

21. Robert Underwood Johnson, "Why Not More Forest Preserves?" *The Review of Reviews*, December, 1894. pp. 651-653.

22. B. E. Fernow, "The Forest Reservation Policy," *Science* (March 26, 1897): pp. 399-493

23. "Forest Policy for the Forested Lands of the United States," extracts from the report of the committee appointed by the National Academy of Sciences, published in *Science*, June 11, 1897, pp. 893-900.

24. Guy La Follette, "The National Forests, As They Appear To The People Who Live In Them," *Overland Monthly*, Vol. 58, October 1911, pp. 284-286.

25. House of Representatives Report No. 152, "Forest Reservations In Colorado," 54 Congress 1st Session, 1896.

26. Senate Document No. 94, "Black Hills Forest Reservation," 55th Congress 3d Session, 1899.

27. Senate Report No. 212, "Settlers in Forest Reserves," 57th Congress 1st Session, 1902.

28. Senate Report No. 860, "Settlers on Forest Reservations," 57th Congress 1st Session, 1902 .

29. House of Representatives Report No. 2078, "Entry of Agricultural Lands in Forest Reserves," 58th Congress 2d Session, 1904.

30. Senate Report No. 1412, "Extending Provisions of Homestead Laws to Certain Lands in Yellowstone Forest Reserve," 59th Congress 1st Session, 1906.

31. Senate Report No. 3291, "Entry of Agricultural Lands Within Forest Reserves," 59th Congress 1st Session, 1906.

32. Shoemaker, "Forest and Range Conservation Also The National Forests," p. 17.

33. Forest Service, USDA, "Court Cases Related to Administration of the Range Resource on Lands Administered by the Forest Service. " Washington, D.C. August 1964.

34. Ibid..

35. Ibid..

36. Ibid..

37. *The Denver Republican*, May 2, 1911.

38. *The Denver Republican*, May 3, 1911.

39. Fernow, "The Forest Reservation Policy," p. 403.

40. Senate Report No. 706, "Right of Way Through the San Francisco Mountains Forest Reserve," 57th Congress 1st. Session, 1902.

41. J. L. Ellis, "Turning National Forests Into Homesteads," *The World Today*, Vol. 16 No. 6, pp. 636-640, June 1909

The Cooperation Imperative: Relationships Between Early Forest Administration and the Southern California Metropolis, 1892-1908

Donn E. Headley
Angeles National Forest

In the years just prior to the turn of the twentieth century, Americans faced serious and severe changes in the political structure of their government. After the watershed election of 1896, both the public at large and the intellectual elite became increasingly disenchanted with the traditional political process. In the years 1897 to 1904, the American public became increasingly aware of and alarmed by impressions "that society's diverse producer groups did not exist in harmony or share equally in government benefits, and that private interests posed a danger to the public's interests."[1]

Spurred by this awareness and alarm, Progressives successfully instituted changes designed to check the dangerous alliance between big business and political parties. Regulatory boards, electoral and campaign reforms passed in state after state from 1903 to 1908; alterations in the land use and distribution system also occurred at this time, culminating in the early conservation movement.[2] In Southern California, this period of "experimentation and uncertainty" made itself manifest in calls for conservation of public lands, the rise of professional forestry on local reserves, and the consolidation of a coalition between officials and corporate interests that mirrored, in many ways, the larger Progressive conservation movement and which would influence regional affairs for decades to come.[3]

At this time in the Los Angeles basin, elites successfully enlisted the aid of a nascent but rapidly evolving federal bureaucracy in order to further legitimize their interests and empower their members in an effort to guide the political system. In this crucial period, representatives of federal forestry became linked to a sub-governmental system that operated not with the supervision of Washington, but in effect answered to the seats of corporate and industrial power, namely New York and Chicago, working through their contacts in Los Angeles.

Just as importantly, with the lack of a substantial national policy that could direct forestry officials in applying a federal system to local conditions, forest lands in

Southern California increasingly came under the influence of interests that sought to develop them for their own purposes, which usually meant the exploitation of the natural resources in order to further urban growth and development. This process dictated conservation policy in the years 1897-1908, as the interests and officials cooperated to devise workable programs for fire prevention and suppression, land use, recreation, and watershed management in the San Gabriel Mountains.

Representing a region that early and readily embraced federal management of its forests, the civic leaders, industrialists, financiers, and developers of Southern California facilitated a remarkably rapid growth in the Los Angeles basin.[4] In this semi-arid land in the years prior to the construction of the Owens Valley Aqueduct (completed in 1913), just about everyone agreed that the future of the community depended upon the health of the watersheds in the mountains above. But protecting those watersheds presented a formidable problem. On one hand, private interests and local communities lacked the legal authority to supervise an area of land that, in the San Gabriel Mountains, embraced over half a million acres. On the other, the federal government lacked both the funding and the personnel to adequately perform the legislative mandate of preventing fires, protecting watersheds, apprehending and prosecuting trespassers, supervising campers, and mediating between the various user-groups.[5]

As this paper proposes to demonstrate, the alliance between civic groups and federal forestry arose, albeit haltingly and unevenly, first out of the negligible, even neglectful supervision under the jurisdiction of the General Land Office (1892-1905), and then out of a spirit of common purpose and amenable philosophies toward land use between professional foresters such as Gifford Pinchot and urban-centered organizations (1905-08, and beyond). In Southern California, forest officials and representatives of user interests, such as land, mining, water, and hydro-electric companies, as well as foothill cities, forged what might be termed a cooperation imperative that provided the expertise (from federal forestry), the manpower (from the users), and funding (from both). This cooperation forged an administrative system even before the arrival of the Forest Service in 1905.

Unofficially from 1897 to 1905, and officially in the years following, Pinchot's decentralized system, driven as much by economic necessity and primitive communications as by any cohesive philosophy or set of standards, actually forced the continued dependence of on-the-ground officials in the forest reserves upon local businesses and industries for the funding and manpower necessary to implement their programs of fire protection and reserve improvement. The cooperation imperative, developed by the first San Gabriel Reserve supervisors, had its liabilities as well as its advantages however, for although reserve programs often received enough funding to be instituted, policy also became tied, for the long term, to the interests and purposes of the urban-based companies. In the San Gabriel Timberland Reserve, this process was more rapid, more visible and had greater significance for the future since the public lands lay so close to the growing urban centers and also possessed the natural resources that those communities saw as vital to their continued growth and development.[6]

Students of this period continue to debate the depth of Progressive convictions and the significance of their achievements. Did the Progressives actually strengthen democratization in the United States, or did they put forth their programs as representatives of one elite battling another? The work of political scientists and historians of Progressive politics offer the best models for beginning to understand the phenomena of early forest administration in Southern California as well as the significance and ramifications of the cooperation imperative. These scholars attempted to explain politics and power in the United States at the end of the nineteenth century and how the governmental system changed in the Progressive period. The models they constructed to interpret these events, whether called "neo-pluralism," "interest-group liberalism," or "corporate liberalism," pointed out that the more government in this period changed, the more politics and the sectors of power in the nation remained, in effect, unchanged, even unchallenged. If anything, a new, technologically innovative elite merely replaced an older one.[7]

In *Private Power and American Democracy*, Grant McConnell presented one of the earliest attempts, along with Samuel Hays' *Conservation and the Gospel of Efficiency*, to place conservation in the Progressive tradition. As McConnell argues, "the conservation movement was characteristically Progressive; its policy was no more than Progressive policy in the field of natural resources." The administration of the forest reserves, indeed federally managed conservation itself, came at a time when the authority of the state began to combine with the "informal and social power" of private groups, a process McConnell called neo-pluralism. This informality resulted in the establishment and eventual entrenchment of sub-legal forms of power that exerted considerable influence on the political and economic affairs of the nation.[8] Progressive legislation allowed these private groups to extend their power until they eventually evolved into varieties of sub-governments.

Shortly thereafter, Theodore Lowi helped explain that breakdown between private and public sectors at the end of the nineteenth century with his concept of interest-group liberalism. He maintained that this breakdown occurred not due to increased public power but due to the appropriation of governmental jurisdictions by private interests. More recently, Jeffrey Lustig effectively demonstrated that the Progressive era merely served to codify corporate liberalism and legitimize its aims, making its agenda that of the federal government's. Samuel Hays, Robert Wiebe, and the organizational school held that, on a national level, big business and the most powerful associations and institutions set the agenda for politics at the end of the nineteenth century. More cogent to our discussion, such corporations, especially those, according to Hays, coalescing around science, technology, and scientific research and pursuing current ideas of efficiency, defined the debates over conservation.[9]

These explanations, however, fall short of explaining the linkage between the public land and public power in turn-of-the-century Southern California. Such scholars, concentrating on events in the capital and in other command centers of the nation, explained *what* happened in the process of this appropriation of power by an American elite, but they did little to explain, specifically with local political systems in mind, *how* it happened. The case study of forest administration in the San Gabriel Mountains of Southern California illuminates the process whereby interest groups formed, consolidated, and gained a foothold in the administration of public lands for their own benefit and profit.

The Forest Reserve Act, passed in 1891, symbolized an early phase in the transition in American public policy when the federal government slowed its distribution of public land and resources and began to withhold and administer them.[10] But beyond the act and formation of the reserves soon after, neither Congress nor the president at first made any provision to supervise and protect the lands they set aside from the very abuses that made their preservation worthy of congressional action.[11] Between 1892, when President Benjamin Harrison established the San Gabriel Timberland Reserve, and 1897, those business and civic interests who had worked so hard to have Southern California lands withheld had complained of the lack of supervision, pointing out continued violations of federal rules and regulations, especially regarding sheep grazing.[12] As early as 1897, the Los Angeles Chamber of Commerce created a fire-prevention committee to supervise reserve lands.[13] Fires in those years had underscored the need for a professional force to administer the public domain.[14] Then, in 1897, when the Sundry Civil Appropriations Bill authorized the secretary of the interior to "make rules and regulations for the protection of the reserves," Congress created the basis for an administrative structure.[15]

In that year, the General Land Office, an agency of the U.S. Department of the Interior, assigned Colonel B.F. Allen, a banker and realtor from Iowa well-versed in land law, to Southern California as Special Forest Agent and Supervisor for the "Western District"—California and Arizona—with headquarters in Los Angeles.

As a newly arrived member of the community, he hoped to demonstrate "to the parties living in the vicinity the policy the Interior Department proposes to make for the care and management of the forest reserves—and at the same time urge upon them the necessity of every one interested giving their personal attention to the danger of fire. . . ." His primary task, then, rested in distributing forest information from the General Land Office to local newspapers and landowners, and notifying the public of the onset of the fire season.[16]

Soon after his arrival, Allen discovered the foundations for cooperative work between his office and private groups already in place. To accomplish his mandate, he knew he had to garner such cooperative relationships. Without men and having little funding, he saw the solution in sharing the expenses of forest management. At first, however, what authority Allen possessed seemed more intended to placate local interests than actually to effect change in reserve administration, because his powers extended slightly beyond his vague orders to enforce General Land Office policy. Eight months after assuming his duties, he could respond to a job request only by stating: "At present I have no authority to employ any one." Even though officials in Washington and civic leaders in Southern California agreed that "during the summer months it will be necessary to have a force of mounted patrollmen [sic] for fire protection . . . ," Allen admitted that he could do nothing to establish such a force, without which fire protection in the Southern California reserves could not progress far.[17]

In response, local water companies led the way in supporting Allen's fire prevention efforts. Allen arrived in the third year of a decade-long drought, and in 1897 he found them "all willing and anxious to cooperate with the U.S. in doing all they can for the prevention and stoppage of fires and timber trespass."[18] These organizations owned land and supply facilities in the mountains and usually had men living at or near the waterworks in order to guard and maintain them. They found it to their advantage to assist in preventing fires in the reserves and watching out for other abuses. For foresters, such companies built and kept roads that eased access to trouble-spots, and some had telegraph or telephone lines that sped the reporting of fires or trespass violations.[19] In the same year, the Los Angeles Chamber of Commerce created a cooperative committee to work with federal foresters to enhance fire protection; this body furthered cooperation in the region for the next ten years.[20]

In July 1898 the General Land Office authorized Allen to hire twenty rangers for his district specifically assigned to fire protection. His two initial appointments to the San Gabriel Reserve became the first rangers assigned to any reserve in the nation. Two years later Superintendent Allen petitioned the General Land Office for funds to begin building ranger stations around the reserve to house his men and their supplies. Washington allocated him one hundred dollars, enough to build a station on the West Fork of the San Gabriel River.[21]

The first San Gabriel rangers served primarily as agents of fire protection, detection, and suppression, working full-time at these tasks in the summer. Year-round rangers had to wait until late fall to do other jobs such as cutting trails and building fire-breaks. When he could, Allen used legal recourse to prosecute violations of fire regulations, for which he received substantial support from state and local officials.[22]

Simultaneously, foresters in Washington began hammering out a national forest policy. The General Land Office's special service division, a forerunner of the Division R formed in 1901, issued a set of rules and regulations in June of 1897. Filibert Roth took charge of this division, assisted by five men from the Bureau of Forestry in the Department of Agriculture. Gifford Pinchot eventually seized this chance to guide forest administration. As one historian has stated, "Pinchot saw Division R as an opportunity to manage the reserves without being held directly responsible."[23]

Under the new division, administrative structure consisted of an inspector in charge of all reserves, a superintendent for each state and territory possessing reserves, a supervisor for each reserve, and a patrol force of rangers or guards. At first, officials stressed a tightly controlled system based on inspections and written reports, with personnel to notify their superiors of all movements. Despite the inspections, the division passed down no comprehensive set of guidelines or policies to direct administrators in how to deal with land use problems, and possessing sporadic and constrained funding, the power of supervisors "was . . . quite limited." Beginning in 1901, possibly with prompting by Pinchot, Division R allocated more responsibilities to supervisors, giving them "more power and permanence."[24] This decentralization of control not only helped stretch the thin resources of federal funds, but it helped foster an *esprit de corps* that attracted competent foresters and professionalized the service.

On the San Gabriel Reserve, unlike many areas in the West, most of the early rangers proved of outstanding merit and capability.[25] The ability of the early supervisors to find and keep such accomplished men placed the day-to-day affairs of the reserve in extremely proficient hands in a period of extreme uncertainty. Everett B. Thomas relieved W.A. Border as supervisor of the San Gabriel Reserve on March 1, 1901 and, upon assuming office, he immediately dismissed as unjustified the criticism recently heaped upon the agency in the wake of disastrous fires that plagued Southern California from 1898 to 1900. By the middle of 1902, however, he commended himself on bringing the Bureau of Forestry back into the good graces of the local community: "I find a keen interest taken in reserve affairs and almost everywhere a friendly feeling is shown."[26] With greater public favor, Thomas found that cooperation came easier. In these years, the role of the reserve in Southern California increased.

A 1901 event illustrated the lengths that Southern California forestry officials would go to forge alliances with influential citizens. In that year, both Western District Superintendent Allen and Supervisor Thomas endorsed the application received from two prominent gentlemen from Los Angeles, the banker Charles S. Forman and wealthy lumberman and developer William G. Kerckhoff. As directors of the Kern Power Company, the two men applied to build a four-mile wagon road on the Kern River in Southern California that made travel to the company's plant facilities faster and more comfortable. In a letter to Sierra Forest Reserve Supervisor Charles Newhall, Thomas vouched for the applicants due to their prominence in local conservation efforts:

> Gen. Forman has taken an active interest in the work of forest protection and in carrying out his company's plans I am sure that the interests of the Reserve will be carefully guarded. . . . Any courtesy that you can extend to him will be appreciated by him and by Superintendent Allen and myself.[27]

Kerckhoff and Forman's company planned to construct power facilities utilizing Kern River water, building the road and using trees from the reserve for power-transmission poles. Thomas urged Newhall to allow the project and "assist them in obtaining a permit for timber required." As leaders in both the business community and in forest preservation organizations, Kerckhoff and Forman stood for their corporation's integrity and stability: "any company which [Mr. Kerckhoff] represents will guard the interests of the reserves." In adding a significant parenthetical aside, Thomas dropped two names of influence: "Mr. Kerckhoff is a close friend of Mr. Hermann's [General Land Office commissioner] and of Gifford Pinchot."[28]

Even following the hiring of rangers, private citizens continued to carry a large share of the burden of fire control in the region, as well as detecting and punishing trespassers. Auxiliary fire brigades from the foothill cities, often formed through the efforts of local water companies, also lent vital assistance. Groups in Ontario and North Ontario, for instance, gained the cooperation of local businessmen; brigade members served through "agreement with their employers who have promised to allow their men to [fight fires] and then return to their positions after the fire is out." In addition, many of the early rangers came from the foothill cities and had gained their familiarity for the San Gabriels through a combination of fire-prevention work and recreational activity. Protective associations, water and land companies also funded support. Supervisor Thomas traveled extensively to local communities to lecture on forest concerns, usually fire control. In the spring of 1901 alone, he addressed the Pomona Board of Trade, the Pomona Farmers' Club, the directors of the Pasadena Board of Trade, and the San Dimas Farmers' Club. Thomas also worked hard to assist the foothill communities in developing their own voluntary fire brigades.[29]

In March 1903 Thomas submitted a summary of complaints regarding General Land Office policies in a long letter to Commissioner Hermann, in which he reiterated his concerns about the close proximity of a large population and highly valued agriculture and industry. The recent drought had intensified the need to protect the public and their welfare, especially the watersheds. The reserves, he stated frankly, held the very future of the region within their mountains: "There is no other section in the United States of a like area and population where the question of water supply is so important or where water and land values are as great. There is no other section containing as large a population with as large an area of highly cultivated land which derives its water supply from such a limited watershed as does this section. . . . Whether the watersheds of these two reserves are thoroughly protected or not effects not only the present wellfare [sic] of this section but it has a very vital bearing on its future growth and prosperity."[30] The Southern California conservationists and community leaders interested in urban growth would have heartily endorsed this sentiment.

After 1902 Gifford Pinchot, with the backing of President Theodore Roosevelt, played an increased role in national administration. He strove to coordinate the conservation policies of the Roosevelt administration with the overarching concept of Herbert Croly's New Nationalism, which sought to strengthen national govern-ment in order to spur local entrepreneurship. Croly had criticized the nation's political party system as too constraining and ineffective. The parties, in his mind, only intruded between the public and its government, making for the inefficiencies so apparent by 1905. Federal agencies would bring efficiency to government, and Pinchot's Bureau of Forestry represented this new breed of scientifically managed department.[31]

The years of 1901-1905 brought a period of experimentation in administrative techniques. Originally, Pinchot's decentralized system revolved around forest reserves loosely administered from Washington, professionalization of the workforce, and nationalized and "impersonal" management guided by scientific principles. The first phase of the institution of this system culminated in the transfer of the reserves from the Department of the Interior and the General Land Office to the Department of Agriculture and Pinchot's Bureau of Forestry in July 1905. As Hays demonstrated, the transfer ended thirteen years of conflict over the purpose and use of the forest reserves and "represented the victory for the development point of view in the Roosevelt administration."[32]

The transfer of the forest reserves into the jurisdiction of Pinchot's Bureau of Forestry also continued the release of the public lands to the influence of local interests. Following the corrupt but highly possessive system of administration under that of the General Land Office, the reserves now fell under a decentralized administration where local officials and corporations gained greater autonomy in the construction and conduct of reserve policy. As set up by Gifford Pinchot, national policy guided local resource development. However, his emphasis upon long-term land-use permits virtually guaranteed that local interests and their needs would take precedence in power and profit over national priorities and federal policies.

In the wake of a graft scandal that led to the dismissal of Everett Thomas as supervisor in September 1905, the young, aggressive Rush H. Charlton assumed the office he would hold for the next two decades, eager to implement Pinchot's ideas to administration on the San Gabriel Reserve.[33] At the same time, local resource development as dictated by alliances between agency officials and regional corporations became codified in the *Use Book*, the Forest Service's official management handbook issued in 1905. One of the most telling of the *Use Book*'s passages states:

> In the management of each reserve local questions will be decided upon local grounds; the dominant industry will be considered first, but with as little restriction to minor industries as may be possible . . . and where conflicting interests must be reconciled the question will always be decided from the standpoint of the greatest good of the greatest number in the long run.[34]

Who recognized, or at least, who defined this "highest good"? In Southern California, a close-knit working organization that included local business interests and federal administrators on local lands came together to devise priorities for management. These priorities most often translated into a pro-development, pro-urban, corporativist, and elitist policy of public lands administration.[35]

As Grant McConnell has shown, the lack of standards for directing and testing policies, since the *Use Book* did not address their implementation save for the vague "highest good" principle, gave the infant Forest Service little guidance to devise a national administration system.[36] In Southern California, this meant that local elites and corporations co-opted the administration of the public land for their own requirements. Their system, in effect, became the official policy of the Forest Service as applied to the San Gabriel Mountains.

In such capacities, San Gabriel officials not only assisted the companies using the water, but the cities they served as well. The Los Angeles and San Gabriel rivers, as well as countless smaller creeks, served a rapidly growing population and served as principal sources of supply for both domestic and agricultural uses in this period. In effect, the federal government served as steward over urban-based and industrially-developed commodities.[37] By the late nineteenth century, for example, small mining operations had given way to larger concerns, and these consistently received permission to develop the lands in the mountains. Forest officials supported their work if it assisted them in their policies and goals. Roads that companies built to bring supplies and workers to the excavations also helped rangers get to fires and patrol their districts. Administrators believed that they could depend more on the larger and better-financed companies, those more likely to continue their activities in the mountains, maintaining trails and roads, and providing fire-suppression assistance to rangers with workers.[38]

By 1908 officials and civic leaders in Southern California had quickly realized that no one agency could accomplish the great work of fire prevention and suppression alone. The *Forest Reserve Manual* had outlined the need for collaboration in 1902: "In and about nearly every reserve it is possible to enlist the cooperation of the better citizens, and thus to have such an agreement that in time of need there can be had a sufficient number of men, and men of the proper kind."[39] In exchange for longer land-use permits and greater say in forest administration through protective and community organizations, these "better citizens" supported officials in their efforts to prevent fires and protect the watersheds.

Gifford Pinchot's structure of forest administration operated on vague and imprecise national policies. In fact, one can argue that his system undertook civil service reform more than political reform or a challenge of existing systems of distribution. The lack of guidance that had typified the General Land Office administration merely transmuted into a vague administrative structure after Pinchot took charge. His influence put a pioneering emphasis on professionalization and technical training, but not on criteria for determining policies and a system to care for the public land.[40]

Professionalization, however, did not address an administrative *system*, or any set of policies that constructed a land ethic that rangers in the field could apply in their day-to-day work; in point of fact, it merely helped construct a highly visible and attractive administrative *style*, one that served the agency well in its attempts to instill an *esprit de corps* throughout the agency, but one that did not serve the public well at a time when leadership and direction regarding conservation and land use were vital.[41] As significantly, Pinchot's system allowed for the betrayal of Progressive principles. Grant McConnell has pointed out that, with the formal channels of responsibility all but closed and with no effective or certain guides for action other than those personal to the administrators, the Forest Service developed its own informal lines of responsibility, its own political ties to a particular constituency. In short, simple insistence upon the virtue of administrators as wardens of the public interest led deviously but certainly to ties with special interests, opposition to which had been the point of Progressive beginnings.[42]

On a regional level, the cooperation imperative also worked imperfectly. Since water and hydroelectric companies showed an interest in fire protection only as it served their immediate needs, cooperation operated in fits and starts. Much depended on the personality, salesmanship, and administrative style of the reserve supervisor.

Foresters and civic interests forged their cooperative relationships with such ease because they readily agreed that urban development in the region depended heavily upon the natural resources within the confines of the San Gabriel Forest Reserve. Southern Californians so readily embraced bureaucratic management of their lands for two important reasons: small, localized, and often disunited interests found such management too large and formidable a task to undertake; more importantly, they realized that, through cooperation and decentralized administration whereon they could participate in forest affairs, federal policy advanced the aims of the Southern California elite to develop the region's industries and cities. In addition federal forestry rapidly rose to prominence in managing the mountain lands in Southern California due to the rapidity with which reserve officials impressed local interests with their professionalism and expertise and, just as importantly, their willingness to support those aims.

The advantages for the forest reserve administration in garnering such allies lay not just in the added funding and manpower for policies and programs. In addition since influential directors and shareholders comprised these corporations, and since these men had interests in local and national banks, real estate concerns, manufacturing and industrial enterprises, forest officials, when they effected an working relationship, tied into a sophisticated network of powerful alliances that helped to bring more public and political support for forest conservation. In so doing, foresters made the preservation of the San Gabriel and San Bernardino Mountains good business, for both mountain-based and purely urban concerns, and for their allies across the nation as well.

Decentralization of power and authority to the individual reserves ensured that the administrators would, in large part, comply with the needs of those interests, being forced to do so from financial considerations. In no way did Pinchot and his allies construct a system of arbitration for the political dialogue between national constraints and local impulses. In Southern California, the Forest Service system, increasingly applied between 1902 and 1908, did little except to codify previously existing operations that gave users, especially private corporate users, great leeway in the development and administration of the public land.[43] Here, in the origins of the administration of the San Gabriel Timberland Reserve, simultaneous with the establishment of conservation principles in the Los Angeles basin, one can glimpse the beginnings of one aspect of the corporate state that dominates American life. The evolution of organized individualism led to a system whereby, as Lustig argues, "America becomes a polity in which the enjoyment of public, constitutional rights is dependent upon one's attachment to private, secondary associations."[44]

Forest administration played no small part in the urbanization of the Los Angeles basin at a period critical to its development, and in later years as well, for the imperative lived on and thrived in subsequent periods even with increases in funding and manpower. The involvement of urban commercial interests and, in more recent years, urban political agencies in the administration of the Angeles National Forest, from the days of its origin as the San Gabriel Timberland Reserve, made it a truly urban wildland, with all the vitality, schizophrenia, and controversy that this paradoxical designation implies.

Notes

The author wishes to thank Michael McIntyre of the Forest Service, Ronald Tobey of the University of California, Riverside, and Richard Wessel of Computer Science Corporation for their assistance in the preparation of this paper.

1. Richard L. McCormick, "The Discovery that Business Corrupts Politics: A Reappraisal of the Origins of Progressivism," *American Historical Review* 86:2 (April 1981): pp. 257; and Lawrence Goodwyn, *Democratic Promise: The Populist Movement in America* (New York: Oxford University Press, 1976).

2. Without attempting to completely list the major works on this subject, the following presents important discussions: J. Leonard Bates, "Fulfilling American Democracy: The Conservation Movement, 1907 to 1921," *Mississippi Valley Historical Review* 44, no. 1 (June 1957), pp. 29-57; Samuel P. Hays, *Conservation and the Gospel of Efficiency: The Progressive Conservation Movement 1890-1920* (Cambridge: Harvard University Press, 1959); Elmo R. Richardson, *The Politics of Conservation: Crusades and Controversies, 1897-1913* (Berkeley: University of California Press, 1962); Roderick Nash, *Wilderness and the American Mind*, 3d ed. (New Haven: Yale University Press, 1982); and John F. Reiger, *American Sportsmen and the Origins of Conservation* (New York: Winchester Press, 1975).

3. Quotation is from McCormick, "Business Corrupts Politics," p. 257.

4. *See* Ronald F. Lockmann, *Guarding the Forests of Southern California: Evolving Attitudes Toward Conservation of Watershed Woodlands, and Wilderness* (Glendale, CA: Arthur H. Clark Co., 1981), especially pp. 23, 62-63, 89, 161. *See* also Hays, *Conservation*, p. 24; and C. Raymond Clar, *California Government and Forestry* (Sacramento: State of California, 1959), pp. 163-64, 172-73.

5. For an early history of Forest Reserve administration, *see* Harold K. Steen, *The U.S. Forest Service: A History* (Seattle: University of Washington Press, 1976), pp. 26-37; and Filibert Roth, "Administration of U.S. Forest Reserves," *Forestry and Irrigation* 8 (May 1902): pp. 191-93, 241-44. For an account of similar problems in other regions, *See also* G. Michael McCarthy, *Hour of Trial: The Conservation Conflict in Colorado and the West, 1891-1907* (Norman: University of Oklahoma Press, 1977), pp. 58-61, 138-48; and Gerald W. Williams, "The USDA Forest Service in the Pacific Northwest: Major Political and Social Controversies between 1891-1945," typewritten MS in Angeles National Forest Library dated 1988, pp. 2-5.

6. No comprehensive, scholarly history of the San Gabriel Reserve, or its successor, the Angeles National Forest, has been written. For informative histories directed at a popular audience, *See* William S. Brown, "History of the Angeles National Forest," typewritten MS in the Angeles National Forest Library, dated 1943; W.W. Robinson, *The Forest and the People: The Story of the Angeles National Forest* (Los Angeles: Title Insurance and Trust Company, 1946); and John W. Robinson, *The San Gabriels: Southern California Mountain Country* (San Marino, CA: Golden West Books, 1977).

7. Grant McConnell, *Private Power and American Democracy* (New York: Alfred A. Knopf, 1966), pp. 43-50, 312; Theodore J. Lowi, *The End of Liberalism: Ideology, Policy, and the Crisis of Public Authority* (New York: W.W. Norton and Co., 1969), pp. 93-97; and R. Jeffrey Lustig, *Corporate Liberalism: The Origins of Modern American Political Theory, 1890-1920* (Berkeley: University of California Press, 1982), pp. 232-40.

8. McConnell, *Private Power*, p. 45, 142, 160, 199-200, 210-11, 243-44, 312.

9. *See* Lowi, *End of Liberalism*, pp. 29, 40, 70-85, 294, and especially Chapter 5, pp. 125-96; Lustig, *Corporate Liberalism*, pp. 232-40, 246-64; *see* Hays, *Conservation*; Robert H. Wiebe, *Businessmen and Reform* (Cambridge: Harvard University Press, 1962); and Robert H. Wiebe, *The Search for Order 1877-1920* (New York: Hill & Wang, 1967).

10. *See* McCormick, "Business Corrupts Politics," p. 268. On the Federal Reserve Act, *See* Steen, *Forest Service*, pp. 26-28; Samuel Trask Dana and Myron Krueger, *California Lands: Ownership, Use, and Management* (Washington, DC: American Forestry Association, 1958), p. 245; John Ise, *The United States Forest Policy* (New Haven: Yale University Press, 1920), pp. 109-15; and Clar, *California Government and Forestry*, pp. 143-44. *See also* A. Hunter Dupree, *Science in the Federal Government: A History of Policies and Activities* (Baltimore: Johns Hopkins University Press, 1986), p. 241.

11. Robert K. Winters, ed. *Fifty Years of Forestry in the U.S.A.* (Washington, DC: Society of American Foresters, 1950), p. 4; *See also* McCarthy, *Hour of Trial*, pp. 46, 50.

12. *See* Abbot Kinney, "The Forest Fires," *Forester* 4 (December 1898), pp. 248-49; and Clar, *California Government and Forestry*, p. 123.

13. Ibid., p. 362; Stephen J. Pyne, *Fire in America: A Cultural History of Wildland and Rural Fire* (Princeton: Princeton University Press, 1988), p. 419.

14. Letter of Supvr. Allen to General Land Office Commissioner (Binger Hermann), July 26, 1897, "Supervisor Correspondence Books," no. 1 (1897-1899), Angeles National Forest Library. *See also* Lockmann, *Guarding the Forests*, pp. 108-09. For similar experiences in Colorado, *See* McCarthy, *Hour of Trial*, pp. 58-59.

15. Roth, "Administration of Reserves," p. 191; and William V. Mendenhall, "Forestry Progress in Southern California," paper presented at meeting of Society of American Foresters, San Diego, 1959, p. 1. *See also* Steen, *Forest Service*, pp. 26-30, 34-37; McCarthy, *Hour of Trial*, p. 56; James Muhn and Hanson R. Stuart, *Opportunity and Challenge: The Story of BLM* (Washington, DC: Government Printing Office, 1988), pp. 28-29; and Supvr. B.F. Allen to W.C. Parsons, June 1, 1898, "Correspondence Books," no. 1 (1897-99). Steen points out that "Congress passed this most important bill without being aware of its content." Steen, *Forest Service*, p. 27, and Steen, *The Beginning of the National Forest System* (USDA Forest Service, 1991).

16. William V. Mendenhall, "History of Past Fires," unpublished MS in Angeles National Forest Library, dated ca. 1931, p. 4. *See also* Clar, *California Government and Forestry*, p. 237, ff. 5; Supvr. Allen to General Land Office Commissioner, July 21, 1897, "Supervisor Correspondence Books," no. 1 (1897-1899).

17. Supvr. Allen to Ernest Klette, February 11, 1898, Ibid. *See also* Allen to W.C. Parsons, June 1, 1898, Ibid.; and Lawrence Rakestraw, "Uncle Sam's Forest Reserves," *Pacific Northwest Quarterly* 44:4 (October 1953): pp. 191, 242.

18. Supvr. Allen to General Land Office Commissioner, August 2, 1897, "Correspondence Books," no. 1 (1897-1899). *See also* Allen's letters to the Commissioner, dated August 31, 1897 and October 24, 1898, Ibid. For references to the drought *See* Supt. Allen's letters to the G.L.O. Commissioner dated October 24, 1898, and March 15, 1899, Ibid.

19. Supvr. Allen to General Land Office Commissioner, August 2, 1897, Ibid.

20. Clar, *California Government and Forestry*, p. 544.

21. Supvr. Allen to General Land Office Commissioner, July 25, 1898, "Correspondence Books," no. 1 (1897-1899); John P. Kaye to Henry Clepper, letter dated November 5, 1941, later reprinted in *Journal of Forestry* 40:1 (January 1942): p. 76. The actual cost of the station was seventy dollars. The building still stands on the Angeles National Forest, having been moved in the mid-1980s to behind the Chilao Visitors' Center.

22. Supt. Allen to Supvr. Langenberg, November 9, 1898, "Correspondence Books," no. 1 (1897-1899). Emphasis in original. *See also* Allen to General Land Office Commissioner, letters dated October 24 and 31, 1898, and to W.C. Bartlett, November 9, 1898, Ibid. *See also* Roth, "Administration of Reserves," p. 192. From 1898-1903, trail and fire- break construction constituted the principal winter activities on the San Gabriel Reserve. *See* Clar, *California Government and Forestry*, p. 203; Supt. Allen to General Land Office Commissioner, January 6, 1899, "Correspondence Books," no. 1 (1897-1899). Emphasis in original.

23. U.S. Department of the Interior, General Land Office, "Rules and Regulations Governing Forest Reserves" (Washington, D.C.: Government Printing Office, 1897); Roth, "Administration of Reserves," p. 191. *See also* Steen, *Forest Service*, pp. 60-61.

24. Roth, "Administration of Reserves," pp. 191, 242; *See also* U.S. Department of the Interior, General Land Office, *Forest Reserve Manual, for the Information and Use of Forest Officers* (Washington, DC: Government Printing Office, 1902), pp. 86-87.

25. For the corruption of General Land Office rangers in Colorado, *See* McCarthy, *Hour of Trial*, p. 60 and ff. 50.

26. *See* Supvr. Thomas' letters to the General Land Office Commissioner, dated August 6, 1901; Thomas to Ranger L.T. Rowley, dated July 6, 1901; Thomas to Commissioner, January 20, 1902; and Thomas to Filibert Roth, Chief, Division R, June 5, 1902, "Correspondence Books," no. 2 (1900-1902).

27. Supvr. Thomas to Chas. S. Newhall, Supervisor, Sierra Forest Reserve, Fresno, California, December 6, 1901 (Letter #1), Ibid.

28. Ibid. Kerckhoff made his initial fortune as principal owner of the Kerckhoff-Cuzner Lumber Company. He established gas and ice companies in Los Angeles. He was a member of a close-knit syndicate of wealthy developers, being allied with railroad magnates E.H. Harriman and Henry E. Huntington, attorney Henry W. O'Melveny, financier Joseph Sartori, and Los Angeles *Times* owner Harrison Gray Otis. These men played prominent roles in the associated construction of the Los Angeles-Owens Valley Aqueduct and real estate development of the San Fernando Valley above Los Angeles as well as hydro electric development in the San Gabriel Mountains. *See* William L. Kahrl, *Water and Power: The Conflict over Los Angeles' Water Supply in the Owens Valley* (Berkeley: University of California Press, 1982), pp. 92-98; *See also* pp. 152-57, 166-68. In addition, Kerckhoff avidly fished and hiked in the San Gabriels, owning a cabin in San Antonio Canyon below Mt. Baldy, the range's highest peak. *See* O'Melveny's eulogistic "The Story of William G. Kerckhoff," *UCLA Magazine* 15, no. 10 (January 1941), n.p.

29. *See* letter of G.A. Steel to the General Land Office Commissioner, January 6, 1900, p. 8, Angeles National Forest Library files; Clar, *California Government and Forestry*, p. 370;

Louis H. Dorr, "Reminiscences of an Angeles National Forest Pioneer," unpublished MS in
Angeles National Forest Library (dated 1940), *passim.*; and letter of Supvr. Thomas to
G.L.O. Commissioner, August 16, 1901, "Correspondence Books," no. 2 (1900-1902);
Everett B. Thomas diaries, dates March 15, April 5, and April 6, 1901, "Supervisor Diaries,"
no. 1 (1900-1901). *See also* letter of Supvr. Thomas to General Land Office Commissioner
Binger Hermann, December 20, 1901, "Correspondence Books," no. 2 (1900-1902). All three
communities are in the San Gabriel Valley of Southern California; Supvr. Thomas to Dr.
Reed, Cucamonga, California, April 16, 1901; Thomas to William G. Kerckhoff, April 30,
1901, Ibid. The Supervisor contacted or visited Boards of Trade, farmers' groups, and water
companies in the Southern California communities of Pomona, Sierra Madre, Cucamonga,
Monrovia, Pasadena, and other cities to elicit support for such brigades. *See also* Supt. Allen
to General Land Office Commissioner, November 22, 1898, Ibid., no. 1 (1897-1899).

30. Supvr. Thomas to General Land Office Commissioner, March 27, 1903, "Correspondence
Books," no. 3 (1903- 1905).

31. *See* McConnell, *Private Power*, pp. 32-38, 41-42; that Gifford Pinchot envisioned the resources
of the reserves as assisting the process of urbanization wherever possible can be deduced from
his comments before the Trans-Mississippi Commercial Congress in Cripple Creek, Colorado,
in 1901, when he stated that "the end of civilization may be described as the founding of
homes . . . and forestry is therefore the handmaid of civilization." Quoted in McCarthy, *Hour
of Trial*, p. 67.

32. Gifford Pinchot, *Breaking New Ground*, repr. ed. (Washington, D.C.: Island Press, 1987), pp.
254-62; Steen, *Forest Service*, pp. 74-78. *See also* McConnell, *Private Power*, p. 44. Five
months later, on July 1, the Bureau of Forestry became the United States Forest Service. In
1907, an Act of Congress [34 Stat. 1269] changed the name of the forest reserves to national
forests. *See* S. LoJacono, "Establishment and Modification of National Forest Boundaries: A
Chronologic Record 1891-1959" (Washington, D.C.: Government Printing Office, 1959), p.
15. The transfer was authorized by Act of Congress, February 1, 1905 [33 Stat. 626]. Ibid., p.
7; Hays, *Conservation*, p. 191.

33. For details and significance of the graft scandal, *See* letters of R.H. Charlton to G.W. Woodruff
[Forest Service's legal officer], October 7, 1905, "Correspondence Books," no. 4 (1905-
1906), and Woodruff to Charlton, October 3 and October 9, 1905, Records Group-95,
National Archives, Washington, D.C. *See also* Steen, *Forest Service*, p. 81.

34. U.S. Department of Agriculture, Forest Service, *The Use of the National Forest Reserves*
(Washington, D.C.: General Printing Office, 1905), pp. 10-11. For origins of the *Use Book*,
See Steen, *Forest Service*, pp. 78-80. The *Use Book* revision committee is pictured Ibid.,
facing p. 17; the gentleman in the back row on the far left is B.H. Crow, Chief Ranger and
Assistant Supervisor for the San Gabriel Timberland Reserve.

35. *See* McConnell, *Private Power*, pp. 43-48.

36. Ibid., pp. 199-200. McConnell states that "[t]he elites to which the agency responded were the
local elites where the [Forest] Service operated, and the values it came to serve were their
values." Ibid., p. 200.

37. For comment, *See* Thomas' letter to General Land Office Commissioner Binger Hermann, dated June 20, 1903, "Correspondence Books," no. 3 (1903-1905).

38. Supvr. Thomas to General Land Office Commissioner, October 22, 1904, and "Report on Right of Way for Wagon Road [for Native Son Mining Company]," of the same date, Ibid. *See* John H. Barber, "A Glimpse of the San Gabriel Forest Reservation," *Forester* 4 (December 1898): p. 241, for a portrait of one mining center in the San Gabriel Mountains, Mt. Gleason, near Acton, California.

39. General Land Office, *Forest Reserve Manual*, p. 29.

40. McConnell, *Private Power*, p. 360.

41. *See* Ibid., pp. 360-66.

42. Ibid.., p. 50.

43. McConnell, *Private Power*, pp. 360-66.

44. Lustig, *Corporate Liberalism*, p. 246.

OTHER FEDERAL AGENCIES

Forests and Reclamation, 1891-1911

Donald J. Pisani
Texas A&M University

Historians of natural resources owe a great debt to Samuel P. Hays' *Conservation and the Gospel of Efficiency: The Progressive Conservation Movement, 1890-1920* (1959).[1] By relating the "conservation movement" to the rise of new scientific disciplines (such as silviculture, hydrology, and agronomy), to the emergence of bureaucratic elites, and to broader campaigns for organization and efficiency, the book broke down the older Progressive view of conservation as a mass *political* crusade directed against corporate monopolization of natural resources, including what remained of the public domain. Above all, Hays argued that the leaders of the conservation movement appreciated the need to coordinate their activities and objectives. In this paper, I will examine his thesis that "the conservation movement of the Roosevelt administration grew out of a fusion of land and water policies which took place around the turn of the century."[2] There was an alliance between forestry and reclamation, to be sure. But the ideas that served as the foundation for that relationship were ambiguous and inconsistent, and the alliance was tense and short-lived. Ultimately, each agency went its own way.

Historians have paid far more attention to the laws, policies, personalities, and controversies of the conservation movement than to the scientific assumptions upon which it was built. Although nineteenth-century science was rooted in natural law, it relied as much on history and experience as on empirical evidence. It was didactic, not just descriptive, and it placed human beings at the center of things. In the last century, no work influenced scientific thinking about forests and streamflow more than George Perkins Marsh's monumental *Man and Nature,* first published in 1864 and reprinted in 1865, 1867, 1869, 1871, and 1874. Marsh assumed that the physical world was one of systems, order, and balance. Heavily forested terrain was normal; deserts, grasslands, and brushlands were somehow abnormal—a symptom of bad health. A humid environment where it rained all year long was healthy; an arid environment where rain fell only during certain seasons was aberrant. Nature preferred light, even rains, not droughts and floods. The history of the ancient world, Marsh argued, had demonstrated repeatedly that the penalty for stripping away the forests was severe. Erosion and flooding washed away the topsoil, rendering the denuded land barren and sterile. Marshes proliferated and malaria epidemics ravaged the cities. Ultimately, fish and game disappeared from streams and their flow became capricious and unpredictable. Industry and commerce sickened and died; society regressed to a pastoral state. Once carried to a certain point, the process of "desertification" was irreversible.[3]

Marsh's cyclical view of human history was infectious. The civilizations of the ancient world had perished because of deforestation and abuse of the land, and, he predicted, so would the United States—unless a certain percentage of forested land was left in its natural state. As *Scientific American* editorialized in 1875, a decade after the publication of *Man and Nature*, "We are beginning to learn . . . that, so far from being incompatible with forests, permanent civilization is impossible without them, that the tree slayer's ambition to bring the whole land under tillage would result, if successful, in making tillage a waste of labor through climatic disturbances. Alternations of drought and deluge, blighting heats and blasting colds, have ever been the penalty for general forest destruction; and many a land once fertile is now a desert for this cause alone. Indeed woodlands are to climate what the balance wheel is to machinery, the great conservator and regulator, without which all other conditions are wasted."[4]

During the last decades of the nineteenth century, several assumptions regarding forests and streamflow became commonplace. Most can be traced back to Marsh. Not all scientists believed that forests caused rainfall, but most assumed that woodlands had a profound influence on the climate *within* their boundaries. They produced a sponge-like humus that soaked up moisture from thunderstorms and heavy rains. They also broke up raindrops, permitting the soil to absorb them more easily; condensed fogs and dews; trapped snow and prevented it from melting as rapidly as in the open; and shielded the ground from the sun and from desiccating winds. Most important, forests provided a natural reservoir that released water slowly, providing a uniform flow. Whether they increased rainfall or not, they conserved it and made it more usable.[5]

In the Far West, boosters, speculators, and irrigation promoters began to publicize the apparent connection between forests and irrigation in the 1870s and 1880s. For example, in 1876 Colorado's constitutional convention insisted that irrigation would be impossible without forests to regulate the water supply, and in March 1885, California's legislature created one of the nation's first state boards of forestry and empowered it "to act with a special view to the continuance of water sources that may be affected in any measure by the destruction of forests near such sources; to do any and all things within their power to encourage the preservation and planting of forests, and the consequent maintenance of the water sources of the State."[6] From 1885 to 1891, the new board repeatedly appealed to Congress to

reserve the entire watershed from Lake Tahoe to the southern tip of the Sierra.[7]
Nevertheless, even as the beneficial influence of forests on streamflow was becoming all but a religion in the West, there were many doubters in the Washington
offices of the U.S. Geological Survey. In 1888 Congress gave the U.S.G.S.,
which John Wesley Powell presided over, the responsibility of surveying the arid
West's reservoir sites and irrigable land. Powell conceived of this job as a long-
term project that might take a decade or more to complete. From the beginning the
survey faced threats from those who favored alternate water sources. A few
westerners believed that rainfall could be produced by detonating explosives on the
ground or in the atmosphere. Others favored drilling artesian wells. But the most
dangerous group insisted that planting trees would increase rainfall, or capture
enough water to make artificial reservoirs unnecessary. The same drought that had
prompted the Irrigation Survey had also given impetus to the crusade for national
reserves, because the drought increased the number of forest fires and exacerbated
the damage done by grazing on the public lands.

In his famous 1878 report on arid lands, Powell had argued that there was plenty
of timber in the arid West—challenging the view of many Cassandras—and he
thought that the timber could better be protected from fire in private rather than
public ownership.[8] In the same report he recommended dividing the West into
grazing and irrigation districts that conformed to natural watersheds. Within those
districts, local residents would excercise full control over *all* natural resources,
including land, water, and forests. The champions of national forest reserves found
much to worry about in Powell's plan, which was embodied in legislation
presented to Congress in 1889. Nevertheless, in an October 1888, letter to the
Kansas City Times, Powell was conciliatory. He denied that trees had any
influence on precipitation, but he recommended protecting the forests from fire and
conceded that forests reduced evaporation from the ground and the severity of
storms, resulting in "more gentle rains."[9]

Still, Powell became increasingly dismayed at the prospect of forest preserves and
the creation of a rival bureaucracy in Interior or Agriculture. He feared that such a
course would "lock-up" potential reservoir sites and prevent the construction of
canals as well as reduce U.S.G.S. appropriations. It would nullify the value of his
work—which he hoped would encourage private land and ditch companies. In the
summer of 1889, he published an article arguing that forests reduced snow-pack by
preventing it from accumulating in great drifts "in the lee of rocks and cliffs and
under the walls of gorges and canyons." The following spring Powell issued an
even more scathing attack on the forests, arguing that 20-40 percent of the rain that
fell there was lost to farmers because forest vegetation captured and used it. In the
Wasatch Mountains of Utah, he noted, research had shown that denudation resulted

in a "great increase in [the] volume of streams." And at a time when many forest-ers wanted to create reserves as a limitation on grazing, Powell went so far as to argue that running sheep in the Sierra Nevada Mountains was a useful way to keep down forest growth![10] Relations between leading foresters and Powell hit rock bottom at the end of the year. Bernhard Fernow, chief of the Division of Forestry in the Department of Agriculture, recounted that at a December 30, 1890 meeting of representatives of the American Forestry Association, American Association for the Advancement of Science, and Forestry Division in Secretary of the Interior John Noble's office:

> "Major Powell, the Director of the Geological Survey, asked permission to be present, which, of course, was politely granted. Before we had an opportunity to state the object of our visit, Major Powell launched into a long dissertation to show that the claim of the favorable influence of forest cover on water flow or climate was untenable, that the best thing to do for the Rocky Mountain forests was to burn them down, and he related with great gusto how he himself had started a fire that swept over a thousand square miles. He had used up our time when our chance came to speak. We consumed not more than two minutes, stating that we had not come to argue any theories, but to impress the Secretary with the fact that it was under the law his business to protect public property against the vandalism of which the Major had just accused himself."[11]

Powell had plenty of allies in the Geological Survey. For example, Henry Gannett, geographer of the Survey, joined Powell in denying that forests had any influence on rainfall and recommended that since trees released enormous quantities of water to the atmosphere through evaporation, "it is advisable to cut away as rapidly as possible all the forests, especially upon the mountains, where most of the rain falls, in order that as much of the precipitation as possible may be collected in the streams. This will cause, not a decrease in the annual flow of streams, as commonly supposed, but an increase. . . . It may be added that the forests in the arid region are thus disappearing with commendable rapidity."[12]

The leaders of the crusade for forest reserves must have winced as they read those words. C. S. Sargent, editor of *Garden and Forest* and after 1890 director of the Arnold Arboretum and professor of arboriculture at Harvard, initially favored the construction of water storage reservoirs by private companies under direction of the national government.[13] That changed after he learned about Powell's bill to create autonomous irrigation and grazing districts and after the Johnstown Dam collapsed in the Conemaugh Valley in the spring of 1889, killing several hundred people and causing enormous property damage. "It is high time," Sargent wrote, "that some organized effort was made to check a movement which has been gathering force . . . until the government seems committed to the construction of enormously expensive works, which all experience has shown to be inadequate for the purpose they are intended to accomplish, and fraught with serious danger to the lives and property of thousands." To capture sufficient water for farmers, huge dams would have to be erected, "reservoirs of death" in his words.[14] Sargent reminded his readers that the head of the U.S.G.S. not only opposed the creation of forest reserves but also opposed the appointment of a special commission to survey and classify the forested lands. He described Powell's article in *Century* as "a rhapsody rather than a sustained and coherent argument." "The serious reader," Sargent fumed, "finds it difficult to persuade himself that a man of science with any clear thought on a matter within the scope of his profession would attempt to give it expression in such a tumefied style."[15]

J. B. Harrison, commissioner of forests for New Hampshire and secretary of the American Forestry Association, also chastised Powell.[16] He warned President Benjamin Harrison that if the forests were stripped away, the rivers, artificial reservoirs, and farmland would be choked with silt and debris. "The Government ought not, I think, to authorize any scheme of irrigation which does not recognize the indispensableness of the mountain forests, as *natural* storage reservoirs, and as auxiliaries to any artificial system."[17]

The war of words continued in 1890. B. E. Fernow contributed an essay to the Senate Select Committee on Irrigation's report in which he argued that "Reforestation on the plains and forest preservation on the mountains is of greater national concern than the location of irrigation reservoirs [by the Irrigation Survey]." The arid West's major problem was not drought or the absence of rainfall, he insisted, but rapid evaporation. Instead of irrigation, he proposed a variation on dry-farming: single rows of trees to reduce the winds that blew across planted fields and removed moisture from plants and the soil. Western streams carried sufficient water, but not at the right time; they lost volume rapidly in late June and July. If the water supply could be preserved for an additional month each summer, there would be much less need for artificial reservoirs. Those structures were intended to extend the growing season of existing farmers as well as open virgin land to cultivation.[18]

Time was on Sargent's side. In 1890 the Irrigation Survey was terminated, in 1892 the U.S.G.S.'s geological and paleontological work was severely curtailed, and in May 1894 Powell resigned from the Geological Survey. The demise of the Irrigation Survey paved the way for the creation of the first national forests. By the end of 1892, fifteen reserves had been created containing over 13 million acres. Most were created to protect the headwaters of important streams, and many were established at the behest of irrigators and real estate promoters who lived in the vicinity of the forest.[19] Nevertheless, the Depression of 1893 stopped irrigation development dead in its tracks, and the West was left with dozens of crippled and paralyzed private land and water companies and little demand for more irrigated land.[20] For a few years that all but eliminated one prime justification for creating national forests. States like Utah and California, which had many acres under irrigation, contained strong supporters of the national forests. However, the states where grazing, mining, or lumbering dominated, as in Colorado, or which had plenty of water, such as Oregon and Washington, were generally hostile.[21]

The partisans of forest protection and arid land reclamation did not formally ally until the end of the 1890s. Throughout that decade, irrigation boosters feared that grazing interests would win control of the entire public domain by capturing the forests and the reservoir sites that had not been set aside by the Irrigation Survey. They also assumed that if the reservoir sites were included in forest reserves that could not be entered by private capital, that would put more pressure on Congress to authorize money to build dams. On the other hand, in the early 1890s the value of many of the reservoir sites reserved by Powell had been compromised by the construction of dams in nearby locations less suitable for storage. Consequently, cession of the public lands to the states also won strong support in many parts of the West as a way to unify public control over land and water.[22]

Because of the depression, the annual irrigation congresses—which began meeting in 1891—did not show much direct interest in forestry until 1897. By that time the depression had begun to lift, and by that time George Maxwell—a paid spokesman of the railroads—had launched a campaign to unite East and West behind a federal reclamation program that would benefit private as well as public lands. The 1897 irrigation congress passed a resolution declaring that "the perpetuation of the forests of the arid regions is essential to the maintenance of water-supply for irrigation as well as the supply of timber for industrial needs." It urged the secretary of the interior to withdraw "all public lands which are of more value for their timber than for agriculture or their minerals."[23] The motto of Maxwell's National Irrigation Association, which was also bankrolled by the railroads, became "Save the Forests, Store the Floods, Make Homes on the Land." Similarly, the motto of the 1900 irrigation congress, which met in Chicago, was "Save the Forests and Store the Floods." In 1901 Maxwell urged Congress to appropriate sufficient money to pay for forest patrols to protect the reserves from fire. "The forests are the source of all irrigation," he wrote. "We cannot irrigate without water. We cannot have water without forests. If we do not preserve them, we will have no irrigation."[24]

Maxwell hoped the support of proponents of the forest reserves, East and West, would make irrigation a national issue and increase the chances of getting Congress to adopt a national reclamation program.

The advantages were mutual. The American Forestry Association had as much to gain from wooing the reclamationists as vice-versa.[25] Both forests and dams promised to mitigate flooding and improve navigation, and since both kept water off the land, the friends of the forests and the friends of irrigation hoped to tap the river and harbor fund. Moreover, in the 1890s many engineers and hydrologists predicted that the increasing public interest in scientific farming would soon make irrigation as common in the East as in the West. That was an another justification for eastern reserves. In addition the "Cleveland reserves" of 1897—created by the president without consulting western politicians and widely denounced in the West— convinced many champions of forest protection that they could not secure their objectives without offering a quid pro quo to the irrigation interests. Finally, after Gifford Pinchot took over the Forestry Bureau in 1898, he began a campaign to transfer control of the reserves from the General Land Office in Interior to his office in Agriculture, a campaign that gained steam after passage of the Reclamation Act of 1902.

The formal marriage between the two overlapping conservation groups was announced at the AFA meeting in Los Angeles in July 1899, in the midst of a great southern California drought reminiscent of the one that had visited the region a decade earlier.[26] Present at the meeting were Abbot Kinney, Elwood Mead, George Maxwell, Frederick Haynes Newell (who became director of the Reclamation Service in 1902), Gifford Pinchot, and many other notables in the two movements. Maxwell was appointed chair of the resolutions committee. It announced the AFA's support for a national reclamation program paid for by leasing the public grazing lands. The honeymoon continued that fall at the Irrigation Congress meeting held at Missoula, Montana. At the beginning of 1902, the title of the American Forest Association's monthly, *The Forester*, was changed to *Forestry and Irrigation*.[27]

Of course political expediency was not the only reason for the alliance. It was also based on personal relationships. In Washington many advocates of forest reserves and irrigation were active members of such organizations as the National Geographic Society and American Philosophical Society. They also formed informal groups within government. Several of Powell's lieutenants in the USGS, including Frederick H. Newell, Arthur Powell Davis (second director of the Reclamation Service), and even Henry Gannett (chief geographer of the USGS) became friends and allies of Gifford Pinchot and his staff in the Forestry Bureau.

During the Roosevelt presidency, these men often lunched together in the "Great Basin Lunch Mess"—a group of department heads mainly from Interior and Agriculture—and Pinchot and Newell were members of TR's "tennis cabinet."

Newell served as secretary and a member of the executive committee of the American Forestry Association from 1892 to 1903. In 1895—the same year he met Gifford Pinchot—he was given charge of the new Division of Hydrology in the USGS along with the responsibility of measuring the flow of streams in all parts of the United States. This increased his interest in the relationship between forests and waterflow. He became fascinated with the difference between streams like Arizona's Gila River, whose flow occurred almost entirely during a three week period at the end of July and the beginning of August and a subsequent three week period from mid October through early November, and rivers in the heavily forested Pacific Northwest, whose flow also peaked in July but which had a fairly large overall volume year round. His work measuring streams convinced him of the close relationship between forests and streamflow, and in 1897, Newell recommended that *all* forest lands be reserved pending a federal survey and classification, a very "radical" position to take at that time. Subsequently, he taught a course in forest hydrography at the Yale Forestry School. Newell and Pinchot often camped out together and served on the boards of many Washington scientific societies. During the Roosevelt years, both were members of the Public Land Commission (1903-1905) and later the Inland Waterways Commission (1907-1908).[28]

Strangely enough, by the end of the 1890s Henry Gannett also became a strong supporter of the national forests. He began his career as a topographer for the Hayden Survey. In 1896 he took charge of the new Division of Geography in the USGS. In 1897 the Forest Management Act reconstituted Gannett's office as the Division of Geography and Forestry and gave it the job of mapping and surveying all new reserves. The USGS was the logical agency to perform this work because it was responsible for topographical mapping and streamflow measurements.

Gannett's office became an enormously important to both the General Land Office and later Pinchot's Forestry Bureau in Agriculture as a source of information about the forested lands. Gannett and Pinchot became fast friends during the summer of 1897, as they inspected many of the new reserves together. By January 1899, in what constituted something of a miracle given his writings ten years earlier, Gannett was listed as one of the directors of the American Forestry Association, along with his friend Pinchot. He had as much to say about the boundaries of the forest reserves as anyone in the GLO or Forestry Bureau. In his autobiography, Pinchot noted: "Henry and I had taken to each other from the first day the work of the National Forest Commission threw us together. He was a man of decided opinions and strong antagonisms, brusque in manner but with a golden heart. He knew more geography than I did, I knew more Forestry than he did, and so we worked together like Damon and Pythias, if those worthies ever did any work. . . . Gannett was . . . a vigorous, forthright, competent man of wide knowledge and varied experience."[29]

This symbiotic relationship between foresters and reclamationists continued for several for several years after passage of the Reclamation Act in 1902. "The recent passage by Congress of the bill inaugurating an irrigation policy," the commissioner of the General Land Office observed in his report for 1902, "may, in its effect, be regarded as amounting, indirectly, to legislation broadening our national forestry work, since to insure effective operation of that law necessitates the forest growth upon all watersheds throughout the public domain, in the States and Territories named, being preserved as an integral part of the work of water conservation. The preservation of these forests as natural reservoirs has, to all intents and purposes, been thereby made incumbent upon the government by Congress. In other words, by ringing into existence a national irrigation system a pronounced impetus has been given to the closely related movement of forestry."[30] And Gifford Pinchot concluded that following passage of the national irrigation law, "the public opinion of the West has become unanimous in favor of forest preservation for the protection of the water supply, and practically so for the perpetuation of the supply of timber." He went on to suggest that not only did westerners appreciate the need to protect forests, they supported reserving land that might be reforested.[31]

The new Reclamation Service quickly proceeded to reserve 40,000,000 acres of land in the West, much of it adjoining national forests.[32] At the beginning of 1906, C. J. Blanchard, the Reclamation Service's chief statistician and publicist noted proudly: "Like Jack Sprat and his wife, they [the Forestry Bureau and Reclamation Service] have proceeded to lick the platter [the public domain] clean; but they have been well-behaved children and have not quarreled over their portions. The forestry infant has shown an exceeding fondness for mountain tops, steep-sided hills, old pine barrens, and high altitudes generally, while the Reclamation Service has selected the valleys and mesas."[33]

Nevertheless, in the years after 1902 the Reclamation Service depended far more on the Forest Service than vice-versa. In 1902 the Reclamation Service had little reliable stream-flow data and little reliable information concerning the water requirements of different crops in different soils. To control the headwaters of the West's streams, and to control its remaining reservoirs, was to control water development; it was one way of blocking speculative water filings that could cripple the national reclamation program in its infancy. While reclamation officials withdrew millions of acres of arable land, they had no authority to reserve land for watershed or streamflow protection. Their greatest fear was that livestock interests would gain control of the national forests, as they had monopolized the public domain. As the director of the Reclamation Service put it, "In general, it may be stated that the officers of the Reclamation Service believe it to be good public policy to keep within forest reserves as much of the catchment area of various streams as may properly be included without detriment to other interests . . . by careful control of the forest reserves, particularly in the matter of grazing." Officers in the Reclamation Service believed that the forests were much more valuable for their impact on streamflow, particularly in the late summer, than for their lumber.[34]

Initially, there was very close cooperation between the two agencies. In 1903, when the 60 million acres of forest reserves were still under the control of the General Land Office, Pinchot wrote to Newell hoping that the Reclamation Service could prevail on the GLO to withdraw additional land prior to their transfer to the Agriculture Department: "Why would it not be a good plan for you to send instructions to all your chiefs of parties or state bosses to send you every case where the watershed or a stream or reservoir should be reserved for its protection? . . . In that way we ought to get a large amount of the most valuable country, and that with very little opposition. It will not matter at all whether or not these areas are wooded now, because if you say they are needed that will settle it. . . ."[35] The Forest Service also promised to measure streamflow on the reserves, provide a supply of timber for use on government water projects, and reforest denuded land adjoining reservoir sites and canal lines.[36]

The 1905 law transferring the forest reserves to Agriculture pledged the proceeds from the forests to the Forest Service, rather than the general treasury, for five years, just as the Reclamation Service had secured independence from Congress by creating a construction fund derived from public land sales. This was only the beginning. Pinchot hoped that the Forest Service would secure control of the 300 to 400 million acres of grazing land in the West as an additional source of income. And as Samuel Hays points out, he also wanted to administer the national parks and consolidate many other features of the Progressive conservation program under his leadership. All this must have worried Newell, who, like Pinchot, was always looking for ways to fund the work of national reclamation.[37] For example, when the sales of public land lagged, Newell informed one of his chief engineers that while there was no money to build new projects, "possibly the Reclamation Fund may be increased by the proceeds, say, of sale of timber or leasing of grazing lands."[38] Nevertheless, no resource bureau grew faster than the Forest Service.

The Division of Forestry's employees expanded from 11 in 1898 to 821 at the time of transfer, when its name was changed to Forest Service. Even before the transfer, the division was conducting field work in twenty-seven states and territories and it indirectly managed over 900,000 acres of private forests.[39]

It was the Forest Service's grazing policy that first tested its relationship with the Reclamation Service. In April 1900, Pinchot informed commissioner of the General Land Office Binger Hermann that the grazing issue was the most important aspect of administering the national forests. "Upon it, more than upon any other," he fretted, "depends the support of the forest reserve policy by the people of the West."[40] Some reserves were created because of pressure from cattlemen, even though Pinchot recognized that this provoked bitter complaints from farmers.[41] In 1906 the Forest Service began charging stockmen a modest fee—considerably lower than that charged on private lands or Indian reservations—to use the reserves. The General Land Office had initially refused to permit grazing, then opened the reserves reluctantly. To Pinchot, however, the reserves had been created to be used and, in the words of historian James L. Penick, "Pinchot shamelessly courted the leading grazing interests."[42] Interior had required a grazing permit after 1898 but did not charge a fee. It had favored local grazers, for example by forbidding any out-of-state herds from entering a reserve. Pinchot favored negotiating with large cattlemen, such as his political allies J. B. Killian of Colorado and Dwight B. Heard and Albert Potter of Arizona, the latter of whom became head of the Forest Service's Grazing Division. By negotiating contracts with livestock advisory boards, he cut administrative costs and ensured better compliance with grazing regulations. In the first years after transfer, proceeds from grazing consistently outstripped those from timber. "The income from the reserves is as yet but a small fraction of what may be expected as they approach full utilization," the secretary of agriculture observed in 1906. The secretary looked forward to the time the Forest Service would be self-supporting, particularly because it was also charging for permits to use reservoir sites, power sites, and to build canals across the public lands.[43]

The conflict over grazing came to a head in 1908. By that time, about 150 million acres of national forest were firmly under the control of the Forest Service, and there was little additional land that seemed likely to be added to the reserves. Therefore the political support of reclamationists—which at one time had been critical—waned in importance. In 1902 boosters had expected federal reclamation to reclaim as many as 60-100 million acres, but the projects launched in the first decade of this century watered no more than a few million acres. Once it became clear that the national irrigation program would be very limited, grazing took on renewed importance. The Reclamation Service clung to the illusion that the national forests existed primarily for watershed protection, but increasingly the Forest Service embraced multiple-use.

In 1907 Pinchot had stocked the national forests "up to the extreme limit of the carrying power of the range."[44] Unfortunately, the winter of 1907-1908 was very dry and, owing to the lack of moisture, Forest Service officials allowed sheep to graze in the high mountains. Reclamation Service engineers perceived this as a direct threat to new settlers on government irrigation projects who needed a supplemental income to tide them over the first hard years, when crops returned little or no revenue. Grazing permits were assigned largely by chronological priority, and in most parts of the West established cattle and sheep growers held older rights than those whose primary job was cultivating the soil. Unfortunately, if government farmers were denied entry to the national forests, some national irrigation projects would be unable to attract new residents.[45] An even more immediate threat came from soil erosion and siltation.[46]

In February 1908, Secretary of the Interior James Garfield, acting on a request from the Reclamation Service, informed Secretary of Agriculture James Wilson that he was becoming increasingly concerned with the damage done by sheep grazing within those parts of national forests that contained streams used for irriga-tion. "I have the honor to request that as far and as rapidly as may be practicable, sheep be excluded from watersheds of streams now or immediately to be used for irrigation, and that as to other watersheds held for future irrigation projects, sheep grazing be carefully restricted." Wilson responded that the 1908 grazing contracts had already been negotiated and could not be rescinded. Besides, the Forest Service had as much of a responsibility to serve the needs of grazers as irrigators. Wilson also reminded Garfield that Republican tariff policies had encouraged the sheep industry: "In the past few years the policies of the present National Adminis-tration have resulted in an enormous increase in the number of sheep in the United States, as well as in almost doubling their per capita value and the value of the wool product. It would be most unfortunate if after thus giving an industry care and support, it should be curtailed by restrictive measures except when such measures are clearly necessary for the proper protection of other and larger agricultural interests." As it was, the market for the products of irrigated lands depended directly on the health of the grazing industry.[47]

In the summer and fall of 1908, Newell, Pinchot, officials of the two services, and stockmen met several times to discuss the grazing question. The Reclamation Service faced strong pressure from groups of water users on its projects. For example, the Salt River Water Association called for a complete cessation of grazing in the Tonto and Verde national forests, which contained tributaries of the

Salt River and, they insisted, had been created solely for watershed protection.[48] However, the secretary of agriculture argued that the cost of maintaining land solely for watershed protection was prohibitive and that the inclusion of so much unforested land within national forests in the southwest had opened the Forest Service to severe criticism, which was "not wholly neutralized by the strong support given by water users of the Salt River Valley." Ironically, local stockmen were just as interested in keeping the land under the jurisdiction of the Forest Service as irrigators. In that way it could not be purchased and developed by private water companies, nor was it likely to be thrown open to rival grazers. The upshot was that the Forest Service became more and more reluctant either to withdraw or protect lands for watershed.[49] In 1910 the secretary of agriculture and secretary of the interior nominally agreed that even land covered with brush or other vegetation should be retained in national forests if it protected streamflow or prevented erosion in rivers "important to irrigation or to the water supply of any city, town, or community. . . ." Nevertheless, the controversy over grazing rights and siltation continued.[50]

Many other changes in the relationship between the Forest Service and Reclamation Service occurred in 1907 and 1908. For example, by that time Pinchot's began to appreciate the future potential of the vast number of power sites within the national forests, and some reclamation leaders feared that since dams designed mainly to generate electricity required a year-round flow to drive turbines, the use of streams to produce power was incompatible with the future of irrigation in the valleys below. The fact that the Reclamation Service routinely used the national forests for the timber needed to build their projects, often without asking permission from the Forest Service, was another source of irritation.

Ironically, although the Forest Service was paying less and less attention to the impact of forests on streamflow in the West, the relationship found new life in the East, due in part to the floods of 1907. The East was actually more subject to wide fluctuations in streamflow than the West, and the cost of a flood in property damage was even more severe than the cost of a drought. Now the Forest Service turned much of its attention to the Appalachian and White Mountains where it wanted to purchase about 1,000,000 acres to protect the watersheds of the Potomac, James, Roanoke, Yadkin, Catawba, Broad, Saluda, Savannah, Chattahoochee, Coosa, Tennessee, New, Cumberland, Kentucky, and Monogahela rivers from floods. Foresters insisted that flood control and navigation improvement were their main motives for adding these private lands to the national forests, but the future of hydroelectric power was equally important. Ironically, the money spent on arid land reclamation in the West was offered as one justification for creating new national forests in the East.[51] As historians have long recognized, the streamflow argument was used to dodge the constitutionality of federal acquisition of private lands. If protecting watersheds improved the navigability of rivers, the Forest Service could not be challenged because the protection and improvement of commerce was a clear responsibility of the central government. By 1920 more than 2 million acres had been purchased and by 1961 more than 20 million. It is interesting to note, however, that west of the Mississippi River there were only nineteen votes cast in favor of the Weeks Bill in Congress and fifty-six against; only one yes vote came from the Far West.[52]

The story of the Weeks Act suggests that "science" in the Progressive Era was not as pure, holy, and disinterested as some historians would have it, nor did it bind together a "scientific community" united by ideals of rationality, order, and efficiency. Then, as now, ideas were political weapons, and they were steeped in the moralism of the time. By 1911 the relationship between forests and streamflow was again under serious question, as it had when the first national forests were created.[53] Not until 1910, following Hiram Martin Chittenden's assault on most of the ideas foresters and reclamationists held so dear, was a full-scale test of the relationship of deforestation to streamflow undertaken.[54] Yet this was not unusual in an age when science was long on theory and short on verification. Look at some of the other ideas that were widely believed among scientists at the time. Powell rejected the idea that forests were natural reservoirs, but on at least one occasion he suggested that once the number of irrigated acres reached a certain point, they would contribute to the spread of cedar, piñon, and pine forests by increasing the ambient humidity.[55] And on another occasion he maintained that water that passed through forests carried natural fertilizers that in and of themselves "will be full compensation for the cost of the process [of irrigation]."[56] And although Gifford Pinchot often criticized the American Forestry Association for being the haven of "tree cranks," he blamed the great 1907 flood in the Ohio Valley on deforestation rather than on heavy rains and he repeatedly predicted that in twenty to twenty-five years the United States would face a severe timber famine that would drive up the price of homes, mining, railroads, and even food—the latter as water supplies decreased.[57] Henry Gannett, ever the skeptic, remained skeptical about "forest influences." "In view of the agitation for the protection of our forests which has been going on for at least a generation, and which has reached such intensity that it has become with many persons almost a religion," he noted in a USGS annual report, "it is strange that there should be practically no knowledge to serve as a basis for such a cult."[58] And in 1908 Bernhard Fernow, who had often fallen victim to rash statements,[59] admitted: "Local conditions vary the forest influence to such a degree, that instead of the forest cover being beneficial it may under some conditions even become detrimental, or at least nugatory, as regards regulation of water flow. To tell the truth, while we know much of the general philosophy of the influence of the forest cover on water flow, we are not so fully informed as to details of this influence as we might wish. . . . [E]ven today we have not very far advanced in the exact knowledge and must still remain doubtful as to the precise function of the forest, and all the general assertions that are found in literature on forest influences, except perhaps those on soil erosion, need more careful investigations."[60]

The year 1911 is a convenient place to end this study. Gifford Pinchot had been fired and the American Forestry Association had changed the name of its official publication from *Forestry and Irrigation* to *Conservation* to *American Forestry*. The publication had come full circle. Moreover, the most prominent irrigation journal, *Irrigation Age*, had strongly challenged the idea that forests benefited arid land reclamation.[61] Although Samuel P. Hays credited the Progressive conservation movement with promoting cooperation, rationality, and efficiency, Gifford Pinchot had a different idea. It was partly self-serving, in that he wanted to take full credit for dreaming up the idea of conservation. But it was also right. He noted that at the end of the Roosevelt administration "every separate Government agency having to do with natural resources was riding its own hobby in its own direction. Instead of being, as we should have been, like a squadron of cavalry, all acting together for a single purpose, we were like loose horses in a field, each one following his own nose. Every bureau chief was for himself and his own work, and the devil take all the others. Everyone operated inside his own fence, and few were big enough to see over it. They were all fighting each other for place and credit and funds and jurisdiction. What little cooperation-operation there was between them was an accidental, voluntary, and personal matter between men who happened to be friends." At least in regards to the Forest Service and the Reclamation Service, that seems to be a pretty fair conclusion.[62]

Notes

1. Samuel P. Hays, *Conservation and the Gospel of Efficiency: The Progressive Conservation Movement, 1890-1920* (Cambridge, MA: Harvard University Press, 1959). The book was reprinted in 1974 by Atheneum Press, New York, with a new preface by the author.

2. Hays, *Conservation and the Gospel of Efficiency*, p. 22 (Atheneum Press edition).

3. George Perkins Marsh, *Man and Nature; or Physical Geography as Modified by Human Action* (Cambridge, MA: Harvard University Press, 1965). Marsh discussed the influence of forests on the physical environment in *Man and Nature*, pp. 113-280.

4. "Waste Land and Forest Culture," *Scientific American* 32 (Mar. 13, 1875), p. 161. *See also* Felix Oswald, "The Preservation of Forests," *North American Review* 128 (Jan. 1879), pp. 35-46 and N. H. Egleston, "What We Owe to Trees," *Harper's New Monthly Magazine* 64 (April 1882), pp. 683-84.

5. Donald J. Pisani, "Forests and Conservation, 1865-1890," *Journal of American History* 72 (Sept. 1985), pp. 340-59. The literature on forests and streamflow is vast. Key articles are cited in "Forests and Conservation, 1865-1890," but for an extended discussion of streamflow arguments *see* Abbot Kinney, ed., *Forest and Water* (Los Angeles: Post Publishing Co., 1900).

6. Herbert A. Smith, "The Early Forestry Movement in the United States," *Agricultural History* 12 (Oct. 1938), pp. 334-35; *Third Biennial Report of the California State Board of Forestry, for the Years 1889-90* (Sacramento, 1890), p. l.

7. Ronald F. Lockmann, *Guarding the Forests of Southern California: Evolving Attitudes Toward Conservation of Watershed, Woodlands, and Wilderness* (Glendale, CA: Arthur H. Clark Co., 1981); Douglas H. Strong, "The Sierra Forest Reserve: The Movement to Preserve the San Joaquin Valley Watershed," *Southern California Quarterly* 46 (June 1967), pp. 3-17.

8. John Wesley Powell, *Report on the Lands of the Arid Region of the United States* (Washington, DC: 1878), p. 17. In his annual report for 1877, Secretary of the Interior Carl Shurz predicted that at its current rate of use, the United States had only a twenty year supply of timber left. *See* the *Report of the Secretary of the Interior, 1877* (Washington, DC: 1877), pp. xvi-xvii.

9. "Trees on Arid Lands," *Science* 12 (Oct. 12, 1888), pp. 170-71.

10. John Wesley Powell, "The Lesson of Conemaugh," *North American Review* 149 (Aug. 1889), pp. 150-56; "The Non-Irrigable Lands of the Arid Region," *Century* 39 (April 1890), pp. 915-22. In an untitled, undated statement to the press probably issued in the 1890s, Powell tried to clarify his position on the forests: "The fact is that I have written and urged with all vigor possible that the forests should be preserved from fire, which is the chief agency of destruction, and on the other hand that the forests should be opened by proper means for the use of the people—that to protect the forests from proper use is bad policy, but to protect them from fire is good policy; and I have further urged that the best way of protecting the forests from fire is to put them in the hands of the people for use." *See* Records Group 57, U.S. Geological Survey, Irrigation Survey, Box #1, D-121, National Archives, Washington, D.C. Powell's views were not novel, particularly in the West. *See* J. M. Anders, "Forests—Their Influence Upon Climate and Rainfall," *The American Naturalist* 16 (Jan. 1882), p. 20.

11. As reprinted in Andrew Denny Rodgers II, *Bernhard Eduard Fernow: A Story of North American Forestry* (Princeton, NJ: Princeton University Press, 1951. Reprinted by the Forest History Society, 1991), p. 154.

12. *Report of the Commissioner of Agriculture, 1888* (Washington, DC: 1889), pp. 603-619; Henry Gannett, "Do Forests Influence Rainfall?" *Science* ll (Jan. 6, 1888), pp. 3-5; Gannett, "The Influence of Forests on the Quantity and Frequency of Rainfall," *Science* 12 (Nov. 23, 1888), pp. 242-44; "The Timber-supply of the United States," *Garden and Forest* 6 (April 26, 1893), pp. 181-82; Harold K. Steen, *The U.S. Forest Service: A History* (Seattle: University of Washington Press, 1976. Reprinted 1991), p. 41.

13. C. S. Sargent, "Irrigation Problems in the Arid West," *Garden and Forest* l (Aug. 8, 1888), pp. 277-78.

14. C. S. Sargent, "The Danger from Mountain Reservoirs," *Garden and Forest* 2 (June 19, 1889), p. 289; Sargent, "Mountain Reservoirs and Irrigation," July 13, 1889, pp. 313-14.

15. C. S. Sargent, "The Forests on the Public Domain," *Garden and Forest* 3 (Jan. 8, 1890), pp. 13-14; "Forests and Irrigation," *Garden and Forest* 3 (June 18, 1890), p. 293.

16. J. B. Harrison, "Forests and Civilization: The North Woods, VII," *Garden and Forest* 2 (Sept. ll, 1889), pp. 441-42.

17. J. B. Harrison to Benjamin Harrison, Sept. 18, 1889, Record Group 57, Records of the U.S. Geological Survey, Letters Received Aug. 5-Oct. 30, 1889, National Archives, Washington, D.C.

18. B. E. Fernow, "The Relation of Irrigation Problems to Forest Conditions," in *Report of the Special Committee of the United States Senate on the Irrigation and Reclamation of Arid Lands* (Washington, DC: 1890), serial 2708, part 4, pp. 112-24. The quote is from p. 120. Fernow made the same points in the *Report of the Secretary of Agriculture, 1889* (Washington, DC: 1889), p. 276.

19. *Garden and Forest* 4 (July l, 1891), p. 301 and Oct. 21, 1891, pp. 493-94. Rodgers, *Bernhard Eduard Fernow*, pp. 158-59; Steen, *The U.S. Forest Service: A History*, pp. 27-28; *Report of the Secretary of the Interior, 1893* (Washington, DC: 1893), pp. 78-79.

20. During the first years of the 1890s, the amount of irrigated land in the West had doubled to over 7 million acres. Paul W. Gates, *History of Public Land Law Development* (Washington, DC: Government Printing Office, 1968), p. 647.

21. John Ise, *The United States Forest Policy* (New Haven, CT: 1920), p. 295-96.

22. *Official Proceedings of the Third National Irrigation Congress, Held at Denver, Colorado, Sept. 3rd to 8th, 1894* (Denver, n.d.), pp. 47-49; Lockmann, *Guarding the Forests of Southern California*, p. 102.

23. *Garden and Forest* 10 (Oct. 27, 1897), p. 420.

24. George Maxwell, "Irrigation and the Forest," *The Forester* 7 (Sept. 1901), p. 233. *See also* Maxwell, "Nature's Storage Reservoirs," *The Forester* 5 (Aug. 1899), pp. 183-85.

25. The AFA was similar to the irrigation congress in many ways. Both were quasi- governmental institutions designed to popularize legislation hatched by elites within government or scientific societies. Both were designed to apply pressure to Congress. Both were infected with a dreamy idealism that often hampered the achievement of practical objectives. And both were designed to bridge the gap between public needs and governmental institutions that could not govern.

26. In January 1899, the drought prompted agricultural and horticultural societies, chambers of commerce, boards of trade, the state miners association, and many other organizations to organize the California Society for Conserving Waters and Protecting Forests. A few months later southern California groups followed suit, and elected Kinney president of their organiza-tion. *See* Donald J. Pisani, *From the Family Farm to Agribusiness: The Irrigation Crusade in California and the West, 1850-1931* (Berkeley: University of California Press, 1984), pp. 294-99; C. Raymond Clar, *California Government and Forestry: From Spanish Days Until the Creation of the Department of Natural Resources in 1927* (Sacramento: Division of Forestry, State of California, 1959-1969), pp. 169-76.

27. "The American Forestry Association," *The Forester* 5 (Aug. 1899), pp. 171-79.

28. For Newell's ideas *see* the annual reports of the USGS, Hydrology Section, for the years from 1896-1901. *See also* Newell's "The National Forest Reserves," *The National Geographic Magazine* 8 (June 1897), pp. 177-87, and Newell, "Forests and Reservoirs," *The Forester* 7 (Sept. 1901), pp. 225-28. Gifford Pinchot describes his relationship with Newell in *Breaking New Ground* (New York: Harcourt, Brace and Company, 1947), p. 316.

29. Pinchot, *Breaking New Ground*, pp. 123, 250. For Gannett's work *see* the reports of the USGS.

30. "Report of the Commissioner of the General Land Office, 1902," in *Reports of the Department of the Interior* (Washington, DC: 1902), p. 320. *See also* Edward A. Bowers, "The Future of Federal Forest Reservations," *Forestry and Irrigation* 10 (Mar. 1904), p. 132.

31. "Report of the Forester, 1903," in *Annual Reports of the Department of Agriculture, 1903* (Washington, DC: 1903), p. 497.

32. *See* the map showing the land reserved for forests and reclamation (Plate 1) in *Fourth Annual Report of the Reclamation Service, 1904-05* (Washington, DC: 1906).

33. C. J. Blanchard, "Mutual Relations of the Forest Service and the Reclamation Service," *Forestry and Irrigation* 12 (Jan. 1906), p. 42.

34. F. H. Newell to Secretary of the Interior, March 17, 1905, RG 115, Records of the Bureau of Reclamation, General Administrative and Project Records, 1902-1919, "783—Establishment and Extension of Forest Reserves," New Mexico file, Box 241. *See also* A. P. Davis to Gifford Pinchot, June 17, 1905 in the same file; Newell to the Secretary of Interior, Feb. 16, 1905, in Colorado file, Box 240; John Whistler to Chief Engineer, Nov. 18, 1903, Oregon file, Box 241; *Official Proceedings of the Thirteenth National Irrigation Congress* (Portland, 1905), p. 72.

35. Gifford Pinchot to F. H. Newell, Sept. 19, 1903, Gifford Pinchot Collection, Box 994, Library of Congress, Washington, D.C. *See also* Pinchot to F. H. Newell, April 17, 1907, RG 115, Records of the Bureau of Reclamation, General Administrative and Project Records, 1902-1919, "783—Establishment and Extension of Forest Reserves," Montana file, Box 241 and in the same file A. P. Davis (Acting Director, Reclamation Service) to the Secretary of Interior, November [date illegible], 1906.

36. Overton Price, Acting Forester, to F. H. Newell, Jan. 4, 1904, in RG 95, Records of the Forest Service, Division of Operation, Box 1, "Reclamation Service" file, and Gifford Pinchot to F. H. Newell, April 26, 1905, RG 95, Records of Letters Sent by the Office of the Associate Forester, 1905-8, National Archives; E. A. Sterling, "Forest Planting About Reservoirs and Along Canals," in *Official Proceedings of the Thirteenth National Irrigation Congress* (Portland, 1905), pp. 82-86. On March 2, 1907, the *Washington Star* reported: "The forestry bureau is not only preserving and cultivating the standing forests on government land, but is beginning to plant trees in different parts of the west. It is undertaking a vast scheme of creative work and will restore, so far as possible, the timber that has been stripped from the mountain sides, where are the sources of the streams that are needed to irrigate the arid plains below. The bureau is working in co-operation with the reclamation service and is also advising, encouraging and assisting private individuals, railway corporations, lumber companies and others to reclothe the denuded hills." Planting new forests or increasing the stand in old forests, it was assumed, would increase the irrigable area of the West by increasing the water supply.

37. Gifford Pinchot, "What the Forest Service Stands For," *Forestry and Irrigation* 13 (Jan. 1907), pp. 27-28; Hays, *Conservation and the Gospel of Efficiency*, p. 72.

38. F. H. Newell to D. C. Henny, May ll, 1908, RG 115, Records of the Bureau of Reclamation; General Administrative and Project Records, 1902-1919, "Sacramento, 340-991," Box 831, National Archives.

39. *Report of the Secretary of Agriculture, 1905* (Washington, DC: 1905), p. lvii.

40. As quoted in E. Louise Peffer, *The Closing of the Public Domain: Disposal and Reservation Policies, 1900-1950* (Stanford, Calif., 1951), p. 74.

41. For example, a memorial from Colorado in May, 1909, charged that less than one- third of the 16 million acres within national forests in that state was actually forested. See *Congressional Record*, Senate, May 14, 1909, pp. 2019-20. Even after Congress cut off this source of income to the Forest Service in 1907, Pinchot and Forest Service officials kept close track of the amount of revenue generated by grazing and timber-cutting permits to remind congressional appropriations committees that the Forest Service largely paid for itself.

42. James L. Penick, Jr., *Progressive Politics and Conservation: The Ballinger-Pinchot Affair* (Chicago: University of Chicago Press, 1968), p. 4.

43. Peffer, *The Closing of the Public Domain*, p. 186; *Annual Report of the Secretary of Agriculture, 1906* (Washington, DC: 1907), pp. 52-53; *Report . . . 1907* (Washington, DC: 1908), pp. 62, 64.

44. "Report of the Forester, 1908," in *Annual Reports of the Department of Agriculture, 1908* (Washington, DC: 1909), p. 426.

45. *Fourth Annual Report of the Reclamation Service, 1904-5* (Washington, DC: 1906), pp. 30-31.

46. Henry S. Graves, "Shall the States Own the Forests?" *Outlook* 102 (Dec. 28, 1912), p. 937.

47. James R. Garfield to Secretary of Agriculture, Feb. 20, 1908 and James Wilson to Secretary of Interior, March 13, 1908, RG 115, Records of the Bureau of Reclamation, General Administrative and Project Records, 1902-1919, "783—Establishment and Extension of Forest Reserves," Box 240.

48. "Report of the Forester, 1909," in *Annual Reports of the Department of Agriculture, 1909* (Washington, DC: 1910), p. 391; A. P. Davis to The Forester, Nov. 30, 1909 and Charles A. Van der Veer (Secretary of the Salt River Valley water Users' Association) to the Director of the Reclamation Service, July 6, 1912, both in RG 115, Records of the Bureau of Reclamation, General Administrative and Project Records, 1902-1919, "783—Establishment and

Extension of Forest Reserves," Arizona file, Box 240; J. B. Lippincott, "Relation of Stream Flow and Suspended Sediment Therein, to the Covering of Drainage Basins," in Abbot Kinney, *Forest and Water* (Los Angeles, 1900), p. 234.

49. Acting Secretary of Agriculture to Secretary of Interior, Aug. 30, 1913, RG 115, Records of the Bureau of Reclamation, General Administrative and Project Records, 1902-1919, "783—Establishment and Extension of Forest Reserves, Arizona file, Box 240.

50. "Report of the Forester, 1911," in *Annual Reports of the Department of Agriculture* (Washington, DC: 1912), p. 349.

51. *Washington Post*, March 2, 1907.

52. Steen, *The U.S. Forest Service*, pp. 127-29; Ise, *The United States Forest Policy*, pp. 207-23; Edwin A. Start, "How the House Voted," *Forestry and Irrigation* 15 (June 1909), pp. 348-57.

53. Gordon B. Dodds, "The Stream-Flow Controversy: A Conservation Turning Point," *Journal of American History* 56 (June 1969), pp. 59-69.

54. Jenks Cameron, *The Development of Governmental Forest Control in the United States* (Institute for Government Research Studies in Administration, Baltimore, MD: Johns Hopkins University Press, 1928), pp. 276, 367-69; "Report of the Forester," in *Annual Reports of the Department of Agriculture, 1910* (Washington, DC: 1911), p. 393. Unfortunately, Hays and others have cast Chittenden's attack mainly as part of the Army Corps of Engineers' effort to defeat the comprehensive and coordinated river basin planning threatened by the Inland Waterways Commission. *See*, for example, Thomas R. Cox, Robert S. Maxwell, Phillip Drennon Thomas, and Joseph J. Malone, *This Well-Wooded Land: Americans and Their Forests From Colonial Times to the Present* (Lincoln, NE: University of Nebraska Press, 1985), pp. 149-50. Chittenden's approach to the streamflow problem was far more "scientific" than the proponents of the idea. Nevertheless, at least one official within the Bureau of Forestry conceded that many factors influenced stream flow besides the existence of trees including precipitation, topography, geology, and the character of vegetation. *See* W. B. Greeley, "The Effect of Forest Cover upon Stream Flow," *Forestry and Irrigation*, ll (June 1905), pp. 163-68.

55. "Trees on Arid Lands," *Science* 12 (Oct. 12, 1888), pp. 170-71.

56. John Wesley Powell, *Report on the Lands of the Arid Region of the United States* (Washington, DC: 1878), p. 20.

57. Gifford Pinchot, "The Upper Ohio Flood," *Forestry and Irrigation* 13 (April 1907), p. 169; Pinchot, "The Conservation of Natural Resources," *Outlook*, Oct. 12, 1907.

58. As quoted in Cameron, *The Development of Governmental Forest Control in the United States*, p. 215.

59. For example, in 1891 he predicted: "Once let woods be spread over the now arid plains of the West and there would be rain in plenty there." *See* "Forests," *Scientific American* 65 (Sept. 19, 1891), p. 181.

60. As quoted in Rodgers, *Bernhard Eduard Fernow*, pp. 128-29.

61. *Irrigation Age*, 22 (Dec. 1906), p. 39; 23 (Feb. 1908), p. 105.

62. Pinchot, *Breaking New Ground*, p. 321.

Early Administration of the Forest Reserve Act:
Interior Department and General Land Office Policies,
1891-1897

James Muhn
Bureau of Land Management

The President, by Section 24 of the Act of March 3, 1891, was permitted to "set apart and reserve . . . public land bearing forests . . . or in part covered by timber or undergrowth, whether of commercial value or not, as public reservations." The provision, attached as a last-minute rider in the Congress, was, in Gifford Pinchot's estimate, "the most important legislation in the history of Forestry in America." To the former Forest Service chief it represented the "beginning and basis of our whole National Forest system."[1]

The Forest Reserve Act, as the legislation has come to be known, was regarded by forestry advocates and federal officials as the first step toward protecting the public domain's remaining stands of valuable timber. The law set aside the public lands withdrawn under its provision from further settlement and appropriation but did little else. There were no specific management provisions or monies provided for the protection of the forest reservations until enactment of the Forest Management Act in 1897.

The absence of specific administrative authority until 1897 has led historians to conclude that, aside from establishing forest reserves, the Department of the Interior and the General Land Office did little in regard to the forest reserves while Congress debated various administrative measures.[2] Want of more specific direction from Congress, however, did not mean that Interior and General Land Office officials did not administer or protect the reserves. Establishment of forest reservations brought up numerous policy questions. Forest reserves had to be selected, access to resources considered, and protection provided. The Land Department gave considerable attention to these issues, doing what it could with the limited means available to them.[3]

Land Department officials saw enactment of the Forest Reserve Act as an important step toward protecting public timberlands from waste and destruction. The

General Land Office had long condemned the rapid disappearance of the public domain's most valuable timber, claiming that inadequate legislation hampered proper protection of the resource from unlawful appropriation and depredation.[4] The Forest Reserve Act, as GLO Commissioner Thomas H. Carter remarked in 1891, promised to "do much in the way of caring for portions of the public lands bearing forest which it is needful to preserve from spoliation."[5] Secretary of the Interior John Noble agreed, adding that if the law was "prosecuted systematically and thoroughly, posterity will look upon the action as that to which the country owes much of its prosperity and safety."[6]

Secretary Noble's statement implied a liberal use of the Forest Reserve Act, but neither he nor his commissioner of the General Land Office intended to use the law indiscriminately. The act, in their view, did not authorize withdrawal of all public timberland.[7] "Wise discretion," as GLO Commissioner Carter put it, was to be used in proclaiming forest reservations.[8] The General Land Office's 1891 circular instructions regarding the investigation of potential forest reserves stated that only those forests "not absolutely required for the legitimate use and necessities of the residents," the promotion of settlement, or the development of natural resources in the immediate vicinity of the timber were to be considered for withdrawal.[9]

The Forest Reserve Act was also seen as more than simply a timber preservation law. Secretary Noble, like many others at the time, believed that the timber at the headwaters of streams had to be protected to prevent devastating floods and to insure a summer-long water supply for the irrigation of lands in the arid West.[10] With that in mind, the General Land Office told its special agents that it was of "first importance to reserve all public lands in mountainous and other regions . . . covered with timber or undergrowth at the headwaters of river and along the bank of streams."[11]

There were, however, other reasons for creating forest reservations. These reserves, as Secretary Noble noted, would "preserve the fauna, fish and flora of our country, and become resorts for the people seeking instruction and recreation."[12] He also expressed willingness to withdraw those areas of "great interest to our people because of their natural beauty, or remarkable features."[13]

The Yellowstone National Park Timber Land Reserve,[14] the first forest reservations proclaimed, reflected these broad considerations. Located adjacent to the east and south boundaries of the park for which it took its name, the reserve's thick stands of timber embraced the headwaters of the Yellowstone River and other streams, but as important, if not more so, the new reserve embraced important wildlife habitat, scenic mountains, and natural curiosities.[15]

Wildlife, scenic, and other considerations figured significantly in the creation of
the other forest reserves prior to 1897. Petitions for the White River Plateau,
Pike's Peak, and Pecos forest reservations called attention the wildlife and scenic
values of those areas. The General Land Office recommendation for the Pacific
Forest Reserve advocated withdrawal of majestic Mount Rainier for its scenic and
scientific significance as much as for the importance of its watershed to flood
control. The Afognak Forest and Fish Reserve in Alaska was made at request of
the U.S. Commission of Fish and Fisheries to preserve natural spawning grounds
and wildlife habitat.[16] The Grand Cañon Forest Reserve stretched interpretation of
the Forest Reserve Act to its fullest. The reservation did contain some timbered
land but mostly embraced the spectacular canyon for which it was named.[17] Still,
as Secretary Noble himself said, these other reasons were subservient to the
"important agricultural and economic purposes" for establishing the forest
reserves.[18]

Most of the early forest reservations were proclaimed only after an exhaustive
investigation by special agents from the General Land Office.[19] The special agents
assigned to the investigations were directed in their work by circular instructions
issued on May 15, 1891, as well as specific guidance from the commissioner. They
travelled throughout the proposed reserves to determine first-hand the character of
the lands and decide which lands, if any, should be included.[20] The men also
assessed public sentiment through personal interviews with local officials and
residents and by soliciting further comment through newspaper notices. These
findings, as well as the other information gathered, were reviewed by the General
Land Office and formed the basis of its recommendations to the secretary of the
interior.[21]

The purpose of establishing forest reservations, as GLO Commissioner Carter
pointed out, was not to cause "injury to the people—the object in their creation
being the present and ultimate benefit to the community at large."[22] The General
Land Office, therefore, took care not exclude whole counties from operation under
the settlement and mining laws.[23] It also made an effort to draw forest reserve
boundaries to eliminate areas known to be chiefly agricultural or mineral in character. The Pike's Peak Timber Land Reserve boundary omitted the newly established
Cripple Creek and Cheyenne mining districts and the Pacific Forest Reserve
excluded coal lands and nearby communities.[24]

It was impossible for the General Land Office to draw boundaries that did not
include some mining and agricultural lands. Hundreds of people as a consequence
found themselves within the forest reservations. The situation did not affect the

interests of private landowners or settlers and miners whose lands were covered by valid entries and locations.[25] Settlers on unsurveyed lands and preemption claimants who had not made entry at the time forest reserves were proclaimed, however, were not protected by the public land laws or legal precedents.[26]. These people faced loss of their homes and expulsion from the reserves as trespassers because they had no "vested interest" in the land that had been withdrawn.[27] Secretary Noble, at the urging of the General Land Office, prevented this from happening by adopting an "equitable administration of the law" that permitted individuals who had made actual settlement in good faith and who were in compliance with the Homestead and Preemption laws prior to withdrawal a forest reserve to make entry and prove up.[28]

The Land Department in adopting this liberal interpretation of law toward settlers hoped that opposition to the creation of forest reservations would be quieted. The controversy, however, was continued by petitions and memorials demanding access to forest reservation resources.

GLO Commissioner Carter did not believe the forest reservations should be locked up. He espoused the American Forestry Association philosophy that the timber and other resources should be made available in a rational and economical manner. Furthermore, Carter felt the law provided sufficient authority for the promulgation of the necessary rules and regulations that would permit such use.[29] Secretary of the Interior Noble, however, did not formulate the needed regulations during his tenure.

Arnold Hague, Bernhard Fernow, and subsequent historians, have argued that Noble's inaction stemmed from his narrow view of the forest reserves as pristine national parks. Noble did urge Congress in 1891 to set the forest reserves apart as national or state parks so that they could be "preserved unimpaired and used for the benefit of the public only." This initial position was undoubtedly influenced by the fact that many of first forest reservations had previously been petitioned for as national parks, but there is little evidence in Land Department files to support this as Secretary Noble's reason for not issuing regulations.[30]

Noble did sympathize with the reasonable use philosophy as advocated by the American Forestry Association. He supported Commissioner Carter's call for the issuance of rules and regulations that would provide for the use of forest reserve resources. In fact, the Interior Department declared that the secretary had the authority needed "to carry into execution the provisions of the law authorizing the withdrawal of such lands and to the realization of the objects of that legislation."[31]

One reason for Secretary Noble's reluctance to approve regulations came from his dislike of exercising discretionary authority in the absence of specific congressional direction. The prerogative, in Noble mind, was a "Pandora's Box," for once the Land Department allowed for the use of forest reserve resources it would be difficult, if not impossible, to limit the privileges granted.[32]

The Land Department also did not have the means needed to administer any rules and regulations it might promulgate. The General Land Office when it advocated rules and regulations for the forest reservations pointed out that the Forest Reserve Act provided no monies for protection, and the small force of special agents at its disposal, given their many responsibilities, would only permit the special agent to give "cursory attention" to the reservations. Such circumstances did not allow for proper supervision of the reserves, and GLO Commissioner Carter worried that permitting use of the forest reserve resources without sufficient control would "only encourage depredations." He, therefore, suggested that no privileges be granted in the forest reserves until Congress provided for protection and supervision.[33]

With these concerns in mind, Secretary Noble turned the matter of opening up the forest reserves over to Congress. He asked Congress to provide a protective force for the forest reservations and to decide how the reserves should be administered.[34] In the interim Noble felt the General Land Office recommendation that timber cutting, grazing, and other uses within the reserves be prohibited was the best course of action to follow.[35]

That was the situation when the Cleveland Administration took office in early 1893. The new secretary of the interior, Hoke Smith, and his Land Office commissioner, Silas Lamoreux, both supported the forest reserve idea.[36] The two men their first annual reports renewed the Land Department plea that Congress enact "legislation which may lay the foundation for a wise, [and] comprehensive forestry system." They also continued their predecessors call for the establishment of a supervisory corps to protect the forest reservations.[37]

The latter was of most immediate concern to the new Land Department officials. They had reports of "widespread destruction by the woodsman and the still greater devastation wrought by . . . forest fires," as well as sheepherding trespass problems.[38] The General Land Office, however, had no hope of effectively patrolling the forest reserves. Congress had not acted on the request for a protective force, and its small corps of special agents, already spread thin, was further diminished because of reduced appropriations.[39] The consequence, as Secretary Smith pointed out, was that the reserves were no better protected than the unappropriated and unreserved public lands. The situation compelled the Land Department to turn to the War Department for assistance.[40]

The idea of using the military as a constabulary force in the forest reserves had arisen in public timberland policy discussions and debates prior to 1891.[41] The Interior Department had used cavalry troops to protect Yellowstone National Park with good results since 1886, and in 1891 it was able to get patrols assigned to Yosemite, Sequoia, and General Grant national parks in California.[42]

When the Yellowstone National Park Timber Land Reserve was established, Secretary of the Interior John Noble had directed the army commander at the adjacent national park "to assume control [of the reserve] and do any and all things as to the accession as you do in the Park itself."[43] The Army could do little more than send occasional patrols through the 1.2 million acre reserve, and could legally do no more than remove trespassers they happened upon.[44] Yet, while this made the situation at the Yellowstone National Park Timber Land Reserve less than satisfactory, the protection provided was more than that the other reserves had.[45]

The Land Department and others considered using the Army to patrol the other forest reserves but no formal request was made until the summer of 1893.[46] By then, Acting Secretary of the Interior William H. Sims, reacting to a General Land Office call for help, told the secretary of war that he needed army patrols because the Land Department felt powerless to protect the forest reservations. The War Department, while sympathetic, refused the request. It pointed out that in the opinion of its acting judge advocate general, the War Department had no legal authority to use soldiers as a "*posse comitatus*, or otherwise, for the purpose of executing the laws," except as might be provided by the Constitution or law. Secretary Smith attempted to get the War Department to change its decision, but his effort was of no avail.[47]

With no hope of receiving assistance from the Army, the Land Department, with the assistance of forestry advocates, renewed its call to Congress for some form of protection and administration for the forest reserves.[48] The debate over forest reserve policy in Congress went, as before, nowhere. Land Department officials, however, were not content with the *status quo*.[49]

The first policy shift came soon after President Cleveland proclaimed the Ashland and Cascade forest reserves in Oregon on September 28, 1893. The Land Department decided not to create any more forest reservations. It made little sense, in the Land Department's mind, to set aside any more reserves until Congress finally provided for their protection and management.[50]

The Land Department's most significant change was its more aggressive stance toward trespass and depredations within the forest reservations. Under Secretary Smith the General Land Office took the position that "the object in creating [the] forest reserves [was] to preserve the lands and timber and undergrowth thereon in a state of nature, as near as possible, and as a conservation for the water supply," and that its only authority was to protect the forest reservations from encroachments and depredations until Congress provided for the proper and judicious use.[51] To do this, the General Land Office, as it told one of its special agents in regard to timber trespass, wanted people to understand that "trespassing on the public lands within these forest reserves will not be tolerated under any pretext, and that those so offending will be prosecuted to the full extent of the law, criminally and civilly."[52]

This policy was formally promulgated in regulations issued on April 14, 1894. Published in local newspapers and posted along forest reserve boundaries, the regulations warned the public against committing depredations and trespass in the forest reservations. No one, it announced, could "settle upon, occupy, or use any of these lands for agricultural, prospecting, mining, or other business purposes."[53] They could not "cut, remove, or use any of the timber, grass, or other natural product," fires were forbidden, and the grazing of livestock was "strictly prohibited." Violators of the regulations, it stated, would be prosecuted for trespass and held financially responsible for any waste and damage—"whether done intentionally or caused by neglect."[54]

The regulations, which simply stated the Land Department's long held policy, was greeted with protest.[55] Stockraising interests were particularly disturbed.[56] California politicians declared that the prohibition would bring "absolute ruin" to the livestock industry and petitioned the Land Department modify its regulations in regard to grazing.[57]

Commissioner Lamoreux was unmoved by such pleas.[58] He contended that the regulations reflected the intent of the Forest Reserve Act that the reserves were to be preserved in their natural state. Until Congress enacted legislation that said otherwise, Lamoreux said, the General Land Office was intent on the rigid enforcement of the regulations of April 14, 1894.[59]

Strict enforcement of the forest reserve regulations was, of course, impossible with its insufficient force of special agents. No sooner was the notice of April 14, 1894, issued than its provisions were openly defied.

In July 1894, for example, it was reported that half the circular notices posted along the Sierra Forest Reserve's west boundary had been torn down by sheep herders. To make matters worse, there were said to be half a million sheep in the reservation, more than anyone had previously remembered seeing. As for the condition of the reserve, it was reported to be "about as bad as it possibly could be, were it not for the tall pine and tamarack trees, which the sheep cannot prey on, it might justly be termed a desert."[60]

The contemptuous attitude of stockmen was a "serious embarrassment" to the General Land Office. When asked in August 1895 if the sheep seen grazing in the Cascade Forest Reserve in Oregon meant the reservation had been excepted from the forest reserve regulations, the General Land Office replied that while the reserve was still closed to grazing, it was unable to enforce the 1894 regulations.[61]

Although the General Land Office's special agents could do little to prevent trespass and depredations, it did not give up hope of enforcing the regulations. There was still another avenue of relief—the federal courts. The prosecution of public land law violators had always been difficult.[62] The General Land Office, however, saw it as the most effective way handling the situation. "Vigorous prosecution . . . ," it was hoped, "if inaugurated and persistently and continuously pushed, case after case, may have some effect" of warning violators from the forest reservations.[63]

The Forest Reserve Act itself stipulated no penalties against trespass or depredations. There were, however, statutes that did provide for fines and imprisonment for trespass upon government reservations. These laws, as well as court rulings that asserted the federal government's right to protect its property like any other owner, provided sufficient authority for Department of Justice to file legal actions.[64]

Suits against timber trespassers were proved particularly successful. A General Land Office official reported in 1896 that timber depredations in the San Bernardino, Trabuco Cañon, and San Gabriel forest reservations in California had nearly stopped because vigorous prosecutions had scared timber cutters with the real possibility of arraignment and imprisonment.[65]

More difficult were grazing trespass cases. The General Land Office perceived grazing—particularly sheep grazing—as the most dangerous threat to the reserves. It claimed sheep did "irreparable damage" by eating "every vestige of green growth as though the ground was swept by fire," and the General Land Office wanted the sheep and other livestock out of the reserves before the animals destroyed them.[66]

The initial suits against stockraisers were filed in California. Special agents of the General Land Office cooperated with the U.S. Attorneys in California in gathering evidence but no convictions were won. The problem, as the U.S. Attorney for the

Southern District of California reported in 1896, was that a "special agent or a witness sees a band of sheep traversing the reservation, but he is wholly unable to testify, when called to the witness stand, whether the destruction of the young growth was by the band of sheep seen by him or by some preceding band of sheep traversing the same territory."[67]

Better results, however, were achieved in Oregon. The attorney general, at the urging of the Land Department, instructed the U.S. Attorney for Oregon to "vigorously prosecute" all case of grazing trespass. Injunctions against any sheep herders who threatened to go upon the forest reserves were to also be filed, and the penalty of contempt was to be enforced against anyone who violated the orders of the court.[68]

Within months the U.S. Attorney for Oregon, aided by a specially appointed deputy U.S. Marshal, had secured one preliminary injunction and commenced eight criminal prosecutions against stockmen.[69] Then in late September 1896, the U.S. Attorney won a significant victory in the federal circuit court for Oregon. In the matter of *United States v. Tygh Valley Land & Live-Stock Co.*, the court held that there was "no implication of a license to use the [forest reserves] to the destruction or injury of these forests," and reiterated the judicial doctrine that the federal government had the right to protect its interests against the threat of trespass and injury.[70] The Oregon livestock industry could no longer ignore the 1894 forest reservation regulations.[71]

The aggressive and successful prosecution of forest reserve timber depredations and grazing trespasses in California and Oregon by the Department of Justice achieved what the Land Department wanted: the enforcement of the 1894 regulations. However, before similar actions could be pushed elsewhere, Congress, reacting to the "Washington Birthday Reserves" made by President Cleveland, enacted the Forest Management Act of June 4, 1897. The law opened the forest reservations to timber cutting, mining, and by implication, livestock grazing, under rules and regulations prescribed by the secretary of the interior. It also provided for the protection of the reserves from fire and other depredations. The forest reserves now entered a new era of administration.[72]

Forest reserve administration by the Department of the Interior and the General Land Office from 1891-1897 was far from satisfactory. This was largely a consequence of Congress' failure to enact legislation that would have provided for the reasonable and judicious use of forest reservation resources, as well as a sufficient force of guardians to protect the reserves from fire, depredation, and trespass. Still, the Land Department did inaugurate a forest reserve system that not only advanced the concerns of forestry advocates but also safeguarded the interests of local communities. These officials also addressed the policy questions that arose as a consequence of the forest

reserve system. Among the most difficult being the supervision of the forest reservations. General Land Office protection, severely hindered by its small force of special
agents, proved particularly frustrating, but by 1896 the Land Department's stance
toward prosecuting violators had begun to have some affect. Land Department supervision of the forest reserves from 1891 to 1897 proved not to be a time of inactivity
and benign neglect, but one of active and concerned administration.

Notes

1. Gifford Pinchot, *Breaking New Ground*, Reprint (Washington, DC: Island Press, 1987), p. 85.

2. *See* John Ise, *The United States Forest Policy* (New Haven: Yale University Press, 1924), pp. 120-
   139; Jenks Cameron, *The Development of Governmental Forest Control in the United States*
   (Baltimore: The Johns Hopkins Press, 1928), 205-207; Harold K. Steen, *The U.S. Forest Service:
   A History* (Seattle: University Press of Washington, 1976), pp. 27-34; Lawrence Rakestraw, "A
   History of Forest Conservation in the Pacific Northwest, 1891-1913," Ph.D. dissertation, University of Washington, 1955: pp. 35-68; Herbert D. Kirkland III, "The American Forests, 1864-
   1898: A Trend Toward Conservation," Ph.D. dissertation, Florida State University, 1971: pp.
   188-246; and Joseph A. Miller, "Congress and the Origins of Conservation: Natural Resource
   Policies, 1865-1900," Ph.D. dissertation, University of Minnesota, 1973: pp. 300-325.

3. "Land Department" was a term commonly used to denote those officials and bureaus within the
   Department of the Interior who administered public land matters. This included the secretary of
   the interior, his assistants, various branch of his office—such as the Lands and Railroads
   Division—as well as, the commissioner of the General Land Office and his agency. *See* Joseph R.
   Rohrer, *Questions and Answers on the United States Public Land Laws and Procedure. . . .*
   (Washington, DC: Joseph R. Rohrer, 1912).

4. Ise, *Forest Policy*, pp. 62-92; Cameron, *Development of Governmental Forest Control*, pp. 100-
   118, 158-178; and U.S. Department of the Interior, General Land Office, *Annual Report of the
   Commissioner of the General Land Office for the Fiscal Year Ended June 30, 1890* (Washington,
   DC: U.S. Government Printing Office, 1890), pp. 80-86. Hereafter cited as *GLO Annual Report*.

5. *GLO Annual Report* (1891), p. 55.

6. U.S. Department of the Interior, *Annual Report of the Secretary of the Interior for the Fiscal Year
   Ended June 30, 1891* (Washington, DC: U.S. Government Printing Office, 1891), I: XV.
   Hereafter cited as *Interior Annual Report*.

7. Congress substantiated that interpretation by extending the Timber and Stone Act of 1878, which
   provided for the sale of public lands chiefly valuable for their timber or stone in California,
   Nevada, Oregon, and Washington, to the remaining public land states and territories in 1892. *See*
   Act of August 4, 1892 (27 Stat. 348).

8. GLO Commissioner to Detailed GLO Clerk G. V. N. Ogden, 21 September 1891, General Land Office, Division "R", Press Copies of Letters Sent to Registers and Receivers [Special Agents, Secretary of the Interior and Miscellaneous Persons] Concerning Saw Mills, Timber Permits, and Forest Reserves, 1891-1908, Record Group 49, Records of the Bureau of Land Management, National Archives, Washington, D.C. [Hereafter cited as GLO, Div. "R", Letters Sent, RG 49, NA].

9. U.S. Department of the Interior, General Land Office, "Circular of Instructions Relating to Timber Reservations," 15 May 1891, *Compilation of Public Timber Laws and Regulations and Decisions Thereunder: Issued January 21, 1897* (Washington, DC: U.S. Government Printing Office, 1897), p. 131.

10. Andrew Denny Rodgers, III, *Bernhard Eduard Fernow: A Story of North American Forestry* (Princeton: Princeton University Press, 1951), p. 199; Miller, "Congress and the Origins of Conservation," p. 281; *Interior Annual Report* (1891), I: XIII; and Secretary of the Interior Noble to Robert Underwood Johnson, 28 August 1891, in *Remembered Yesterdays*, by Robert Underwood Johnson (Boston: Little, Brown, and Co., 1923), p. 295.

11. General Land Office, "Circular of Instructions Relating to Timber Reservations," 15 May 1891, *Compilation of Public Timber Laws*, p. 132; and GLO Commissioner to Special Agent B. F. Allen, 10 October 1891, GLO, Div. "R", Letters Sent, RG 49, NA.

12. *Interior Annual Report* (1891), I: XV.

13. Secretary of the Interior Noble to President, 25 March 1891, Department of the Interior, Patents and Miscellaneous Division, Miscellaneous Letters Sent, 1894-1908, Record Group 48, Records of the Office of the Secretary of the Interior, NA [Hereafter cited as DOI, P & Misc. Div., Letters Sent, RG 48, NA].

14. During the period 1891 to 1897, the forest reservations were called "Timber Land" and "Forest" reserves. The research found no significance in the differing names. It appears to be simply a change in title. The term "Timber Land" reserve was used from the establishment of the Yellowstone National Park Timber Land Reserve on March 30, 1891, to the creation of the San Gabriel Timber Land Reserve on December 20, 1892. Prior to San Gabriel, the term "Forest Reserve" was used twice—first with the Pecos and then the South Platte. After San Gabriel, the term "Forest Reserve" was consistently used when naming the new forest reservation. All forest reservations were renamed "National Forests" by act of Congress in 1907.

15. *Interior Annual Report* (1891), I: CXXXVII-CXXXVIII; Eliza Ruhamah Scidmore, "Our New National Forest Reserves," *Century Magazine* 46 (September 1893): 795; Thomas G. Manning, *Government in Science: The U.S. Geological Survey, 1867-1894* (Lexington: University of Kentucky Press, 1967), pp. 155-165; and Aubrey L. Haines, *The Yellowstone Story*, 2 vols. (Boulder: Colorado Associated University Press, 1977), II: 94-95.

16. *See* correspondence in files for Santa Fe National Forest, Pike's Peak National Forest, and White River National Forest, GLO, Div. "R", National Forest Files, RG 49, NA; GLO Commissioner to Secretary of the Interior, 18 January 1893, GLO, Div. "R", Letters Sent, RG 49, NA; Edgar T. Ensign, "Forest Reserves of the Western Mountain Region," *Proceedings of the American*

270 Origins of the National Forests

Forestry Association at the Tenth, Eleventh, and Twelfth Annual Meetings, Washington, December, 1891, 1892, and 1893, and at the World's Fair Congress, Chicago, October 18 and 19, 1893, Vol. 10 (Washington, DC: American Forestry Association, 1894), pp. 116-122; and Lawrence W. Rakestraw, A History of the United States Forest Service in Alaska (Anchorage: U.S. Department of Agriculture, Forest Service, 1981), p. 10.

17. There were limits to this broad interpretation of the Forest Reserve Act. When it was proposed that the "Petrified Forest" in Arizona be set aside under that law, the General Land Office convinced the secretary of the interior that it was not the character of "forest" contemplated by the act. Assistant GLO Commissioner to Secretary of the Interior, 14 February 1893, GLO, Division "E", Press Copy Letters Sent to Surveyors General [and Others], 1872-1908, RG 49, NA; Scidmore, "Our New National Forest Reserves," p. 795; and Ensign, "Forest Reserves," p. 119.

18. Interior Annual Report (1891), I: XV; Ibid. (1892), I: IV; Rakestraw, "History of Forest Conservation in the Pacific Northwest," pp. 35-53; Douglas H. Strong, "The Sierra Forest Reserve: The Movement to Preserve the San Joaquin Valley Watershed," The California Historical Society Quarterly 46 (March 1967): 5-13; GLO Annual Report (1893), p. 78; and the General Land Office final reports for forest reservations in GLO, Div. "R", Letters Sent, RG 49, NA.

19. The Yellowstone National Park, White River Plateau, and Battlement Mesa forest reservations were all established by Secretary of the Interior Noble without benefit of reports from special agents.

20. The investigation of potential forest reservations was time-consuming. Examination of many areas—often covering hundreds-of-thousands, and at times millions, of acres—took weeks, sometime months, to complete. During that time the potential forest reserves were threatened with being overrun by settlers, speculators, and others before the lands were withdrawn by presidential proclamation. The situation prompted the Land Department to adopt a policy of making "temporary" withdrawals of the public lands selected for examination. These temporary withdrawals withheld the public lands affected from entry and location, and allowed the Land Department to maintain the status quo in an area until its final deposition was determined. See Pike's Peak Park (20 July 1891) in Decisions of the Department of the Interior and General Land Office in Cases Relating to the Public Lands, U.S. Department of the Interior (Washington, DC: U.S. Government Printing Office, 1892), Vol. 13, p. 54-55 [Hereafter cited as L.D.]; Battlement Mesa Forest Reserve, 16 L.D. 190-192 (25 January 1893); and GLO Commissioner to W. B. Harlan, Como, Montana, 28 September 1891; GLO Commissioner to Secretary of the Interior, 16 February 1892; and GLO Commissioner to Secretary of the Interior, 23 January 1893, GLO, Div. "R", Letters Sent, RG 49, NA.

21. General Land Office, "Circular of Instructions Relating to Timber Reservations," 15 May 1891, Compilation of Public Timber Laws, p. 131-133.

22. GLO Commissioner to Senator Henry Teller, 2 April 1892, GLO, Div. "R", Letters Sent, RG 49, NA.

23. GLO Commissioner to Special Agent Edgar T. Ensign, 19 October 1891; GLO Commissioner to Special Agent M. J. Haley, 11 January 1892, Ibid.

24. GLO Commissioner to Secretary of the Interior, 28 January 1892; and GLO Commissioner to Secretary of the Interior, 18 January 1893, Ibid.

25. *See* the discussions regarding this principle in *Military Reservation—Entry—Power of President*, 1 L.D. 30 (15 July 1881); *Albert White*, 1 L.D. 451, 452 (10 February 1881); *Fort Maginnis*, 1 L.D. 552 (21 October 1881); *Staltz v. White Spirit et al.*, 10 L.D. 144 (11 February 1890); *Emma F. Zumwalt*, 20 L.D. 32 (19 January 1895).

26. *See* discussions in *Military Reservation—Entry—Power of President*, 1 L.D. 30 (15 July 1881); *Rees v. Churchill*, 1 L.D. 450 (4 January 1882); and *Jefferson Davenport*, 16 L.D. 526 (16 June 1893).

27. GLO Commissioner to J. W. Ryder, Hayden, Colorado, 2 December 1891; and GLO Commissioner to Register and Receiver, Glenwood Springs Land Office, Colorado, 10 December 1891, GLO, Div. "R", Letters Sent, RG 49, NA.

28. GLO Commissioner to Secretary of the Interior, 29 January 1892; GLO Commissioner to Register and Receiver, Glenwood Springs Land Office, Colorado, 20 February 1891, GLO, Div. "R", Letters Sent, RG 49, NA; Secretary of the Interior to GLO Commissioner, 2 February 1892, Department of the Interior, Lands and Railroads Division, Letters Sent by the Lands and Railroads Division of the Office of the Secretary of the Interior, Microfilm Publication M620, Record Group 48: Records of the Office of the Secretary of the Interior, NA [Hereafter cited as DOI, L&RR, Letters Sent, RG 48, NA]; GLO Commissioner to Secretary of the Interior, 13 January 1892, GLO, Div. "R", National Forest Files, Bitterroot National Forest, RG 49, NA; and *Battlement Mesa Forest Reserve*, 16 L.D. 190 (25 January 1893).

29. GLO Commissioner to Secretary of the Interior, 24 November 1891, and GLO Commissioner to Secretary of the Interior, 22 March 1892, GLO, Div. "R", Letters Sent, RG 49, NA; American Forestry Association, *Proceedings of the Tenth, Eleventh, and Twelfth Annual Meetings* (1894), 14-15; Rodgers, *Fernow*, p. 157; and Kirkland, "The American Forests," pp. 191-194.

30. *Interior Annual Report* (1891), I: XIV; Rodgers, *Fernow*, p. 157; Kirkland, "The American Forests," p. 190; and Steen, *U.S. Forest Service*, p. 28.

31. Kirkland, "The American Forests," pp. 189-190; Secretary of the Interior to Chairman, House of Representative Committee on Public Lands, 13 January 1892, and Secretary of the Interior to Chairman, Senate Committee on Public Lands, 13 January 1892, DOI, L&RR, Letters Sent, RG 48, NA; and *Instructions*, 15 L.D. 284-285 (10 September 1892).

32. Noble's sentiment as to the use of discretionary authority is best illustrated by his remarks regarding the regulations for the Timber Permit Act of 1891. See *Interior Annual Report* (1891), I: XIV; and "Address of Hon. John W. Noble, Secretary of the Interior," *Forest Leaves* 3 (March 1892): 114.

33. GLO Commissioner to Secretary of the Interior, 24 November 1891; and GLO Commissioner to Secretary of the Interior, 6 July 1892, GLO, Div. "R", Letters Sent, RG 49, NA.

34. Secretary of the Interior to Chairman, House of Representative Committee on Public Lands, 13 January 1892, and Secretary of the Interior to Chairman, Senate Committee on Public Lands, 13 January 1892, DOI, L&RR, Letters Sent, RG 48, NA; and *Interior Annual Report* (1892), I: V.

35. The restrictions did not apply to travel through or hunting and fishing in the reserves. *See* Secretary of the Interior to GLO Commissioner, 15 July 1892, DOI, L&RR, Letters Sent, RG 48, NA; and Acting GLO Commissioner to Editor, *The Avalanche*, Glenwood Springs, Colorado, 2 November 1891; GLO Commissioner to Secretary of the Interior, 6 July 1892; and GLO Commissioner to E. W. Parker, White Oaks, New Mexico, 8 February 1893, GLO, Div. "R", Letters Sent, RG 49, NA.

36. The extent of the new administration's support is illustrated by the appointment of Edward A. Bowers as assistant commissioner of the General Land Office. Bowers was a leading forestry advocate and prominent member of the American Forestry Association. He had also worked as a special agent in the General Land Office, and in that capacity outlined a timberlands policy for the public domain. Ise, *Forest Policy*, pp. 95, 111; Rodgers, *Fernow*, pp. 154-156; Steen, *U.S. Forest Service*, pp. 26, 39-40; Scidmore, "Our New National Forest Reserves," p. 797; U.S. Congress, House of Representatives, Committee on Public Lands, *Public Timber Lands*, Ex. Doc. 242, 50th Congress, 1st sess., 1888.

37. *Interior Annual Report* (1893), I: IX, LX-LXI; and *GLO Annual Report* (1893), p. 79.

38. Ibid.

39. In fiscal year 1893 the General Land Office had responsibility for 571 million acres of unappropriated and unreserved public lands (exclusive of Alaska), as well as the 13 million acres of forest reserves. To investigate frauds, illegal fencing, timber depredations, and other problems on these lands it had 82 part-time special agents, 13 less than the previous year. The 1894 budget allowed for only 40 special agents, and the number of special agents remained around that number through 1897. See *GLO Annual Report* (1892), p. 390; Ibid. (1893), pp. 78, 135, 301; Ibid. (1894), p. 435; Ibid. (1895), p. 399; Ibid. (1896), p. 368; and Ibid. (1897), p. 349.

40. *Interior Annual Report* (1893), p. LXI.

41. *GLO Annual Report* (1890), p. 82; Kirkland, "The American Forests," p. 147, 198.

42. *GLO Annual Report* (1890), p. 82; Kirkland, "The American Forests," pp. 147, 198; and H. Duane Hampton, *How the U.S. Cavalry Saved Our National Parks* (Bloomington: Indiana University Press, 1971), pp. 81-112, 146-151.

43. Secretary of the Interior Noble to Captain George Anderson, Acting Superintendent, Yellowstone National Park, 14 April 1891, DOI, P & M Div., Letters Sent, RG 48, NA.

44. Haines, *The Yellowstone Story*, II: 95; and Captain George S. Anderson, Acting Superintendent Yellowstone National Park to W. P. Couper, Chief, Patents and Miscellaneous Division, Department of the Interior, 1 November 1895, GLO, Div. "R", National Forest Files, Yellowstone National Forest, RG 49, NA.

45. When possible the General Land Office did send special agents and other officials to investigate problems in forest reserves. *See* for example GLO Commissioner to Special Agent Edgar T. Ensign, 25 March 1892, GLO, Div. "R", Letters Sent, RG 49, NA; and Acting Secretary of the Interior to GLO Commissioner, 23 June 1893, DOI, L&RR, Letters Sent, RG 48, NA.

46. *Interior Annual Report* (1891), I: XV; and Ibid. (1892), I: V; Secretary of the Interior to Chairman, Senate Committee on Public Lands, 13 January 1892, DOI, L&RR, Letters Sent, RG 48, NA; GLO Commissioner to Secretary of the Interior, 24 November 1891; GLO Commissioner to Secretary of the Interior, 6 July 1892; GLO Commissioner to Secretary of the Interior, 26 January 1893, GLO, Div. "R", Letters Sent, RG 49, NA; F. D. W. French, "The Forests and the Army," *Garden and Forest* 6 (22 February 1893): 95-96; and U.S. Congress, Senate, *Committee on Public Lands, Report to Accompany S. 3235*, Senate Report 1002, 52d Cong., 1st sess., 1892, pp. 11-12.

47. Acting Secretary of the Interior to Secretary of War, 20 July 1893 and Secretary of the Interior to Secretary of War, 16 August 1893, P & Misc. Div., Letters Sent, RG 48, NA; Assistant GLO Commissioner to Secretary of the Interior, 23 June 1893; Acting Secretary of War to Secretary of the Interior, 27 July 1893; Chief, Patents and Miscellaneous Division, "Memorandum for the First Assistant Secretary," n.d.; Acting Judge Advocate General to Secretary of War, 23 August 1893; Acting Secretary of War to Secretary of the Interior, 28 August 1893; Assistant Attorney General to Secretary of the Interior, 16 September 1893; P & Misc. Div., Records Relating to Forest Reserves, RG 48, NA; and *Interior Annual Report* (1893), I: LX-LXI.

48. In spite of the War Department's ruling, the Department of the Interior was able to have troops at Yellowstone National Park continue patrolling the adjacent Yellowstone National Park Timber Land Reserve. The patrols, which were extended to include the Teton Forest Reserve set aside in 1897, did not end until 1902. Haines, *The Yellowstone Story*, II: 95, 97.

49. *Interior Annual Report* (1893), I: LXI; Ibid. (1894), I: XVIII, LXXI-XCIII; Ibid., (1895), I: XXII, LXIII-LXIV; Ibid., (1896), I: XVI; *GLO Annual Report* (1893), p. 79; Ibid. (1896), pp. 71, 73; Ise, *United States Forest Policy*, pp. 122-128; and Miller, "Congress and the Origins of Conservation," pp. 300-307.

50. In many respects this was a continuation of a policy adopted by the Harrison Administration in its last weeks. *See* Assistant GLO Commissioner to George H. Parsons, Colorado Springs, Colorado, 5 October 1893, GLO, Div. "R", Letters Sent, RG 49, NA; *Interior Annual Report* (1895), I: LXIII; Ise, *Forest Policy*, p. 120; Rakestraw, "History of Forest Conservation in the Pacific Northwest," p. 54; and Scidmore, "Our New National Forest Reserves", p. 796.

51. Acting GLO Commissioner to S. C. Smith, Bakersfield, California, 28 March 1893; GLO Commissioner to Secretary of the Interior, 1 August 1894; and Acting GLO Commissioner to Secretary of the Interior, 5 June 1896, GLO, Div. "R", Letters Sent, RG 49, NA.

52. GLO Commissioner to Special Agent C. G. Coleman, 11 August 1893, Ibid. Also *See* Assistant GLO Commissioner to Special Agent Frank Powell, 18 November 1893, Ibid.; and Special Agent Frank Powell to GLO Commissioner, 25 November 1893, GLO, Div. "R", National Forest Files, Gifford Pinchot National Forest, RG 49, NA.

53. By the Act of February 20, 1896 (29 Stat. 11), the Pike's Peak, Plum Creek, and South Platte forest reserves were opened to mining.

54. General Land Office, "Notice," 14 April 1894, *Compilation of Public Timber Laws*, pp. 133-134.

55. It should be noted under Sections 18-21 of the Act of March 3, 1891, private companies could receive rights-of-way to construct reservoirs, ditches, and canals needed for irrigation purposes.

The law, which applied to public lands and government reservations, was amended in 1896 to include electric power generation purposes. No applications under the law were made in the forest reserves until 1893. The rights-of-way could not "interfere with the proper occupation [of the reservations] by the Government," which prompted Secretary of the Interior Hoke Smith in 1895 to stipulate that companies granted easements could not take any timber from outside the area of their reservoirs or water ways. *See* Act of March 3, 1891 (26 Stat. 1095, 1101-1102); Act of May 14, 1896 (29 Stat. 120); *H. H. Sinclair et al.*, 18 L.D. 573 (7 March 1894); *Hamilton Irrigation Co.*, 21 L.D. 300 (18 October 1895); and GLO Commissioner to Secretary of the Interior, 2 March 1893, DOI, L&RR, Letters Received, 1881-1907, File 1893-2357, RG 48, NA.

56. Frederick V. Coville, *Forest Growth and Sheep Grazing in the Cascade Mountains of Oregon*, U.S. Department of Agriculture, Division of Forestry, Bulletin No. 15 (1898): 10-11; and William D. Rowley, *U.S. Forest Service Grazing and Rangelands: A History* (College Station: Texas A&M University Press, 1985), p. 24.

57. California State Senator G. G. Goucher to U.S. Senator Stephen M. White, 10 May 1894; Senator Stephen M. White to Secretary of the Interior, 17 May 1894, GLO, Div. "R", National Forest Files, Sierra National Forest, RG 49, NA.

58. Commissioner Lamoreux took a more lenient attitude toward mining activity. When Oregon Congressman Binger Hermann petitioned that the Cascade Forest Reserve be opened to prospecting and mining, Lamoreux recommended that the reserve's proclamation be modified to permit the location and entry of mineral lands under the mining laws. Secretary Hoke Smith, however, opposed opening the forest reservations to any form of entry and disposal and refused to consider Congressman Hermann's request. *See* GLO Commissioner to Secretary of the Interior, 31 May 1894, GLO, Div. "R", Letters Sent, RG 49, NA; and Secretary of the Interior to GLO Commissioner, 16 June 1894, DOI, L&RR, Letters Sent, RG 48, NA.

59. This policy stance shows that the Land Department under Secretary Hoke Smith had a narrower interpretation of the Forest Reserve Act than during John Noble's tenure. GLO Commissioner to Secretary of the Interior, 1 August 1894, GLO, Div. "R", Letters Sent, RG 49, NA.

60. Captain James Parker, Acting Superintendent, Sequoia National Park to Secretary of the Interior, 10 July 1894, GLO, Div. "R", National Forest Files, Sierra National Forest, RG 49, NA.

61. Acting GLO Commissioner to Secretary of the Interior, 23 August 1895, GLO, Div. "R", Letters Sent, RG 49, NA; *GLO Annual Report* (1895), pp. 85-86; and *Interior Annual Report* (1895), I: XXII.

62. *See* Homer Cummings and Carl McFarland, *Federal Justice: Chapters in the History of Justice and the Federal Executive* (New York: The Macmillan Co., 1937), pp. 260-269; and Harold H. Dunham, *Government Handout: A Study in the Administration of the Public Lands, 1875-1891* (New York: Da Capo Press, 1970), pp. 261-274.

63. Acting GLO Commissioner to Secretary of the Interior, 14 July 1896; and Acting GLO Commissioner to Secretary of the Interior, 16 August 1894, GLO, Div. "R", Letters Sent, RG 49, NA.

64. Act of March 3, 1891 (26 Stat. 1095, 1103); Act of March 2, 1831 (4 Stat. 472); and Act of March 3, 1875 (18 Stat. 481).

65. Detailed Clerk J. R. Hampton to GLO Commissioner, 25 March 1896, GLO, Div. "R", National Forest Files, Cleveland National Forest, RG 49, NA; Detailed Clerk J. R. Hampton to GLO Commissioner, 1 April 1896, GLO, Div. "R", National Forest Files, San Bernardino National Forest, RG 49, NA; and Detailed Clerk J. R. Hampton to GLO Commissioner, 3 April 1896, GLO, Div. "R", National Forest Files, San Gabriel National Forest, RG 49, NA.

66. Assistant GLO Commissioner to Secretary of the Interior, 23 June 1893; GLO Commissioner to Secretary of the Interior, 1 August 1894; GLO Commissioner to Secretary of the Interior, 26 June 1895; and Acting GLO Commissioner to Secretary of the Interior, 5 June 1896, GLO, Div. "R", Letters Sent, RG 49, NA.

67. United States Attorney, Southern District of California to J. R. Hampton, Detailed GLO Clerk, 7 March 1896, GLO, Div. "R", National Forest Files, San Bernardino National Forest, RG 49, NA.

68. Secretary of the Interior to Attorney General, 22 July 1896, DOI, L&RR, Letters Sent, RG 49, NA; and Attorney General to U.S. Attorney for Oregon, 10 January 1896, Department of Justice, Letters Sent by the Department of Justice: Instructions to U.S. Attorneys and Marshals, Microfilm Publication No. 701, Record Group 60: Records of the Department of Justice, NA [Hereafter cited as DOJ and RG 60].

69. U.S. Attorney for Oregon to Attorney General, 3 September 1896, DOJ, Year Files, 1884-1903, File 1895-8757, RG 60, NA.

70. *United State v. Tygh Valley Land & Live-Stock Co.*, 76 F. 693, 695 (1896) concerned a pleading of demurrer. The defendant claimed in affect that even if the allegations made as to grazing trespass were correct, the legal consequences were not such that required them to be answered or for the proceeding to continue. The trespass complaint against the Tygh Valley Live-Stock Company, therefore, still had to be tried.

71. Coville, *Forest Growth and Sheep Grazing in the Cascade Mountains*, p. 11; and Lawrence Rakestraw, "Sheep Grazing in the Cascade Range: John Minto vs. John Muir," *Pacific Historical Review* 27 (November 1958): 374-375.

72. Act of June 4, 1897 (30 Stat. 11, 34-36).

Yellowstone and its Borders: a Significant Influence Toward the Creation of the First Forest Reserve

Mary S. Culpin
National Park Service

One hundred years after the creation of the Yellowstone Park Timber Land Reserve and one hundred and nineteen years after the creation of the Yellowstone National Park, the federal land managers in this area face many of the same concerns that the late nineteenth century conservationists encountered—the protection of the watersheds in Yellowstone National Park and providing sufficient habitat for the game animals of this region. Today the pertinent federal land managing agencies, the National Park Service, the United States Forest Service, and the Bureau of Land Management, have developed a strategy with common goals for the protection of this "Greater Yellowstone area." Although the late twentieth century goals go beyond the earlier concerns, many are directly or indirectly related to the earlier protection issues. But for 1991, the centennial year of the national forests, perhaps a look at the very early concerns for protection and preservation of Yellowstone National Park may offer an additional view for the establishment of the first timber reserve.

In the early 1880s, several prominent Americans realized that the boundaries established for Yellowstone National Park "bore no relation to the surrounding mountains, which in most cases were high and conspicuous."[1] The 1872 boundary was drawn to include the principal natural features of the park—the geysers, Lake Yellowstone, Mammoth Hot Springs, and the Grand Canyon of the Yellowstone. Since the area had been inadequately explored and the promoters were anxious for its establishment, a expedient and simple method to include the major features was used:

> The north line was drawn through the junction of the Gardner and the Yellowstone Rivers; the east line was drawn north and south through a point ten miles east-ward from the most eastern point of Yellowstone Lake; the south line was drawn through a point ten miles south of the most southern point of Yellowstone Lake; and the west line was drawn through a point fifteen miles west of the most western point of Madison Lake.[2]

One of the earliest men to recognize the inadequate boundary was Civil War hero General Phillip Sheridan, who had had an interest in the Yellowstone country since 1870. In his role as commanding general of the Division of the Missouri, Sheridan had approved several military-led expeditions into the area, including the Washburn-Langford-Doane party in 1870, the Barlow-Heap party in 1871, the Jones expedition in 1873, and the Ludlow party in 1875.

Sheridan made three visits to the Yellowstone, but his trip in 1882 generated public concern for the lack of protection being afforded in the park, the infant concession policies, and the inadequate boundaries for a vital game habitat. Sheridan turned to the public for support of his plan to add 250,000 acres which extended the boundary 40 miles to the east and 10 miles to the south. In addition to congressional support, it was to the naturalist, George Bird Grinnell, who the general had been requested accompany the Black Hills expedition of 1874, and who a year later was a member of the Ludlow expedition to Yellowstone, that Sheridan relied on for publicity. As editor-in-chief of the *Forest and Stream,* Grinnell kept Sheridan's plight before the public.

Sheridan also enlisted the support of a former military aide, who was now the territorial governor of Montana, John Schuyler Crosby, and even the Wild West showman, "Buffalo Bill" Cody, who by that time felt that the killing of game animals "does not find favor in the West as it did a decade or so ago."[3] Sheridan's most vocal and influential supporter was Missouri senator George Vest, to whom he appealed to support his Yellowstone cause. With a copy of his plan, which proposed the extension of the boundaries, protection of the wildlife, prohibition of monopolies for concessioners, sufficient appropriation for administering the park, and the management of the park assigned to the military, Sheridan also sent this message to Vest, "The suggestions made in my report are the only thing left for us to do to save the noble game."[4] Vest's first bill, submitted in January of 1883, failed to pass the Congress, but a revised bill did pass in March of 1883, giving some protection for the park. However, Sheridan's vision of an extended boundary for the game habitat was not included in the 1883 legislation. The March 8, 1883 edition of *Forest and Stream* stated, "It is a matter of regret that the bill which provided for the extension of the limits of the Park could not have been passed during the present sessions of Congress, but we trust that at the next steps may be taken, in time, to set aside from settlement a considerable additional tract of territory on the south and east of the present Park."[5]

Despite the recent failure for full protection for the park, Sheridan organized a grand tour of the park for the summer of 1883 for President Chester Arthur and a party of influential friends, which besides Sheridan included Senator Vest. The presidential visit brought more public attention to the park and a few months later, Grinnell wrote in *Forest and Stream*, "The trip . . . is already, as we predicted last summer would be the case, resulting in action for the proper preservation of the Park."[6]

During the trip, Senator Vest visited with the United States Geological Survey geologist Arnold Hague at Lake Yellowstone. Senator Vest requested Hague to submit his views and suggestions for the protection and preservation of Yellowstone. Hague, who by that time was very familiar with the park, wrote to Vest in December of 1883 pointing out that "The most important object to be gained in maintaining the National Park is the preservation of the forests which now cover the greater part of the Park plateau and neighboring mountains."[7]

Hague drew attention to the problems and expense of buying and controlling surrounding forests for the protection of the Adirondacks in order to provide a uniform flow of water for the Hudson River. He pointed out to Senator Vest that "No such reason exists today against forever protecting the forests in the neighborhood of the Park, while the reasons for so doing are equally urgent. In a country like the Far West, with its vast tree-less areas, rapidly being taken up by settlers, it is all the more important that certain exceptionally situated timber regions should be carefully protected by law before seized upon by settlers."[8] Hague urged for a greater expansion of the boundary than the one suggested by Sheridan and included in the earlier, unsuccessful Vest bill. Hague called for extending the east and south, but also called for modifying the northern and western boundary. Hague felt that "little would be lost in the way of timber land or natural scenery needing protection" if the northern boundary was moved to the south to coincide with the Montana-Wyoming territories boundary. A similar alteration on the Western boundary would move the boundary to coincide with the Wyoming line, thus placing the entire park with the Wyoming Territory. Hague believed that the original western boundary was the result of a misunderstanding of the name of Shoshone Lake which was labeled Madison Lake in the 1872 legislation. A similar change had been proposed by the park's second superintendent, Norris, after his 1881 survey of the boundaries.[9]

On the southern boundary, Hague wrote, "In my opinion the 44° Parallel of latitude would make the most suitable southern line, by extending the Park as far south it would take in a rough mountainous country mainly made up of volcanic lavas but densely covered with forests and a resort for large game."[10] Hague did not agree with moving the southern line as far south as Sheridan suggested for fear of including some areas that "might prove upon exploration to be valuable mineral lands as well as lands favorable for summer patronage."

Hague suggested to Vest that the eastern boundary be extended 30 miles to the east of the present line. This, in addition to adding "largely to the domain of timber and protected game area," would include all of the streams draining westward to the Yellowstone River, and the headwaters of the majority of the streams running eastward. Hague's eastern line differed from Sheridan's in that it did not extend to Cedar Hill and it would not include "lands already occupied by ranchmen as grazing country upon which a number of people have already settled. It is also more likely to embrace valuable mineral land and is moreover a far less definite point than a standard meridian line."[11]

Hague contended that if the national park was set aside as it should be, for the preservation of game, the existing boundaries were not sufficient "to make the place one where large game will naturally roam, particularly when driven in from outside for protection." He noted that the "mountains lying to the south, east and west abounding in game, presents all the natural advantages sought for by deer and elk. Enlarge the park, and you make the whole area a game country."[12] He called upon the government in managing the park, "to protect above everything else the timber and game." Hague felt that this policy should be a good defense against the threat by the railroad of building a line across the northern tier of the Park. The encroachment of a railroad would introduce a high risk of fire for the timber and damaging noise and traffic driving the game from the area.[13] The following month, Arnold Hague responded to a request from the secretary of the interior regarding his views for Yellowstone's preservation and protection, by sending a near identical letter to the one that he had sent to Vest.

Concurrently with Hague's petitions for redefining the boundaries to offer greater protection and preservation, commercial interests were seeking changes to the northern boundary including moving the line to the Lamar River and making the eastern boundary the Yellowstone River. However, strong conservation supporters argued that the extreme boundary change would exclude one of the preferred buffalo grazing ranges along the Lamar Valley.

Senator Vest introduced a new protection bill to Congress which also included boundary changes heavily influenced by Arnold Hague's case. The bill did not pass, and several more bills presented during the next two years failed to pass.

During the summer of 1885, Secretary of the Interior Lamar assigned Washington D. C. lawyer William Hallet Phillips as a special agent of the Interior Department to investigate the conditions of Yellowstone Park. Many of Phillips' issues related to leases within the Park, but he did address the continuing threat from railroad and nearby Cooke City mine interests to adjust the northern boundary to allow for a line to Cooke City. Phillips wrote "I think the Department should strenuously oppose this project. The country proposed to be cut off is one much frequented at times by the game, and its retention within the boundaries of the Park is necessary for the protection of game. If the parties interested in the mines really are desirous of a railroad reaching that place, I am satisfied from diligent inquiry that a route from Billings, Montana, to Cooke is practicable. Such a route would lie wholly outside the boundaries of the Park."[14]

Five months after the Phillips report was submitted to the Interior Department, Arnold Hague continued his campaign for the enlargement of the park. In the preface to a letter from Hague to Senator Charles Manderson published in *Forest and Stream*, George Bird Grinnell calls Hague the "highest authority we can have on the subject [the preservation of the forests] and should be convincing to every intelligent man."[15] Grinnell calls this subject "one which will interest every practical man and which has an especial and particular meaning for all those who live on the plains, to the east or to the west of the Continental Divide."[16]

In Hague's published letter, he states that the issue of timber preservation is "gradually attracting more and attention in all the more settled parts of the country. The necessity for some proper restrictions, rigidly enforced, is now very generally admitted." He proposes that "certain areas, favorably situated for the growth of trees, should be set aside forever as forest reservations." Again illustrating the difficulty the state of New York was undergoing regarding the Adirondacks, he reminded the senator that "Today no such difficulties exist against forever setting aside the country in the immediate vicinity of the Park, while the reasons for so doing are manifest to all who have given the subject any attention."[17]

Hague predicted that future settlement in the lower Yellowstone Valley would necessitate the protection of the immediate area along the sources of the drainages into Yellowstone Lake, the East Fork of the Yellowstone, and the headwaters of the many southern branches of Clark's Fork and the Stinking Water. Hague informed Senator Manderson that the proposed extension "So far as known carry no minerals of economic importance, and judging from the volcanic character of the country, the indications are against any discovery of valuable ore bodies. These mountains are useless for settlement and should be withdrawn from the public lands."[18]

Hague warned the senator that unless these areas are not withdrawn from public use, settlement was surely to take place or the forests could be timbered to supply the growing demand for railroad ties, which annually amounted to approximately

60,000,000 ties. Tamarack and black pine seemed to be the tree of choice in Montana and Wyoming, with a young tree from ten to twelve inches in diameter supplying two railroad ties. Another worry to Hague was the potential of a growing mining center and need for large amounts of charcoal at Cooke City, near the northeast border of the park.

Finally Hague championed the preservation of the wild game in the area, suggesting to the senator that the demise of so many wild game in the Rocky Mountains for the past twenty years could be halted with the protection within a "natural zoological reservation, sufficiently large to allow all wild animals to run free without molestation." In a possible appeal for a larger audience, Hague suggested that "By rigidly enforcing the game laws the Park will, in a few years, become so densely stocked that the surplus, seeking new haunts, will run outside the limits for its own protection. In this way ample sport will be afforded the hunter shooting under territorial laws."[19]

The following year, S. 283 was introduced by Senator Vest; but with the addition of an amendment authorizing the Montana Mineral Railway right-of-way, the bill was never passed. In 1890 another bill was considered for the protection and extension of the park. The bill which was comparable to the ones supported by the past four secretaries of the interior was again met with opposition and interference of Representative Payson, who again added a railroad authorization for the park. An offering of an alternative to the line through the park, the commissioners on public lands and other park supporters suggested a right-of-way on the eastern side of the park, but the Washington speculators were banking on obtaining a franchise for a railroad through the park and then selling it to the Northern Pacific or its competitor, the Manitoba Railroad Company. Thus their influence blocked any passage of park extension bill.[20]

The shenanigans practiced in the House of Representatives in regard to the bill to extend the boundaries of Yellowstone National Park produced a persistence in the park's congressional supporters to prefer a postponement of the passage of such a bill until the dreaded railroad feature was deleted. This never came to pass. In 1891 the Congress successfully enacted "An Act to Repeal the Timber-culture Act, and for Other Purposes," which authorized the president to create forest reserves. The first forest reserve had essentially the same boundaries promoted by Arnold Hague during the 1880s for Yellowstone National Park's protection and preservation. Because the 1891 act had no "penalties for depredations committed, and no power to enforce them if there were any," the reserve was placed under the supervision of Yellowstone National Park.[21] The military superintendent of Yellowstone supervised the timber reserve for about ten years. During part of that time, the secretary of the interior made an annual request for the inclusion of the reserve into the park with no success.[22]

It should be noted that the persistence for the preservation and protection of the "Greater Yellowstone Area" shown by Arnold Hague, Senator George Vest, and countless others is found in the federal managers today. Also Theodore Roosevelt's letter to the editor of the *Forest and Stream* on December 5, 1892, holds out the same counsel that we 100 years later adhere

> It is the utmost importance that the Park shall be kept in its present form as a great forestry preserve and a National pleasure ground, the like of which is not to be found on any other continent than ours; and all public-spirited Americans should join with *Forest and Stream* in the effort to prevent the greed of a little group of speculators, careless of everything save their own selfish interests, from doing the damage they threaten to the whole people of the U.S., by wrecking the Yellowstone National Park.[23]

Notes

1. Horace Albright, "Report on the Proposed Revision of the North, East, and South Boundary Lines of Yellowstone National Park and the Extension of the Park Southward to Include the Teton Mountains, the Headwaters of the Yellowstone, and the Area Lying Between these Regions," July 10, 1925. National Archives, Record Group 79. Entry 6, Yellowstone NP Tray No. 564.

2. Albright, "Report On The Proposed Revision Of The North, East and South Boundary Lines Of Yellowstone National Park And The Extension Of The Park Southward To Include The Teton Mountains. The Headwaters Of The Yellowstone River And The Area Lying Between These Regions."

3. Paul Hutton, "Phil Sheridan's Crusade for Yellowstone", *American History Illustrated*. 19 (1985): 13.

4. Hutton, "Phil Sheridan's Crusade for Yellowstone," 13.

5. "Mr. Vest's Victory," *Forest and Stream* (March 8, 1883).

6. "The Yellowstone Park," *Forest and Stream* (December 20, 1883): 401.

7. Arnold Hague to Senator George Vest, December 28, 1883. National Archives, R.G. 57, Arnold Hague Papers, Box 26.

8. Hague to Vest, December 28, 1883.

9. Richard Bartlett, *Yellowstone: A Wilderness Beseiged* (Tucson: University of Arizona Press, 1985), 226.

10. Bartlett, *Yellowstone: A Wilderness Beseiged*, 226.

11. Hague to Vest, December 28, 1883.

12. Ibid.

13. Ibid.

14. W. Hallet Phillips Report found in letter to Secretary of Interior L. Q. C. Lamar from W. Hallet Phillips, September 12, 1885. Yellowstone National Park Library, Yellowstone National Park. Microfilm No. 63 Roll 3. The William Hallet Phillips Papers can be found at the Library of Congress.

15. "Needs of the Yellowstone Park," *Forest and Stream* (February 25, 1886): 89.

16. Ibid.

17. Ibid.

18. Ibid.

19. Ibid.

20. "The Yellowstone Park Bill," *Chicago Daily News*, May 13, 1890.

21. "Yellowstone National Park," *Garden and Forest*, December 16, 1891, 589. *See* Harold K. Steen, *The Beginning of the National Forest System* (USDA Forest Service, 1991).

22. Albright, 1-2.

23. Robert Underwood Johnson, *Remembered Yesterdays* (Boston: Little Brown and Company, 1923), 309.

INDIVIDUALS AND THE

NATIONAL FORESTS

Wooden Politics: Bernhard Fernow
and the Quest for a National Forest Policy,
1876-1898

Char Miller
Trinity University

Governmental forestry in late nineteenth century America was a joke. No one knew this better than Bernhard Eduard Fernow, a German-born and -trained forester, who became the third head of the Division of Forestry in the spring of 1886. Indeed, his first day on the job was rich in Dickensian humor. After climbing flight after flight of stairs in the even-then historic Agriculture building, he finally reached the tiny office of the division, tucked in the attic. If its size and locale had not convinced him of the disdain with which his profession was held within the federal bureaucracy, then the attributes, if such they be, of his two assistants did. One of these, Nathaniel Egleston—"a reverend, white haired gentleman"—had been the previous division head, and had been demoted to make way for Fernow. This less than ideal work environment was made all the worse by the fact that Egleston was incompetent. His "knowledge of the whole subject was even less than that of his predecessor [Franklin Hough]," Fernow observed, and his administrative abilities were such that he "was at his wits end [about] what to do with the [division's] munificent appropriation of $8,000" per annum. Witless was how the second assistant might best be described; a political appointee, he had no scientific knowledge of nor interest in forestry. But both of Fernow's subordinates knew the central fact of political sinecures: when he came upon them that first morning, they were "cosily, but by no means amicably, ensconced in a little garret room with two small oval windows, quarreling as to whom the credit for their performances really belonged." For Fernow, this was a bad joke.[1]

He fully expected to infuse a more serious note into the division's proceedings, however. That, after all, is why he reveled in the telling of this anecdote. The laughter it was designed to provoke, the sympathy for Fernow it was to elicit, helped distinguish him from that comic pair. So did the anecdote's punchline. Fernow's antidote for his office's languid and slothful air was simple: he introduced a typewriter. This was an "innovation highly resented by the two," not only because it disturbed their quiet, but because it signaled a sharp shift in orientation:

there was work to be done. Work that would be done in a rational and efficient manner, work that would be regularized and codified in ways that only a typewriter could then produce. With Bernhard Fernow, modernity had arrived.[2]

So, too, had a certain prolixity. In 1898, for instance, Fernow proudly noted in his final report as chief of the Division of Forestry that his record of publication had far outstripped that of his predecessors combined; in the ten years that Hough and Egleston had been in office they had managed to produce only four annual reports. The ever exact Fernow knew that annual meant each year, and published the requisite number. Moreover, he tabulated his publications in another way, noting that more than 6,000 pages of reports, bulletins, circulars, and other forms of "propaganda for [the] more rational treatment of our forest resources" poured out of the division's typewriter during his tenure. On top of that he had filled nearly 20,000 pages of letterbooks, "largely containing specific advice given to correspondents." So that none would think that this productivity was but a waste of energy and funds, Fernow calculated that in fact his costs per page ($24.00: "hardly a fair charge for expert writing") were 20 percent less than those incurred "during the preceding period of nonprofessional writing." Efficiency, diligence, and economy were the hallmarks of his administration, or so this telling of the history of federal forestry would imply, a telling that left no doubt but that Fernow had exorcised the ghosts of Egleston and Hough.[3]

There was, however, more to Fernow's governmental service than this. Indeed, the significance of his contribution to the forestry movement in his adopted country— he had become a citizen of the United States in 1883—emerged most fully not in the number of pages he composed as America's first professional forester, but in the meanings embedded within those texts. For it is only by analyzing these writings, these many bulletins, circulars, reports, and lectures, that one can begin to evaluate the philosophical principles that formed the foundation of his work. And that is an important task; these principles, which shaped his understanding of the proper role of government in developing, maintaining, and controlling the American landscape, were at once the product of his training in the Prussian Forestry Department and of his later immersion in the intellectual currents sweeping America at the turn of the century. There was more to his commitment to forestry, in short, than the mere study of trees.[4]

He had had some sense of this even in his youth. Born in 1851 in Inowrazlav, Prussia, a favored son of an elite landed family, Bernhard Fernow was expected to inherit his grandfather's great estate in eastern Prussia. But he never did, because in fulfilling one of the conditions for his inheritance, which family legend has it was that he study law and forestry, he fell in love not with his studies but with a woman.

His pursuit of forestry was what did him in. He had begun his apprenticeship in the Prussian Forestry Department, and after that had received advanced training for two-and-a-half years at the department's famed academy at Muenden, where he studied under G. Heyer, among others, and worked at several of the department's forests. His future seemed assured; his family pleased.

That assurance and pleasure vanished when Fernow, in the midst of his academic career, met Olivia Reynolds, an American living in Gottingen, sometime in the early 1870s; she was keeping house for her brother, a medical student at the university, one of many Yankees absorbing the German academic scientific concepts that would forever transform the American pursuit of knowledge. To this marriage of cultures, Olivia and Bernhard would contribute quite literally. They became engaged in 1875, over the Fernow family's objections, and when Olivia returned to the United States shortly thereafter, Bernhard followed, after having wrangled an appointment as an official Prussian observer of the American Centennial celebration to be held in Philadelphia in 1876. He remained, and the couple was married several years later, a train of events that reinforced Fernow's philosophical fatalism. "I am a . . . believer in chance and accidents shaping to a large extent our lives," he once observed, the social consequences of which Olivia Reynolds Fernow was quick to claim credit for: "If anyone should ask me who was the originator of the forestry movement in this country, I should modestly reply, 'It was I.' She had seen the forest for the trees.[5]

Few in her generation shared her insight. That is forestry, as it was practiced in much of Europe, was generally unknown in the United States. Or to be more precise, few considered large-scale management of forested lands necessary, since the supply of lumber here seemed so great. That perspective had a decided and economic impact on the new Fernow household, of course. Without a culture in support of forestry, there was no call for foresters, and in the decade before Fernow became head of the forestry division, he held a variety of jobs, few directly related to his chosen profession. But he kept up with his field, continued his studies of North American trees, and of economic conditions of the lumber-based industries, published a number of relevant articles, improved his English to the point where he was no longer embarrassed to speak in public, and emerged as a driving force in the fledgling American Forest Congress which had been established three years before Fernow had arrived in America. He had become such a presence within forestry circles that he was the obvious choice to succeed Nathaniel Egleston in 1886. But so difficult had been his struggle to establish himself in this country that two years later, when a Yale undergraduate wrote inquiring about America's future need for "educated foresters," Fernow could only reply "Qui en sait?" Well, Fernow did know, and in his reply to Gifford Pinchot, the Yalie destined to create the U.S. Forest Service, he urged the young man to study forestry with an eye on its usefulness "in other directions," including "landscape gardening, nursery business [or] botanist's work. . . ." Pinchot's prospects, the head of American governmental forestry assumed, were as dim as had been his own.[6]

Fernow's present was not all that exciting, either. Although he was chief of the forestry division in the Department of Agriculture, that title masked a bureaucratic maze in which he labored. Public lands, after all, were under the purview of the General Land Office (GLO) in the Department of the Interior, which meant that the forester had no forests under his direct control. The GLO might ask his advice about how to manage the forests, but that assumed that management was both desirable and possible. It was not. When Fernow assumed his office in 1886, there was, for instance, no delineation of a federal forest system, no public lands set aside for the practice of his profession. Such regulations would emerge in time, and Fernow was active in their initiation. This was as true for the Federal Reserve Act of 1891, Section 24, which enabled the president to "set apart and reserve, in any State or Territory having public land bearing forests . . . as public reserva-tions," an addition to the bill for which Fernow took perhaps more credit than he deserved, as it was in ensuing ancillary legislative initiatives that sought to protect these new forest reserves. By the early '90s, there were approximately 18 million acres set aside, a total President Cleveland sought to more than double with the so-called Washington's Birthday Reserves announced in 1897. The concept of national forests, and by extension of forestry, was coming of age.[7]

These dramatic changes notwithstanding, Fernow's work in Washington remained largely a matter of giving advice and serving as a conduit of information about forestry. These alterations in the numbers and sizes of forest reserves, then, did little to change his early and rather gloomy assessment of the forestry division's activities: "under present conditions," he had written a friend in 1887, "no practi-cal work will be done and we might as well satisfy ourselves, that all we can do is talk."[8]

Talk was not cheap with Fernow, however. Indeed, it is in his public discourse and private musings about how a system of forestry management ought to develop and function in the United States that the radical quality and political impact of his ideas emerge most clearly. For him, forestry was more than just an applied science, it was also an art, an art whose success would require the reformulation of the philosophi-cal basis of American political life.[9]

The first step, acquiring the plans for systematic forestry management, was simple enough. The United States need but look to Europe for its models. The European nations, after all, had been experimenting with increasingly centralized forms of control of forested lands. It is not surprising that Fernow, educated within the German forestry system, would believe that its methods were the most effective and most culturally adaptive. They were, he observed, as applicable in British India as in Japan, two diverse Asian societies that had hired German foresters, adopted their silviculture strategies, and then created forestry schools modeled after German educational programs, so as to perpetuate this methodology. There was little reason why the United States could not follow suit, reaping the benefits of his homeland's technology and expertise.[10]

Fundamental to this transfer of knowledge was the adoption of a set of principles of forestry management that assumed a central place in what Fernow called his "propaganda work" on behalf of the federal government. In report after report, in bulletin after bulletin, he argued that forestry was best defined as the Germans had defined it: "forest growth is to be treated as a crop to be reproduced as soon as harvested," and thus involved the idea of a "continuity of crops." In this, foresters were like farmers. Husbanding the "natural forces and conditions upon which the thrifty forest growth relies" was also part of the forester's charge, however, for it was no less critical that foresters produce "the largest amounts of material (or revenue) in the shortest time without impairing the condition and capacity for reproduction of the forest." That made foresters more like bankers than farmers, in fact, for proper forest management "involves the curtailment of present revenue for the sake of a continued greater revenue in the future"; this in turn required "continuity and stability to a greater extent than agriculture." Timbered land, then, was "permanently invested capital, from which the only the interest is used." One never cut into this capital, either: "the amount harvested or the revenue to be derived" should be "as nearly corresponding to the annual accretion" as possible. Good foresters balanced the books.[11]

To set up these books in the first place, to establish these principles on the ground, required intensive planning, as the Germans' experience so vividly demonstrated. During the nineteenth century, Fernow reported, the various states had begun to invest heavily in topographical surveys of state-owned lands, both to record boundaries and topography, but also to determine the location of markets, and thus the cartographic relationship between forests and consumers. On to these maps were then platted forest districts that established administrative and supervisory lines of authority running between the *Oberlandforstmeister*, or director of the agency, and the *Foersters*, or district rangers. The Germans were nothing if not organized.[12]

That organization extended to the very construct of the forest itself. A key task of the *Foersters*, for example, was to conduct a survey of the district that would be carried out "to the utmost minutae." Each district—especially those in relatively flat terrain—would be divided up into "oblong compartments" of 60 to 75 acres, along each side of which, and at evenly spaced intervals, were cut a series of "openings or avenues" that ran north and south, east and west; each of these received a particular alphabetic designation depending on its orientation on the compass. At the intersections of these avenues, the Foerster would place "a monument of wood or stone" that carried the identifying marks of compartment and avenues, "rendering it easy to find one's way or direct any laborer to any place in the forest." In Fernow's revealing commentary, this structure gave the German landscape the look "of an American city regularly divided into blocks." The forest had become a gridiron.[13]

This artificial quality, this emphasis on what Aldo Leopold denounced as the German penchant for "slick and clean forests," appalled generations of American foresters; such detailed plans would not go into effect in the National Forest System, either. But for Fernow, and the tradition of which he was a part, there was a larger point to regularizing the land in this fashion. Once this was accomplished, then human activities upon it could be controlled and rationalized. This involved establishing a set of legal regulations that determined rights and uses of the forests, drafting fire protection policies, and ascertaining what Fernow called the forest's "arithmetical basis"; among other things this meant evaluating soil conditions and conducting precise tree measurements to create a database from which to assess rates of growth, timber yield capacity, and future productivity. On the basis of these facts was "rational management" of the land defined, a definition that accommodated neither wilderness nor irresponsible resource exploitation.[14]

This was the kind of management that Fernow expected to import to the United States, too, though he was shrewd enough to know that the German experience, born as it was of different historical, social, and political circumstances, was not an exact model for the American republic. "We in the United States are fortunate in that we can learn from the experience and profit from the assiduous work of these careful investigators," even if "we may never adopt [their] admirable administrative methods." But of necessity would Americans adopt the "technical measures" of German forestry, for these were based on "natural laws and proved by experience"—hundreds of years of experience Fernow was quick to point out— and thus were essential to the attainment of "proper forest management."[15]

Yet even these technical measures would not be adopted readily without a wholesale change in Americans' conception of the powers and obligations of government, local, state, and national. With this, Fernow happily elbowed his way into the then-raging debate over the appropriate relationship between the individual citizen and governmental authority. He had no sympathy with what he conceived to be the contending parties in this issue, however, either with the "individualists" or the socialists, groups he disagreed with on intellectual and professional grounds: neither political posture meshed well with the principles that guided forestry, and that thus shaped his political philosophy.

The individualists, those for whom a Social Darwinian conception of society held great explanatory power, were misguided, Fernow declared. "It will be part of my theme," he wrote in essay, "The Providential Functions of Government with Special Reference to Natural Resources," which contains the most mature expression of his political ideology, "to point out the danger and impropriety of considering the social development of man as closely analogous to, nay, as of the same order as the biological development of plant and animal." That analogy, favored by Herbert Spencer and his American acolytes, perpetuated the notion that humanity had little control over its environment, that biology was destiny.[16]

Not so for Fernow. He deftly separated the idea of biological and social development and argued that the latter was well within our control. After all, there were "two qualities by which the human individual differs from the brute, the head and the heart, the intellect and the soul, the reason and the emotions. . . ." And these "have had, and will in the future have still more influence upon the social development of the race." This must be so, he concluded, for "if we content ourselves to accept these [biological] forces as the only ones now at work in shaping *social* development, we shall fail in understanding, explaining or directing that development."[17]

No human society could evolve under these conditions, he affirmed. Progress could not "depend or . . . shape itself entirely under the working of the natural law of competition," a law the individualists championed. True, Spencer and others believed that individuals would "independently of society, develop the social instinct," and would "do so sooner and with less friction if let alone." But Fernow believed that a *laissez-faire* approach was by definition absurd: "It is not very clear why such a result should occur, how the free exercise of competition is to produce cooperation, which is its very antithesis."[18]

How then obtain social cooperation? Not through coercion, Fernow argued, an argument that set him apart as well from those whom he labeled as "rational socialists," those who proclaimed not the principles of *laissez-faire* but those of *faire-marcher*. Their detailed prescriptions for social improvement, their propositions "to hasten the millennium," depended on "making cooperation compulsory and reason rule supreme." Those goals, however laudable in the abstract, could only be achieved at a great social cost: the socialist alternative would only suppress "the individual as in a colony of ants," Fernow declared, "each existing only as a part of the whole." The forester could hardly accept such social regression.[19]

There was, of course, a third path to social cohesion. Standing between the individualists and socialists, those twin peaks of American political thought of the late nineteenth century, was the "true democrat, in whose creed society, the demos, stands recognized as the supreme ruler with the ideals of progressive civilization as the goal of associated effort." This figure was confronted with a tricky balancing act, negotiating between the needs of society and its individual members. As Fernow put it, the democrat must give "all liberty possible to individual activity that does not interfere with the good of society," a good that included "the moral and intellectual development and material comfort of all its members, present and future." To fulfill this required the acceptance of a new understanding of government, required a recognition that government was not an "evil," not something separate from its people, "but as a good created by [the individual] for the attainment of his highest human ideals." This was a government to which Fernow could pledge allegiance, this, he confirmed, "is the creed to which I subscribe."[20]

His subscription makes sense in more than just political ways. In granting that this was the only form of governance that could secure not only "social existence, but social progress," in affirming that this meant that government had certain "providential functions," Fernow laid the ground work for the development of a welfare state whose hand was quite visible in directing the present and future well-being of its citizens.

This overt guidance was especially necessary in terms of a society's natural resources. Of these it is not surprising that Fernow focused on the forests. This resource was particularly prone to exploitation, he noted, exploitation that was legitimate under the then-reigning economic theories. But when the profit motive and speculative greed confronted a seemingly inexhaustible supply of timber in the United States, the end result was an environmental disaster: lumber interests razed this well-wooded land, leaving behind a landscape filled with stumps. At the mercy of the "unrestricted activity of private individual interests," Fernow concluded, the forest "is quickly exhausted, its restoration is made difficult and sometimes impossible, its function as a material resource is destroyed." No progressive nation should accept such despoilation, and its only protection lay in the "exercise of the providential functions of the state to counteract the destructive tendencies of private exploitation."[21]

In this sharply etched critique of American political culture, Bernhard Fernow was not alone. Indeed, he was but one of many government scientists—C. Hart Merriam and Frank Lester Ward among others—who argued for a dramatic rethinking of Americans' fervid commitment to unrestrained individualism. These new professionals were convinced that their academic training alone had fully prepared them both to understand the necessity for social restraint as well as to direct its evolution. That is one reason why Fernow had been so dismissive of his amateur predecessors at the Division of Forestry, Nathaniel Egleston and Franklin Hough. Why, too, he thus applauded the government of New Jersey when, in 1894, it appropriated funds for a study of the conditions of the state's forests and then entrusted this task "not to a commission of ever so respectable, intelligent and patriotic citizens . . . but to an existing bureau of technically educated men, who were equipped to do this work thoroughly and authoritatively." For Fernow and his peers, government should not be left to dilettantes.[22]

Neither should it have been left to those he called the "cheap men," to politicians. Alas for Fernow, he spent a dozen years surrounded by such cheapness, rubbing shoulders with those for whom compromise was an addiction, men whose social graces and political perspectives were equally coarse. They more than anything else had inspired his quest for a "providential government," they most of all were a daily reminder of how wide was the gap between the ideal and real forms of governance. His job was thus a constant source of frustration; indeed, he spoke of it as a "leaden anchor" that weighed him down. Each time the division's budget was slashed or other bureaucracies encroached on his already small terrain, he was pressed down farther, and his "vigor and enthusiasm" were sapped anew. Things went from bad to worse when congressional leaders periodically pressured Fernow to shut down his beloved studies of timber physics in favor of conducting constituent-pleasing weather modification research, and became worse still when each secretary of agriculture—he suffered through four of them—proved no more supportive than the next. Not surprisingly, Fernow constantly spoke of retirement from governmental service, and yet even when this came to pass in 1898 were his interests frustrated. He had hoped, even expected, that his able assistant, Charles Keffer, would replace him. Instead, Secretary James Wilson selected Gifford Pinchot, for whom Fernow held no great love. Moreover, in his letter of transmittal to Fernow's last report from the Division of Forestry, Wilson made it clear that not only was Pinchot working in "distinctly different channels" from his predecessor, but that these meet with the secretary's "full approval." Things had come full circle: Fernow, who had dealt roughly with those whom he had succeeded, now knew something of their pain.[23]

There had been a greater irony in the year before he left that accelerated his departure. In 1896, at the urging of a National Academy of Sciences Commission on

National Forests, President Cleveland set aside 20 million acres of national reserves on which forestry would be in time be practiced. Fernow should have been pleased with the president's actions, given their implicit endorsement of his professional concerns and the bright prospects they offered for finally establishing governmental management of forested lands on a large scale; these Washington's Birthday Reserves could have marked the debut of germanic forestry in the New World.

But that was not how Fernow interpreted the presidential proclamation, instead arguing that it was injudicious and perceiving it more as a repudiation than a triumph. One key to his response lay in the politics surrounding the call for a National Academy of Sciences' Commission in the first place. Particularly galling was the fact that the call had originated within the American Forestry Association at its 1895 meeting, had been brought forth by Gifford Pinchot who had had the temerity to claim that the Association, and indirectly Fernow, had failed to protect America's forested domain. Affronted, Fernow fought to rebut Pinchot's "harangue," pointing out that congressional action was forthcoming, and that the formation of such a commission might imperil the legislative process, but to no avail. The association's executive committee was charged with formulating a call for action, and in February of 1896 the secretary of the interior signed a letter requesting the National Academy to establish a commission.[24]

Fernow was no more pleased with the commission's composition than he was with its creation. Although its membership included both academic and governmental scientists, some were more professional than others; one whose academic credentials were smaller than his ambition was large, was the ubiquitous Gifford Pinchot, chosen as the commission's secretary. Then there was the chairman, Charles Sprague Sargent. He, John Muir, an unofficial member of the commission, and others demanded that the military protect the reservations and that the forests therein be forever preserved, twin blows to the very concept of foresters and forestry. Finally, there was an even more personal snub: Fernow was not selected as a member of the commission. As he confided to one correspondent, "I have neither been consulted nor in any way asked to contribute my share, nor recognized in my existence as the representative of the Government of this question." Having not chosen to consult its resident expert, the government should expect little from the commission's junket tour of the national reservations during the summer of 1896.[25]

Fernow could not have been more wrong, as President Cleveland's startling announcement of 20 million acres in new reserves demonstrated. His action, based on the commission's report, dramatically upstaged Fernow's own decade-long and painstaking labor to establish a national forest system by working within the tortuous maze of congressional politics. Fernow also believed that the Cleveland reserves threatened what success he had been able to achieve. They infuriated western representatives in Congress, who were fearful that the reserves would be closed to development, touching off a legislative battle to rescind the president's action. Although the reserves were saved, and Fernow figured prominently in their salvation, the whole affair deepened his disenchantment. He felt unappreciated within the federal bureaucracy and challenged, if not outmaneuvered, within the forestry movement that he had done so much to establish. More, he now seriously doubted that a full-fledged national forest policy, complete with a centralized system of forest management, could ever develop, given in the fractured character of American politics, a doubt he readily shared with his successor, Gifford Pinchot. The government had not proved to be providential after all.[26]

Neither would Cornell University. In the summer of 1898, he resigned as division chief to become the first head of Cornell's new state-funded school of forestry, believing that his vision for the profession could best take root in the groves of academe. That was not to be: Fernow encountered many of the same problems that had dogged his efforts in governmental service. Although the curriculum that he devised drew heavily on "the most advanced German ideas in forestry education," as did his working plan for the school's 30,000-acre demonstration forest, his budget was never large enough to sustain his ambitions. The program was also understaffed. It did not help that the Pinchot-led Bureau of Forestry lured away Cornell faculty and snapped up most of the graduating students, depleting the numbers who could work for Fernow. The chief blow, however, came in the guise of a crippling lawsuit filed against the school when it failed to produce the amount of lumber it had contracted to cut. In its wake, the state legislature withdrew the school's operating funds, thus killing the Cornell program in 1903, less than five years after its commencement. This effectively ended Fernow's career in the United States, too, for in 1907 he become the dean of a new forestry school at the University of Toronto.[27]

Cornell's fall aside, Fernow could take comfort, ironically enough, from the fact that many of the ideals he had hoped to institute at the governmental and academic levels were taking hold. In 1905 Gifford Pinchot and President Theodore Roosevelt shifted responsibility for the national forests from the Department of the Interior to the Department of Agriculture, established the U.S. Forest Service and its regulatory powers, and pumped up its budget. Fernow could take partial credit for all this, for although he had had strong doubts that this level of governmental management of forests would ever come to pass, he had been one of the first to articulate its necessity. More credit still belonged to him in terms of the growth in academic forestry; through Cornell, and later at Toronto, he had helped establish the idea of forestry within the university curriculum, an idea that advanced with the increased social need for professional foresters. Their professional status, in the end, is perhaps his most important legacy: New World forestry was no longer a laughing matter.

Notes

1. Bernhard Fernow, "Birth of a Forest Policy," Bernhard Fernow Papers, Cornell University.

2. Ibid.; this anecdote fits within a larger pattern of the professionalization of American science in the late nineteenth century: A. Hunter Dupree, *Science in the Federal Government: A History of Policies and Activities,* (Baltimore: Johns Hopkins University Press, 1986), p. 157-169; 239-244; Ronald C. Tobey, *The American Ideology of National Science, 1919-1930* (Pittsburgh: University of Pittsburgh Press, 1971), p. 3-18; Charles E. Rosenberg, "Science and American Social Thought," in David D. Van Tassel and Michael G. Hall, eds., *Science and Society in the United States* (Homewood, IL: Dorsey Press, 1966), p. 135-162; Carrol W. Pursell, Jr., "Science and Government Agencies," in Ibid., p. 223-250; George H. Daniels, ed., *Nineteenth-Century American Science: A Reappraisal,* (Evanston: Northwestern University Press, 1972).

3. Bernhard Fernow, "Government Forestry, 1876-1898," U.S. Governmment Printing Office, 1899, p. 7; He added to his extraordinary publication record, so that by the time of his death in 1923 he had published more than 250 articles and bulletins, as well as several books—a productivity that might just put contemporary, computer-aided scholarship, to shame.

4. Ben Twight, "Bernhard Fernow and Prussian Forestry in America," *Journal of Forestry* (February 1990): p. 21-25; Char Miller, "The Prussians are Coming! The Prussians are Coming: Bernhard Fernow and the Roots of the USDA Forest Service," *Journal of Forestry* (March 1991): p. 23-27, 42.

5. Andrew Denny Rodgers, III, *Bernhard Eduard Fernow: A Story of North American Forestry* (Princeton: Princeton University Press, 1951. Reprinted by the Forest History Society, 1991), p. 14-17; on Germany's extensive influence on American scientific culture, and the belief, that Fernow also embodied, that science had a social responsibility, *see* Rosenberg, " Science and American Social Thought," in Van Tassel and Hall, eds., *Science and Society in the United States*, p. 145-158; Tobey, *The American Ideology of National Science*, p. 3-18; Dupree, *Science in the Federal Government*, p.221, and passim.

6. Bernhard Fernow to Gifford Pinchot, May 10, 1888, Gifford Pinchot Papers, Library of Congress.

7. Fernow, "Government Forestry," pp. 6-9; Rodgers, *Fernow*, Chapter II-III; Harold K. Steen, *The U.S. Forest Service: A History*, (Seattle: University of Washington Press, 1976. Reprinted 1991), Chapter II.

8. Fernow to J. G. Kern, March 10, 1887; Fernow to Kinney, April 6 1887, quoted in Steen, *U.S. Forest Service*, p. 40.

9. Samuel P. Hays, *Conservation and the Gospel of Efficiency: The Progressive Conservation Movement, 1890-1920*, (Cambridge: Harvard University Press, 1959); Dupree, *Science in the Federal Government*; Donald Worster, *American Environmentalism: The Formative Period, 1860-1910*, (New York: John Wiley & Sons, Inc., 1973), p. 73, all suggest that Fernow accomplished little during his tenure as division chief, believing, as Worster has put it, that all he was able to do was keep his "desk tidy." Only Worster has read Fernow's political commentary with some sense of its implications for a new form of governance.

10. Fernow, "Forest Policies and Forest Management in Germany and British India," H. Doc. No. 181, 55th Congress, 3d Session; Fernow, *The Economics of Forestry* (New York: Thomas Y. Crowell, 1902), p. 330.

11. Fernow, "Forest Policies and Forest Management In Germany and British India"; Fernow, *Economics of Forestry*, Chapter 9 & 10; Fernow, "What is Forestry," Bulletin no. 5, (Washington: Government Printing Office, 1891), p. 7-31; Fernow, "Economic Conditions Antagonistic to Conservative Forest Policy," *Proceedings* of the American Association for the Advancement of Science, 1897, p. 329-335.

12. Fernow, "Forest Policies and Forest Management," p. 238-239.

13. Ibid.

14. For a discussion of Americans' reactions to German forestry, *see* Miller, "The Prussians are Coming," *Journal of Forestry* (March 1991): p. 23-27, 42; Fernow "Forest Policies and Forest Management in Germany and British India," p. 239.

15. Ibid.; Fernow, "What is Forestry," p. 14-15. Fernow's emphasis on the historical validity of German methods was over-emphasized. As he recognized, European forestry, or at least his idealization of it, had not been fully realized either in Europe generally, or in his beloved Germany. What his historical investigations revealed, in fact, was that the United States was not as far behind the Europeans as Fernow implied. Most countries had not begun a serious program of rational management until the nineteenth century, until after Napoleon. Indeed, many had only begun to buy up large tracts of land after mid-century, and some not until the 1890s. The German states were more advanced than most, but even here Fernow acknowledged that more than half of German forests were owned by private interests, and majority of these did not employ systematic and rational forestry. Germany was thus a model for American by its successes *and* its failures. See Fernow, "Forest Policy and Forest Management in Germany and British India," passim; Fernow, "Economic Conditions Antagonistic to Conservative Forest Policy," *Proceedings* AAAS, 1892, p. 330; Twight, "Bernhard Fernow," *Journal of Forestry* (February 1990): p.21-25; Miller, "The Prussians are Coming," *Journal of Forestry* (March 1991): p. 23-27, 42.

16. Fernow, "The Providential Functions of Government with Special Reference to Natural Resources," *Science* (August 30, 1895): p. 252-254.

17. Ibid.

18. Ibid., p. 255. In this set of arguments, Fernow was indebted to the insights of Frank Lester Ward, and especially to his *Dynamic Sociology* and *Psychic Factors of Civilization*, both of which he cited in his text. Fernow was thus allying himself with one of the progenitors of 20th century liberalism.

19. Ibid., p. 255-257.

20. Ibid., p. 256-257; like other scientists in this debate, Fernow tended to exaggerate the extent to which *laissez-faire* policies guided the American polity: Howard S. Miller, "The Political Economy of Science," in George H. Daniels, ed., *Nineteenth-Century* American Science, p. 99-114.

21. Ibid., p. 262-264.

22. Fernow, "Address on Forestry," *The Forester* (February 1, 1897): p. 22-28; Hays, *Conservation and the Gospel of Efficiency*; Rosenberg, "Science and American Social Thought," in Van Tassel and Hall, eds., *Science and Society in the United States*, p. 154-58; Dupree, *Science in the Federal Government*

23. Fernow, "Address on Forestry," *The Forester*, p. 26-28; Rodgers, *Fernow*, p. 232-241; Steen, *U.S. Forest Service*, p. 37-42.

24. Gifford Pinchot, Diaries, June-December, 1895, Gifford Pinchot Papers, Library of Congress; Fernow, "The Birth of a Forest Policy;" Fernow to H.H. Chapman, Jan. 4, 1912, quoted in Rodgers, *Fernow*, p. 220, indicates that Fernow wrote the letter for the Secretary of Interior, but did so grudgingly, to "satisfy the parties which held with Mr. Pinchot." Fernow would later take credit for initiating the letter, and thus creating the commission; *see* Steen, *U.S. Forest Service*, p. 30-31.

25. Rodgers, *Fernow*, p. 209-210; 220-225; Pinchot, *Breaking New Ground*, (New York: Harcourt & Brace, 1946), passim; Fernow to Abbot Kinney, October 9, 1896, quoted in Steen, *U.S. Forest Service*, p. 32; Fernow, "Address on Forestry," *The Forester*, p. 25 on preservationists; Char Miller, "Before the Divide: John Muir, Gifford Pinchot and the Early Conservation Movement," (Washington: Society of American Foresters, in press), on the commission's internal debates.

26. Rodgers, *Fernow*, p. 227, argues that Fernow left Washington, having completed "the job on which [he] had set his heart." That is only partly true, for Rodgers provides even better evidence of Fernow's disgruntlement, his belief that at Cornell he would gain the respect and support so missing during his Washington years; Fernow to Henri Joly, March 21, 1896, quoted in Rodgers, p. 232. *see also*, Miller, "The Prussians are Coming," *Journal of Forestry* (March 1991): p. 23-27, 42; Hays, *Conservation and the Gospel of Efficiency*, p. 29-35; Dupree, *Science in the Federal Government*, p. 239-246.

27. Fernow, "The New York State College of Forestry," *Science* (October 14, 1898): p. 494-501; Rodgers, *Fernow*, Chapter VI; Filibert Roth to Gifford Pinchot, March 10, 1900, Pinchot Papers; Filibert Roth, "Great Teacher of Forestry Retires," *American Forestry* (April 1920): p. 209-212.

Congressman William Holman of Indiana: Unknown Founder of the National Forests

Ron Arnold
Northwoods Studio

The origins of the Forest Reserve Act of 1891 have at last come to light. For nearly a century, the "who" and the "why" behind its famous Section 24 remained shrouded in mystery and mythology.

Gifford Pinchot in his autobiography called Section 24 "the most important legislation in the history of Forestry in America . . . [and] the beginning and basis of our whole National Forest system."[1] This "most important legislation" reads:

> Sec. 24. That the President of the United States may, from time to time, set apart and reserve, in any State or Territory having public land bearing forests, in any part of the public lands wholly or in part covered with timber or undergrowth, whether of commercial value or not, as public reservations; and the President shall, by public proclamation, declare the establishment of such reservations and the limits thereof.[2]

This 68-word clause baffled everyone because it gave the president power only to *proclaim* forest reserves. It did not confer the power to administer the reserves nor did it provide appropriations for management of any kind, nor did it state the purpose of the reserves.

Dr. Harold K. Steen, executive director of the Forest History Society, has pointed out that the clause doesn't even make sense grammatically: The first sentence lacks a necessary noun, it doesn't say *what* the President may set apart and reserve as public reservations.[3]

As a result of this sketchy, seemingly incomplete law, the earliest forest reserves were simply off-limits and their resources totally locked up. Homesteading was prohibited. Timber cutting and livestock grazing were prohibited. Hunting and fishing on the reserves were prohibited. Tourism and scientific research were prohibited. One could not even legally set foot within the reserves. This triggered a serious rebellion in the West, and it took Congress until 1897 to write a law providing administrative guidelines and appropriations for the forest reserves. Even then it was added as an emergency rider to a Sundry Civil Appropriations bill. And the 1897 law was written in the dark about the intent of the 1891 act.[4]

One of the undisputed facts that has always been known about the original Section 24 is that it was a rider tacked on to "An act to repeal timber culture laws, and for other purposes," a huge bill reforming public land law. Another undisputed fact is that the rider was added at the last minute in a House-Senate conference committee but was not referred back to the originating Public Lands Committee of either the House or the Senate, which is an illegal procedure. The bill went straight to a floor vote where both chambers passed it, unaware of Section 24, according to most historians. President Benjamin Harrison signed the bill into law March 3, 1891.[5]

Beyond that, the picture dissolves into confusion. Politicians and conservationists in 1891 and in the years since had no idea who added Section 24 or what its legislative intent was. Why did the origins of such a momentous forestry law lay hidden for so long? The answer that we will discover is that everybody was simply looking in the wrong place, because the facts were in the public record all along. However, there were enough red herrings to justify the lapse. At least half a dozen unlikely people have taken credit for attaching the rider. At least half a dozen likely explanations of its origin have been offered. The controversy over Section 24 is as murky as the clause itself.[6]

The most generally accepted account tells a story something like this: The idea of creating forest reserves goes back to the 1870s, so it was nothing new when Section 24 was passed in 1891. More than 200 forestry bills had been introduced in Congress during the twenty years from 1871 to 1891 and they all failed.[7]

But the reservation clause is thought by professional historians to have originated in 1889 with the law committee of the American Forestry Association, a citizen's organization founded in 1875. AFA's law committee consisted of three distinguished professionals: Bernhard Eduard Fernow, an immigrant German forester who in 1889 was the chief of the Division of Forestry in the U. S. Department of Agriculture; Nathaniel Egleston, the immediate past chief of the Division; and Edward A. Bowers, commissioner of the General Land Office in the U. S. Department of the Interior.[8]

This law committee met with President Benjamin Harrison in April 1889, presenting a petition advocating an efficient forest policy. The president was cordial but took no action. The following year the American Forestry Association memorialized Congress to create forest reserves and to provide a commission to administer them. Congress likewise took no action.

The law committee tried again, this time with Secretary of the Interior John W. Noble. Fernow, Bowers, and Egleston were joined by others, including John Wesley Powell, head of the U. S. Geological Survey. Fernow impressed upon Secretary Noble his responsibility to protect the public domain.

As Dr. Steen wrote of the meeting in his book *The U.S. Forest Service: A History*, "Accounts vary as to who said what, but it is generally accepted that as a result of the meeting, Noble personally intervened with the congressional conference committee at the eleventh hour to get Section 24 added."[9]

If this story is true, the intent of the rider that authorized forest reserves was clearly forestry, i.e., the professional management of reserves for both protection and use. However, the first forest reserve actually created under Section 24 was not even related to forestry, but added a huge section to Yellowstone National Park by presidential proclamation after Congress had just rejected a bill proposing the identical enlargement.

However, John Ise, the historian who in 1920 wrote the first comprehensive history of U. S. forest policy, seems to have confirmed that Noble added the rider. He wrote: "Noble, who had been influenced by Fernow and Bowers, and perhaps by other members of the American Forestry Association, asked the committee to insert a rider authorizing the president to establish reserves."

He based his assertion on a letter from Fernow, who replied to Ise's correspondence, "My memory is, that at the time the story was current, Mr. Noble declared at midnight of March 3, in the Conference Committee, that he would not let the President sign the bill . . . unless the Reservation clause was inserted. Since these things happen behind closed doors, only someone present can tell what happened, Secretary Noble or one of the conferees. All we, that is, Bowers and myself, can claim is that we educated Noble up to the point."[10]

But no government documents corroborate that any of this really happened. Dr. Steen wrote, "Much of the original documentation has been lost for what is now called the Forest Reserve Act of 1891."[11]

Noble's secretarial papers would probably tell the tale. But those papers are lost. They were given to the Missouri Historical Society by Noble's sister-in-law shortly after his death on March 21, 1912. On February 19, 1928, a Mr. Tibbott, who was writing a book on President Benjamin Harrison, asked to examine Noble's papers, but they were missing. Somewhere between 1912 and 1928 Noble's papers had disappeared. I consulted with Senate Historian Richard Baker. He could find nothing about Noble and what had happened in that House-Senate conference committee meeting. He observed that there is little likelihood that any executive-branch officer could violate the separation of powers doctrine so blatantly as to thrust himself into a closed-door legislative session making imperious demands and threatening a presidential veto. Baker suggested that the Noble story was probably fabricated. The only professional historian who had suggested the same thing was Dr. Steen, who said in a footnote that the writer of a 1971 Ph.D. dissertation had cast doubt upon Noble's specific role and whether Fernow was even aware that the amendment was under consideration.

I read the thesis of Herbert D. Kirkland, a young doctoral candidate who had sifted through massive amounts of documentation that others had missed. Primarily through letters that have been gathering dust in the National Archives for nearly a century, Kirkland showed decisively that neither Forestry Division chief Fernow nor Interior Secretary Noble even knew that Section 24 had been added, much less had anything to do with putting it there.

Kirkland wrote, "nothing at all appears on the Forest Reserve Act in the Division of Forestry papers until March 16, 1891, almost two weeks after it became law. These papers indicate that it was quite likely that Fernow was not even aware of this legislation until after it had passed." Yet, as a result of Fernow's statements and their interpretation by Ise and others, nearly everyone gives Noble credit for initiating the Forest Reserve Act.[12]

In fact, Noble found out about Section 24 on Monday, March 16, 1891, when Arnold Hague, an Interior Department employee in the U.S. Geological Survey assigned to Yellowstone, took the news to Noble in a private meeting.

Hague's letters show that he and Washington lawyer and Yellowstone advocate W. Hallett Phillips discovered the enactment of Section 24 late the previous week. Hague, an ardent preservationist, realized the implications of Section 24 in rectifying the recent crushing defeat of a bill asking Congress to expand Yellowstone National Park. Hague took Section 24 to Noble, who asked him and Phillips to draft an appropriate proclamation establishing a Yellowstone Forest Reserve with the same boundaries as the failed proposal to Congress. Hague delivered the draft proclamation to Noble on March 25. Noble forwarded it immediately to President Harrison, who signed it March 30, not two weeks after Noble found out about Section 24.[13]

Why did Noble get credit for inserting Section 24? Arnold Hague's letters reveal that answer, too. In an April 4, 1891 letter to *Forest and Stream* magazine publisher George Bird Grinnell, Hague provided "such data as you may need in order to make up an editorial for your paper" about the Forest Reserve Act. After citing Section 24 verbatim, Hague guessed: "It was put in, I suppose, as a sop to those who believe in timber preservation." He did not know who did it. But he advised Grinnell, "In your editorial you had better give the Secretary of the Interior a little taffy for his seeing the necessity for this thing." Grinnell obliged. And that's how the Noble myth entered American literature.

But if Noble didn't add Section 24, who did? And why? Doctoral candidate Kirkland, who so brilliantly uncovered Hague's key role in throwing credit to Noble, could not penetrate further. "This writer," he concluded, "has been unable to determine who specifically drafted the forest reserve clause and attached it to the Act to Repeal Timber-Culture Laws. It appears, however, that it came from someone within the conference committee rather than from Noble, Bowers, Fernow, Hague, Phillips, or the variety of other people sometimes given credit for publicizing the idea of reserving forest land."

And that's exactly where it came from. My staff searched the *Congressional Record* for the names of those assigned to the conference committee. The three senators and three representatives were not hard to find: For the Senate there was Public Lands Committee chairman Preston B. Plumb, Republican of Kansas; Richard E. Pettigrew, Republican of South Dakota; and Edward Carey Walthall, Democrat of Mississippi. For the House there was Public Lands Committee Chairman Lewis Edwin Payson, Republican of Illinois; John Alfred Pickler, Republican of South Dakota; and William Steele Holman, Democrat of Indiana.

Six men. None of them stellar names in the firmament of American history. Certainly none of them recognizable champions of forestry, or preservation, or any of the things for which today's national forests are noted. One of them is the actual father of the national forests. But which one? The papers of each of these men are still extant and fail to set one conferee apart as a forest reserve advocate.

There was one thing left: to go over the *Congressional Record* with a fine tooth comb. The conference report containing the Section 24 rider was debated on February 28, 1891 in both the House and the Senate.[14]

First the Senate. Senator Preston B. Plumb, chairman of the Public Lands Committee, submitted the conference report to the Senate and recommended that it Do Pass (with the new Section 24). The secretary of the Senate proceeded to read the conference report. Immediately, Senator Wilkinson Call of Florida interrupted the reading, saying he felt the conference version should be printed "so that we might all understand it before acting upon it." Plumb blandly asserted, "there is nothing in the report on any subject whatever that has not already undergone the scrutiny of this body, and been passed by this body."

That was true of everything in the bill except Section 24. The Senate had never seen it before. But why would Plumb lie? Was it he who added Section 24, but for some secret reason?

Upon the reading of Section 24, Senator Call pounced on the amending rider and said, "I shall not willingly vote or consent . . . to any proposition which prevents a single acre of the public domain from being set apart and reserved for homes for the people of the United States who shall live upon and cultivate them." Senator Plumb then told a real whopper: "no bill has passed this body or any other legislative body that more thoroughly consecrates the public domain to actual settlers and home-owners than does the bill in the report just read." As we have seen, President Harrison would soon use Section 24 to consecrate the Yellowstone Forest Reserve to keeping actual settlers and home-owners out forever.

The Senate voted its approval of the bill, and was perfectly aware of what Section 24 contained. They had just heard it read to them. Senator Call of Florida clearly pointed out its flaws. The charges that Section 24 was passed in ignorance are false.

In the House, a similar drama played itself out. Representative Payson, chairman of the Public Lands Committee, presented the conference report to the House, where the clerk began to read it. The chief objector here was Mark Dunnell, who back in 1873 had originally introduced into the House the Timber Culture Act, which this bill repealed.

Representative Payson patiently answered Dunnell without lying about the bill's contents. The clerk then read the whole bill, including Section 24. Dunnell regarded himself as a champion of forestry, but he vociferously opposed Section 24, feeling it important enough to merit its own fully detailed law. A number of representatives asked questions, mostly about details that might affect their constituencies. Payson and conference committee member William Steele Holman answered them.

Thomas Chipman McRae of Arkansas arose and said, "I do believe, Mr. Speaker, that the power granted to the President by section 24 is an extraordinary and dangerous power to grant over the public domain, and, if I could, I would move to amend by striking out that section. I would cordially vote to strike it out, and am sorry that it is in the bill."

Mr. Holman asked, "What section?" Mr. McRae answered, "Section 24. I do not believe, Mr. Speaker, in giving to any officer, either the head of a Department or the President, power to withdraw from settlement at will any part of the public lands that are fit for agricultural purposes and not required for military purposes. There is no limitation upon this extraordinary power if the land be covered with timber."

McRae continued for two more paragraphs, deeply worried about the power granted by Section 24. Then Mr. Holman said, "My friend will remember that the bill in regard to the withdrawal of forest land is exactly the same as the bill passed last session, after very careful consideration."[15]

That was the clue everybody had missed. The true story had been staring us all in the face in the pages of the *Congressional Record* for nearly a century. During the 50th Congress, 1888, H.R. 7901 was introduced, "A bill to secure to actual settlers the public lands adapted to agriculture, to protect the forests on the public domain, and for other purposes." The bill was introduced by William Steele Holman, Democrat from Indiana, one of the 1891 conferees. But in 1888 he had been chairman of the Public Lands Committee! The Democrats ruled the House in 1888 and a Democrat therefore chaired every committee. The Republican-dominated 51st Congress relegated Holman to ranking minority member of the House Public Lands Committee in 1891, and therefore to lowest man on the totem pole of the famous conference committee.

In Holman's bill was the answer. Section 8 says:

> "That the President of the United States may from time to time set apart and reserve, in any State or Territory having public lands bearing forests, any part of the public lands designated in this act as timber lands, or any lands wholly or in part covered with timber or undergrowth, whether of commercial value or not, as public reservations, on which the trees and undergrowth shall be protected from waste or injury, under the charge of the Secretary of the Interior; and the President shall, by public proclamation, declare the establishment of such reservations and the limits thereof, and may employ such portion of the military forces as may be necessary or practicable in protecting such or any other reservations, or any other public timber land from waste or injury; and all the provisions of this act, or of any law touching the public domain which relates to timber lands, shall be subordinate to the provisions of this section."[16]

This is the original model for Section 24, but here it stands in its entirety. There is no question about it. There were plenty of forest reserve bills introduced in both the 50th and 51st Congresses, but none contained language even close to that of Section 24. Its similarity to Section 8 is too precise to be coincidence. And Section 8's grammar is correct.

Section 8 immediately answers several questions, the most obvious being why Section 24 is grammatically incorrect. Someone in the 1891 conference committee cloned Section 24 word for word from the template of Section 8 but purged the clause which referred to designated timberlands because the 1891 act made no such designation. A splicing phrase had to be added, which was evidently done under pressure of time, because no one seems to have noticed that the splice added the innocent-sounding word "in" at just the wrong place. Here is the 1888 prototype with the extracted words of the 1891 paraphrase shown in boldface type and the added splicing phrase shown in italics within brackets, i.e., the boldface and italics are Section 24.

> Sec. 8. **That the President of the United States may from time to time set apart and reserve, in any State or Territory having public lands bearing forests,** [*in*] **any part of the public lands** designated in this act as timber lands, or any lands **wholly or in part covered with timber or undergrowth, whether of commercial value or not, as public reservations,** on which the trees and undergrowth shall be protected from waste or injury, under the charge of the Secretary of the Interior; **and the President shall, by public proclamation, declare the establishment of such reservations and the limits thereof**[.], and may employ such portion of the military forces as may be necessary. . . [et cetera]

At least now we know the paradigm for Section 24. And we are sure that the conference committee knew it, too. We see that they deliberately eliminated the power to administer the forest reserves, not wishing to entrust them to the secretary of the interior for some reason, and also deliberately eliminated the power to allocate military appropriations to protect the reserves with troops.

Holman's 1888 bill was accompanied by a full report from the Committee on Public Lands explaining exactly why Section 8 said what it said. The protection of watersheds received a great deal of discussion, as did the creation of timber reserves for the sale of timber by sealed bid to the highest bidder, the prevention of large landed estates being illegally built from the public domain, and provision for settlement by actual settlers in opposition to corporations. A key passages states:

It seems proper here to remark that in the preparation of this bill the purpose of making the public lands a source of revenue to the national Treasury has been wholly ignored . . . *in securing homes for our people, so that only mineral lands, timber lands, town sites, and reserved lands made especially valuable by the improvement of surrounding lands and forest reserves are to be exempt from the homestead principle.* . . . The committee submit that the bill, in its purpose, general scope, and in its details, is essentially a homestead measure, and carefully guards against any form of monopoly of this the most valuable of the public wealth . . . [italics in the original][17]

That is the legislative intent of Section 24. The documentation wasn't lost. We were simply looking for it in the wrong place. But there is a good reason it appeared to be lost: Holman's 1888 bill passed the House but died in the Senate. Bills that die tend to vanish from history.

The forest reserves had no original primary purpose, but a mixed one not too different from today's multiple use principle. Forest reserves were intended to specifically preserve watersheds, to provide for controlled timber cutting within reserves, to prevent fraud, monopoly, speculation and the buildup of private landed estates, and to generally intersperse settled areas with non-settled timberlands where nothing but commercial quality trees could be cut under government control. The original forest reserves were intended for both preservation and use.

Had we known that fact, had we known the legislative intent of the original forest reserves, had we known that Gifford Pinchot's 1905 policy that forest reserves (national forests) are for the purpose of preserving a perpetual supply of timber for home industries, preventing destruction of the forest cover which regulates the flow of streams, and protecting local residents from unfair competition in the use of forest and range was virtually identical to the original legislative intent, modern court cases such as the Monongahela lawsuit, Izaak Walton League v. Butz, would likely have had an outcome more favorable to wise use. We would have known that the Forest Service's long traditional practice was right on target with the actual legislative intent behind the 1891 forest reserves.

The report bears the signature of William Steele Holman, chairman, Public Lands Committee, House of Representatives, United States Congress. So does H.R. 7901. Although we cannot say for certain that Holman wrote the language of Section 8 and Section 24 (he probably did, as we shall see), we can certify that he is legally responsible for that language as committee chairman and signator. That makes him the father of the forest reserves. And the unknown founder of the national forests.

Ironically, there's probably not a forester alive today who ever heard of William Steele Holman. The Forest Service has raised no monument in memory of him because they have no memory of him. Sadly, Holman died in 1897 without realizing what he had set in motion.

Who was William Steele Holman? He was a pioneer lawyer born on a farm near Aurora, Indiana, September 6, 1822, who lived to serve more terms in Congress than anyone else had at the time. He became a classic Jeffersonian Democrat of unquestioned integrity, embodying the ideals of a nation of frugal yeoman farmers and mistrusting every kind of intemperance or concentration of power, political or economic. His entire life was without scandal of any sort and he remained ever a stickler for the proprieties. He was self-effacing and personally modest. Were it not for a dedicated and capable biographer's scholarship in the 1940s we would know almost nothing of him today.

Early in his career as Democratic Representative from Indiana, Holman stood one day on the House floor listening to a measure he found unacceptable and uttered the cryptic but lawyerly response, "Mr. Speaker, I object." It became his trademark. Whatever Holman didn't like met with "Mr. Speaker, I object." Newspaper reporters tagged him The Great Objector and efficient *Congressional Record* printers paid him the unintended compliment of stereotyping the line: Mr. HOLMAN. Mr. Speaker, I object.

As a member of the Appropriations Committee he slashed funding for every imaginable project, characterizing government spending as a carnival of luxury and extravagance. His zeal for thrift became legendary and he gained the title Watchdog of the Treasury. Committee chairman and future president James A. Garfield had to deal with Holman regularly, good-naturedly explaining the merits of an appropriation or cajoling him to remove an objection. Frequently to avoid delay, Garfield accepted Holman's suggestions on small points.

In 1885 Holman was appointed chairman of a congressional committee to investigate the expenditure of appropriations for Indian Schools and for Yellowstone National Park. The inquiry would take three and a half months, out to the Pacific coast by the northern route and return through Arizona by way of the southern. The investigators included Joseph G. Cannon of Illinois and other high ranking members of Congress. Holman exasperated the committee by forcing them to practice a rigid economy on the entire trip. He would honor requisitions for Pullman berths only at night, making the members ride coach by day or pay their own Pullman fares. Holman refused to use a sleeper at all, sitting up all night while his colleagues rode in comfort. He lectured committeemen that he and his wife had traveled in an ordinary coach all the way from Indiana to California and back. At hotels he demanded rooms without bath, but the committee rebelled and made him approve rooms with baths. The watch-dog of the Treasury barked at every requisition.

He saw Yellowstone first hand, visited many homestead settlers, and traversed public lands that would one day encompass more than fifty national forests. He was well aware of the many measures that had been introduced to Congress proposing forest reserves and felt personal sympathy for such protection. His biographer, Israel George Blake, described Holman as a botanist of no mean ability. He also noted that, "Holman saw to it that his farm contained many beautiful flower gardens filled with unusual plants. He transplanted trees from various historic spots which formed a sort of arboreal avenue of history. It is said that when one or another of these old friends of the forest was marked for the axe he would be heard to say in as startling tones as he ever addressed to the Speaker of the House, "I object."

Three years after his investigative trip west, Holman led his Public Lands Committee in writing H.R. 7901. It is clear that even if he was not sole author of the Section 8 forest reserve clause he concurred with it completely. As chairman of the committee he would have had the power to force its alteration or removal.

Holman the Jeffersonian Democrat was fanatically against land monopoly of any kind. A speech he gave on the floor of the House in 1870 denouncing railroad grants and other land monopolies and sympathizing with the landless and laboring people was reprinted in booklet form and widely circulated. He believed that the whole tendency of the government since the Civil War had been to foster the growth of gigantic businesses and overgrown estates, and that these corporations now considered themselves responsible to no one, not even to Congress itself. Holman could not tolerate that idea and did everything he could to prevent public land monopoly and help the actual settler.[18]

Knowing this about the man who is legally responsible for the language of Section 24, we can conclude how it actually came to be added to the 1891 bill to repeal the timber-culture act.

There is no reason to believe that anyone but Holman inserted the rider. No one on the Senate side of the conference committee had any vested interest in the language of H.R. 7901, certainly not enough to copy it almost verbatim: Remember, after H.R. 7901 passed the House in the 50th Congress it died in the Senate Public

Lands Committee. The Senate conferees of the 51st Congress knew Section 8's forest reserve language but clearly held it in no special regard. The other House conferees were Republicans who had no particular interest in forest reserves. Holman came to the conference committee as the sole House Democrat, and a dethroned one at that. Republican Lewis Edwin Payson of Illinois had replaced Holman as House Public Lands Committee chairman and John Alfred Pickler of South Dakota was second ranking majority member. These party relationships are important. The Republicans in the 51st Congress held only a slender majority of seven votes in the House. They knew their control was precarious, and that a powerful Democratic minority could easily block any Republican legislation. So Speaker Thomas B. Reed promulgated new rules that allowed the chair to entertain no motions whose purpose would be to block legislation. Holman, watch-dog of the Treasury, seethed with resentment, censuring the Republicans as a petty oligarchy. He entered the conference committee meeting in no fine mood.

Holman certainly insisted on the minority having some say in shaping the new law. He seized upon the forest reserve clause of his H.R. 7901 because it thwarted the Republican tendency to favor corporate capitalists. It was sufficiently technical and obscure that the other conferees would scarcely risk the whole bill just to keep Holman from adding a pet provision, especially one that had already passed the House in an earlier version.

So Holman, during the conference committee meeting, inserted Section 8 of H.R. 7901 as the new Section 24, eliminated the administration and appropriations provisions and also removed the inapplicable reference to designated timberlands, hurriedly patching up the language as best he could. Nobody in the conference cared a whit about Section 24 anyway, so nobody checked the grammar. Just as James A. Garfield had done earlier, the conference committee gave in to Holman on a small point to avoid delay.

And that is how the Forest Reserve Act of 1891 really happened. Where elite forestry professionals and their counterparts in the elite preservationist guard could not legislate forest reserves into existence, a curmudgeon lawmaker from Indiana who wanted to keep forests for many uses did the trick because he was in the right place at the right time.

It is time to recognize Congressman William Steele Holman of Indiana, 1822-1897, as the man behind Section 24—the unknown founder of the national forests.

Notes

1. Gifford Pinchot, *Breaking New Ground* (New York: Harcourt, Brace, and Company, 1947), p. 85.

2. 26 Stats. 1095 (March 3, 1891).

3. Telephone interview with Dr. Steen, September, 1988.

4. Wayne Hage, *Storm Over Rangelands* (Bellevue, WA: Free Enterprise Press, 1989), p. 116ff.

5. Harold K. Steen, *The U. S. Forest Service: A History* (Seattle, WA: University of Washington Press, 1976. Reprinted 1991), p. 26.

6. K. A. Soderberg and Jackie DuRette, *People of the Tongass: Alaska Forestry Under Attack* (Bellevue, WA: Free Enterprise Press, 1988), pp. 108ff.

7. Bernhard Eduard Fernow in 1897 produced a chart for the American Forestry Association listing 93 pieces of legislation introduced in Congress from 1871 through 1890. See *Proceedings of the American Forestry Association*, XII, p. 41-58.

8. Andrew Denny Rodgers III, *Bernhard Eduard Fernow: A Story of North American Forestry* (Princeton, NJ: Princeton University Press, 1951), p. 142-43. Reprinted by the Forest History Society, 1991.

9. Steen, *The U. S. Forest Service*, p. 26.

10. John Ise, *The United States Forest Policy* (New Haven, CT: Yale University Press, 1920), p. 115.

11. Steen, *The U. S. Forest Service*, p. 27.

12. Herbert D. Kirkland, "The American Forests, 1864-1898: A Trend Toward Conservation," unpublished Ph.D. dissertation, University of Florida, 1971: p. 175.

13. All of Hague's letters discussed here are in Record Group 57, Hague Papers, letter book 3B, National Archives. Hague to E. M. Dawson, March 16, Hague to Noble, March 25, 1891, Hague to Grinnell, April 4, 1891, Hague to Grinnell, April 6, 1891.

14. *Congressional Record*, Senate, 51st Cong., 2d sess., February 28, 1891, *passim*.

15. *Congressional Record*, House, 51st Cong., 2d sess., March 2, 1891, pp. 3611-16.

16. U. S. Congress, House, *House Resolution 7901*, 50th Cong., 1st Sess., 1888.

17. U. S. Congress, House, 50th Cong., 1st Sess., 1888, *Report No. 778*.

18. William Steele Holman's biography is in Israel George Blake, *The Holmans of Veraestau* (Oxford, OH: The Mississippi Valley Press, 1943).

John B. Waldo and William G. Steel:
Forest Reserve Advocates for the Cascade Range of Oregon

Gerald W. Williams
Umpqua and Willamette National Forests

The struggle to have forest reserves (now called national forests) in Oregon began in the mid-1880s. Two men, John B. Waldo and William G. Steel—both active members of the Progressive wing of the Republican Party—fell in love with the pristine mountain land along the backbone of the Cascade Range. The Cascades are dotted with mountain peaks that climb to over 12,000 feet, glaciers which cling to the steep rocky slopes, and evergreen trees that blanket the approaches below timberline. Acutely aware of the policy of the federal and state governments to transfer all the public land to private ownership as soon as possible, the two men resolved to save the Cascades for the public, and for future generations. They undertook this effort at a time when there were national arguments about the appropriate use or disposal of the public domain timber lands. Their struggle in this effort is a remarkable story of fortitude and courage in the face of often overwhelming odds.

Origins of the Cascade Range Forest Reserve

The origin of the Cascade Range Forest Reserve goes back to the summer of 1885, after William G. Steel, of Portland, visited the wondrous Crater Lake near the southern end of the Cascade Range. On his return from the lake, Steel visited Roseburg to confer with Congressman Binger Hermann, who encouraged him to seek federal protection for the area.

> When returning to Portland, [I] stopped at Roseburg, to confer with Hon. Binger Hermann, Congressman from Oregon, in reference to having the land surrounding the lake withdrawn from the market, with the intention of creating a national park. A petition to President Cleveland was at once drawn up, and signed by Mr. Hermann. It was circulated, signed by a large number of prominent citizens, and forwarded to its destination.[1]

Several bills were introduced in Congress in late 1885 to create the national park, but opposition was too great. Finally, on February 1, 1886, President Grover Cleveland suspended by executive order ten townships around Crater Lake from homestead entry and sale.[2] This land withdrawal encompassed Crater Lake and an area northward including Diamond Lake and surrounding country. This was the first withdrawal of public land in the state for scenic or forestry purposes.

However, this was a tenuous triumph because without congressional designation as a national park, the land could be restored to homestead or mineral entry by a future president. There were several attempts in Congress during 1886 and 1887 to formally establish a Crater Lake National Park, but every effort failed due to opposition by Oregon ranching and sheepherding interests. There were bills in 1888-93 to give the land to Oregon to be held in trust for a state park.[3] It wasn't until 1902 that Crater Lake National Park was established.

In January 1886, while the Crater Lake situation was still unsettled, Steel conferred with John B. Waldo. (In his 1932 account of this meeting, Steel wrote that it occurred in October of 1885.) Waldo suggested that the best course of action was to seek federal protection for the entire Cascade Range.

> I met Judge John B. Waldo, who asked me why I did not apply for the entire Cascade range. Taking it as irony, I made a factitious reply, when he assured me that he was in dead earnest and asked me to call at his office, which I did. We talked the matter over at considerable length and I was deeply impressed with his knowledge of the situation and the value of such a move.[4]

Protection for the remainder of the Cascade Range would have to wait for action by Waldo, Steel, Congress, and eventually the president.

Waldo's Forest Reserve Memorial of 1889

John B. Waldo, former judge and chief justice on the Oregon Supreme Court, was well known throughout the state as "an ardent conservationist, . . . [who] was associated with the [Crater Lake] National Park movement. With his brother William, and John Minto, he explored and named many features of the Cascades." John Waldo "was a mountain lover, who spent his summers exploring the mountains and lakes in the Cascades. Each year he would leave the valley in early summer, and head for the wildest and remotest parts of the Cascades, either alone or with . . . friends. . . . A man of wide learning, and possessor of a large library, he had become concerned about the permanent losses to the country by the policy of land disposal."[5]

John B. Waldo decided to lead an effort aimed at obtaining a forest reserve along the crest of the Oregon Cascade Range. After his reelection defeat in 1886, Waldo was elected to the Oregon Legislature in the fall of 1888, upon completing the first documented journey along the crest of the Cascades from Mt. Jefferson to Mt. Shasta. Inspired by the examples of Colorado and of California in their attempts to establish state forest reserves as well as by the successful Steel effort, he introduced House Joint Memorial No. 8 on January 14, 1889. The memorial was a petition to the Congress, urging the establishment of a forest reserve or preserve along the crest. It was to be twelve miles on either side of the divide and was to be managed by a joint state and federal commission. The memorial read, in part:

> To the Honorable, the Senate and House of Representatives in Congress assembled: Your memorialists would most respectfully represent that this portion of the Cascade range of mountains in the State of Oregon hereinafter described consists of the summit of said range and a portion of the slopes extending down either side thereof. . . . Your memorialists therefore suggest and earnestly request that your honorable body pass an Act withdrawing the whole of said strip of land from sale and granting the same to the State of Oregon, to be held in trust for the people of the State of Oregon and of the United States, to be used as a public reserve or park, and for no other purpose.

The proposed forest reserve was designed for a variety of purposes. One clause in the memorial stated: "That the altitude of said strip of land, its wildness, game, fish, water and other fowl, its scenery, the beauty of its flora, the purity of its atmosphere, and healthfulness and other attractions." The memorial also cited the low commercial value of the forest but paramount value of its streams and lakes, the effects of the forests on climate, soil fertility, streams and lakes stocked with fish, and the hiding places for "fast-perishing herds of elk, deer, antelope and other game." Management of the proposed forest reserve would have been by a combined state and federal board which was to be headed by the governor of Oregon. The governor was to appoint to the board six commissioners and the president of the United States another six.

There were a number of special provisions in the memorial. The commissioners would have been granted the power to grant leases for hotels (not greater than forty acres each) and for grazing. Grazing animals would have been authorized if the animals were in transit across the reserve, or if stock animals were being used for forest visitors, tourists, or campers. Hunting was to be allowed but not for commercial sale or profit. Railroads were to be allowed to cross the reserve, but they could use only as much timber and stone as was necessary for the construction of the railroad. Other timber harvest and homesteading would have been prohibited. Mining was permitted under the U.S. mining law of 1872.

On introduction [to the Oregon House] the memorial was referred to a special committee, consisting of one member from each of the counties on either side of the range boarding the proposed reservation. Amendments were made in committee, largely to please the grazing interests. . . . Also prohibition of grazing was postponed for a period of ten years, allowing sheepmen to find new ranges. As amended, the memorial was recommended for passage, and passed by a unanimous vote. In the Senate, however, the memorial met a different fate. The sheep interests had gathered their forces, and the measure, after being referred to the Committee on Public Lands, was tabled.[6]

The Forest Reserve ("Creative") Act of 1891

Within three months of the defeat of Waldo's memorial, the American Forestry Association's (AFA) law committee, consisting of Bernhard Fernow, Nathaniel Egleston, and Edward A. Bowers of the GLO, met with President Harrison. They urged him to adopt a forest policy, but their efforts failed. In the spring of 1891, a twenty-three section bill was being considered to repeal the overly generous and much abused Timber Culture Act of 1873, the Preemption Homestead Act, and abolish the sale of public domain lands. Complex events transpired at the eleventh hour to get Section 24 added."[7] This section was a one paragraph amendment (rider) to the Act, allowed the President to proclaim by executive order "forest reserves" from any public domain land that was forested or covered with undergrowth. The act since known as the "Creative" of "Forest Reserve" Act (26 Stat. 1095) was signed into law on March 3rd.

President Benjamin Harrison established the first forest reserve on March 30th, 1891, some three weeks after passage of the act. This forest reserve was called the Yellowstone Park Timber Land Reserve and included around 1.2 million acres of land on the south and east sides of Yellowstone National Park (now part of several national forests). John Waldo commented on the Forest Reserve Act:

> The friends of the reservation would have proceeded, probably, under the highly useful and practical act of 1891, had that act been in force in 1889 or before. That act puts a business face on the matter, which renders procedure

under it comparatively easy; and, while it arrests the further divestiture of the public domain, it leaves the way open and unhampered, at the same time, for any future and further action.[8]

The Cascade Range Forest Reserve of 1893

Passage of the Forest Reserve Act of 1891 did not go unnoticed by the friends of forest reserves for Oregon. William "Will" Gladstone Steel revived Judge Waldo's idea for a large forest reserve along the crest of the Cascade Range. In a letter to Judge Waldo on March 30, 1891, Steel wrote: "Do you think there is any significance in the fact that the recent congress gave the president greater powers in reference to the withdrawal of public lands from the market? If so might it not be an opportune time to have the [Oregon] Alpine Club [which was founded by Steel] petition for the withdrawal of the summit of the Cascade Range?" Waldo wrote back on April 4th saying: "I am glad to see that your interest has not abated concerning the question of a Cascade Mt. public reserve. The action of congress you referred to had not come to my attention. . . . My view now is that the entire Cascade Range should be reserved."

A great deal of preliminary work had been accomplished, when the matter was brought to the attention of the Oregon Alpine Club, and thereafter pretty much everything was done through that organization [and its successor—the Mazamas]. . . . Judge [Waldo] volunteered his legal services for the period of the conflict. He prepared a petition, which I circulated throughout the state, getting many signatures, some of the signers, however, subsequently fought us bitterly.[9]

However, Stephen A.D. Puter, self-exclaimed "King of the Oregon Land Fraud Ring," and other land speculators reportedly were the ones that prompted Steel to revive and support the Waldo proposal for the forest reserve. Puter and his friends believed they could enrich their pockets in illegal land fraud schemes through illegal transfer of land from the public domain to "homesteaders" who would, as soon as they took legal possession of the land, transfer their property rights to a land speculator or timber company (who often paid the claimant to file their claim in the first place). In other cases, the land fraud artists exchanged their claims (either homestead or cheaply purchased school lands) within the forest reserve for higher quality timber land at lower elevations. They were confident that by establishing a forest reserve along the crest of the Cascades it would bring them "success" in their illegal ventures:

> The "School Land Ring ". . . finally conceived the idea of establishing an immense forest reserve in the Cascade range of mountains, upon the theory

> that the State would be entitled to indemnity for all the unsurveyed schools
> sections within the limits of the proposed reserve. . . . We had an elaborate
> map made of the country that was proposed to be withdrawn, indicating that
> its boundaries extended along the Cascade range from one end of the State
> to the other, and embraced a strip about 30 or 40 miles in width. This map
> indicated that there were fully 195,000 acres of unsurveyed school sections
> within the proposed reserve, for which the State would be entitled to
> indemnity. We then engaged the services of Will G. Steel, of Portland,
> giving him the map and all other data at our command, and started him
> back to Washington for the purpose of promoting the establishment of the
> reserve.[10]

There is no information from the Steel letters to indicate that Puter and the school
land fraud ring actually paid Steel to circulate the petition or his travel expenses to
Washington. In any event, by the spring of 1892, petitioners were circulating
around the state gathering signatures in support of the creation of a forest reserve
in the high Cascades. The renewed proposal had the support of many Oregonians,
including the Oregon Legislature. The numerous petitions and endorsements
flooded the General Land Office, Congress, and the president. There was a delay
as there was the suspicion that the land looters had already taken advantage of the
situation by excessive filing on land that was to be reserved. The Department of
the Interior took several months to investigate the situation during which time the
Bull Run Timberland Reserve came into existence on June 17, 1892, to protect the
water supply for the City of Portland.[11]

> There were many delays that seemed to us wholly unncessary [sic], so that
> matters dragged along until an exciting presidential campaign was upon us.
> Soon after election I went to Washington [in January 1893], to look the
> ground over and found [Bernhard] Fernow and [Edward] Bowers on guard
> and wide awake to the situation. While there I was brought into close
> relations with Secretary Noble, of the Interior Department, whom I found
> deeply interested, but Cleveland had just been elected, consequently the
> Harrison administration [1889-93] objected to issuing the proclamation [due
> to suspicions that land fraud might occur].

The Waldo idea to create a forest reserve along the crest of the Cascade Range for
the people of the State of Oregon and the United States was finally within grasp.
On September 28, 1893, President Grover Cleveland created the Cascade Range
Forest Reserve (Executive Order 28 Stat. 1240) which contained 4,883,588 acres,
and the Ashland Forest Reserve containing 18,560 acres. The Cascade Range
Forest Reserve was the largest in the nation. On the same day, he also proclaimed

the establishment of the very small Ashland Forest Reserve, which was designated to protect the watershed for the City of Ashland in southwest Oregon. These two reserves, the sixteenth and seventeenth in the nation, were last ones to be established for almost four years, as President Cleveland said that he would not establish any more forest reserves until Congress provided some means for their protection and management.[13] Very little opposition was expressed to the creation of this forest reserve.

There were continuing beliefs that the basic reason for the establishment of the Cascade Range Forest Reserve was not for the people of the United States, but rather a select group of land fraud artists. *The Roseburg Review*, on November 20, 1893, reported on the new reserve with this observation: "There is no doubt [about] the secret of the Cascade forest reservation scheme, and the people of the state should take prompt measures to defeat it." Puter and his friends were ready to take advantage, until the state entered the scene. However, the reserve was established and the land fraud ring suffered a setback through the state legislature:

> Governor Pennoyer . . . had been laying for us . . . notifying Clerk Davis not to receive or file a single application for any tract based upon Cascade Forest Reserve indemnity, and stating further that it was his intention to have a bill introduced before the next Legislature raising the price of all school indemnity lands [from $1.25] to $10 an acre. The vigorous stand taken by the executive was a body blow to the school land ring, for we had figured upon making an enormous "killing" in connection with the sale of the 195,000 acres of base existing within the limits of the proposed reserve, there being a profit of from $1.50 to $2.50 an acre thereon. . . . Several measures were introduced [in the state legislature], raising the price all the way from $5 to $10 an acre, but the ring succeeded in holding the price down to $2.50 an acre.[14]

Now there was time to reflect not the process for establishment, but the reasons for its existence. Judge Waldo, much more philosophical and reflective than Steel, stated his rationale for reserving the mountains that he loved:

> During the life time of men now living, the greater part of this inhabitable continent has been given into private hands. 'The end of the land' has been reached. . . . An urgent need of the hour would seem to be, not more land to cultivate, but some change for the better in our ideas. . . . There are educational uses in mountains and the wilderness which might well justify a wise people in preserving and reserving them for such uses; and such a people might find this [Cascade Range Forest] reservation not only wisely

reserved, but to be none too great a tract for such a purpose....Not only fields to toil in, but mountains and wilderness to camp in, to hunt and fish in, and where, in communion with untrammeled nature and the free air, the narrowing tendencies of an artificial and petty existence might be perceived and corrected, and the spirit enlarged and strengthened.[15]

Opposition to the Cascade Range Forest Reserve Mounts

Opposition to the Cascade Reserve soon mounted from central Oregon sheep owners, Waldo's old nemesis from 1889. On April 14, 1894, the secretary of the interior issued a public notice which prohibited sheep grazing on all forest reserves. The situation came to a head in early 1896 when the Oregon congressional delegation backed an effort to eliminate or severely reduce the size of the reserve. The sheep interests

> appeal to the public in print, circulate petitions for party conventions, and load the air with denunciations of the outrage which has been done them. And yet, the most careful inquirer will fail to find that these complaints are based on any other ground than these sheep owners are liable to be prohibited from appropriating public property to private uses for private profit—prohibited from committing what is, strictly, a trespass.[16]

In his letter to Cleveland, Waldo wrote on the matter of retaining the Cascade Range Forest Reserve: "I learned, if not with astonishment, certainly with regret, that the Oregon [Congressional] Delegation at Washington, or some of them had applied to you to abrogate, in great part, this reservation. . . . I am not alone, here, in thinking this action of our delegation to be far astray."[17] The Oregon delegation in Congress, consisting of senators John Mitchell and George W. McBride and representatives William R. Ellis and Binger Hermann, was ready to totally eliminate the Cascade Range Forest Reserve. This, of course, was at a time when all U.S. senators were elected by the state legislatures, not by direct election, which increased the potential for wheeling and dealing by the political parties.

> An aggressive organization of sheep men was perfested [sic] and notice given to the Oregon delegation in congress that every member was expected to fifgt [sic] the Cascade reserve to a finish and have the lands composing it restored to the market. Unless such action was taken at once, sheep men would fight them at the polls, and do everything possible to defeat them for re-election. Members of the delegation immediately loved the sheep men from the depths of their great hearts, and and [sic] manifested a disposition

to take their orders [from the sheep owners], regardless of the best interests of the state. Here was a political organization with money, votes, axes to grind, and what more do you want? All they asked was that the delegation represent their interests, which they were willing to do, so there you are. Sheepmen soon heard the voices of their minions in the halls of congress, shouting of their downtrodden rights and demanding satisfaction at government expense.[18]

Steel spent several months in the spring of 1896 orchestrating a lobbying campaign in Washington, D.C., because Waldo and members of the Mazamas (a Portland-based mountaineering and lobbying organization that was formed by Steel on the summit of Mt. Hood on July 19, 1894, from the remains of the defunct Oregon Alpine Club) convinced him that his presence at the Capitol was critical to defeat the opposition. When he first arrived in Washington, Steel took temporary employment with Senator Mitchell in order to get enough money to pay rent and purchase food. Steel soon found out that Mitchell was the leader of the opposition.

> I had always been an enthusiastic Mitchell man, and once my brother, his manager, pulled him through a doubtful election, when everybody else had given up. I felt strongly attached to him, so called upon him immediately after arriving in Washington [during December 1895]. I was paying my own expenses and it was a heavy tax, so I asked for and was given employment at the munificent salary of ten dollars per week and remained with him for a month. In the meantime I gradually discovered that there was a deep chasm between us.[19]

While Steel was in Washington, Waldo and others from the Mazamas kept up a campaign to eventually defeat the opposition. At one point Steel ran so low of funds that he was forced to ask Waldo for money to pay living expenses. Steel was very effective at meeting with government officials and making his position known. The fact that he had tremendous support from Oregon certainly helped the situation, as he could by telegram send a message to Waldo or the other supporters and within days the government office would be flooded with letters, telegrams, and petitions.

> [Mitchell] finally told me . . . that a proclamation was then prepared "to wipe the Cascade reserve off the map," and would be signed by the president before the close of the week. Next morning I called upon [Assistant Commissioner of the GLO] Bowers, who confirmed the statement, adding that Mitchell had interceded with the president, and stated in the most positive terms, that the people of Oregon were unanimous in demanding

that lands within the reserve be restored to the market. There was no division of sentiment whatever, and indignation was simply unbounded. I denied the statement and asked time to prove my assertions. Bowers quickly got in touch with the White House, then suggested that I call upon S. W. Lamoreaux, commissioner of the general land office, and a bosom friend of Mitchell, and ask for 30 days delay.

As early next morning as conditions would permit, I called at Lamoreaux's office and sent in my card. He was busy, so I waited. After a while the clerk told me he [Lamoreaux] would probably be busy a long time. I thanked him and said I would wait a long time. Again he came and told me flatly I could not see him. "Did he say so?" The clerk returned an evasive answer, so I told him that was satisfactory to me provided Mr. Lamoreaux would say it. I had my own ideas as to what would happen, and soon imagined the commissioner had the same idea in his noodle, for I was immediately invited into his presence. I found him a large man, physically, who seemed impressed with his own importance and vast dignity and an utter insignificance for other people, which I failed to appreciate, so greeted him pleasantly and was met with, "Well, what do you want?" I stated my case and asked for a delay of 30 days, that I might show the president wherein Mitchell had deceived him. He refused and I started for the door. He followed me and suddenly seemed anxious to talk, but I wanted to escape. He contended that the time was unreasonably long, to which I responded, I have your answer Mr. Lamoreaux." However, before I could get away he granted the 30 days time. I immediately reported to Bowers, who seemed to enjoy my report. I hired a typewriter [person] and spent my time sending telegrams and letters to Oregon.

Bowers had informed me that the president would appreciate a legal opinion on the situation, by some attorney fully informed on the subject, so I carefully prepared a letter to Judge Waldo, giving details as fully as possible and asked him to prepare such a document, which he began immediately. Judge C. B. Bellinger was then on the federal bench in Portland and was working heartily with us, so Waldo conferred with him, while working on the brief and when finished, they went over it together. Waldo suggested that it would have a better effect if Bellinger would sign and forward it, which he did. It was an unusually strong document and the president was greatly pleased with it and sent to Bellinger a long autograph letter of commendation.

In about a week I again called on Bowers, who informed me that the president had received a large number of telegrams from Oregon, protesting against Mitchell's statements and he had come to believe the senator had lied to him. I had previously gone to the business office of the commissioner and asked to see certain papers I knew to be on file there, but was flatly refused by a man who seemed to be in authority. Bowers suggested that I go back and present my request to the same official, which I did. He was very busy and sent a clerk to see me, but I insisted on dealing with the man in charge, who finally came and I asked to see the papers, which were at once shown to me. I examined them carefully and made notes, although I then had no use for them, and at once reported to Bowers, who chuckled to himself, just as though it was fun. At this point it was thought a little publicity would help, so a meeting of the American Forestry Association was called and certain resolutions passed, given to the Associated Press, and next morning appeared all over the country.[20]

Arguments for and Against the Cascade Range Forest Reserve

The various factions fighting over the Cascade Range Forest Reserve published articles in the *Portland Oregonian*, a daily newspaper that was read state-wide, and a variety of city and county newspapers around the state. Space does not permit a lengthy evaluation of the hundreds of often vitriolic articles and letters that steamed between the major players.[21] In many cases, responses and counter-responses were written by Steel, Waldo, and others in support of the reserve, while arguments against the reserve were from John Mitchell, John Minto, John Williamson, and others.

The following is a summary of the main contentions that were expressed over a period of about six years during the height of the controversy over the Cascade Range Forest Reserve. Many of the same arguments have turned up in attacks and defenses of other forest reserves across the nation.[22] Basically, the arguments and counter arguments fell into eight major categories:

> *Use of the land contentions*: The arguments for reserving the Cascade Range Forest Reserve came early in the debate. Waldo's 1889 proposal stated that it is to be "kept free and open forever as a public reserve park and resort for the people of the State of Oregon and the United States . . . and for no other purpose." Later there were statements about "wise foresight," "preservation for the people of Oregon and the U.S.," and like reasons. The people against the reserve expressed that the reserve was too large, not reserved for the future based on unwarranted scientific theories, and that it would inhibit the future growth and development of the state.

Also, opponents felt that the reserve gave the "timber sharks" (land fraud ring) the opportunity to steal land that would adversely affect the future generations.

Water contentions: There were many arguments and counter arguments over water in the Cascades. Generally, those in favor of the reserve mentioned the need for protection of the streams that rise in the Cascades. The water would be necessary for drinking water, industrial use, and irrigation. This argument was often couched in terms of compaction of the soil by sheep, preventing forest fires, and prevention of timber cutting. Those opposed to the reserve often commented that western Oregon already had too much rain and that sheep grazing or timber cutting might actually improve the climate. They also thought that trees used the water that was needed by the farmers, thus if there were fewer or no trees, the farmers would have a greater water supply for their crops and the people in the cities would have more water for their needs.

Sheep grazing contentions: Initially, those in favor of the reserve did not consider sheep grazing to be a big problem, but it became obvious that the establishment and defense of the reserve would hinge on this issue. Those in favor of the reserve believed that sheep were a menace to the reserve, eating all the grass and seedlings, trampling the soil, and damaging the water supply. Also the herders frequently set fires in the fall to promote new grass growth in the spring. Those against the reserve contended that sheep grazing was a right of the public, that sheep do not destroy the trees and that their eating the grass would actually prevent fires. They felt that herders did not burn the forest and that elimination of sheep grazing would severely damage the economy of central and eastern Oregon.

Mining and mineral claim contentions: Generally, the proponents were not opposed to mining and mineral production on the Cascade Range Forest Reserve, although they believed that the potential for minerals was quite low except in a few areas. Opponents rallied hundreds of miners and investors in mining property to attempt a massive reduction in the reserve so that mining and prospecting could go on unhampered. There was even the comment made that trees standing on the land were a hindrance to mining as they hid potential new discoveries. This opposition melted away after the laws and regulations were clarified to allow mining and prospecting to continue with very little interference.

Fish and wildlife contentions: Waldo and the other early promoters of the Cascade Range Forest Reserve believed that the abundant species of fish and wildlife were being decimated by hunters and anglers. The reserve would be a place for restricted or no hunting and fishing. The opposition did not specifically criticize these contentions, but implied that deer and elk compete for the grass needed by sheep and cattle, and that the wolf, cougar, and bears were very threatening to the production of meat, wool, and leather. Basically, they felt that the land was needed for production not for the wildlife that reside in the forest.

Scenery and recreation contentions: Scenery and recreation were important considerations from the very beginning. As early as 1885, Steel was successful at convincing influential people that Crater Lake and its surroundings would be important factors in the development of the state. The proponents believed that the Cascade mountains would quickly become a mecca for tourists, a resort for the people of Oregon and the U.S. who would come to see the grand scenery. Opponents, on the other hand, thought that scenery was fine, but the forest reserve as it then existed included too much land. At the most, perhaps two or three areas would be sufficient for recreation, the remainder should be put back on the "market" and sold to homesteaders and others who would use the land.

Timber supply contentions: Proponents of the Cascade Range Forest Reserve felt that the timber had little commercial value in the high mountains, however the lower elevation stands were potentially very valuable. They felt the need to preserve or reserve the timber supply for the future, and that, if properly managed, there would be enough for the next century. Opponents of the reserve believed that the timber was practically worthless, but they wanted to make sure it was available to homesteaders and miners. They also felt that the eastern lumber barons were not seeking the timber in the reserve, as they had plenty in the lower elevations and besides, the trees were rapidly regrowing in areas where it had been cutover a few decades earlier.

Money for schools contentions: With the establishment of the Cascade Reserve, land which was available for the state (sections 16 and 36 in every township) to sell was preempted by the federal government. As many of the preempted sections within the reserve were located very high in the mountains, it was unlikely that anyone would have purchased thousands of these acres of land. Since most of the new state land was at lower elevations, the state was able to make a considerable amount of money for the schools in the state upon the sale of the land. Proponents of the reserve fought successfully for the state to raise the prices of their land for sale to increase the money available for the schools. Opponents, however, looked at this as a conspiracy to charge "excessive" amounts for the land ($5 per acre vs. $2 per acre) to homesteaders who couldn't afford the increased fee. They also saw this as a method for the well known Oregon land fraud ring to step in and take over valuable land that the homesteaders could not afford, which would eventually end up in the hands of a very few timber owners or land speculators.[23]

In spite of the opposition, Steel's personal efforts were very effective in countering the opponents arguments and the Cascade Reserve emerged intact. Had the largest forest reserve been dismantled, the fledgling national forest system in Oregon might have never developed into its present form. As soon as the fight in Congress was considered won, Steel returned to Oregon to join the Mazamas for a summer outing to Crater Lake. He was interrupted on his outing by a request to lead the National Forest Commission in a study of the Cascade Range Forest Reserve.

National Forest Commission of 1896-97

The National Forest Commission was funded by Congress through the National Academy of Sciences. It was sent to investigate the forest reserve situation in the West and to report on their findings to Congress. The following people were selected as members of the commission: Charles S. Sargent—chair of the commission; General Henry L. Abbot; Alexander Agassiz; William H. Brewer; Arnold Hague; Gifford Pinchot—secretary; and Wolcott Gibbs—member ex officio.

> Late in August 1896, the Mazamas visited Crater Lake and I accompanied them. While in Ashland I received a telegram from the commission, asking me to return to Portland and accompany them to Crater lake. I continued with the club until we got to the lake, then, at six o'clock Friday morning [I] left for Medford, 85 miles distant, walked and arrived in time to catch the North bound five o'clock train Saturday, arriving in Portland Sunday morning, where I conferred with the commission, then we returned to Ashland, where I fitted out and we went to Crater Lake over the Dead Indian road. We spent a night at the lake and returned to Medford by the Rogue River road.[24]

At the same time as the commission was visiting the lake, Henry Graves was studying portions of the Cascade Range Forest Reserve "to see parts of the Reserve we had missed, study the rate of growth of the Douglas-fir, that most wonderful tree, and make himself familiar with the effect of sheep grazing on the forest . . . it was original firsthand information."[25] After the National Forest Commission left the smoke-filled Crater Lake, they traveled to the Sierras in California, then on to southern California and Arizona with its Grand Canyon, then to New Mexico, Colorado, and home. The commission proposed that thirteen new forest reserves be created totalling 21,378,840 acres. On February 22, 1897, President Cleveland issued the proclamations to establish these reserves, which were afterward known as the "Washington's Birthday Reserves." "News of the reserves, which came simultaneously with the report's recommendations that grazing be eliminated from the forests, caused predicted furor in the West."[26]

There was an immediate outcry from the western states to have the reserves cancelled. Arguments against the new forest reserves were almost identical to the earlier protests about the Cascade Range Forest Reserve, although some wanted all the reserves eliminated.[27] As before, much of the opposition was led by western stockowners who "did not command broad based support outside their region. Rather, they spoke for a narrow, but highly organized user group whose activities inspired suspicion on the part of conservationists. . . . [However,] the political power of the grazing interests in the West compelled attention."[28] Yet, there were many who were favorable to the forest reserves, but they were barely heard over the opponents outcries.

Management of the Forest Reserves—The Organic Act of 1897

While the Sundry Civil Appropriations Act of 1897 (the yearly act to fund governmental operations) was being considered by Congress, opponents to the thirteen "Washington's Birthday Reserves" amended the bill to suspend the new reserves for a nine-month period. The Sundry Appropriations Act of June 4, 1897, also provided for the first on-the-ground management of the forest reserves. This "Organic Act," as it became known, authorized funds for the administration of the reserves, directing the General Land Office (GLO) in the Department of the Interior to organize a ranger force. GLO's head, Binger Hermann, a former Oregon congressman, was responsible for appointing superintendents for each state and forest supervisors and rangers for each reserve. When Steel failed to receive an appointment as Oregon's forest superintendent in July of 1897, he suspected that Hermann was using the Cascade Reserve for political ends.[29] Steel thereafter became an adamant opponent of continued GLO administration.

During the summer of 1897, USDA botanist Frederick V. Coville studied the grazing situation in the Cascade Range Forest Reserve to scientifically measure the damage caused by sheep. His report of the following year suggested that sheep grazing was a danger to the forest only if it were unregulated.[30] Coville also "contradicted the earlier [National Forest Commission] report's main assertions regarding the commercial value of the sheep-raising industry to the region, fires caused by herders, and the extent to which erosion problems occurred because of overgrazing."[31]

Steel and Waldo both saw the General Land Office administration as the greatest threat to the forest reserves. The GLO's hold on the reserves began to weaken when land fraud scandals throughout the western states received widespread publicity in 1899. An enlargement of the Cascade Reserve in 1901 brought allegations that GLO officials had taken bribes from speculators who stood to benefit from the expansion. As a result of an investigation and a grand jury indictment, President Theodore Roosevelt allowed Forest Superintendent Salmon B. Ormsby to resign so that the position could be abolished in January 1902.

Management Transferred From Interior to Agriculture in 1905

Congress transferred all of the forest reserves to the Department of Agriculture on February 1, 1905. This occurred amid a backdrop of federal land fraud trials in Oregon (1903-1910). Hermann was dismissed from his post by Roosevelt in early 1903 for trying to cover up his involvement in the frauds. Steel testified against the ex-commissioner at a subsequent trial but Hermann avoided conviction by destroying key GLO files and letters while he was still in office. One of Oregon's senators was not so fortunate. After a sensational trial that lasted for several months in 1905, Senator John H. Mitchell was convicted of receiving bribes to expedite some fraudulent land claims.

After the transfer, Pinchot moved quickly to make federal forest administration above reproach. The USDA Forest Service was created from the old Bureau of Forestry on July 1, 1905. Forest Service employees were appointed through the Civil Service Commission, rather than by political appointment under the GLO. Meanwhile, President Roosevelt continued to make proclamations creating new forest reserves and enlarging existing ones.

The president's power to establish forest reserves in most western states ended on March 4, 1907, when the annual agricultural appropriation bill became law. Oregon's Senator Charles Fulton, who had been implicated in the land fraud trails, attached an amendment to the appropriation bill which made Congress the only government branch which could create new forest reserves in most states. However, in the few days before the bill was to become law, Roosevelt, with frantic work by Pinchot and his staff, completed the establishment of an additional 16 million acres of land as forest reserves (subsequently called the "midnight reserves") in the states where his power to proclaim forest reserves was to be eliminated. In large part, these forest reserves became the basis for the present national forest system in the West. The same piece of legislation also changed the designation "forest reserve" to "national forest" because Pinchot wanted to show that the federal forests were for use, and not just reserved or preserved.[32]

After the Cascade Range Forest Reserve was enlarged on January 25, 1907, the name was changed to the Cascade Forest Reserve on March 2, 1907. Two days later it became the Cascade National Forest. The large Cascade National Forest was broken into the Oregon (now Mt. Hood), Cascade (now Willamette), Umpqua, and Crater (now Rogue River) national forests on July 1, 1908. Another division followed three years later when the Santiam National Forest was established from portions of the Oregon and Cascade national forests. On the same date, the land area east of the crest of the Cascade Range was given to the new Deschutes and Paulina national forests. The Cascade National Forest name disappeared as a distinct entity in 1933 when it was combined with the Santiam National Forest to form the Willamette National Forest.

Conclusion

Waldo and Steel, both Progressive Republicans with a passion for state politics and the Cascade Range Forest Reserve, intended their efforts to be regional in scope, not national. Steel, especially, quickly learned to very effectively play the role of lobbyist in Washington D.C. His effectiveness at lobbying is even more remarkable considering that he had no role model to learn the "ropes" from and that there were no organizations or people to help him in his appointed rounds. Steel realized that personal and official messages from Oregon were effective methods to make decision-makers take notice. It was here that Waldo and the Mazamas were effective in their organization to bombard the president, Congress, and the executive branch with petitions, letters, and telegrams at critical times. They used their best judgment to overcome overwhelming odds and decisions previously made to promote, establish and defend the largest forest reserve in the nation—the Cascade Range Forest Reserve—for more than two decades.

Notes

1. William Gladstone Steel to John B. Waldo, 30 March 1891.

2. William Gladstone Steel, "Petition for a National Park," special issue of *Steel Points* 1:2 (January 1907): 68-74.

3. Harlan D. Unrau, *Administrative History: Crater Lake National Park, Oregon*. NPS D-71, 2 vols. (Washington: NPS 1988).

4. William Gladstone Steel, "Cascade Range Forest Reserve: A History." Unpublished mss., 1932. National Park Service Archives, Crater Lake.

5. Howard McKinley Corning, *Dictionary of Oregon History* (Portland: Binford & Mort, 1956); Lawrence Rakestraw, "A History of Forest Conservation in the Pacific Northwest, 1891-1913," Ph.D. diss., University of Washington, 1955: p. 31. Reprinted by Arno Press, Inc., 1979.

6. Rakestraw, "History of Forest Conservation," 33-34.

7. Harold K. Steen, *The Beginning of the National Forest System*, USDA Forest Service, 1991.

8. John B. Waldo, "The Cascade Forest Reservation," *The Forester* 4:5 (May 1898): 102.

9. Steel, "Cascade Range Forest Reserve," 1.

10. Stephen A. Douglas Puter and Horace Stevens, *Looters of the Public Domain* (Portland: Portland Printing House, 1908): 322.

11. Rakestraw, "History of Forest Conservation."

12. Steel, "Cascade Forest Reserve," 1.

13. Harold K. Steen, *The U.S. Forest Service: A History* (Seattle: University of Washington Press, 1976). Reprinted 1991.

14. Puter and Stevens *Looters of the Public Domain*, 322.

15. John B. Waldo to Grover Cleveland, 28 April 1896, Oregon Historical Society Archives.

16. Ibid., 10-11.

17. Ibid., 1.

18. Steel, "Cascade Forest Reserve," 2-3.

19. Ibid., 3.

20. Ibid., 3-4.

21. Gerald W. Williams and Stephen R. Mark, compilers, *Establishing and Defending the Cascade Range Forest Reserve: As Found in Letters, Newspapers, Magazines, and Official Reports, 1885-1912.* Roseburg, OR: Umpqua and Willamette National Forests and Crater Lake National Park, 1991.

22. *The Forester*, "War on the Forest Reservations," 4:5 (May 1898): 96-101.

23. Puter and Stevens, *Looters of the Public Domain*.

24. Steel, "Cascade Forest Reserve," 5.

25. Gifford Pinchot, *Breaking New Ground* (New York: Harcourt, Brace and Company, 1947): 102.

26. William D. Rowley, *U.S. Forest Service Grazing and Rangelands: A History* (College Station, TX: Texas A&M University Press, 1985): 27.

27. Pinchot, *Breaking New Ground*; Rowley, *Forest Service Grazing and Rangelands*; Steen, *U.S. Forest Service*.

28. Rowley, *Forest Service Grazing and Rangelands*, 24.

29. Williams and Mark, *Establishing and Defending*.

30. Frederick V. Coville, "Sheep Grazing in the Forest Reserves," *The Forester* 4:2 (February 1898): 832-835; Coville, *Forest Growth and Sheep Grazing in the Cascade Mountains of Oregon*. Bulletin No. 15 (Washington: USDA Division of Forestry, 1898).

31. Rowley, *Forest Service Grazing and Rangelands*, 33.

32. Steen, *U.S. Forest Service*.

Author Affiliation

Arnold, Ronald
Executive Vice President
Center for the Defense of Free
Enterprise
Bellevue, WA 98005

Conners, Pamela A.
Historian
Stanislaus National Forest
Sonora, CA 95370

Culpin, Mary Shivers
Historian
National Park Service
Denver, CO 80225-0287

Dempsey, Stanley
Royal Gold, Inc.
Denver, CO 80202

Gillis, Peter
Director, Information Management
Practices Division
Treasury Board of Canada
Ottawa, Canada K1A 0R5

Headley, Donn E.
Forest Historian
Angeles National Forest
Arcadia, CA 91006

Hendricks, Robert L.
International Forestry
USDA Forest Service
14 St. & Independ. Ave., S.W.
Washington, DC 20250

Larrabee, Stephen
Forest and Wood Sciences
Colorado State University
Fort Collins, CO 80523

Limerick, Patricia Nelson
Department of History
University of Colorado, Boulder
Boulder, CO 80309-0234

Lynch, Dennis L.
Forest and Wood Sciences
Colorado State University
Fort Collins, CO 80523

McCarthy, Michael
Community College of Denver
Denver, CO 80217-3363

Miller, Char
Department of History
Trinity University
San Antonio, TX 78212

Miller, Joseph A.
Yale School of Forestry and
Environmental Studies
360 Prospect St.
New Haven, CT 06511

Muhn, James
Land Law Historian
Bureau of Land Management
Div. of Resource Services
Denver, CO 80225-0047

333

Palmer, Kevin
Historian
Modoc National Forest
Alturas, CA 96101

Pisani, Donald J.
Department of History
Texas A&M University
College Station, TX 77843

Reiger, John F.
Department of History
Ohio University, Chillicothe
Chillicothe, OH 45601-0629

Rowley, William D.
Department of History
University of Nevada
Reno, NV 89577

Ryan, Mike
Beaverhead National Forest
Dillon, MT 59725

Shands, William
Pinchot Institute for
Conservation Studies
3601 Whispering Lane
Falls Church, VA 22041

Steen, Harold K.
Executive Director
Forest History Society
701 Vickers Avenue
Durham, NC 27701

White, Richard
Department of History
University of Washington
Seattle, WA 98195

Williams, Gerald W.
Umpqua National Forest
Roseburg, OR 97470